New Imaginaries

# New Imaginaries
*Youthful Reinvention of*
*Ukraine's Cultural Paradigm*

Edited and Translated by
## Marian J. Rubchak

## berghahn
NEW YORK · OXFORD
www.berghahnbooks.com

First published in 2015 by

Berghahn Books

www.berghahnbooks.com

© 2015, 2019 Marian J. Rubchak
First paperback edition published in 2019

**Library of Congress Cataloging-in-Publication Data**

New imaginaries : youthful reinvention of Ukraine's cultural paradigm /
edited and translated by Marian J. Rubchak.
   pages cm
Includes bibliographical references and index.
  ISBN 978-1-78238-764-0 (hardback : alk. paper) —
  ISBN 978-1-78238-765-7 (ebook)
  1. Women—Ukraine. 2. Feminism—Ukraine. 3. Ukraine—
Civilization—21st century. I. Rubchak, Marian J.
  HQ1665.45.N49 2015
  305.409477—dc23

                                        2014039962

**British Library Cataloguing in Publication Data**

A catalogue record for this book is available from the British Library

ISBN 978-1-78238-764-0 hardback
ISBN 978-1-78920-521-3 paperback
ISBN 978-1-78238-765-7 ebook

# Contents

# Illustrations

## Figures

# Tables

# Foreword

## Martha Kichorowska Kebalo

Once again, Marian J. Rubchak has provided a great service in producing another volume of collected works on women and gender issues in Ukraine. The present study differs from her previous volume, *Mapping Difference: The Many Faces of Women in Contemporary Ukraine,* that was made up of contributions from both Western- and Ukraine-based researchers. This time she has deliberately chosen to showcase a generation of researchers born and educated in Ukraine, who came to maturity after Ukraine's independence in 1991. She presents this collection as evidence of a "New Imaginaries" paradigm that is emerging within this feminist academic community, finding a parallel in Anna Fournier's ethnography of Kyivan high school students as they responded to the Orange Revolution of 2004 (*Forging Rights in a New Democracy: Ukrainian Students Between Freedom and Justice,* 2010). Fournier describes the process of political change in Ukraine as one of "constant engagement or conversation" rather than one based upon imported models. In the same vein, Rubchak is suggesting that the contributors to this collection constitute a cohort that has creatively experimented with Western research practices and combined them with their own academic conventions acquired through their formative (late-Soviet) education. The multiple research approaches taken by contributors throughout are explained as stemming from these dynamics as well.

This collection comes at a time when Ukraine's territorial integrity and sovereignty are under grave threat from Russia's invasions, and illegal annexation of Crimea. The contributors' cohort, which experienced the Orange Revolution as young adults, now has yet another bond—the experience of Ukraine's Euromaidan from the fall of 2013 to the spring of 2014. But their chapters were written at a time before this ongoing crisis. That prior time will be remembered as a period of unprecedented state corruption, steeply increasing social inequality and mounting oppression of human rights and freedoms. As Oksana Yarosh in chapter 2 observes: "Sadly, contemporary society is apathetic, when what is so urgently needed is outrage!" Ultimately it *was* outrage that fueled the specifically pro-Ukrainian civil disobedience against (now ex-) President Victor Yanukovych when he declined to sign a Ukraine–European Union Association Agreement on 21 November 2013. Those who had since 2004 longed for more personal freedom and opportunity underpinned by European values, good governance, and democracy would not accept this veering away from the European integration they saw as their country's destined path. At first peaceful, the revolution eventually met with violence and death, making it very different in tone from the earlier Orange Revolution of the authors' youthful years. Dissent in Ukraine had grown up to face stark adult realities.

The years of the Yanukovych administration, despite the hobbling of state structures that might have effectively monitored the implementation of gender equality legislation, were also years of feminist ferment and innovation. There was growing a more solid, confident feminist resistance and a refusal to shrink at the backlash. There was a strong and self-aware feminist agency within the opposition movement of the Euromaidan too. Women acted heroically, not only in the medical, media, and provisioning spheres of battle, but also in creating their own fighting formations. Failures to recognize them are being called out (see Christina Paschyn's blog, www.femitup.com/euromaidan-ukrainian-women-are-heroes-too/); women's contributions to the Euromaidan protests are now a serious irrepressible topic of both popular and academic discussion. A new paradigm is indeed being forged. The cover art for this volume marks a move from the woman's face as an icon of Ukraine (victim/saint/mother) to the face of woman—cheeks marked with the colors of the Ukrainian flag in the style of a football player's face paint—as a metonymic symbol of a feminist Ukraine ready to do battle in the arena. The next battle and what is at stake now is the integration of women in the interim government of Ukraine (they were not well integrated), and in its new government elected in May 2014 (also not integrated).

The offerings in this volume provide a snapshot of the pre-2013 arenas of feminist engagement, conversation, contention, and dissent. They will take us through the expected topics of women's representation in politics; the question of the role of women's movement in earning political agency; the effects of state gender policies; the kinds of models society supports for women's behavior, and the way their images are being used in commercial advertising; demographic changes brought about by women's behaviors; and more, as they were documented from a pre-Euromaidan viewpoint. The chapters are valuable resources for student, policy maker, and social activists alike. Future research will provide updates on the new directions subsequently taken. One thing is certain, this feminist movement has been a long time brewing, and, in true Euromaidan fashion, it will not back down.

# Acknowledgments

Inspired by a desire to move closer to the West as they renegotiated their citizenship, Ukraine's post-Soviet youth launched a protest in late 2013 against a retrograde regime; it was soon joined by people from all walks of life to constitute a popular and ultimately successful opposition movement that came to be known as Euromaidan. This was the beginning of yet another facet of the New Imaginaries cultural paradigm shift that is the focal point of the present anthology.

Scores of people, too many to list, deserve my gratitude for their assistance in moving this book from inception to completion. I am indebted to the anonymous reviewers for their thoughtful comments and helpful suggestions. I especially want to thank Molly Mosher of Berghahn Books for her unflagging support and assistance through the many changes and revisions as work on the book progressed. In addition my gratitude goes out to the editorial staff at Berghahn Books whose scrupulous editing and helpful suggestions helped to refine this collection and bring it to a successful completion. I also extend my thanks to Asya Kucherevska, originally from the beleaguered eastern Ukrainian city of Luhansk, for permission to feature her painting on the cover of this book. Her dramatic portrayal of a woman revolutionary was conceived as a tribute to the women activists who found their feminist voice during those Euromaidan protests in Kyiv. Resisting the conventional role ascribed to them as women, many of these protesters formed all-women *sotni* (squadrons) and fought on the barricades alongside the men—to them I dedicate this volume.

My appreciation also goes to Valparaiso University, my home institution, for its ongoing confidence in my research and writing, and continuing financial support as work on this collection progressed. In addition, I gratefully acknowledge the Shevchenko Scientific Society in New York, together with its John and Elizabeth Chlopecky Fund, for a generous grant that facilitated the completion of this volume.

On a final anecdotal note, in my youth I followed a long-running cartoon, "Born Thirty Years Too Soon," featured daily by my hometown newspaper. A memory of its message often came to mind as I struggled with various technological difficulties, the solutions to which so frequently eluded me. Luckily, my son-in-law Homi Byramji was on hand to offer guidance and remedies.

Thank you everybody for your assistance and encouragement.

# Introduction

Marian J. Rubchak

In 1990 students from the National University in Kyiv formed a movement of youthful activists committed to social change. Dissatisfied with the absence of democracy, and inspired by the example of the Chinese students' hunger strike in Tiananmen Square, they erected a "tent encampment" on *Maidan Nezalezhnosti* (Independence Square), where on 2 October a core of 150–200 students commenced a hunger strike. It quickly attracted about 2,000 new participants and continued to build support by the thousands each day until the students staged a demonstration in front of the Ukrainian Parliament building on 15 October. One of their leaders, Oles Doniy, presented a list of demands before the legislative body, and urged students everywhere to coordinate supportive sit-ins at their own institutions.[1]

That same day some of the protestors took possession of the University building in Kyiv, while those demonstrating at the Supreme Soviet (parliament) broke into smaller groups and carried their message to schools and factories throughout the city, with a significant measure of success. Pro-communist workers from the Arsenal factory—a communist stronghold—soon joined the youthful activists. This was a major turning point in the students' protests, strengthened by the fact that their peers from all over the country were adding their endorsements. The "blindsided" authorities capitulated and on 17 October agreed to some of the protesters' demands. Among them were resignation of the authoritarian prime minister, Vitaly Andreyevich Masol, multiparty elections, and deployment of Ukrainian men in military service only within their home territory. The Revolution on Granite had scored a huge victory, although much of it proved short-lived as the result of an eventual government rollback of its concessions. The demonstrators did score an important victory in the resignation of the prime minister, seen as a major impediment to liberalizing the country's Soviet-style economy, and symbol of abhorrent authoritarianism. Doniy also pronounced the students a crucial factor in the impending defeat of the communist regime.

But why now? What had motivated these youthful protesters to erect barricades and agitate for reforms while the Soviet Union, under which they had all been socialized, was still intact? Of significance was their interpretation of human rights, representing imported Western values that the students engaged, redefined, and shaped to fit their own needs. In so doing, they took the first crucial step toward achieving the creation of that New Imaginary—neither Soviet nor Western--that is the focus of this volume. In the Ukrainian context such a "floating signifier ... [came to] represent a new form of human dignity and moral worth" (Goodal 2007: 160, cited in Fournier 2010: 180). Since the 1980s new principles had been filtering in from the West, and by 1990 they had firmly engaged this late Soviet generation—ideas which gained currency as the students reconciled selected elements of Soviet modernity with an articulation of their own quest for freedom and democracy (Fournier 2010: 180).[2] Although it was not yet about gender, the revolution was also important for the fact that it encouraged open opposition to the existing ideology, the dominant values, and a regime of hated practitioners—all of which would soon fire up female activists to seek reforms as well.

The next game-changing event would be Ukraine's Orange Revolution in 2004, in which youths once again took the lead, acting as organizers, strategists, and active participants. Without the prior organizational expertise (acquired during the 1990 revolution), the mounting student protests that helped to launch that revolution, and the financial backing of many of those who went into business (especially in Lviv) after the1990 revolution, the "Orange Days" might not have happened. Unlike the Revolution on Granite, the Orange Revolution introduced an important feminist tenet when it elevated to power an outstanding political leader—Yulia Tymoshenko. In 2005 she became Ukraine's first female prime minister, and was named by *Forbes* as the third most powerful woman in the world that same year. Although Tymoshenko remained on the *Forbes* list in various positions for the next few years, her ability to influence events gradually diminished over time until it stalled in August 2011 when, in a political ploy, she was imprisoned by President Victor Yanukovych for alleged corruption. Even in prison Tymoshenko remained a female public figure to be reckoned with for much of the time, however. Moreover, despite her disavowal of "feminist" as a self-descriptor she became, to borrow a description from Martha Bohachevsky-Chomiak, "a feminist despite herself."[3]

## Women and Revolution

In 2010 a newly installed chauvinistic regime began exemplifying, as Ukraine's Euromaidan Revolution would confirm, unexampled corruption, intimidation, authoritarianism, and capacity for savage violence.

Under Yanukovych, whose electoral victory was hailed by Western pundits as "open and democratic,"[4] Ukraine began its backward slide toward authoritarianism. Late 2013 brought a spiraling political crisis; it spawned yet another mass protest, spearheaded by several thousand students demanding that Ukraine sign an Association Agreement with the European Union. The protesters were quickly joined by others, people of all ages from all walks of life.[5] In evidence this time were large numbers of women, although other than Ruslana Lyzhychko (more on her below) no woman came close to approximating Tymoshenko's stature as a leader. Nonetheless, as Sarah Phillips suggests, "Maidan was a productive space for Ukraine's feminists, providing opportunities for the articulation of divergent yet reconcilable perspectives on women's activism. The imaginative responses of Ukraine's feminists to the challenges of the Maidan have paved the way for a potential broadening of the base of Ukrainian feminism."[6]

That said, it is important to emphasize that a number of women began to ascend to prominence, with one literally taking center stage. She was the already-mentioned Ruslana Lyzhychko, a parliamentary deputy and songstress who had placed first in the 2004 Eurovision contest, an achievement that was followed by other international triumphs. After her term as a parliamentary deputy expired in 2006 Ruslana became a tireless social activist and an important symbol of hope during those agonizing months of protests. She took to the stage erected on revolutionary Maidan to belt out inspirational songs urging protesters to stay the course. Ruslana also visited a number of European countries in early 2014, to which she carried Maidan's message. During a plenary session of the European Economic and Social Committee (EESC) meeting in Brussels on 21 January 2014 she issued an urgent appeal to EU leaders, asking them to enact sanctions against the corrupt Yanukovych regime. We now are fully aware that the regime was nothing more than Russia's puppet, carrying out under Putin's guidance acts of sadistic brutality, intimidation, Soviet-style propaganda, and a massive misinformation campaign in an attempt to move Ukraine into Russia's ambit. In a press conference held during the Brussels' EESC meeting, requested by its President Henri Malossi, Ruslana repeated her plea for sanctions to help resolve the escalating crisis in Ukraine. Sadly, little of the fervent support expressed by members of the European Union moved beyond lip service.

In recognition of her unwavering commitment to peaceful resistance and national unity in the fight against corruption and human rights violations, Ruslana Lyzhychko received the 2014 International Women of Courage award from First Lady Michelle Obama.[7] By this time she had already garnered considerable international attention. On 7 March 2014 CNN's Wolf Blitzer cast her as the "voice of Ukraine."

A second outstanding female dissenter was Tetiana Chornovol, a muck-raking journalist, brilliant political analyst, and uncompromising activist during the Euromaidan conflict. She began exposing the astounding wealth stolen from the Ukrainian people by a handful of oligarchs—most notably President Yanukovych's "family" (biological and political), and Attorney General Viktor Pshonka. It was her relentless investigation and revelation of the assets criminally amassed by yet another prominent politician, Interior Minister Vitaly Zakharchenko, however, that precipitated a brutal attack on her person shortly after midnight on 25 December 2013. While driving home from Maidan that night, Chornovol was followed by men in a black SUV that eventually ran her off the road. She was dragged from her vehicle and savagely beaten about the head and face by three young assailants, who left her for dead in a ditch.[8] Astonishingly, she survived this attack to become a major galvanizing force for the growing radicalization of the antigovernment protesters who subsequently forced President Yanukovych from office. The post-Yanukovych interim government named Chornovol chair of the government's anticorruption committee, but she was not offered a ministerial post, either in the interim administration or its succeeding male-dominated governing body.[9]

I also wish to call attention to the names of two women taken from a long list of female volunteers who labored selflessly on Maidan providing medical services to the injured. The first is that of Maidan's medical coordinator, Dr. Olha Bohomolets. Later when Ukraine's post-Maidan government was being assembled, she rejected an offer of minister for humanitarian issues on the grounds that there was much left to be done to improve the quality of medical treatments for Maidan's victims. The other is emergency medical worker Nina Matviyiv, who arrived on 18 February 2014 as the only female among thirty protest volunteers from the town of Busk (Lviv region in western Ukraine). Without a helmet, shield, or bulletproof vest Matviyiv tended to the wounded with unexampled courage and total disregard for her own safety under the hail of snipers' bullets raining down on Maidan.[10] During the protests Ukrainian society consolidated as a nation. That same impulse was to motivate women to assert themselves as fully-valued human beings.

## Rethinking Gender Equality

As the conflict wore on, a surge in violence extended it to nearby Hrushevsky Street by mid-January (2014), where it escalated into a full-blown war zone. Female protesters began to seek approval to join the men in active combat on an equal footing. Whether from a misplaced idea of chivalry, or decision stemming from some deeply-rooted gender prejudice, on 20 January 2014 Maidan's commandant Andriy Parubiy ordered a ban on female fighting, justifying his decision with a concern for the safety of women untrained for combat. Their response was to organize themselves into All-Women's Squadrons. To highlight this initiative Nadia Parfan organized a "Night of Women's Solidarity," featuring marches among other forms of opposition to the patriarchal system under which they lived. "This evolved into an informal, nonhierarchical grassroots initiative ... called 'Half the Maidan: Women's Voices of Protest.'" Gradually women would become visible not as mere auxiliary volunteers but as active fighters on the barricades.[11]

Meanwhile, on 4 February 2014 the newspaper *Volyn Post* informed its readers that Maidan's women had begun organizing self-defense squadrons (*sotni*).[12] Soon these would be replicated elsewhere in Ukraine, in locations such as Lviv, Lutsk, Kharkiv, and Ternopil (Oblast), among others. Ruslana Panukhnyk, one of the organizers of Kyiv's first and most prominent women's formation—the 39th All-Women's Self-Defense Squadron—explained that having been turned away from fighting on the barricades they were forced to break ranks with the men and establish themselves as independent units. Ironically, although this was an important example of a female civil initiative, with potentially far-reaching consequences, the endeavor had its limits. Too many women remained relegated to distributing sandwiches and tea, and cleaning up garbage ("The Untold Story," note 14).The head and founder of a second women's squadron, Irma Krat, was also motivated by the same deeply felt outrage over what she perceived as men's hypocrisy. A third volunteer, Nina Potarska coordinated the work of these two units, with their core membership of thirty, plus some eight hundred (and growing) external supporters.[13]

Ruslana Panukhnyk instituted women's training sessions, and professional athlete Olena Shevchenko, one of the initiators of the 39th Squadron, quickly began offering master classes in self-defense, initially designed to train women to protect themselves.[14] By late February 2014, however, women wearing helmets could be seen in active combat alongside the men.[15] Feminist activists had carved out a space for themselves on Maidan, and their involvement soon escalated to active combat as the protests were followed by a war in Ukraine's East. Will the women extend their efforts to deconstruct traditional gender roles once that fight comes to an end, as it surely must? This remains an open question.

In early March 2014, as hostilities in Kyiv wound down on Maidan, the women's post-Maidan objective became a twofold one: to join their male counterparts in active combat against the Russian forces and separatists when the violence moved to Ukraine's eastern region; and to become a permanent force in the struggle against the nation's entrenched patriarchy. The ongoing conflict opened up two questions: will Sarah Phillips' observation that fighting in the conflict zone had a transformative experience,[16] that it opened up a host of exciting possibilities for effecting change, for participating in a successful social movement designed to overthrow patriarchal discourses, for discouraging a willingness to tolerate discrimination hold true?[17] Or will remarks such as that pronounced by Right Sector leader Dmytro Yarosh: "Through the experience of frontline fighting, a new Ukrainian identity is being forged ... From this group of men a new political culture will also emerge ... They will be the post-war core for a renaissance society,"[18] foreshadow the women's own willingness to leave forging that new political culture to the men?

Although nominally combat has remained a masculine domain, women did start to penetrate its ranks, on Maidan and especially in the war in Ukraine's east. By the end of 2014 the media were routinely featuring them in battle fatigues fighting alongside the men, and commanding military formations.[19] Of course, not all women elected this way of contributing to the war effort. Some chose traditional female means to support the war effort, such as preparing food packs to be sent to the troops at the front, for instance. A variety of women's Squads sprang up throughout Ukraine and many of them organized kitchens to produce packaged meals for those doing the fighting, an activity reminiscent of the kind of work in which many women had engaged on Maidan. The 39th All-Women's Self Defense Squad, the very one that had spearheaded the feminist initiative on Maidan for inclusion of women in active combat saw some of its own members turn to such auxiliary activities during the war raging in the East.

Clearly, attitudes toward achieving gender justice varied just as widely in the post-Maidan period as they had during the protests in Kyiv. And so I ask yet again: Will women finally create that social movement "designed to overthrow patriarchal discourses," and "discourage discrimination," as Sarah Phillips has suggested? This is likely to remain an open question for some time to come.

## Nation in Transition

In the year that followed those first student protests in 1990 Ukraine became a sovereign state and Soviet barriers to the outside world collapsed, producing an ideological vacuum. Distancing themselves from their dictatorial socialist past, reform-minded women hastened to help fill the void. That same year the late Solomea Pavlychko lobbed the first feminist salvo with her article "Do Ukrainian Literary Studies Need a Feminist School?"[20] In 1993 this preliminary feminist initiative expanded its reach to a Kyiv launch of the self-proclaimed "first truly feminist magazine," *Piata Pora* (Fifth Season), aimed at a popular readership. For most Ukrainian readers feminism was an alien concept representing a Western importation that no one understood or desired, yet it refused to disappear. In the end, a lack of funding caused the publication's demise before the third edition could be brought into print. Following that early attempt to raise a feminist consciousness in Ukraine, in May 1994 the literati commenced a serious literary engagement with the West in the form of a serialized publication in translation of Simone de Beauvoir's *The Second Sex*.[21]

July 1995 was pivotal for those early post-Soviet reform-minded women pursuing gender justice, although the term *gender* itself was yet to make its way into the Ukrainian lexicon. They had been lobbying for a special parliamentary hearing on women's issues for some time and one was finally scheduled for the twenty-sixth of the month. Little of consequence changed as a result of those initial proceedings, but media coverage did raise a measure of public awareness, setting off an early round of discourses on women's rights. In September a delegation of Ukrainian women, headed by a male spokesman, attended the Fourth Women's Conference in Beijing. In preparation for their report on Ukraine's implementation of the "UN Convention on the Elimination of All Forms of Discrimination against Women," to which Soviet Ukraine was a signatory, the delegates conducted extensive research. Their efforts revealed much about discrimination against women in Ukraine that was not widely known. In Beijing these women were introduced to some of the ways in which gender justice was dispensed in other countries. Still reflecting the patriarchal mindset to which they were habituated, however, when asked why they had entrusted their leadership to a man, and authorized him to speak on their behalf in Beijing, they all agreed that his presence in both capacities was calculated to enhance the prestige of the delegation.[22] Nonetheless, the predictability of such reflexive patriarchally conditioned responses did begin to diminish somewhat as reformers threw themselves into the work of organizing gender-oriented seminars, retreats, workshops, and conferences featuring dialogue on women's problems.

During the first half of the 2000s unremitting pressure from the early female activists yielded a series of initiatives addressing abuses against women. On 25 November Ukraine signed on to the UN-sponsored "16 Days of Activism against Gender Violence," scheduled to run annually between 5 November and 10 December, and unveiled a nationwide crusade for gender awareness titled "Ukraine 2015: Millennium Development Goals." Legislative reforms followed, beginning with the law on "Prevention of Violence in the Family" enacted on 15 November 2001. Following this, in an effort to expand gender parity throughout the various governmental institutions, the Ministry of Internal Affairs issued a decree in 2003 calling for cooperation from all enforcement agencies.[23] After passage of a series of (albeit imperfect) laws addressing women's rights, an unprecedented piece of legislation was introduced on 8 September 2005. This was the landmark Law on Ensuring Equal Rights and Opportunities for Women and Men, considered the most important legislative act on equal rights in Ukraine to date. It entered into force on 1 January 2006 as the first legally established definition of prejudice based on sex in Ukrainian history. This was the realization of a decade-long campaign by the early post-Soviet women activists to persuade tradition-minded legislators that gender inequality was indeed a painful reality in Ukrainian society. Without the political will to establish guidelines for enforcing this and other laws on gender justice, however, the laws remained static declarations of intent. And before they could even take root as instruments of practical applications women's rights issues they were shunted to the margins with the accession to power of the Yanukovych administration in 2010. The newly installed regime's indifference to gender problems emboldened police, those "criminals in uniform" who extorted sexual favors from violated women in return for registering their complaints, to continue turning a blind eye to abuses against women (Amnesty International 2007; Network Women's Program 2009). Societal norms also exacerbated the continuing absence of gender justice with the general public frequently condoning the criminal behavior of male assailants while impugning their female victims (Network 2009).

For their part, although two earlier parliamentary hearings (1995, 2004) registered only minor modifications in their rhetoric, the sessions did keep discourse on women's rights alive. A hopeful note was struck on 21 November 2006 when participants in yet another parliamentary session on women's issues no longer focused mainly on pleas for creating an environment conducive to the special needs of "women as women"— appeals that had so dominated the earlier hearings. For the first time advances in gender education became a topic of serious discussion, stressing the proliferation of gender-oriented programs in schools, and the founding of centers for gender studies throughout Ukraine—an umbrella organization based in Kharkiv, and gender centers in Kharkiv, Kyiv, Ternopil, Dnipropetrovsk, Mariupil, Zhytomyr, Uzhorod, Slovianska, Cherkassy, and Zaporizhzhia. Most recently a women's studies program was added to the offerings of Lviv's Catholic University.[24] Papers and dissertations on the subject were/are also written, and the number of scholars working on gender issues continues to grow. On a discordant note, however, the drumbeat of calls for reform and more effective laws also went on, testifying to the ongoing absence of implementation mechanisms, along with an imperfect comprehension of questions surrounding women's rights.

At the 2006 hearing Olga Kobets, chair of the Parliamentary Subcommittee on Gender Policy, summed up the need to shift from words to deeds:

This is not the first time that we have met to discuss gender parity ... each time promises followed, "solutions" were proposed and duly registered, but they never materialized.... Why? Because the political will was not there. Our politicians live in a virtual world of their own power structures. This is one problem. Another is the relentless use of catchphrases, the endless posturing.... In this chamber we can identify representatives of public organizations who still remember the first All-Ukrainian Congress of women held back in 1994 where question of establishing quotas for political representation by women were high on the agenda. The issue was raised yet again in 2001. Unfortunately, as before the politicians heard but did not listen.

The session concluded with an all-too-familiar assurance from the chair that a special committee would be appointed to systematize the day's recommendations, to be presented before the legislature for consideration. In the immortal words of Yogi Berra, "It's like déjà vu, all over again."

## Women and Nation

In nations like Ukraine, which have achieved independence after a protracted period of foreign domination, it is not unusual for scholars and quasi-scholars to draw inspiration from the past in order to validate the age-old existence of some idealized nation, albeit constructed in the present by "masculinized imaginings." As Akhil Gupta so aptly phrased it: "One of the first things that new nation states do is write the history of the nation ... [as one that stretches] into the distant past, where women are generally recognized only in their role as producers of citizens and are thus precariously positioned as subjects of the nation."[25]

During the first decade of Ukraine's independence, narratives of the country's past followed this traditional trajectory. Ideologically driven historical and pseudo-historical books of varying quality were marked by rosy-hued versions of the primordial existence of Ukraine as a nation, and heavily charged with ethno-nationalist rhetoric. In such authors' eyes their patriotically driven historical narratives authenticated Ukraine's being as a discrete entity following a teleological path toward its ultimate destiny as a modern European nation.

Women's history was eclipsed by this nation-building discourse. Women themselves have been complicit in such a suppression of their contributions to the nation's historical evolution. As an early example I offer a statement made on the eve of Ukraine's independence, in 1990, by Oksana Sapeliak, president of the Ukrainian Association of Women in Lviv, in which she insisted that before she and her sisters begin liberating women they must first turn their attention to the liberation of the nation.[26] Soon the nation would be liberated, but the old essentialist arguments remained.

By 2010 women's history had received a boost with the founding of "The Ukrainian Association of Researchers of Women in History."[27] In 2012 the work of the Association was augmented by the inauguration of the Women's Studies Program at the Ukrainian Catholic University in Lviv.

All progress to the contrary, among the most compelling markers of the women's continuing inferior status were the annual condescending greetings from prominent males on "International Woman's Day." Oksana Kis captured their all too predictable form:

> Leading politicians in the state (including the presidents of Ukraine, parliamentary speakers, as well as local political authorities) keep on publishing their greetings on this occasion. Despite their connections to different, or even opposite, segments of the political spectrum (from liberal to conservative, from nationalist to communist, etc.) the rhetoric is almost identical. Politicians of all stripes and genders unanimously continue to essentialize Ukrainian women.[28]

During the Soviet era the political meaning of International Women's Day was modified to reflect communist propaganda exhorting women to participate in the formation of a radiant Soviet future. Eventually, this socialist greeting evolved into one celebrating spring and extolling women's beauty, with men being urged to mark the occasion by presenting flowers, candy, and other such tokens of affection to their wives, sweethearts, female acquaintances, employees, etc.[29]

By 2011 this persistent Soviet tradition, with its unremitting "canned" sexist greetings from politicians, was infuriating many reform-minded women. In an expression of their outrage Kis authored and distributed via the Internet an open letter to the president, following the publication of one of his "Hallmark" felicitations. In her statement she emphasized the women's outrage. An excerpt reads:

> Do we truly merit the men's gratitude only for our family output? What about our creativity, knowledge, professionalism, experience, talents, leadership? We believe that the President of Ukraine has to value us—full-fledged Ukrainian citizens—especially for these features. ... We are not the "weaker sex," and do not want to be considered an embellishment of [male] society—its "beautiful half"; we demand to be regarded as equal and competent citizens of a democratic country.[30]

Sadly, on 10 March 2015 Kis felt compelled, yet again, to raise her voice in protest. Although, she explains that the nation has undergone a radical transformation, there are new functionaries in office, Ukrainians have become aware of themselves as a political nation, yet we continue to see in the latest round of greetings to women on 8 March the same mindless clichés, the same tired refrain extolling "spring, beauty, love, and femininity."[31] Recovery of women's missing history and assertion of their equality has been undertaken in a different way in the eastern Ukrainian city of Kharkiv, where members of a gender studies center have established the nation's first Women's (now Gender) Museum dedicated to reclaiming women's history from its obscurity. Supported by the "Global Fund for Women," on 3 March 2009 its founder Tetiana Isaieva and her fellow organizers mounted their inaugural exhibit on the premises of Kharkiv's national university (the museum was still searching for a permanent home at this time). In due course they produced four panoramas of male and female roles in society, and assembled twelve exhibits—one of which was titled "Stop Sexism." A recent key event was the launch of a sixteen-page interactive digital display *Pravda pro 8 Bereznia* (The Truth about 8 March). It was posted on the Internet at the beginning of March 2011 to commemorate the 100th anniversary of International Women's Day. Its portal lists the museum's activities and special events, and reports on the work of NGOs. Articles and rare photographs pertaining to women's history are also posted, and consciousness-raising gender forums are routinely organized. The founders of the museum announced their intent to make their own history as well. In the voice of Isaieva: "We are … rewriting history as it has been recorded up to now."[32] With the advent of Maidan, much of their material highlights the activities of the Women's Squads.

## Whither FEMEN?

The year 2008 represented a watershed in Ukraine's quest for change in its gender dynamic. Visible signs of economic and social progress were everywhere. Cheerless Soviet cities had given way to vibrant European-like metropolises, filled with brightly lit modern shops and teeming with young people—products of a free society with a view of life that would not sanction a return to a communist past.[33] In the spring of that year a new female force with an unorthodox approach to civil disobedience was preparing to emerge. Members of this first free generation in Ukraine organized themselves into a colorful if bizarre group of mostly female university students dedicated to challenging sexism, prostitution, and abuses against women.

The first women activists to begin agitating for reforms in independent Ukraine had been schooled in the Soviet authoritarian principles of a now-disgraced Moscow-centered regime that, to borrow a phrase from Brian J. Forest (2010), was "stretching its claws to reclaim influence"[34] and socialized to have a firm respect for authority. Not surprisingly, they were motivated to advocate changes by working within the dominant social structures. Among their youthful offspring, who came to maturity in Ukraine's post-Soviet open society, there arrived a fearless postmodern assemblage of women who had reached adulthood with a set of values that prompted them to challenge the status quo—not from within but through direct confrontations. Styled a "most daring and unorthodox protest group" by Jeffrey Tayler,[35] they formed an organization of dissenters in the spring of 2008 under the leadership of Anna Hutsol,[36] labeled themselves FEMEN, adopted pink as their signature color, announced their disavowal of feminism as a self-descriptor, and put forth an ambitious goal of reversing the exploitation of women—with a special emphasis on prostitution, coerced sex, and violence.

The nature of FEMEN's dissent is without historical precedent in Ukraine. The group began its rise to prominence by appropriating a public arena typically inhabited by men—the street. Protests challenging abuses against women, and the negative stereotyping that encouraged such behavior, took the form of street theater. FEMEN filled it with daringly innovative tongue-in-cheek parodies of crimes against women performed for passers-by on Kyiv's main thoroughfares, with role-playing simulating prostitution, sex-for-grades, political corruption, etc., designed to ridicule these practices. It did not take long for FEMEN's leaders to recognize the limitations of this kind of theater in advancing the group's cause, however. Accordingly, they resolved on more daring modes of expression, and topless demonstrations soon became FEMEN's hallmark.[37]

During the early stages of the group's existence Ukrainian authorities took scant notice of it, but by 2010 this began to change as Ukraine commenced its backward slide toward authoritarianism under the newly installed Yanukovych regime. In this atmosphere FEMEN came under increased scrutiny and persecution even as the organization was catapulting to worldwide fame. This, accompanied by increasing harassment and traumatic physical attacks, caused FEMEN"s leaders to turn their gaze Westward. Soon they were mounting dramatic protests on foreign shores, their methods described by a New York reporter writing in Europe as "a new age art form."[38]

Today, FEMEN's Ukrainian saga appears to have ended,[39] its mission compromised by global notoriety, and growing addiction to publicity and self-promotion, augmented by a series of ill-chosen acts of defiance. Under severe pressure from domestic authorities, who did not eschew subjecting women to brutal attacks, three members of the core leadership were driven to seek asylum in France, where they established a second base. Once again, organized resistance against entrenched authority in Ukraine had fallen short of its goal, this time without leaving a legacy of protest. Unlike the students in 1990 who had attracted a nationwide following, FEMEN never drew the critical mass support required by such a cause and never evolved into the cutting-edge feminist movement of its early promise,[40] although, to be fair, the organization did broaden public discourse, often producing passionate debates on the relevance of gender and women's rights.

After establishing their alternate headquarters in Paris, FEMEN recruited new members to its cause, but by early 2014 signs of erosion in their new home were palpable, added to which was a serious drop-off in membership. Contributing to its difficulties, a disaffected French recruit left the movement and announced that she is writing a book about her disillusionment over the disorganized internal mechanism of FEMEN's organization, and its lack of adherence to feminist principles.[41] A handful of its foreign members do appear to be continuing FEMEN's struggle against patriarchy, but interest and associated coverage began falling off dramatically as the revolutionary events started to unfold in Ukraine. A recent example showed Simferopol police dragging a topless activist away from the scene of her protest against Putin's invasion of Crimea. The scene did not attract much interest, only a brief reference noted that one of the two protesters was savagely beaten about the legs.[42]

Even as FEMEN was losing much of its relevance in Ukraine, an alternative organization arose calling itself *Ofenzyva* (Feminist Offensive), an overtly feminist grassroots women's group dedicated to changing Ukraine's patriarchal culture that had been agitating for women's rights since 2010. In a bid to reinstate the political significance of International Women's Day *Ofenzyva*'s stated objective was to turn its organization away from the candy and flowers celebration of women's beauty that the holiday had become. Unlike FEMEN, fully clothed *Ofenzyva* members eschewed exhibitionism, choosing instead to express opposition to anti-women prejudice in the form of annual marches on 8 March, mount appropriate displays, and organize "dialogue-enriched conferences."[43] Also unlike FEMEN, it neither rejected feminism nor confounded its meaning. The core decision-making body was limited to women because, as *Ofenzyva* organizers argued, they were not represented in the highest echelons of political power where resolutions affecting their lives are passed, therefore they must have a female alternative to advance women's needs.[44] The group was recently dissolved.[45]

## Winds of Change

Although in large part shaped by its past, today's Ukraine is part of a changing world as well. One has only to walk the streets of major cities to appreciate the physical alterations to the cityscapes that have occurred over the past two and a half decades. As for the young post-Soviet generation, it seems more willing than ever to take to the streets in defiance of outdated cultural norms.[46] Without abandoning their traditional Ukrainian values, the first-generation female activists had broken new ground in promoting public awareness of the absence of women's rights, establishing thereby a solid foundation for reforms that the younger activists might build upon.

Today, gender—unrecognized or simply dismissed until recently—has become something of a buzzword, especially within the proliferating gender studies centers and university programs. Rallies and protest marches, no longer confined to student groups, are also on the rise. In March 2009, for instance, women took to the streets to voice their indignation over ongoing gender discrimination,[47] and in 2011, in observance of the Centennial of International Women's Day, a march consisting of a diverse crowd of supporters chanted feminist slogans as it made its way from the parliament and surrounding government buildings to Independence Square. For the first time in Ukraine's history the term feminism was heard on a broad public scale.[48]

Rising acceptance of gender as a viable concept also had its dark side. It spawned a severe backlash in the form of an anti-gender campaign labeled "STOP Gender." Assisted by a well-planned, well-funded organizational structure, the campaign attracted support from a large segment of the Ukrainian population. Its success was based upon a program of message consistency,[49] a standard package of disinformation, and the use of familiar channels of the negative publicity that permeated every sector of society, right on up to the various levels of government.[50]

The axis—an "imagined" divide between the democratic Western-tilting part of the nation and its Eastern, Russian-oriented, counterpart—represents a dichotomous relationship of competing interests, but the two poles of that axis are united in their abhorrence of feminism and gender (misunderstood by supporters and detractors alike). Western Ukraine has become a particular focus of the movement's anti-gender misinformation campaign owing to the perceived hazards of its shared borders with Western Europe through which dangerous ideas are certain to flow.

STOP Gender's range of (mis)information posted on one website warned Ukrainians that a successful gender policy represents a menace to the nation's traditional family values, that it is bound to result in the dictatorship of a pro-homosexual minority over the tradition-oriented majority. In sum, a positive gender policy allegedly would provide a "road map" of tolerance for trans-sexuality that leaves women and men free to determine their own sex, condones sadomasochism, invites pedophilia, and tolerates the ritual killing of children. Legislators were routinely pressed to avoid European integration, the result of which purportedly would increase the influx of those treacherous Western values, with their promotion of the freedom to practice homosexuality, engage in same-sex marriage, and subscribe to a variety of alternative lifestyles.[51] The threat of homosexuality alone represented a compelling argument in a homophobic country such as Ukraine still struggling to validate its national identity as an age-old society of traditional values.

The rogue Ukrainian Orthodox Greek Catholic Church—an unofficial NGO—fueled the STOP Gender campaign, with many of the country's religiously oriented organizations falling into line. Some of the uninformed or misinformed government officials organized public disinformation campaigns of their own in which they portrayed gender as a dangerous Western import (a throwback to Soviet propaganda). Such forces argued that the proliferation of the very notion of gender must be halted before it, together with gender studies centers, women's studies programs, and the Western values that they stand for lead to a Ukrainian genocide (Hankivsky).

## About the Book

In 2011 my first volume of collected works brought together an interdisciplinary group of Ukrainian and American scholars who wrote on the status of women in Ukraine during the opening decade and a half of the nation's independence.[52] Meanwhile a new breed of scholar was coming of age—researchers who reached maturity in an independent Ukraine, or were born after 1991. The current collection features chapters written by such rising young scholars who provide us with a more nuanced appreciation of the cultural tectonic shifts in Ukraine since independence. Having been spared the constraints imposed by a regime that shaped the worldview of the previous generation, the young contributors to this volume work in an atmosphere that is free of the dictates that once stifled individual thought and creativity. This latest generation of researchers populates a country that, at least in the popular imagination, aligns itself more closely with a Western model of society, although blind adoption of Western-centric values is no more acceptable to them than nostalgia for a lingering Soviet past.[53] Nonetheless, to quote Tetyana Bulakh: "Soviet-constructed dominants of political, social, and cultural life continue to impact the value system of even the new generation" (chap. 4). One of the most glaring residues of the Soviet legacy is to be found in Ukraine's still heavily centralized educational system.[54] Although this does not act as a necessary constraint on the scholarship of the current post-Soviet generation, its young researchers are products of this system, and their writing style, presentation, and argumentation have been shaped, to a greater or lesser degree, by its traditions. Thus one can appreciate all the more readily the impact of Western influences on current Ukrainian research and writing practices, as they interact with the residue of Soviet scholarly conventions to produce a paradigm shift—a New Imaginaries scholarly paradigm.

In their scholarly pursuits today's researchers engage, and are at liberty to modify, the ideological theories and practices arriving from the West in an atmosphere of unobstructed intellectual creativity and uncensored scholarship. Transforming the former stultifying conventions dictated by state-sponsored scholarship into a dynamic intellectual force marked by an independent outlook on life, these youthful scholars are infusing them with elements to which they can relate despite the lingering vestiges of Soviet-imposed ideas, research methodology, and scholarly apparatus. Such interactive principles are creating what Anne Fournier, in her pioneering work on Ukraine's new democracy, describes as the interplay between Soviet and Western methods capable of beginning an articulation of New Imaginaries that are neither Soviet nor Western.[55]

To date this latest Ukrainian scholarship, viewed through a gender prism, has attracted surprisingly little scholarly attention in the West, where neither here, nor elsewhere, does such an English-language anthology, written exclusively by the young Ukrainian authors, exist.[56] The present volume offers these pioneering contributions in an attempt to help fill that lacuna. Aside from drawing attention to indispensable priorities for future research on gender policy development in Ukraine, the contents of this book lend themselves to comparisons with studies of similar changes throughout the post-communist world, as well as to critical cross-disciplinary, cross-cultural communication on paradigmatic alterations and enhancement of gender relations.

The present volume is divided into four sections—gender politics; interpretations of the arts and literature; changing demographics; and paradigm shifts—fourteen chapters in all, with an introductory essay and a preface. The collection opens with a section on politics in recognition of the vital role that they play in the organization of people's lives. Notwithstanding that Ukraine was among the first of the former Soviet countries to implement the kind of progressive gender legislation that should have facilitated an equitable gender distribution in mainstream politics, as well as in the corridors of power, the post-Soviet parliamentary component of women has scarcely ever exceeded 10 percent, and is unlikely to rise anytime soon. Tamara Martsenyuk probes for answers to this unequal distribution of power. She begins by examining the political landscape using a combination of in-depth interviews, Ukraine's compliance with the international documents to which it was a signatory, the results of sociological polls and surveys on women's political activity, women's NGOs, grassroots initiatives aimed at achieving women's empowerment, and the overall public controversy surrounding gender party quotas designed to reverse the political injustice. Using quantitative and qualitative methodologies as analytical tools, Martsenyuk creates a composite portrait of Ukraine's turbulent political life.[57]

Oksana Yarosh asks questions about the way that both society and Ukraine's political system work to determine gender representation: How do electoral models impact gender distribution in mainstream politics? Is a reformed political system possible with Ukraine's deeply entrenched biases against women? To what extent does women's lack of solidarity play a role in their own underrepresentation? Do many women even aspire to prominent roles in mainstream politics? How do neo-traditional values inhibit women's representation on the highest rungs of political power? A richly detailed overview of Ukraine's electoral process leads Yarosh to conclude that in and of itself the electoral model does not necessarily determine women's political agency—the key lies in its interpretation. Women have it in their power to expand their influence—their organizations number in the hundreds. Instead of pursuing competing agendas they would do well to unite in the pursuit of some collective goals. At present, a "women's movement," aptly described by psychologist Valentyna Bondarovska during the 2006 parliamentary hearing on women's issues as extremely weak to nonexistent, has little prospect of breaking into that male citadel of politics any time soon unless women themselves make some effort to coalesce into a nationwide movement with readily identifiable and uniform goals.

Art critic, curator, and feminist scholar Tamara Zlobina moves the political needle from the electoral process to the effects on people's lives of political decisions and their accompanying rhetoric. She suggests that the so-called guaranteed private space for women, as articulated in the Soviet Union, represented a useful framework from which to begin developing policies on the women's private lives in post-Soviet Ukraine. What did happen in reality? During the 1990s two conflicting models evolved. The first reflected a conservative paradigm of womanhood as embodied in the "Berehynia" image of domesticity (widely and wildly popularized during the late Soviet period) that in post-Soviet Ukraine resonated with its allegedly age-old national traditions of spirituality and acceptable morality. The second paradigm was rooted in the evolving post-Soviet market economy, where an ideology of commodifying and commercializing women's bodies emerged as a reflection of the "Barbie" image, representing Western-style glamour.

This binary was widely publicized in the media. Together the two images—Berehynia and Barbie—were promoted simultaneously to convey a double standard for the socialization of young girls. They were somehow to be reconciled as young women to this construction of their individual identities. Despite this seeming binary, argues Zlobina, in actual fact none is in evidence. No double standard emerged, there was no need to reconcile two opposites because these seemingly opposing views simply reflected two sides of a single coin, with each designed to serve men.

Like Zlobina, Tetiana Bureychak and Oksana Kis discuss the commercialization and exploitation of women's bodies, and they too attend to public policy. Instead of the media at large, however, although the media are addressed in the chapter, the authors target the advertising industry. In contrast to Zlobina's argument for the nonexistent binary, Bureychak and Kis see the Barbie/Berehynia trope as the embodiment of two opposing and separate values—one symbolizes glamour and the other traditional womanhood (more on this later).

Part 2 opens with Tetiana Bulakh's study of the phenomenon of glamour in post-Soviet Ukraine as a distorted overcompensation for the deprivations of the Soviet past, as well as the desire to create an exclusive social space for an emerging bourgeoisie. As she observes: "In its contemporary application glamour correlates with the creation of an illusory reality, an enchanting world of magic, luxury, and perpetual leisure." This myth was eagerly embraced on the heels of Ukrainian independence by a class of post-Soviet nouveaux riches, known as New Ukrainians, who adopted Western values and patterns of conduct while preserving only their externals. Re-imagined Western influences drew on, and challenged, Soviet consumption styles to produce a New Imaginary best exemplified as a nouveaux riche cliché.[58] It embodied the contrast between the evolution of Western glamour as a succession of authentic cultural expressions, and its Ukrainian imitation that reflected the country's Soviet past during which glamour was demonized as a decadent Western import. The resulting New Imaginary, expressed in fashion, was forged within a social milieu that lacked an uncompromised cultural legacy. As Bulakh reminds us, "the Soviet system had not simply detached the Ukrainian upper class from its cultural moorings, it had effectively cut it off from the cultural traditions of the West as well." In post-Soviet Ukraine the initial result was a tendency toward vulgarism, ostentatious display, excessive ornamentation, and tasteless immoderation. This comprised the new aesthetic—kitsch from its very inception. Although the Soviet connection is diminishing, vestiges of it have not died out altogether. They can still be discerned in their contrast with incoming Western values.

As mentioned, Bureychak and Kis in their collaborative effort scrutinized public representations of a newly conceived post-Soviet prestige marker—the female body, positioned in degrading poses, and featuring the luxurious objects being offered for purchase. This "status-conferring merchandise" emerged as the most up-to-the-minute validation of success in Ukraine, with images designed to appeal to male pride, exaggerated masculinity, and exhilarating sense of power.

The authors offer a critical analysis of the way that Western theories of gender and advertising play out in this non-Western cultural setting. Western modes s of commercial advertising have flooded the Ukrainian media and the nation's public spaces. They work as agents of socialization to the new values that are systematically replacing the lingering Soviet ideals. This leads us to the inescapable conclusion that the absence of laws regulating advertising will continue to sustain the exaggerated eroticization of women's bodies in ways that degrade them, for use as marketing devices.

The authors also provide a content analysis of videos that appear on Ukrainian television, but their primary focus is on outdoor advertising, with its special outreach capability. Sexism pervades the public space in the shape of billboards, posters, and displays in shop windows assault the viewer at every turn. They cannot be turned off at will in the way that a television message or a print ad might simply be ignored or disconnected with a click of the remote or setting aside a published piece. Outdoor messages that objectify and commodify women are organized in such a way as to capture the attention of passers-by on both the liminal and subliminal levels during the few seconds that they remain in sight. Their messages, devoid of surplus images and captions, do the work of transmitting the new capitalist creed in a manner that is reminiscent of the Soviet political poster. In so doing, they offer a facet of the evolving New Imaginaries paradigm—neither Western nor Soviet—in a non-scholarly setting.

In her second contribution to this volume, that comes in Chapter 6, Tamara Zlobina ushers us into the world of women's contributions to the contemporary art scene. She centers this piece on the oeuvre of three outstanding female artists struggling for recognition in a patriarchal climate. For the sake of their art and the feminist message they wish to convey, the artists resort to a form of subterfuge that Zlobina labels "masquerade." It functions as a guerilla strategy acting as a protective shield that permits a woman to create and disseminate an independent female agenda while feigning conformance to the patriarchal ideology that supports the socially approved needs, desires, and fantasies of men. This masquerade of womanliness veils the traditionally perceived "inappropriateness" of feminine behavior as active agent (still a male monopoly), rendering the artist's installations more palatable to a conservative viewing public. At the same time the approach appeals to the sophisticated viewer, capable of understanding its cloaked message. Zlobina examines the encoded feminist philosophy that disguises, facilitates, and stresses its capacity for conveying meaning through a medium that transcends the knowable on the surface of a typical woman's existence. Imperceptibly, this masquerade transports the viewer's gaze to the inner recess of the mind where the feminist message resides.

Maria Tytarenko turns to a different medium in her examination of what it means to be a professional woman in a country experiencing a dynamic transformation from authoritarian control to an open democratic society. She shines her spotlight on the achievements of Ukrainian women in literary journalism. Centralized Soviet control over intellectual discourses made it impossible for Ukrainian journalists to adopt the transformative world patterns of literary journalism active in the free world during the twentieth century, where Western women made their mark. As latecomers to such changes, post-Soviet Ukrainian journalists incorporated the imported mature ideas and practices into their own literary/journalistic tradition by a process of "leap-frogging"—adapting Western progress to the needs of a modernizing post-Soviet society (somewhat reminiscent of the earlier Soviet push for rapid industrialization). Together with residual, albeit declining, Soviet influences something fresh and innovative was born—a New Imaginaries literary paradigm. This adaptation of the achievements of their Western counterparts to their own current needs enabled Ukrainian "witnesses of history" to reconstruct their historical memory through the application of formerly inaccessible forms of experimentation, using mixed genres to portray more precisely the historical periods about which they wrote.

Part 3 moves on to an exploration of some of the underlying causes and effects of Ukraine's changing demographics as women become de facto breadwinners, despite the continuation of traditional rhetoric favoring an ideology of the hegemonic patriarchal system. Victoriya Volodko opens with an in-depth look at the direct impact on families sending female workers to foreign shores in pursuit of desperately needed income.[59] Laboring under intense feelings of guilt, migrant women leave behind children who are unable to understand why their mothers must remain absent for so long, with many of these offspring exhibiting signs of psychological traumas as a result. To be sure, remittances sent home made it possible for the children to enjoy a higher standard of living, better nutrition, and an otherwise unaffordable education, perhaps even an apartment, but the social costs came high. In some instances, with the passage of time the children's dependence on these remittances grew, and the goods that the money earned abroad led to an inversion in values, as possessions surpassed family ties in value, and led to a multitude of social problems.

For their part, the men left behind faced the dangers inherent in their loss of status as breadwinners, a loss that might generate mounting feelings of inadequacy. Such consequences are capable of producing broken relationships, alcoholism, drug abuse, and other forms of antisocial behavior. Meanwhile, the women's relatively high earnings rendered them vulnerable to suspicions of immoral behavior abroad, inflamed by the envy of those left behind to struggle in a broken economy.[60] Indeed, at one time President Kuchma referred to all Ukrainian women working in Italy as prostitutes.[61] Others are now often known to accuse such migrant women of being bad mothers.

Galyna Gorodetska limits her focus to a case study of women migrant workers in Basque country. Like Volodko, she argues that the bleak economic picture—hyperinflation, falling wages, unemployment, mounting debts, a defunct social safety net that excessively impacts women, and the high incidence of domestic violence—are factors that motivate female outmigration. A contributing cause, Gorodetska argues, is Spain's long-standing attraction as a desirable country of destination. This appeal is augmented by the more recent influx of family members and friends. In Basque country, as elsewhere in the world of migrant labor, workers tend to concentrate in similar occupations, around which diasporan communities form. With their ability to provide social, psychological, and material support communities such as the one in Spain are in a favored position to serve as powerful magnets for the new arrivals.[62]

Halyna Labinska studies women's migration more narrowly, centering it primarily on a single Ukrainian region—the Lviv Oblast. Her case study serves as a microcosm of the national process, but also takes into account an internal migration pattern—from village to city. The author rounds out her chapter with a discussion of reproductive processes in the region, and its high male mortality rate, both of which are said to contribute to the unstable demographic balance.

Against this backdrop Labinska also weighs in on the labor migration from this westernmost Ukrainian territory to nearby foreign destinations; clearly, geography matters. Among the factors that determine the women's decisions to migrate abroad the author cites proximity to potential host countries as a compelling incentive. Labinska concludes with a discussion of the transformative process that brings together the residue of ideas and practices formed in a discredited Soviet system, and incoming Western tenets that lead to heightened expectations, to the framing of a New Imaginaries cultural profile, although she does not apply the term itself.

The closing chapter in this section provides an interesting counterpoint to the post-Soviet Ukrainian migrations, both in kind and in motivation. Liudmyla Males analyzes a series of celebratory wedding songs for evidence of what can be termed the internal migrations of newly-married women during the early modern era of Ukraine's historical development. Her primary source consisted of papers written by senior college students on the subject in partial fulfillment of their practicum requirements.[63] Pre-existing symbolic structures still lodged in popular memory confirmed a tradition of women's historical freedoms persisting in early modern times. As the nation progressively morphed into a patriarchal social order[64] these freedoms were gradually eroded until they applied exclusively to single females. Unmarried women preserved their traditional liberties, but upon betrothal an internal "migration" to the husband's family commenced, ending with the young wife's subordination in a new authority structure. Wedding songs illustrating this "migration" are replete with references to her unhappy fate, particularly if a mother-in-law existed to exercise her not always benevolent, yet unquestioned, authority.[65]

The single most important factor that unites all four patterns of migration is female sacrifice, regardless of historical time, setting, or motivation, and in each case family plays a decisive part as women take up their migrant roles. Contemporary workers make sacrifices for the benefit of established families, while pre-modern women relocated to new and unfamiliar settings in the expectation of forming a family, although clearly this was not their sole motive for marriage.

Marfa Skoryk opens the fourth and final section with her interpretation of the ways in which both Soviet and Western influences have conflated to create a New Imaginary paradigm in the study of psychology, and its relationship to gender studies. She starts with a brief historical summary of the evolution of psychology as a discipline during the twentieth century in the West, where biology came to define sexual differences. Akin to what occurred in literary journalism, as described by Maria Tytarenko in her chapter, the long reign of Soviet ideology behind the iron curtain precluded any reception and adaptation of Western achievements and values. When the latter ultimately made their way into post-Soviet Ukrainian academic psychology programs they were considered a viable point of entry for all gender studies. In addition, consistent with the Soviet practice of insisting on practical applications in every sphere of life, during the initial period of reception and adaptation of the mature Western conventions psychologists in post-Soviet Ukraine tended to consider the fact that the study of gender must have a practical function, that it needs to be applied to "concrete" spheres such as the economy, for instance. Not unlike the adaptation of mature Western developments to post-Soviet Ukraine's literary journalism, foreign achievements in psychology also provided a "jumping-off point" for bringing that discipline up to contemporary Western professional standards in Ukraine. Contrary to developments in other disciplines, however, psychologists also adopted measures to provide an autonomous space for gender (a gender "ghetto") where it, together with psychology, might progress undisturbed toward creating a paradigm shift that serves those professional interests.

Hanna Chernenko's succeeding chapter channels the discussion toward Ukraine's persistent attraction for hegemonic patriarchy. Her research rests primarily upon reader's comments found in a single, long-running journal known today as *Zhinka* (Woman). Although a seemingly overly narrow primary source base for scholarship, this journal's extensive run and huge popularity render it a useful vehicle for gauging women's reactions to patriarchal influences and ideals over the course of nearly a century, and vicissitudes of frequent and dramatic political changes in contemporary Ukraine.[66] The concept of an egalitarian family as defined in the West began inserting itself in independent Ukraine only when it was no longer possible to ignore the influence of women's emancipation theories flowing in from abroad. This collision of cultural values reflected Soviet conditioning and the uneven pace of adaptation of Western theories to locally specific needs, forging yet another component of the emerging New Imaginaries paradigm.

The volume concludes with Tetyana Bureychak's concentration on men in crisis, a subject that was influenced by the kind of Western scholarship that had received serious academic attention for decades before beginning to engage Ukrainian scholarly discourse. The continuing institutionalized patriarchy that defines post-Soviet Ukrainian values does pay rich dividends in privileges for men, privileges they enjoy but that come at a price. These include social constructions of masculinity to which men are no longer able to respond adequately. Accordingly, they tend to induce a lifestyle or social behavior in men that can lead to death as the most serious of their consequences. The mass media play a critical, if negative, role by publicizing conflicting solutions to the men's dilemma. On the one hand they valorize an environment that reinforces traditional masculinity, and on the other the media encourage a modification in the social expectations of men by suggesting that certain obligations might be best met by women and the state. Nowhere is there a reference to men's accountability for their own weaknesses, or their impotence in shaping their own destiny.

Volodko and Gorodetska also address the potential consequences of men's inability to adapt to the post-Soviet alteration in their status. Male feebleness is traceable in part to the Soviet era when women gained in strength as a result of assuming by necessity that infamous Soviet-style double (even triple) burden. Meanwhile, men were progressively weakened as their responsibilities virtually contracted to public service alone. In addition to working full-time, women were charged with child rearing, tending to domestic duties, taking care of the elderly, and performing public service. At the same time, "backed by tough state regulations," men's obligations to their families were so diminished that they were pushed to the sidelines of private life. The disparity widened between an exaggerated publicly-created image of "macho" masculinity and men's inability to rise to its publicized level. In this way, "the totalitarian regime … ushered in a spirit of servility … among males, [especially] those more or less involved in the socio-political sphere."[67] A merger of Soviet-induced limitations on men's responsibilities, and Western scholarly attention to male issues as an integral part of gender studies filtering into Ukraine, yielded an impressive set of building blocks for use in the construction of a new and different kind of paradigm for the study of gender relations.

This volume is equipped to serve a wide audience across the various branches of learning. It brings together studies from a range of disciplines, diversity of views, and methodologies, produced by a generation of post-totalitarian Ukrainian researchers who are recasting normative axioms in the context of their rapidly-changing world. Rather than imposing a Western model of scholarship generally requiring, by way of one example, an abstract that presents a thesis and proposed methodology, I have chosen to preserve the texture of Ukrainian scholarly conventions in writing patterns: organization, flow of argumentation, and presentation. In the interest of technical consistency, however, transliterations that did not conform to uniform Western conventions were reformatted. Accordingly, *yu, ya, ye* have been rendered as *iu, ia, ie,* for example, and the soft sign' in proper names has been eliminated. Exceptions to this last modification are the names of authors in the bibliography or notes section, where they appear as they did in the original publications, or as the authors themselves commonly render them.

The offerings in this collection portray a range of pre-2013 arenas of feminist engagement, conversation, and debate. They take us through the expected topics of women's representation in politics; the role of women's movements in achieving political agency; the effects of state gender policies; the kinds of models society supports for women's behavior, ways in which their images are used in commercial advertising; demographic changes produced by female behavioral patterns; and more, all offered from a pre-Euromaidan perspective. Any attempt to analyze the full impact of recent events in Ukraine on future developments would be premature.

Inasmuch as no overall theme was imposed on the authors, no reconciliation of divergent perspectives was considered necessary. In bringing together the individual views of each author for a discussion on contemporary Ukraine, the diverse strands of their scholarship were woven into an intriguing tapestry of its post-Soviet life. By scrutinizing the diverse aspects of that life through a gender prism the contributors have created a new and unique form of women's scholarship—the nuanced New Imaginaries paradigm exemplified in this volume.

**Marian J. Rubchak** is a member of Phi Beta Kappa, twice a senior Fulbright scholar, and is currently a senior research professor of history at Valparaiso University. She has traveled extensively throughout Ukraine, and has taught and lectured in several institutions of higher learning there, including Kharkiv University's Summer School in Foros, Crimea for senior scholars of women's and gender studies. Rubchak translated, annotated, and provided the introduction to volume 17 of Sergei Soloviev's *History of Western Russia*; her most recent publication is an edited collection, *Mapping Difference: The Many Faces of Women in Contemporary Ukraine*, for which she also provided an introduction. Her current research interests include identity construction in various contexts, gender studies, and the impact of historical memory on the formation of a feminist consciousness.

# Notes

Since the original publication of this volume, considerable progress has been made in promoting the concept of equal rights for women in Ukraine. This continues, but largely on the elite level as before. In response, some members of the rank and file have taken matters into their own hands, forming new programs and institutions to continue the campaign against Ukraine's patriarchal culture.

1. The Revolution on Granite initiative was instrumental in mobilizing the youth to protest in the next, the Orange Revolution of 2004. Doniy's commitment also extended to the 2013 Euromaidan Revolution. Some of the "Orange" student activists, having gone on to become businesspeople in their turn, offered organizational skills and monetary assistance. The same was true of the Revolution on the Granite generation. In 2014 Oles Doniy was elected as a non-affiliated member of the Ukrainian parliament.
2. The young people were articulating a new formulation of rights discourses and strategies that embrace neoliberal self-regulation and Soviet-style governmental care.
3. Martha Bohachevsky-Chomiak 1988.
4. The electoral process was in fact riddled with corruption, but the media, as well as some historians, simply kept mindlessly repeating the same "free and fair" election characterization that someone initially (for whatever reason) put out there.
5. The impetus and leadership provided by the youth—comprising largely university students—has been widely acknowledged.
6. Phillips 2014.
7. "Ukrainian pop star Ruslana honored with an International Women of Courage award!" *Voices of Ukraine*. 6 March 2014.
8. Documents recovered after Yanukovych and his bodyguards fled Ukraine point directly to the president ordering the attack that three of his bodyguards executed. A notebook belonging to the head of his bodyguards was retrieved after his hasty retreat in late February. It offers evidence of a planned attack and its price. See http//stories.yanukovychleaks.org/notatki osobystogo oborontsya/.
9. One woman holds a cabinet position: Minister of Social Policy Liudmyla Denisova.
10. Yuriy Butusov 2014.

11. Phillips 2014.
12. Radio Liberty was its source. Nataliya Trach. 2014. "Standing Guard: The men and women protecting Euromaidan" in which one of the protest leaders, Havryliuk, announced that women were welcome as participants but would not form an actual component of any self-defense unit. See also *News Global.* 15 February 2014.
13. See http://euromaidanpr.wordpress.com/2014/02/05/a-female-squadron-forms-for-euromaidan.
14. For a fuller account, see *Kyiv Post* 14 February 2014; and *Volyn Post* 14 February 2014. *Ukrainska Pravda: Zhyttia* 2 March 2014. And "The Untold Story of the Ukrainian Revolution." 27 February 2014. All were posted on the Euromaidan listserve on 25 June 2014.
15. Female Squadron (*Zhinocha Sotnia*), 16th Squadron of "Maidan Self-Defence" (*Samooborony Maidanu*). Reference sent to author by a female activist on Maidan on 5 March 2014. On 15 May 2014 I received an email notification from *Fulbright Ukraine* that several women's organizations in Ukraine, including *Zhinocha Sotnia* (organized during the January 2014 protests in Kyiv), in conjunction with a number of Fulbright programs were inaugurating a photo exhibition titled *Zhinky Maidanu* (Women of Maidan) documenting their selfless dedication to the cause of an open Western-oriented democratic society.
16. See also Trina R. Mamoon. 2012.
17. Phillips. 2014. It was reprinted online without pagination. Accessed on line on 15 August 2014.
18. "All efforts for the front: Everything for victory." Internet post, 31 August 2014.
19. On 10 Nov 2014 Oksana Kis posted a notification of a video aired on Channel 1+1 about other women in active combat. See http://tsn.ua/.../zhinki-viyskovi-u-zoni-ato-voyuyut-na-rivni...
20. Vira Aheieva, ed. 2002.
21. In 1992 Solomea Pavlychko launched her publishing house (*Osnovy*), dedicated to the production of important Western literature on feminism in translation. She headed it until her untimely passing on New Year's Eve, 1999.
22. From personal conversations with female deputies following the 1995 parliamentary hearing that I witnessed.
23. Responses to this legislation are available in Halyna Fedkovych. 2005.
24. Shortly after this change in the curriculum, the program began to attract considerable opposition, however; although it continued to function it still faces an uphill struggle.
25. Akhil Gupta 1992. Cited in Rubchak. 1996.
26. In *News from Ukraine.* 1990, no. 5. During a personal conversation with her some years later she reiterated her conviction that the women's only priority must be nation building.
27. Oksana Kis. 2013: 18–21.
28. Oksana Kis. 2012. Men's Day is also observed in Ukraine, on 23 February, but unlike International Women's Day it is not a national holiday.
29. During one of my numerous stays in Kyiv men were out on the streets on 8 March offering women small nosegays of mimosas attached to cards bearing the customary saccharine greetings.
30. Kis. 2011.

31. "Spring's irritation." 2015.
32. Materials received from Tetiana Isaieva, director of the Gender Museum, in 2013.
33. Events playing out on Euromaidan at the time of this writing between Westward-leaning forces in opposition to the Yanukovych regime and pro-Russian supporters to the east and south are signaling the danger of Ukraine's return to its authoritarian past.
34. As late as 24 November 2013 Kyiv's bilingual newspaper *Den'* characterized this same force as: "Saber-toothed tigers ... roaming nearby."
35. Reported by *Radio Liberty,* Jeffrey Tayler. 2013.
36. In *Ukraine is Not a Brothel,* a film produced by Kitty Green, a 32-year-old male political scientist, Victor Sviatsky, hinted obliquely that he might have been the founder of FEMEN, a claim that FEMEN's leaders vehemently deny.
37. See Rubchak. 2013 on the Berghahn Books blog site, from which some of this text was excerpted. http://www.berghahnbooks.com/history/.
38. Herszenhorn. 2013.
39. It finds itself in serious difficulty in the West as well.
40. Rubchak 2012a. Also in Ukrainian in *Krytyka.* XIV: 4(174); and Rubchak. 2012b.
41. Announcement of the forthcoming book appeared online on 12 February 2014 on the *Myr* site. By this time FEMEN had begun referring to itself as *feminist* without being able to articulate what it means. Its leaders resorted to terms like *ultra-feminists* but offered no definitions.
42. "Stop Putin," *Euromaidan SOS.* 1:7 March 2014: 11.
43. Rachkevych 2012.
44. Ibid.
45. For a spirited debate on this turn of events, see dialogue in *Krytyka* between Mayerchyk 2014b and Martsenyuk 2014. Cited in Phillips. 2014
46. An example of continued student involvement is the 27 February 2013 rally protesting hearings by the Parliamentary Committee on Education on new laws and regulations that, if passed, would have paralyzed institutional autonomy, academic freedom, and student mobility to a graduate study curriculum of choice. http://youtu.be/edKACcsBFTY.
47. Kis. 2012.
48. All such initiatives transpired before the tragic events of 2013–2014 on Kyiv's Euromaidan, and the subsequent incursions of Russian armed forces and Russian-supported separatists in eastern and southern Ukraine. The landscape—human and physical—has changed dramatically, and the outcome of this warfare is yet to be determined as of late 2014.
49. "A lie told often enough becomes truth," Lenin once pronounced in a statement paraphrased from William James (1842–1910), father of modern psychology, who declared earlier: "There's nothing so absurd that if you repeat it often enough, people will believe it." The anti-gender movement STOP Gender appears to be operating according to the same principle.
50. Olena Hankivsky (unpublished). "STOP Gender! The current situation and potential responses to the anti-gender movement in Ukraine," with the author's permission.

51. It is important to mention in this context that Ukraine already holds the distinction of a society with a serious breakdown of the traditional family structure.
52. Rubchak. 2011.
53. The Euromaidan uprising since mid-November 2013 has demonstrated how much of the Soviet past still lingers. The corrupt authorities and their oligarchic allies are resorting to coercion, brutal force by the Special Forces (*Berkut*), savage attacks by unidentified assailants, intimidation, and unconstitutional mandates that include Soviet-style "show trials" to keep themselves in power and consistently above the law.
54. This changed recently. A new bill on higher education has been introduced providing greater autonomy and scope for reforms within the inherited Soviet-era system controlled by a retrograde Ministry of Education.
55. Anna Fournier. 2012.
56. Partial exceptions to this include my *Mapping Difference. The Many Faces of Women in Contemporary Ukraine*, but it also includes chapters by Western researchers.
57. The final chapter of Ukraine's struggle for an open democratic society that played out for three months in 2013–2014 has yet to be written, but protesters scored a massive victory (at the cost of scores of lives) when parliament voted on 22 February to remove the Yanukovych regime and allow the formation of a provisional government. Elections to bring in a new slate of officers were held on 25 May 2014. They returned a male-dominated governing body.
58. "Clothes that accentuated a woman's figure were banned.… Ukrainian women wore no low necks, used padded shoulders, and were clad in long, loose skirts." For a further explanation, see "Gender in the USSR." 2012. 18 April: 3.
59. Official figures place the entire process of women's labor migration at 233,000. Unofficially this is estimated at closer to 1.8 million.
60. This also reflects former Soviet attitudes toward any woman's travel abroad to such "dens of iniquity" where women are said to work in the sex trade. Today it can determine a women's decision to remain in the host country.
61. Olena Fedyuk. n.d.
62. The author earned her PhD here. Her residence in the country provided ample opportunity for extensive research on the Ukrainian diaspora in Spain.
63. Practicum is the practical application of previously studied course material (theory).
64. Although this thesis is generally accepted, the emphasis on matriarchy that accompanies it remains a contentious issue, but it is a suitable subject for a separate study.
65. Not surprisingly, of course, that authority has given way to serious opposition in today's world.
66. The journal was founded back in 1920 under the title *Communard*, then changed in 1929 to *Radianska Zhinka* (Soviet Woman), and finally it became simply *Zhinka* after Ukrainian independence was declared in 1991.
67. Oleksandr Pahiria. 2012.

# Bibliography

Aheeva, Vira, ed. 2002. *Solomea Pavlychko, Feminism.* Kyiv: Osnovy.

Bohachevsky-Chomiak, Martha. 1988. *Feminists Despite Themselves: Women in Ukrainian Community Life 1884–1939.* Edmonton: Canadian Institute of Ukrainian Studies, University of Alberta.

Butusov, Yuriy. 2014. "Heroes of Maidan: Nina Matvijiv," *Tilamuse.*

"Changing face of Ukraine's resistance," *News Global,* 15 February 2014.

"Lifestyle," *Kyiv Post,* 14 February 2014.

*Den'.*

Fedkovych, Halyna. 2005. *Legislative Trends and New Developments: Stop Violence against Women.* http://www.stopvaw.org/Legislative-Trends,_and_New_Developments24html.

Fedyuk, Olena. n.d. "Ukrainian Labor Migrants: Visibility through Stereotypes," *MigrationOnline.cz.*

Fournier, Anna. 2012. *Forging Rights in a New Democracy: Ukrainian Students between Freedom and Justice.* Philadelphia: University of Pennsylvania Press.

"Gender in the USSR," *The Ukrainian Week.* 18 April 2012: 3.

Gupta, Akhil. 1992. "The Song of the Non-aligned World: Transnational Identities and the Reinscription of Space in Late Capitalism," *Cultural Anthropology.* 7: 70–72.

Hankivsky, Olena (unpublished). "STOP Gender! The current situation and potential responses to the anti-gender movement in Ukraine."

Herszenhorn, David M. 2013. "Ukraine's Feminist Shock Troops," *New York Times.* 31 May.

Kis, Oksana. 2015. "Spring's aggravation, or how are public servants greeting Ukrainian women on International Women's Day?", *Ukraina Moderna.*

———. 2013. "What is/what kind of women's history does Ukraine need?" *Krytyka* XVII 1–2(183–184): 18–21.

———. 2012. "Ukrainian women reclaiming the feminist meaning of International Women's Day: A Report about Recent Feminist Activism," in *The International Yearbook of Central, Easter, and Southeastern Women's and Gender History,* vol. 6, 219–232.

———. 2011. *Zakhidna Analitychna Grupa,* 18 March. http://zgroup.com.ua/article.php?articleid=260.

*Krytyka.* XIV 4(174).

Mamoon, Trina R. 2012. "'Black Widows: Women as Political Combatants in the Chechen Conflict," in: *Embracing Arms. Cultural Representation of Slavic and Balkan Women in War,* Helena Goscilo and Yana Hashamova, eds. Budapest and New York: Central European Press.

*Myr.*

*News from Ukraine.* 1990.

Pahiria, Oleksandr. 2012. "Gender in the USSR," *The Ukrainian Week,* 18. ukrainianweek.com/Society/?page=4.

Phillips, Sarah. 2014. "The Women's Squad in Ukraine's Protests: Feminism, nationalism, and militarism on the Maidan," *American Ethnologist* 41: 414–426. Doi: 10:1111/amet.

Rachkevych, Mark. 2012. "New Feminist Offensive aims to lift women," *Kyiv Post*, 22 March.

*Radianska Zhinka*. 1939.

Rubchak, Marian J. 2011. *Mapping Difference: The Many Faces of Women in Contemporary Ukraine*. Oxford and New York: Berghahn Books.

———. 2013. Berghahn Books blog site: http://www.berghahnbooks.com/history.

———. 2012a. "The Charge of the Pink Brigade," *Eurozine*, 3 July.

———. 2012b. "Discourse of Continuity and Change. Legislature and the Gender Issue in Ukraine," in *Gender Politics and Society in Ukraine*, eds. Olena Hankivsky and Anastasiia Salnykova. Toronto: University of Toronto Press.

Tayler, Jeffrey. 2013. "Femen: Ukraine's topless warriors," *Radio Liberty*, 8 November.

Trach, Nataliya. 2014. "Standing Guard: The men and women protecting Euromaidan in which one of the protest leaders, Havryliuk, announced that women were welcome as participants but would not form an actual component of the self-defense units," *in Kyiv Post*, 10 February.

*Ukrainska Pravda: Zhyttia* 2014.

*Voices of Ukraine*. 6 March 2014.

*Volyn Post*.

*Zakhidna Analitychna Grupa*. 8 March 2011.

# PART I

# Gender Politics in Post-Soviet Ukraine

# CHAPTER 1

# Women's Top-Level Political Participation
## Failures and Hopes of Ukrainian Gender Politics

Tamara Martsenyuk

More than twenty years of Ukrainian independence passed before women's representation in *Verkhovna Rada* (Ukrainian Parliament) rose to 10 percent (in 2012). As the United Nations Development Program (UNDP) states in their Ukrainian records, however: "No women currently serve as oblast [regional] governors, only one woman was recently appointed to the governmental ruling body, and few were recruited as candidates in the last election. It was only as late as February 14, 2012 that one female was appointed Minister of Health (and Vice-Prime Minister)—Raisa Bohatyriova—Party of Regions. In short, Ukraine's record on women's inclusion in mainstream politics is abysmal."[1] At the same time, the State Committee of Statistics of Ukraine indicates that women make up 64 percent of the management cadres of all civil servants,[2] yet most serve at the local level. Gender discrimination against women's access to political power at the upper levels is reducible to the following: the greater the power, the fewer the women.

Ukraine was among the first of the former Soviet republics to implement gender equality legislation. It had (and continues to have) a number of international gender equality projects that are financed by the UNDP, EU, Swedish Institute of Development (SIDA), etc. The country boasts the most famous female politician in the world (especially after the Orange Revolution)—Yulia Tymoshenko—who might have served as an excellent role model for Ukrainian women had she not disavowed feminism. What are the main barriers that have limited the position of women at or near the top of the political pyramid? This chapter will consider both the negative and positive trends in recent years (2010–2012).

Various levels of analyses will be employed to provide some insights into the reasons for the current political situation. They include: the results of international reports and Ukraine's obligations concerning gender equality implementation; gender politics in Ukraine during the previous decade affecting female empowerment; a discussion of the most popular political party, and the position of its leadership on questions of women's empowerment; results of sociological polls on women's political participation; women's NGOs and grassroots initiatives to translate their empowerment into a viable political agenda; and the controversy surrounding implementation of gender party quotas as an expedient designed to reverse female parliamentary underrepresentation. Both quantitative and qualitative methods as well as empirical data will comprise the methodological approach.

Primary quantitative data analysis is based on public-opinion surveys ("Opinions and Attitudes of the Ukrainian Population," 1999, 2007, 2008, 2010)[3] provided by the Kyiv International Institute of Sociology.[4] Secondary quantitative data analysis draws on recent reports such as the Global Gender Gap Report 2011 and UNDP Human Development Report 2011, and the Women in National Parliaments and Women in Politics databases, collected by the Inter-Parliamentary Union. Findings also include an evaluation of the progress to date toward fulfillment of Ukraine's Millennium Development Goals. In addition, a discussion of affirmative action will take into account projects such as "Quotas: A Key to Equality?"[5] and the Global Database of Quotas for Women,[6] compiled by a research team from the Political Science Department at Stockholm University.[7] In-depth interviews conducted in Ukraine in 2011[8] by experts with ten or more years experience in Ukrainian gender politics implementation, and my own participation in various public initiatives since 2004, round out the body of this research.

## Gender in Reports: International Level

According to the Global Gender Gap Report 2011, provided by the World Economic Forum (Hausman, Tyson, and Zahidi 2012: 338), Ukraine places 64th among 135 countries in the world measuring gender-based gaps in four fundamental categories: economic participation and opportunity, educational attainment, health and survival, and political empowerment.

The political empowerment subindex includes the male/female gap in political decision making at the highest levels; the ratio of women to men at the ministerial level and in parliamentary positions; and the ratio of women to men according to years spent in executive office—prime minister or president—during the past fifty years. It lacks the variables that capture the differences in government at the local levels, but its authors are cognizant of the problem and assure us that should such data become

**Table 1.1.** *Ukraine in the Global Gender Gap Report 2011.*

| # | Subindex | Rank (among 135 countries) | Index Score (0.00 = inequality; 1.00 = equality) |
|---|----------|----------------------------|--------------------------------------------------|
| 1 | Economic participation and opportunity | 44 | 0.704 |
| 2 | Educational attainment | 24 | 1.000 |
| 3 | Health and survival | 56 | 0.976 |
| 4 | Political empowerment | 106 | 0.065 |
| 5 | Total | 64 | 0.686 |

*Source:* Hausman et al. 2011: 339.

available for the global level they will be considered for inclusion in the Global Gender Gap Index (Hausman, Tyson, and Zahidi 2012: 4).

In other subindices, such as educational attainment and economic participation, Ukraine delivered much better scores. The nation's women are well educated and in general participate dynamically in the labor market (primarily at the lower levels), yet they are virtually excluded from top political decision making here as well. In the Global Gender Gap Report 2011 political empowerment subindex, Ukraine is positioned behind a number of other post-Soviet countries such as Latvia (33rd), Lithuania (65th), the Kyrgyz Republic (68th), the Russian Federation (84th), Estonia (87th), Moldova (88th), etc.

The Gender Inequality Index (GII) of the UNDP Human Development Report also focuses on women's participation in political decision making, highlighting the fact that women lag behind men everywhere. The UNDP Human Development Report for 2011 ranks Ukraine 76th out of 187 countries (UNDP 2011), yet it is considered a country with a high human developmental level.[9] The GII ranking puts Ukraine in 57th place, with only 8 percent (currently 9.7 percent) of the seats in the National Parliament occupied by women (UNDP 2011: 140). Finally, when we search the Inter-Parliamentary Union database of Women in Parliaments,[10] Ukraine takes 120th place (sharing it with Algeria) among 190 countries classified in descending order by percentage of women.

Ukraine set out to meet the Millennium Development Goals by 2015 (UNDP 2012). The goals were adapted to the nation's values, taking into account the specifics of the country's augmented evolution. In particular, Goal 3 is connected to ensuring gender equality. There are two main targets here: gender equality in political life and gender equality in Ukraine's labor market.

According to the UNDP Millennium Development Goals for 2015, ratified by Ukraine, its parliament is under obligation to reach a target of at least 30 percent women (table 1.2). By 2007 the Ukrainian state planned to raise the women's presence in *Verkhovna Rada* to 13 percent (UNDP 2012), but this number fell far short of the country's international obligation of a 3.1 subgoal. Following the 2007 parliamentary elections *Verkhovna Rada* continued as an almost totally male-dominated body, consisting of only 8 percent women. Since independence Ukraine has shown little augmentation of this number, a clear indication that it will prove difficult to achieve the 30 percent objective in three years.

**Table 1.2.** *Goal 3: "Promote Gender Equality" in UNDP Millennium Development Goals: Progress in Achievement*

| | |
|---|---|
| Target 3.A: Ensure gender representation at the level of no less than 37 percent in representative bodies and high-level executive authorities | 3.1. Gender ratio among the members of the Parliament of Ukraine, number of women / number of men<br>3.2. Gender ratio among the members of local authorities, number of women / number of men<br>3.3. Gender ratio among the higher-level civil servants (one–two categories), number of women / number of men |
| Target 3.B: Half the gap in incomes between women and men | 3.4. Ratio of average wages between women and men, percent |

| | 2000 | 2001 | 2002 | 2003 | 2004 | 2005 | 2006 | 2007 | 2008 | 2009 | 2010 | 2015 |
|---|---|---|---|---|---|---|---|---|---|---|---|---|
| 3.1 | 8/92 | 8/92 | 5/95 | 5/95 | 5/95 | 5/95 | 9/91 | 8/92 | 8/92 | 8/92 | 8/92 | 30/70 |
| 3.2 | 42/58 | 42/58 | 42/58 | 42/58 | 42/58 | 42/58 | 35/65 | 35/65 | 37/63 | 37/63 | 37/63 | 50/50 |
| 3.3 | 15/85 | 15/85 | 14/86 | 16/84 | 13/87 | 19/81 | 19/81 | 17/83 | 18/82 | 23/76 | 25/75 | 30/70 |
| 3.4 | 70.9 | 69.7 | 69.3 | 68.6 | 68.6 | 70.9 | 72.8 | 72.9 | 75.2 | 77.2 | 77.8 | 86 |

*Source.*[11]

To sum up, according to the primary international reports on gender inequality throughout the world—the Global Gender Gap Report 2011, the Gender Inequality Index in the UNDP Human Development Report 2011, and the Inter-Parliamentary Union database of Women in Parliament—Ukraine ranks very low in female empowerment and political participation compared to neighboring post-Soviet countries. Moreover, gender equality in Ukrainian politics has the worst value compared to other areas such as education, health, and the economy.

## State Level: Gender Politics in Ukraine

The negative macro-picture of Ukrainian women's participation in top-level politics might be better explained by analyzing it at the state levels.

During the past ten years some of the goals have been achieved. For example, *Verkhovna Rada* adopted the groundbreaking law "On Ensuring Equal Rights and Opportunities for Men and Women" (Law no. 2866-IV) in September 2005, which came into effect on 1 January 2006. The government of Ukraine also ratified the decree "On Adoption of the State Program of Ensuring Gender Equality in Ukrainian Society for 2006–2010" (Decree of the Cabinet of Ministers no. 1834), and developed a subsequent one for 2011–2016. More than a decade ago Ukraine became the first post-Soviet country to introduce domestic violence legislation ("On Prevention of Domestic Violence"). In 2011 separate pieces of legislation on prevention of human trafficking (a critical gender-based problem) were adopted. De jure gender equality is supported by national institutional mechanisms and legislation. International and national NGOs monitor the results of state and regional programs and propose solutions for improvement.

One might persuasively argue that despite so many promising proposals, legislative attempts, and government programs, etc., not much has been realized. Without a doubt, there is a lack of governmental accountability for meeting its legislative initiatives. The all-important Ukrainian legislation "On Ensuring Equal Rights and Opportunities for Men and Women" is a clear example of such ineffectiveness. Yet it is also significant that the law introduced such vital gender-sensitive terminology as equal rights and opportunities for women and men, gender equality, discrimination on the basis of sex, sexual harassment, etc. (Law no. 2866-IV, Article 1). Concrete bodies, institutions, and organizations are specified as those with the power to ensure equal rights and opportunities for both sexes. All of this is nothing more than a "tempest in a teapot," however. Most articles are simply declarative, without any real mechanism for executing them (particularly the administrative or criminal codes), or sanctions for violating them. For example, according to Article 17, "employers are prohibited to offer jobs targeting specifically women or men in their advertisements." But in the absence of any sanctions the Ukrainian labor market ads are full of such discriminatory descriptions.

In October 2010 the Ukrainian population was surveyed regarding its acquaintance with the law "On Ensuring Equal Rights and Opportunities for Men and Women."[12] Despite the fact that the law came into force back in 2006, 43 percent of the respondents had never heard of it; the same number had heard something, but only about 10 percent of the respondents were familiar with the contents.[13] The answers of women and men did not differ significantly, leading to the conclusion that relatively few Ukrainians of either sex are familiar with any major gender legislation.

For some time the Ministry of Ukraine for Family, Youth, and Sports (Ministry for Social Policy at the time of this writing) was the main body responsible for ensuring equal rights and opportunities for both sexes. The title alone attests to the fact that perception of gender issues is limited. Under current economic and social conditions the entrenched stereotypes of men as breadwinners and leaders in the public sphere (particularly in politics), and of women as mothers and wives, limit any real prospects for gender equality. In its effort to become gender specific Ukrainian legislation is still crafted with a view to protecting women, family, and children, thus perpetuating traditional gender roles, and what amounts to the infantilization of women.

The second largest problem regarding gender issues besetting Ukrainian society can be analyzed by the content of public speeches delivered by top authorities. Since 2010 sexist speeches by high-level politicians have received wide attention in Ukraine: "Ukrainian women berate 'Neanderthal' PM for sexist remarks."[14] Other sexist pronouncements by Mykola Azarov received extensive coverage as well: "Some say our government is too large; others that there are no women," he observed. "There's nothing to look at during cabinet sessions, nothing but boring faces. With due respect to women, however, conducting reforms is not women's business." Foreign newspapers like *The Guardian* reported the incident.

Azarov's remarks made it plain that Ukrainian women are nothing more than "a beautiful commodity" to look at and to inspire politicians to great deeds. To add insult to injury, in his recent greetings to women on International Women's Day on 8 March 2012, Azarov failed to offer Ukrainian woman any hope for positive change, or even to suggest the need for such practical benefits as state support for parents with children, for instance. Instead, he resorted to the well-worn wish for their "personal happiness" and "unfading beauty."[15]

As for women as beautiful objects, the Ukrainian president has vigorously promoted the notion of objectified womanhood: "Welcome to Ukraine to see our beautiful girls" was the message sent to an international delegation that met in Davos in 2011.[16] In an effort to improvise on the EURO 2012 promotion "Switch on Ukraine," Yanukovych declared, "it is enough to see it with one's own eyes, when the chestnut trees are in bloom as the weather grows warmer, in Ukrainian cities women start to take off their clothes. To see such beauty is an amazing thing!"In the eyes of many men Ukrainian women have two roles to play: as objects of beauty (inspiration to men) and as mothers (reproducers of the nation). One woman—Yulia Tymoshenko—seemingly embodied both profiles in the role of a stylish woman and "mother of the nation" (especially during the Orange Revolution), but she never rose to the challenge of knowingly becoming the role model she might have been.

# Political Parties

What can we expect of politics in Ukraine when the nation's most famous female politician never exhibited any gender sensitivity? During the 2007 parliamentary elections, for example, the woman who came after her on the party list was in thirtieth place. Tymoshenko's failure to address this could account, at least in some measure, for the failure of Ukrainian women's organizations to make a show of solidarity during their International Women's Day demonstrations on 8 March 2012 against her unjust imprisonment, or to mount a grassroots protest against her persecution and incarceration.

On 1 March 2012 the National Democratic Institute (NDI) and the United Nations Development Program (UNDP) hosted a remarkable event in Kyiv, an open discussion on "Empowering Women for Stronger Political Parties." Arseny Yatseniuk ("Front of Change" party leader), Vitaliy Klychko (*Udar* party leader), Leonid Kozhara (Deputy Head, Party of Regions), Borys Tarasiuk (*Rukh* party leader), etc., all assembled to discuss women's political empowerment.

In an effort to share their main proposals with male party leaders, NDI and UNDP presented a comprehensive manual on the development of political parties through the enthusiastic and effective engagement of women as activists, members, and voters. According to these associations, internal party organizational strategies include: addressing gender equality in the party's legal framework; making a statement on gender equality in the founding document; and advocating for internal quotas that would ensure women's participation on governing boards (NDI 2011: 4). NDI also examines the benefits accruing to political parties when they involve women in their public activity. It notes, "findings from the case studies suggest that those political parties augmented their support base and gained electorally after adopting reforms to promote women's empowerment" (11). Spinoffs for political parties implementing reforms would be renewed public interest in their parties; increased flow of funding; an increase in new members, etc. (12).

Ukrainian political parties have their own specific attitudes toward involving women in politics, however, especially at the top level. These differences are visible in their party programs and lists. All the most popular Ukrainian parties (such as Our Ukraine, the Bloc of Yulia Tymoshenko, the Party of Regions, and so on) tend to be gender insensitive, and ignore important gender equality implementation measures in their programs (Plotian 2006; Melnyk, and Kobelianska 2006).

In 2010 members from the Ukrainian Women's Fund interviewed eight of sixteen political parties in *Verkhovna Rada* to determine the deputies' attitudes toward women in politics. Results proved contradictory. Political parties declared equal opportunities for women and men, and the absence of discriminatory policies, but as a rule made no special effort to engage more women. The latter's very low numbers at the top level are explained by competition among candidates themselves, with men proving to be more adept at securing the top positions (UWF 2010: 2). Although an analysis of the first five party lists demonstrated that in electoral campaigns parties declare their intent to follow the "at least one woman in the first fifth" rule, female candidates never seem to rise to such positions.

In April 2010 three focus groups (in Kyiv, Chernihiv, and Lutsk), with representatives of leading political parties in attendance,[17] were conducted under the auspices of the project "Analysis and Recommendations for the Reform of Political Parties' Legislation and Regulation in Ukraine" (Kovryzhenko 2010: 15).[18] Once again, results confirmed that politicians are less than eager to support affirmative action that would raise the number of female representatives in mainstream politics. General sentiment indicated that "women's participation in political life should be promoted indirectly, not through mandatory quotas" (84).

In his personal blog on "Ukrainian Pravda" the Deputy Head of the Party of Regions[19] Leonid Kozhara[20] provided some allegedly gender-sensitive statistics that confirmed gender segregation. According to Kozhara, women constitute 53 percent of all registered Party of Regions members, yet only half, or 25.5 percent, are deputies at any level. There is no hierarchical specification, perhaps to avoid portraying an even bleaker picture. Women comprise a mere 30 percent of the Party of Region's local boards, where so-called women's issues are normally considered, disparities that Ukrainian parties vow to correct.

## Public Opinion: Attitudes toward Women in Politics

Monitoring public opinion demonstrates that, contrary to the actions of political parties, Ukrainian society is becoming more egalitarian-oriented in its consideration of female participation in the political life of the country. This positive dynamic can be traced for the years 1999–2007 (table 1.3).

In 1999 nearly 63 percent of respondents (more than 65 percent men and nearly 61 percent women) were of the opinion that most men are better suited for politics than most women. Results of the same public opinion survey taken in 2007 demonstrate a visible change in attitudes. The number of respondents with patriarchal views decreased by almost 20 percent—from 63 percent to just over 45 percent of all respondents, but the growing difference between male and female views became more

**Table 1.3.** *"Most men are better suited for politics than most women"* (percent)

| | 1999 | | | 2007 | | |
|---|---|---|---|---|---|---|
| | Total | Men | Women | Total | Men | Women |
| Don't agree / prefer to disagree rather than agree | 19.5 | 18.2 | 20.4 | 34.7 | 29.6 | 39.0 |
| Difficult to say | 15.8 | 15.0 | 16.4 | 18.2 | 17.9 | 18.5 |
| Prefer to agree rather than disagree / agree | 62.5 | 65.3 | 60.4 | 45.3 | 50.9 | 40.8 |
| No answer | 2.2 | 1.5 | 2.7 | 1.7 | 1.7 | 1.7 |

*Source:* KIIS, February 1999 (n=1588), April 2007 (n=2009).

apparent, with 51 percent of men and 41 percent of women agreeing with the "most men are better suited for politics than most women" sentiment. Clearly, Ukrainian society still favors the male-breadwinner family model. Respondents of both sexes prefer to sustain the traditional division of public and private spheres—reinforcing the belief that women should make support of men's careers a top priority.

For all of the positive changes in public attitudes a persuasive argument is building that on the whole Ukrainian society continues to perceive women only as mothers and homemakers. Paradoxically, women might also hold a full-time position outside the home because so many families are unable to survive on a man's salary alone. Although traditional stereotypes still hold, Ukrainian society simply cannot afford many full-time homemakers. Of course, this is no indication of women's growing equality with men, either in jobs or in salaries. Clearly, gender discrimination remains endemic in the Ukrainian labor market as well.[21] All such negative sentiments aside, however, recurring references to the low number of women in Ukraine's parliament do suggest that the majority of Ukrainians might be amenable to the idea of women in top political positions.

**Table 1.4.** *"For a wife it is more important to support the husband's career than to pursue her own"* (percent, 2010)

| | Total | Men | Women |
|---|---|---|---|
| Don't agree | 17.7 | 12.8 | 21.7 |
| Prefer to disagree rather than agree | 17.1 | 13.2 | 20.2 |
| Difficult to say | 24.5 | 25.7 | 23.5 |
| Prefer to agree rather than disagree | 16.0 | 18.6 | 14.0 |
| Agree | 20.3 | 25.3 | 16.1 |
| No answer | 4.4 | 4.4 | 4.5 |

*Source:* KIIS, October 2010 (n=2038).

**Table 1.5.** *"How many female deputies belong in the Ukrainian Parliament?"* *(percent, 2010)*

|                              | Total | Men  | Women |
|------------------------------|-------|------|-------|
| More than half               | 5.6   | 3.9  | 6.9   |
| About half                   | 30.5  | 23.0 | 36.5  |
| One-third                    | 19.8  | 19.2 | 20.2  |
| One-fourth                   | 10.7  | 13.3 | 8.6   |
| One-tenth                    | 6.6   | 8.8  | 4.8   |
| None                         | 6.7   | 10.0 | 4.0   |
| Difficult to say / don't know| 17.5  | 18.7 | 16.6  |
| No answer                    | 2.6   | 3,1  | 2.4   |

*Source:* KIIS, October 2010 (n=2038).

To summarize, almost 60 percent of all respondents replied that the number of women in Ukraine's parliament should equal at least one-third or more. Approximately one-fifth of the respondents were unable to supply an answer, while 10 percent of the men and 4 percent of the women indicated that the Ukrainian parliament should remain a male-dominated preserve.

Public opinion on the presence of women in mainstream politics does appear contradictory, but it is also undeniable that for the past ten years views have become somewhat less patriarchal. Ukrainian society (women especially) supports (at least nominally) the idea that the Ukrainian parliament ought to comprise no less than 30 percent women, and the figure rises to 50 percent in some cases. Also, an argument can be made that in recent years at least a good portion of Ukrainian society has come to see a positive role model in the person of Yulia Tymoshenko, who has played such a constructive role in Ukrainian politics. At the same time, our data indicate that a segment of society seems unable to jettison the gender stereotyping of women as unsuitable for politics. This paradox remains to be worked out.

## Women's Activism

A lack of female solidarity in both civil society and politics in Ukraine is consistent. Notwithstanding the rising numbers of women who actively support gender parity, they are still in the minority. No women's movement worthy of the description *strong,* with a focus on feminism and the capacity to promote actively the idea of increasing women's participation in politics, exists in contemporary Ukraine. The country boasts hundreds of women's NGOs—local and national—but these tend to focus more on social issues such as women's health, childhood, and poverty than on equal rights and opportunities in the political sphere or the labor market. Examples include such organizations as the National Council of Ukrainian Women (1999), the Women's Union (*Zhinocha Hromada*), the Ukrainian Women's Association (*Soiuz Zhinok Ukrainy*), Women and Children of Ukraine, etc. Their visibility fell between 2010 and 2012, particularly in media coverage and attendance at community meetings on women's empowerment. This is yet another sign of the changing political climate after Yanukovych became president in 2010. A single exception is FEMEN, a group of radical grassroots activists demonstrating for women's rights, but the effectiveness of FEMEN's protest activity is a topic for a separate discussion.

An outstanding example of a pro equality individual activist is Kateryna Levchenko, former MP and current leader of an international antiviolence NGO that goes under the name La Strada-Ukraine. Her organization launched an attempt to sue Prime Minister Azarov for his sexist speech in 2010, although it proved unsuccessful.[22]

Among the new grassroots organizations rejecting prevailing anti-women cultural values we also find initiatives like *"Ofenzyva"* (Feminist Offensive),[23] which in 2011 introduced an alternative model of celebrating International Women's Day on 8 March. It organized a women's art workshop, an international conference on feminism, and a march bearing the slogan "Church and State, the time has come for them to live apart." Its 200-person street protests, however, are hardly large enough to raise any genuine awareness of gender inequality. At the same time stronger public awareness, especially at the grassroots level, and in books and brochures, is manifest in the so-called antigender initiatives (like "STOP Gender"). They publish materials on gender politics, LGBT liberations (called gay-dictatorship), and children's rights (juvenile justice), calling attention to threats to family values. According to the Centre for Societal Research,[24] Ukrainian Protest and Coercion Data in Ukraine in 2010 and 2011, there were only twenty to twenty-three protests on the subject of women's rights (that is approximately 1 percent of all protests mounted). Almost all progender protests are executed by FEMEN, while a third are antigender protests (especially antiabortion demonstrations), which are on the rise and becoming increasingly strident.

Meanwhile, in late 2011 an "Equal Opportunities" caucus was formed in the Ukrainian Parliament.[25] It comprised twelve female and three male deputies from the pro-presidential and opposition factions and advocated gender equality in all spheres of life. The group was left with a large agenda after the 8 March 2012 holiday had passed. For instance, on 12

March Deputy Andrii Shkil introduced a bill on the prohibition of abortion. Under the existing law a woman can have an abortion only during the first trimester of her pregnancy. This bill and unresolved gender-based violence, especially rape, are subjects of increased attention,[26] constituting potential incentives for women's NGOs and activists to unite in a common protest against the use of women as objects of manipulation by a patriarchal society.

## Yulia Tymoshenko: Controversial Female Empowerment Model

Yulia Tymoshenko is the most famous woman in Ukraine's mainstream politics: she heads the All-Ukrainian Union "Fatherland" party and Bloc of Yulia Tymoshenko. Whatever her personal convictions, including her self-descriptor as a nonfeminist, she still represented a useful role model for women in Ukrainian politics as prime minister in 2005, and again in 2007–2010. During the Orange Revolutions she inspired a multitude of people and was proclaimed "The Orange Princess." According to the Ukrainian magazine *Focus,* "Lady Yu" placed first in the annual ranking of the most influential women in Ukraine between 2006 and 2010. In the presidential election of 2010 Tymoshenko lost to Victor Yanukovych by only 3.5 percent of the votes (45.4 percent vs. 48.95 percent), owing to questionable circumstances, although she did win the popular vote. All such achievements rendered her a positive role model whether or not she personally sought the label.

Yulia Tymoshenko has not offered any special evidence of gender sensitivity, and shows no particular concern for the problem of gender discrimination or issues such as gender-based violence, etc. Perhaps for this reason Ukrainian women's organizations failed to support her when she was sentenced to seven years' imprisonment for her alleged abuse of office in brokering an unfavorable gas deal with Russia.

We might argue quite convincingly that in her role as a famous female politician Tymoshenko has generally supported the patriarchal stereotypes that characterize Ukrainian public opinion. She was also known as "a beautiful feminine object," and named by the *Huffington Post* "a world leader of style." In her defense, however, in *Mapping Difference: The Many Faces of Women in Contemporary Ukraine* (Rubchak 2011: 314) we can read: "In Ukraine, where the term gender is only beginning to gain acceptance, where feminism is anathema, Tymoshenko is aware that a public declaration of support for the feminist point of view can be political suicide."

# What is to be Done? A Gender Quota Debate

In recent years a number of Ukrainian researchers have discussed the introduction of gender quotas by political parties (Oksamytna 2006; Melnyk and Kobelianska 2006; Martsenyuk 2007; Plotian 2006). Experts on gender issues support the idea of their implementation. In the words of the head of the Committee for European Integration Serhii Plotian: "Implementation of gender quotas is widely seen as leading to more equal representation of women and men in elective bodies" (2006: 34). Among his recommendations is that much-discussed party quota of thirty females in the candidate lists (34). In particular, he proposed changes to the laws "On Ensuring Equal Rights and Opportunities for Men and Women," "On the Election of People's Deputies of Ukraine," and "On the Political Parties of Ukraine" by adding a phrase requiring the presence of at least 30 percent of *either* sex on the lists. All such recommendations aside, in 2006 party lists of eligible candidates for election to the Ukrainian parliament still showed that men appear four times more frequently than women (34).

The political sphere in Ukraine is highly corrupt. According to the Corruption Perception Index Report 2011 data (Transparency International 2011) Ukraine placed 152nd among 180 countries. Ukrainian politics are closely connected to business, and dominated by men. Unlike the men, women have less money and fewer social networks at their disposal, a situation that impedes their ability to break into mainstream politics. That said, it must also be emphasized that according to data from the International Centre for Policy Studies,[27] Ukraine has made approximately ten legislative attempts to introduce gender party quotas, four of them connected with gender quotas in political candidate lists (International Center for Policy Studies 2007: 10). Each of these attempts failed, however. Article 1 of the law "On Ensuring Equal Rights and Opportunities for Men and Women," discussed above, defines "positive actions" as "special temporary actions designed to overcome the imbalance between opportunities for women and men to implement equal rights given them by the Constitution and the Laws of Ukraine" (Law no. 2866-IV). Article 3 of the same law refers to affirmative action as the primary focus of state politics on ensuring equal rights and opportunities for women and men. The main gender legislation of Ukraine refers only to general definitions and statements about positive actions but offers no concrete quotas for eliminating the gender imbalance. By contrast, on the international scene in recent years more than one hundred countries have adopted such quotas (Krook 2009: 304). Electoral quotas for women might be constitutional, legislative, or in the form of a political party allocation (International IDEA).

Such quotas are controversial instruments, with their pluses and minuses. They put the responsibility on individual parties for nominating women. As Drude Dahlerup (1998: 102) explains, the main advantage of the party quota system is that "it forces the nominating bodies, especially political parties, to engage women in an active recruitment process." It is essential that voluntary party quotas be adopted by a number of parties simultaneously, however. Should only one party decide to participate, then "if the support of that party declines, the representation of women will also drop" (Tripp et al. 2006: 132–133). In such an eventuality, blaming women can serve the interests of the nominating party.

Gender quotas aim to augment female representation in particular state bodies, eventually bringing it to a level equal to the proportion of women in the general population. When women constitute approximately half of the population clearly their views should be presented at the highest state level—a "critical mass" issue. As Dahlerup also observed, 30 percent is a crucial threshold for changing the political scene. This was one of the reasons why Ukraine signed on (in 2000) to the UNDP-sponsored Millennium Development Goals requiring that level of representation as a means of publicly conveying compliance with the objective of promoting gender equality and empowering women, but the signatories' intent to implement such equality objectives remains open to question.

In the KIIS-conducted poll the question was posed: "What is your attitude toward the introduction of gender quotas in order to increase women's representation in Parliament?" Results of public opinion surveys conducted in 2008 and 2010 demonstrate that Ukrainians tended to support the idea of implementing quotas. Approximately 47–51 percent of the population (depending on the particular year) appeared to favor the initiative. For example, the number of declared supporters in October 2010 totaled almost half the adult population (47.6 percent), exceeding opponents of the plan by more than double.

Not surprisingly, women tended to be more quota-friendly than men. For example, 59 percent of the women compared to 42 percent of the men supported affirmative action policies in 2008. By the 2010 election year, men had become twice as likely to oppose quota implementation. More than a quarter of the total respondents ventured no opinion, offering answers like "difficult to say" or "don't know" (28 percent in both 2010 and 2008). The fact that such a high percentage of the population had not formed an opinion on the subject is another issue. It might well reflect an absence of debates on gender equality and party quotas in the media and public discourse.

Supporters of different political parties also held divergent views. Respondents who supported Our Ukraine, the People's Self-Defence Party, the Bloc of Yulia Tymoshenko, and the Party of Regions were studied in

**Table 1.6.** *Attitudes toward the Introduction of Gender Quotas for the Purpose of Raising the Female Representation in Parliament (percent)*

| | 2010 | | | 2008 | | |
|---|---|---|---|---|---|---|
| | Total | Men | Women | Total | Men | Women |
| Agree | 47.6 | 39.9 | 53.8 | 51.3 | 41.4 | 59.4 |
| Disagree | 22.2 | 30.0 | 15.8 | 18.1 | 25.2 | 12.3 |
| I do not have an opinion on this issue | 16.9 | 17.5 | 16.3 | 17.8 | 19.5 | 16.5 |
| Difficult to say / don't know | 11.1 | 10.4 | 11.7 | 11.6 | 12.5 | 10.8 |
| No answer | 2.2 | 2.2 | 2.3 | 1.2 | 1.4 | 1.1 |

*Source:* KIIS, September 2008 (n=2036), October 2010 (n=2038).

April 2007, prior to the parliamentary elections. As shown in table 1.7, adherents of the Our Ukraine Party (57 percent) and the Bloc of Yulia Tymoshenko (57.5 percent) tended to have a more positive attitude than supporters of the Party of Regions (40.7 percent).

Approximately 28 percent of the Party of Regions membership offered no opinion, compared with 16 percent of the respondents supporting the Bloc of Yulia Tymoshenko, and 19 percent from the Our Ukraine Party.

Both Tamara Melnyk, gender equality adviser to Yury Pavlenko, minister of family, youth, and sports in the Yushchenko government, and the UN-led women's rights program Equal Opportunities and Women's Rights in Ukraine Program Coordinator Larysa Kobelianska endorsed the idea of affirmative action (2006: 8). They also remind us that when pass-

**Table 1.7** *Attitudes of Respondents with Different Political Views toward Gender Party Quotas (percent, 2007)*

| | | If we have now elections and you voted which party would you support? | | |
|---|---|---|---|---|
| | | Our Ukraine Party | Bloc of Yulia Tymoshenko | Party of Regions |
| There is a proposal to introduce gender quotas in order to increase the number of female deputies in the *Verkhovna Rada.* What is your opinion? Do you support the measure or not? | Agree | 57.0 | 57.5 | 40.7 |
| | Disagree | 19.9 | 23.0 | 27.5 |
| | I have no opinion | 13.3 | 9.1 | 16.0 |
| | Difficult to say / Don't know | 5.9 | 6.6 | 11.7 |
| | No answer | 3.8 | 3.8 | 4.4 |

*Source:* KIIS, April 2007 (n=2009).

ing the law "On Ensuring Equal Rights and Opportunities for Men and Women" the legislative body ignored a gender analysis of the structure of *Verkhovna Rada,* as well as the international mandate of implementing gender equality through affirmative action (8).

What can we expect from Ukraine's current situation? Is it possible that the introduction of quotas would reduce political corruption, or address the low level of women's grassroots activism, patriarchal gender stereotyping, and sexism in Ukrainian society? Ukraine's international obligations and the positive experience of other countries are among the reasons for considering them a potential route for Ukraine to follow in order to begin addressing the issues under discussion here. When all is said and done, however, whether or not this can happen under the current misogynistic Yanukovych regime continues to be an open question.[28]

## Conclusion

Our evidence indicates that Ukrainian women, well educated and actively involved in the labor market, are excluded from the decision-making process at the highest political levels. Vertical gender segregation in Ukrainian politics is rampant. Malfunctioning legislation on gender, and sexist speeches from high-level politicians exert a negative influence on governmental gender politics. Ukrainian party views on a female presence in their bodies are also contradictory. On the declarative level, lawmakers make a show of supporting gender equality, yet at the same time they are shown to be averse to implementing their own recommendations.

A press release from the "Equal Opportunities" parliamentary caucus states that members "plan to raise the issue of introducing voluntary quotas for women in the party election lists."[29] Political strategist Taras Berezovets argues that Ukrainian parties already have an undeclared agreement on a quota of 20 percent for the representation of women in each of the political forces, but even these are far from being met.[30] As observers point out, "quota talks" connect mostly to election campaigns, when political forces are courting women voters.

The Ukrainian parliamentary election in October 2012 was based upon a mixed electoral model—50 percent from party lists and the remaining 50 percent from simple-majority constituencies—with a 5 percent candidacy threshold. This electoral system is considered by many to be one of the major negative factors influencing the low number of women elected (Matland 1998). Conventional wisdom has it that the majoritarian system tends to cut women's representation,[31] whereas in contrast the proportional electoral rule (PR) favors the election of more women. According to a National Democratic Institute analysis of future elections the current mixed voting electoral system will produce only twenty-eight women (6.2 percent) in the Ukrainian parliament.[32] Volunteer party quotas could be helpful in raising this percentage. As gatekeepers, political parties are in a position to influence the level of women's political participation via affirmative action, should they manifest the political will to do so.

At the same time, it is important to remember that time is a vital resource for active participation in political life. Gender scholars (Bryson and Lister 1994; Bryson 2007) argue that women's "double burden" results in a decrease in the length of time available for their political participation. In her book *Gender and Politics of Time* Valerie Bryson underscores the idea that shared domestic responsibilities is a key issue for implementing equality between the sexes (2007). Domestic work, assigned to the "female" sphere of activity, when added to full-time involvement in the labor market, leaves women with a much-reduced time horizon for politics. This is a crucial issue for Ukrainian society—on both the state and family levels. Emancipating women from domestic drudgery and care giving would require active involvement from men. It is incumbent upon the Ukrainian state to confront this head-on as yet another challenge for nondiscriminatory gender politics.

**Tamara Martsenyuk** holds a candidate of science degree in sociology. Her research interest focuses on the social structure of society, especially gender relations. She is an associate professor in the Department of Sociology at the National University of Kyiv-Mohyla Academy (Ukraine), and is currently a visiting scholar at the European University of Viadrina (Germany). She has authored more than forty articles and chapters in books, including most recently "Ukrainian Societal Attitudes towards the Lesbian, Gay, Bisexual, and Transgender Communities," in *Gender, Politics, and Society in Ukraine,* published by the University of Toronto Press in 2012.

## Notes

1. News as of 5 March 2012: http://www.undp.org.ua/en/media/41-democrat ic-governance/1286-empowering-women-for-stronger-political-parties.
2. *Statistical data on civil servants and officials of self-governmental bodies (as of 31 December 2008).* Main Department of Civil Service of Ukraine, http://www.guds .gov.ua/control/en/publish/article?art_id=167381&cat_id=39077.
3. February 1999 (n=1588), April 2007 (n=2009), September 2008 (n=2036), October 2010 (n=2038).
4. Kyiv International Institute of Sociology (KIIS) is one of the leading research institutions in Ukraine. http://www.kiis.com.ua.
5. http://www.statsvet.su.se/quotas/.

6. For comprehensive information about the project, see Global Database of Quotas for Women, A Joint Project of International IDEA and Stockholm University, http://www.quotaproject.org/.

7. For further details about the project see Research at the Department of Political Science, The Quotas Project, http://www.statsvet.su.se/quotas/.

8. Full results of these interviews can be found in the report: http://gender.undp .org.ua/images/lib/gender_portret_kryma_ukr.pdf.

9. Among others are the forty-seven countries at a very high human developmental level, and those at medium and low human developmental levels. http://hdr .undp.org/en/statistics/hdi/.

10. The situation as of 31 December 2011, http://www.ipu.org/wmn-e/classif.htm.

11. Ukraine: Progress toward Millennium Development Goals. Fact sheet 2011. http://www.undp.org.ua/en/millennium-development-goals/mdgs-in-ukraine.

12. KIIS database (n=2038); my analysis.

13. One might argue that in general Ukrainians have a low level of acquaintance with legislation, that they do not trust the rule of law.

14. See the full article at http://www.guardian.co.uk/world/2010/mar/24/ukraine-mykola-azarov-women.

15. Full text of the greeting is available at http://www.partyofregions.org.ua/ru/news/politinform/show/9208.

16. More information can be found on the Ukraine Watch blog, http://ukrainewatch .wordpress.com/2011/01/31/yanukovych-invites-to-ukraine-for-sex-tourism/.

17. Such as "Our Ukraine," the Ukrainian People's Party, the political "Civic Party Pora," the Communist Party of Ukraine, the party "Reforms and Order," All-Ukrainian Association "Motherland," the Party of Regions, and the People's Party.

18. Funded by the European Union and implemented in Ukraine by the OSCE Office for Democratic Institutions and Human Rights (ODIHR). The result is *Regulation of Political Parties in Ukraine: The Current State and Direction of Reforms,* a comprehensive report that thoroughly analyzes the particular problems and issues in Ukraine's legislative and regulatory framework for political parties.

19. Headed by Yanukovych before he was ousted.

20. See text in Ukrainian at http://blogs.pravda.com.ua/authors/kozhara/4f4f74 fcb7d1d/.

21. The EU project "Gender Equality in the World of Work" (2009–2011) implemented by the International Labor Organization, was dedicated to this problem. http://ge nder.ilo.org.ua.

22. More information is available from Kateryna Levchenko's column in *Ukrainska Pravda*: http://www.pravda.com.ua/columns/2010/04/1/4904154/. An interview in September 2011 revealed that the courts found no evidence of discrimination. Azarov's pronouncement was ruled a personal judgment. This led to an appeal in the international courts that remains to be resolved.

23. It is an independent public feminist initiative that fights to overcome patriarchal forms of power in its various manifestations (sexism, homophobia, transphobia, ageism, racism, and chauvinism) and stands for economic and reproductive rights for women. It wants to change discriminatory social and legislative practices, to create space for critical gender studies and independent political activism, to de-

velop and share emancipatory feminist knowledge and nonsexist language. http://ofenzyva.wordpress.com.
24. Centre for Social Research was created to carry out a study of social problems and collective protests in Ukraine. http://cedos.org.ua.
25. More information can be found at http://www.undp.org.ua/en/media/41-democratic-governance/1238-equal-opportunities-caucus-formed-in-the-ukrai nian-parliament.
26. The Oksana Makar case is a particularly virulent example of an egregious miscarriage of justice in Ukraine.
27. The International Centre for Policy Studies is an independent research organization whose function is to promote the concept of public policy and related processes as a guarantee of effective democracy in Ukraine and other post-Soviet countries. http://www.icps.kiev.ua/eng/.
28. By the time this chapter had been submitted the Euromaidan Revolution had successfully deposed Yanukovych as president and he fled Ukraine. Revolutionary events followed at an accelerated pace, as did Russia's illegal involvement in Ukraine's internal affairs. They continue to unfold, but the "woman question" was put on hold yet again.
29. The press release of "Cross-faction Group on 'equal opportunities'" is formulated by the *Verkhovna Rada,* 6 December 2011.
30. See text in Ukrainian at http://ukrainian.voanews.com/content/women-preside nt-in-ua-2012-03-09-142080573/918840.html.
31. The electorate votes for a party, and the winning party forms a government.
32. See text in Ukrainian at http://portal.rada.gov.ua/rada/control/uk/publish/arti cle/news_left?art_id=285306&cat_id=37486 Women's representation in the Ukrainian parliament in 2012 remained the same—just under 10 percent.

# Bibliography

Bryson, Valerie. 2007. *Gender and the Politics of Time: Feminist Theory and Contemporary Debates.* Bristol: Policy Press.

Bryson, Valerie, and Ruth Lister. 1994. *Women, Citizenship and Social Policy.* Department of Applied Social Studies, University of Bradford.

Dahlerup, Drude. 1998. "Using Quotas to Increase Women's Political Representation," in *Women in Parliament: Beyond Numbers,* ed. Azza Karam. Stockholm: International IDEA Publications, 91–106.

Decree of Cabinet of Ministers no. 1834, 2007. "On the Adoption of the State Program on Ensuring Gender Equality in Ukrainian Society for the Period up to the year 2010." 27 December.

Hausman, Ricardo, et al. 2011. "Global Gender Gap Report." Geneva: World Economic Forum. http://www3.weforum.org/docs.

International Centre for Policy Studies. 2007. *Varieties of a Balanced Representation of Men and Women in the Organs of Ukraine's Elective Organizations.* Kyiv: The International Centre for Policy Studies.

International IDEA 2012. *About Quotas: Global Database of Quotas for Women*. A joint project of International IDEA and Stockholm University. http://www.quotapro ject.org/aboutquotas.cfm.

Kovryzhenko, Denys. 2010. *Regulation of Political Parties in Ukraine: Current State and Directions of Reforms*. Kyiv: Agency for Legislative Initiatives, and OSCE/ODIHR.

Krook, Mona Lena. 2009. *Quotas for Women in Politics: Gender and Candidate Selection Reform Worldwide*. New York: Oxford University Press.

Law no. 2866-IV. 2008. "Zakon Ukrainy pro Zabezpechennia Rivnykh Prav I Mozh-lyvostei. dlia Cholovikiv i Zhinok." *Verkhovna Rada* of Ukraine.

Martsenyuk, Tamara. 2007. "Gendernyie kvoty v Ukraine. Byt' ili ne byt'?" *Yi* 1(17): 18–22.

Matland, Richard. 1998. "Enhancing Women's Political Participation: Legislative Recruitment and Electoral Systems," in *Women in Parliament: Beyond Numbers*, ed. Azza Karam. Stockholm: International IDEA, 65–90.

Melnyk, Tamara, and Larysa Kobelianska. 2006. *Chas Obyraty Zhinok: Genderny Analiz Vyboriv 2006 Roku v Ukraini*. Kyiv: K. I. C. Publ.

NDI and UNDP. 2011. *Empowering Women for Stronger Political Parties: A Good Practical Guide to Promoting Women's Political Participation*. http://www.undp.org/ content/dam/undp/library/gender/gender%20and%20governance/Empowering WomenFor%20StrongerPoliticalParties.pdf.

Oksamytna, Svitlana, and Jan Sverdliuk, eds. 2005. *Zhinky v Politytsi: Mizhnarodny Dosvid Dlia Ukrainy*. Kyiv: NAUKMA. www.dfc.ukma.kiev.ua/books/women_ politics_ukr_text.pdf.

Plotyan, Sergiy. 2006. *Genderny Analiz Parlamentskykh I Mistsevykh Vyboriv 2006 roku*. Kyiv: A.D.E.F. Ukraine Publ.

Rubchak, Marian J. 2011. *Mapping Difference. The Many Faces of Women in Contemporary Ukraine*. New York and Oxford: Berghahn Books.

Transparency International. 2011. *Corruption Perception Index 2011*. http://cpi.trans parency.org/cpi2011/results/#CountryResults.

Tripp, Aili. 2006. "Sub-Saharan Africa: 'On the fast track to women's political representation'," in *Women, Quotas, and Politics*, ed. Drude Dahlerup. New York: Routledge, 112-137.

UNDP. 2011. *Human Development Report*. "Sustainability and equity: A better future for all." http://hdr.undp.org/en/media/HDR_2011_EN_Complete.pdf.

———. 2012. *Ukraine in 2015: Millennium Development Goals adapted for Ukraine*. http://www.undp.org.ua/en/millennium-development-goals/mdgs-in-ukraine.

UWF. 2010. *Zbil'shennia Predstavnytstva u Protsesi Pryiniattia Rishen' u Politychnykh Partiiakh Presdtavlenykh v Ukraini: Zvit Za Rezul'tatamy Opytuvannia Politychnykh Partii Predstavlenykh u Verkhovnii Radi*. Kyiv: Ukrainian Women's Fund. http:// www.uwf.kiev.ua/Political%20parties%20final%20report.pdf.

# CHAPTER 2

# Gender Transformations in the Political System of Contemporary Ukraine

## *Will Ukraine Remain Gender Blind?*

### Oksana Yarosh

Would Ukraine's political system profit from a reformation or is a total reconstruction needed? The goal of this chapter is to illuminate some aspects of that system as refracted through a "gender prism." We will examine the gender component of the legislative process, the functioning (or not) of its implementation mechanisms, as well as the evolution of self-government toward a more balanced representation of the sexes. Upheavals in both national and local self-governmental bodies engaged in constructing gender-parity mechanisms are apparent, but we need to determine if they are permanent, or even functional. Several thousand NGOs have been registered in Ukraine—are they catalysts for change or mere transitional gender lobbying instruments in the political process?

This chapter will address the question of the gender factor in Ukraine's electoral process and its party systems. As a higher organ of the legislative process in a democratic country, the composition of parliament should reflect the interests of all constituents, but no such legislative body exists in today's Ukraine. Urban parliamentarians are not known to promote any legislation favoring a village agenda. Senior legislators do not advocate resolutions sympathetic to the interests of youth. Representatives of the capital are unwilling to support effective programs for regional development. The worldwide women's and gender movement introduces yet another problem of the disconnectedness between legislators and constituents—family development programs and enactment of laws on motherhood and maternity leave without any input from those whom they affect. Nominally, Ukraine's current parliamentary body represents both sexes, yet it actively discriminates against a majority with only minority rights. Theoretically, the country's roughly 45 million inhabitants are all represented in the 450-member parliamentary body, but bona fide representation depends upon the existing "rules of the game," in which the electoral model appears to play a determining role. In 1991 Ukrainians began experimenting with assorted electoral systems, none of which has done much to improve the underrepresentation of women.[1] The obvious conclusion is that the problem does not lie in the nature of the electoral system.

As of 1 January 2011 women comprised 70 percent of Ukraine's work force, yet they still fail to occupy decision-making positions.[2] All evidence points to the fact that the less ability to influence decisions a position offers, the greater the likelihood of women staffing it. This is true at all administrative levels, from the regional on up to the national.

The most recent changes in the political elite (in 2010) dealt a painful blow to the national mechanism designed to introduce gender equality. Earlier legislative advances such as "The State Law on Guaranteeing Equal Rights and Opportunities for Women and Men," the presence of advisers in the ministry on gender questions, an Interdepartmental Gender Council, and others, are gradually being eroded by the loss of their institutional status. At issue are questions such as: Can the slogan 'separate but equal' be enforced or must the Ukrainian state remain gender blind? Will Ukrainian society remain forever disposed to tolerate inequality? How can the current gender imbalance be corrected in favor of the equal rights guarantee as sanctioned by the Ukrainian Constitution and its Laws?

## Gender and the Ukrainian Constitution

Political systems in countries throughout the world exist in a state of perpetual restructuring—minor tinkering with electoral laws is commonplace. International obligations are subjected to external pressures and the institutions themselves are susceptible to internal strains. The importance of building democracy in Ukraine is not at issue here; it is its quality, rather, or that level at which any system conforms to the will of the entire people, assumes responsibility, and adopts a policy of commitment to equality as well as the participation of both sexes. This begs the question: Which political model can most effectively eliminate the existing gender gap, if indeed the model itself becomes the determining factor?

A host of criteria exist for measuring democracy. Arend Liiphard's comparative analysis of democratic systems argues that of all the historical forms, the highest level of democracy is to be found in the parliamentary majoritarian system—with people voting for a party. The party that garners the most votes becomes the government (Hadenius 2005). All indicators point to the fact that women's representation, the level of political participation in families, and popular involvement in the voting process are best in countries where the parliamentary form of administration[3] is joined to the proportional electoral system. Framers of new constitutions would do well to take heed.

The parliamentary-proportional model works well wherever the system boasts well-established traditions, where influential political parties and an activist political culture exist. Inasmuch as these are lacking in Ukraine, we can speak only of possibilities. The 1996 Constitution of Ukraine instituted a presidential-parliamentary model. During the Orange Revolution in 2004 constitutional reform altered the substance of the constitutional order to reflect a parliamentary-presidential model. In 2010 the Constitutional Court overturned the 2004 reform, leaving the 1996 variant in effect once again, with deleterious results.

All four of Ukraine's presidents have endeavored to introduce changes to Ukraine's constitution, and they established "constitutional assemblies" to publicize their efforts, yet none has observed the clearly stated rules or strategic vision of the future, as required of a transitional society enacting reforms. The "laws alter stereotypes" thesis is axiomatic, but for a long time now parliamentarians have declared that Ukraine has excellent laws, but they are not being implemented.

In a discussion with participants at a conference in Kyiv, organized by the Warsaw office of ODIHR,[4] Monika Platek, a long-standing expert from the Council of Europe, aptly observed: "If a law remains unimplemented, it is a bad law." But can we truly expect superior legislation from inferior representatives? Ukraine has many inconsistent, contradictory, and difficult-to-implement laws. As an example we refer to one on providing social aid to mothers of children up to three years old replete with ambiguities making implementation virtually impossible. Neither the individuals who enacted it nor the holders of high office are prepared to take the responsibility for its deficiencies, however. The burden falls to employees of the various departments in the workplace, and social services personnel at the local level. They have spent the past few years in the courts being called to account for incompetence, a failing that stems from the terms of the official document itself, crafted by incompetent parliamentarians who wrote defective laws.

On the surface, the will to unify legislation seemingly exists. Working committees have been formed to address electoral, tax, excise tax, and other codes, but we still see no evidence of sociopolitical reforms that would benefit society. Chaotic evolution is the relentless political exercise in Ukraine, with every new political elite beginning its work with a blank slate, thereby negating all former progress. The outcome is not the ideal social model being sought, but chaos that serves the interests of the privileged, those with money, status, connections, etc.

The "State Law on Guaranteeing Equal Rights and Opportunities for Women and Men," ratified in 2005 and coming into effect on 1 January 2006, is considered by Ukrainians to be "gender specialized." Although it required certain compromises for passage, that law opened the way to speaking of gender in legal terms for the first time. It also made possible alterations to other governmental documents—the law on "Ombudsman of the Ukrainian Parliament," to the body of laws on labor, the law on the "Union of Citizens," and the law on "Collective Resolutions and Agreements." They all are remarkably resistant to realization and so remain on paper, but the fact that the "State Law on Guaranteeing Equal Rights and Opportunities for Women and Men" was passed helped to raise public awareness of issues like gender inequality, sexual discrimination, and sexual harassment symbolizes progress. It generates public discourse— an important preliminary step in acknowledging and perhaps eventually changing the prevailing exploitation of women. Meanwhile, the ministry has cited its concern regarding discriminatory provisions regarding men in the Codex. Whereas it introduces the idea of generating an environment that allows women to combine household obligations with a professional life, the law fails to offer men similar concessions—flexible, shorter working hours, and time off for domestic obligations. According to the minister of justice those discriminatory norms have been forwarded for scrutiny to the parliament—the organ that approved the law in the first place.

Many countries have chosen to address the issue of gender justice by establishing an office of ombudsman on equal rights and opportunities. According to jurist Tamara Melnyk,[5] the post of ombudsman for gender equality exists in countries with functioning integral laws on sexual parity. In Ukraine's patriarchal climate, despite legislative safeguards, and ombudsman oversight in the implementation of the gender-friendly law, no mechanism exists for its execution. Currently, a single Ukrainian ombudsman (with a staff of approximately one hundred) is unable to cope with the deluge of requests. Reports indicate that each day this government department receives half a dozen requests for assistance—a staggering and rising workload suggesting that the time has come to create a pool of ombudsmen throughout Ukraine, at the regional and national levels.

Under Yushchenko Ukraine's parliament included a subcommittee on International Legal Questions and Gender Policy, headed by Olena Bondarenko, parliamentary deputy from the Yulia Tymoshenko bloc, *"Bat'kivshchyna"* (Homeland). It was created on 12 April 2007 and since 6 April 2011 eight members have staffed it.[6] This low number testifies to its priority. Personnel authorized by the previous parliamentary session began its work by establishing committees charged with introducing gender equality. A secretariat of twenty-seven parliamentary members was formed to offer advice and methodological help on issues of equal rights and possibilities for women and men, organized according to the agendas of each of the committees.

As both foreign and domestic experience testifies, irrespective of party affiliation members of such structures are in a position to lobby parliament for solutions to gender problems, but willingness on the part of deputies or representatives of political factions to address issues that determine the outcome is required.[7] For their part, female deputies are united, but only on the local level. As members of these groups argue persuasively, only unified action on voting for the protection of health, education, and social services irrespective of party affiliation insure their success.[8]

The construction of state organs in Ukraine began in 1996 in the aftermath of the Peking Conference. They were organized that year by what was then the Ministry of Family and Youth. Since 1999 it has undergone a series of reorganizations, culminating in its 2005 title change when it became the Ministry of Family, Youth and Sport. In April 2010 the Department of Family and Gender Policy, with twenty-three staffers, came into being. The years 2006–2009 witnessed significant progress with the naming of gender representatives to ministries, gender councils, as well as to the formation of consulting bodies and working groups, but the 2010 elections heralded a backward slide.

In accordance with the presidential Decree No. 389/2011, as of 6 April 2011 the Ministry of Social Policy became the coordinator of gender policy transformations. Irrespective of which government executive organ acts as the primary executor of change, advances will become a reality only when such a mechanism becomes truly functional. Every government organ will then be obliged to adhere to this gender-sensitive governmental policy if one is in fact established.[9]

As a document, the governmental program for strengthening gender equality in Ukrainian society by 2010 is significant. This is the first instrument of its kind to espouse consolidation of equal rights and opportunities for women and men. The process of adopting oblast (regional) programs on strengthening gender equality is also defined by Ukrainian law, but like all such laws it reflects the national model, and seldom makes concessions to gender issues specific to individual regions. Generally speaking, innovative propositions are deleted when the project is submitted for approval to oblast financial boards, if it is argued that the national agenda lacks certain stipulations, such as sensitivity to local circumstances. Not surprisingly, this is especially true when the new propositions mandate significant financial outlays.

Solutions to these problems require a complex systemic approach. If there is no universal plan to take up gender issues these can be transferred to the agendas of individual branches, or groups. For instance, regional special-purpose programs on "Improving the people's reproductive health by 2015" can address the needs of men as a special-purpose group. Unlike those of women, men's mammary glands are more susceptible to aggressive diseases, such as cancer of the breast. In Ukraine during 2010, 138 cases of a particular kind of cancer were diagnosed, 67 of them fatal. Exacerbating the situation is the fact that men are more reluctant to seek medical advice, the problem surfaces at a more advanced stage, and then it is too late, as noted by the surgical oncologist in Kyiv's polyclinic clinic Volodymyr Nod (Sviatoshyn district).[10]

Women's health appears to be more or less protected, yet at the same time the quality of care is an issue. Ukrainian experts Oksana Kyseliova and Natalia Musiienko have noted that tightening budgets and rising medical care costs have impacted women disproportionately, and families headed by women are particularly vulnerable. Diminished access to medical services and reductions in the length of postoperative hospital stays (both attributable to shrinking financial resources) shifts the obligation to provide care onto family members. As a rule this falls on the already overburdened shoulders of women. The need to reform the health care system, enabling it to offer reasonable costs and provide timely access to medical services at all levels, particularly primary medical and sanitary support in the villages, is acute.[11] Instead, changes such as the plan to consolidate all maternity buildings at the *raion* (district) level by 2011 offer dramatic testimony to further constraints on access to qualified health care for women.

Women are victimized in other sectors of Ukrainian society as well. We have learned from the "Alternative Report on Ukraine's Implementation of the UN Convention on the Liquidation of All Forms of Discrimination against Women" that banks, credit unions, and other financial institutions create insurmountable hurdles for women when they come to them looking for answers, or to apply for credit, mortgages, and other forms of financing. Banks have now agreed to grant women credit, but only at the inflated interest rates of 17–28 percent, limited to one year, and with the proviso that women provide personally owned immovable assets as collateral. Very few of those wishing to embark on a business venture are able to meet these criteria. The terms are especially onerous for aspiring entrepreneurs in rural areas.[12]

The election-monitoring process also needs improving; without effective oversight we cannot begin to speak of its efficacy. The Ukrainian Ministry of Family, Youth, and Sport tracks the process, but this has routinely been done by the office holders themselves, even though external monitoring is acknowledged as superior to the seldom-objective internal oversight. Admittedly, alternative (nongovernmental) supervision is evolving as well, but it is proceeding at a snail's pace.

We will pay special attention to gender profiles as a jumping-off point for the inauguration of gender-friendly programs. Equality cannot become a reality before describing the agenda currently in force, illustrated by a list of existing problems. Such profiles are required for any development of a regional gender policy, yet not all regions have been able to assemble the requisite data. In Vinnytsia, Chernivtsi, Volynia, and Khmelnytsky oblasts (districts) gender profiles are compiled only when international assistance is offered.

Advisers on questions of gender are appointed to the prime minister of Ukraine. They comprise parliamentary heads; the Ministry of Family, Youth, and Sport; the Ministry of Defense; the Chairman of the State Committee on Television and Radio; and heads of eighteen oblast state administrations. Between 2007 and 2010 we saw cadre fluctuation when heads of regional administrative offices were replaced. This also led to changes in the cadres of advisers, and on occasion even elimination of gender issues altogether.

Regional coordinating councils on advising and consulting organs on gender issues have been created under various names nearly everywhere throughout Ukraine, but the efficacy of their work depends upon the political will of its heads and members alike. Although their creation marks a positive developmental moment, it begs two questions: how prepared are NGOs to play a constructive role in promoting gender justice, how willing are governmental organs to hear them?

Gender centers are promising resources for gender-policy reconstruction. The task of such centers is to provide informational and consultative assistance to both government and society. Ministerial data indicate that Ukraine recently witnessed the opening of its twenty-first gender center.[13] Unfortunately, some exist only on paper, and some regional centers are known to send only pro forma copies of their membership lists to the Ministry. As one Lviv activist observed sarcastically—if we can believe ministerial reports on the family we must conclude that Ukraine has no gender-related problems whatsoever!

Social improvement depends upon capable and stable cadres. The EU-UNDP program for Equal Opportunities and Women's Rights in Ukraine has completed a series of sessions for trainers, equipping them with the necessary skills for instructing new cadres. They offer extensive teaching resources on basic gender politics that are designed to increase an understanding of gender issues among government officials. This training is indispensable because in their ignorance of the meaning of the term *gender* officials frequently enter what they believe to be a "tender" program.[14] They are oblivious of the law that they are directed to implement, and in the end these training programs tend to attract a minimal number of participants at best. This confirms the existence of professional gender segregation—that "fir tree" or "Cheop's pyramid" with women concentrated at its base.[15]

We appreciate the special, if sporadic, contributions that international development programs, international institutions, funds and agencies make to our country's modest progress on gender issues, but believe that our own government should also share in such initiatives. Moreover, with all of their laudable intentions, without a thorough understanding of the needs of a given society, international donors do not always deploy their resources where they will do the most good.

## The Electoral System

Elections have a special meaning for the citizenry at large inasmuch as they are the single most important symbol of their participation in the country's political life. Electoral results depend not only upon citizens exercising their will through the ballot box, but upon the way the electoral process is organized. Although Ukraine has experimented with various systems, women's parliamentary representation has never exceeded 10 percent after 1991, a number reached as a result of the 2012 elections.

The present political situation represents more than a problem with the nature of the electoral system. A gender analysis of electoral measures has demonstrated that raising women's representation is achievable under any type of electoral system, although proportional representation, based on gender-balanced lists, is still the most promising vehicle. As it stands now, in a majoritarian electoral system with single-mandate electoral district political parties, the most acceptable candidate, or the one considered most likely to win, is put forward, yet for a variety of reasons that candidate is seldom a woman. A majoritarian system is also able to take advantage of district pairing (districts represented by pairs), with women and men nominated in turns. Fiona Beveridge, Sue Nott, and Kylie Stephen, authors of *Gender and State Politics,*[16] look to the practices of the Welsh parliament in the United Kingdom as a viable model. It numbers sixty parliamentary members elected according to a majoritarian system that draws on party lists for candidates. Women constitute 40 percent of its body. The party determines both who will run and the order of their appearance on the electoral list, leading to the inescapable conclusion that if a party or electoral bloc has the political will to produce gender-balanced representation, any electoral model will work as long as women's names appear at or near the top of their lists.

Since 8 September 2005 the "Law of Ukraine on Equal Rights and Possibilities for Women and Men" has mandated that political parties and blocs nominating candidates for parliamentary office in a multi-mandate government electoral district must include both sexes in their list of candidates[17]—but there is no oversight, with predictable results. The first principle of our gender law correlates with the proportional electoral model. In the event of change, attaching a gender-balance mechanism would ensure that any electoral model would promote gender justice. When the proportional system is in force, electoral lists must be transparent, as well as regionally and gender balanced. In order to ensure a high number of qualified female and male representatives on every level of government this law obliges the compilers of lists to nominate qualified candidates who enjoy the backing and trust of the electorate.

The 2012 parliamentary elections proceeded according to a mixed electoral system.[18] In the opinion of both international and domestic experts, that process failed to conform to democratic criteria. Runoff elections in five districts confirmed these assessments. Of all 445 women registered by the Central Electoral Commission of Ukraine, only 43 women, or 10 percent, were elected to the legislature (*Verkhovna Rada*). Experts predict that a move to an electoral system with a majoritarian component will decrease the women's representation further. On the county level, approximately seventy political parties failed to register a female candidate for national office. Five counties in a single region, Rivne, fall into this category.

## Electoral Culture

A poorly informed electorate creates a serious problem. The general level of the Ukrainian people's education is high, but the quality of their knowledge and understanding of the political process is deficient. An intelligent government requires intelligent citizens. How to find them in a post-totalitarian country—or, as James Mace once characterized it, a "post-genocidal" country—where for decades individualism was destroyed, as was freedom of critical thought? Germany provides an excellent comparative example illustrating what is meant inasmuch as it has expended considerable effort and resources on the political education of its citizenry, and continues to do so. No German politician will permit him/herself to be photographed in front of a column, for example, lest it evoke an association with the former regime. Such an enlightened citizen is difficult to manipulate. Electoral activity is extremely important, but it is less so than the nature of the vote itself, one that displays sound voter judgment [19]

No less important in the electoral process is the nature of the body that guarantees the suitability of its cadres. The Central Electoral Commission (CEC) is charged with certifying the voting procedure as well as protecting the rights of the voting public, but can it insure adherence to the demands of Ukraine's legislation? Today's CEC consists of four women (27 percent) in the body of fifteen. How can such low numbers inspire confidence in the commission's ability to guarantee gender parity in the national electoral process without a gender balance in its own composition? County electoral commissions have a different tradition with their relatively equal representation of the sexes. In 2012 women comprised 56 percent of its membership. In 225 county electoral commissions 106 women functioned as heads, 114 filled deputy head positions, and 155 served as secretaries. Four women of every fifteen members of the commission occupied posts as both deputy heads and secretaries.[20]

Each new administration and parliamentary majority in Ukraine initiates changes in the electoral model. In 1994 the majoritarian system was 50 percent majoritarian and 50 percent proportional. In 2006 and preterm 2007 it became proportional, with a closed list requiring a minimum 3 percent threshold of party backing. In 2012 a mixed electoral system was introduced once more, with the backing requirement raised to 5 percent.

Democracy is a dynamic process subject to fluctuations, but freedom in political contests and respect for the results of democratic elections must remain constant. The *Washington Post* informed us recently that Ukraine has been removed from the democratic to the "partially democratic" category.[21]

Currently, the Law of Ukraine on electing parliamentary deputies is based upon a mixed system. We will examine the gender aspects in the evolution of Ukraine's political parties. During the second half of the 1990s women's parties were founded: the Ukrainian Christian Women's Party (established in 1991); the All-Ukrainian Party of Women's Initiatives; the Party of Women of Ukraine (1997); and the Party of Women's Solidarity of Ukraine (1999). In 2001 the All-Ukrainian Political Union "Women for the Future" came into being. In 2013 the Ukrainian Women's Christian Party suspended its activity, leaving three parties: the Party of Women of Ukraine, the Party of Women's Solidarity of Ukraine, and "Women for the Future." None was able to cross the threshold of minimum support to move on to the elections. Worldwide experience has demonstrated that single-sex parties are seldom able to meet that requirement. Of the 200 political parties registered by the Ministry of Justice as of January 2012 in Ukraine, only 21, or 11 percent, were headed by women.

A large majority of political parties throughout the world have voluntarily introduced gender quotas in their ranks. The Ukrainian political culture and absence of solidarity on the national level in gender movements, as well as the capability for effective lobbying, testify to the continuing low probability of such representation in future.[22] Only two parties—Udar and the Party of Regions—included gender equality in their pre-election platforms. In most party programs economic questions and socioeconomic development head the agenda. Issues like demographics, family policy, and combined domestic and official obligations placed second on the lists of priorities. An additional hurdle for the women's participation in mainstream politics is the high national registration fee imposed (nearly

1.92 million *hryvna* [240 thousand USD]). The "Solidarity of Ukrainian Women" was the only women's party to run in the 2012 election, but it yielded no successful candidates.

Left-wing parties manifest the greatest readiness to advocate for gender parity. The Democratic Alliance Party was the first to apply the party "Zipperlist" for this purpose, that is to say a methodical formation of an electoral list according to the model woman-man, woman-man, etc. In order to get its candidates on the ballot a high registration fee was required. The party introduced a major innovation to Ukrainian politics by soliciting political donations from the citizenry at large to meet this requirement. Although the funds raised proved insufficient, this attempt to introduce fiscal transparency to the political process marked a pioneering effort with game-changing potential.

## Gender Constituent of Municipal Self-Governing Organs

The introduction of gender parity is a systemic process affecting the municipal level of government. In the most recent elections (2012), the mean proportion of women in regional councils matched their national representation at 10 percent. General information gathering also proved problematic because no government executive organ publicizes a summary of a gender distribution in municipal elections. In the oblasts, community organizations turned to regional apparatuses for information, and received analyzable data. The 1994 municipal election resulted in a 30 percent female representation. In 1998 the figure rose to 38 percent, and 42 percent in 2002. Village and rural elections returned a significant percentage of female office holders because villagers tend to place more faith in women leaders. As one head of a rural council in the Khmelnytsky region once was heard to ask a candidate for office: "Why do you think that you will make a better head than your male predecessor?" "I don't drink," was her response! She was elected in 2006. Alcoholism is an omnipresent "men's" disease. The results of municipal elections on 30 October 2010 demonstrated a similar tendency. Women have a better chance of prevailing at the village level; their chances diminish at the district and municipal levels.

In 2010 Poltava (central Ukraine) was the scene of an unusual phenomenon. Of the fifty deputies in the city council, seventeen, or 34 percent, were women, with an average age of forty-two. Of those seventeen women, thirteen came from a relatively obscure political party calling itself "Ukraine's Conscience" (formed in 2005). This new party with its catchy name resonated with the voters, among whom the demand for ethical deputies and new faces was high. Mayoral candidate Mamai Oleksander, local leader of "Ukraine's Conscience," received a whopping 62 percent of the votes. He was forty-two years old, and up to 1996 worked as a loader, janitor, and painter-plasterer. Between 1996 and 2010 he went from entrepreneur to prosperous businessman. In 2009 he founded a community association called "Our Home—Poltava" calculated to provide assistance to the socially unprotected stratum of society. It became his support base in the next electoral campaign. The Poltava city council also has the highest indicator of female representation of all city councils in Ukraine but, as the record shows, deputies are not yet sensitive to gender problematics.

Execution of the 2010 law in local elections brought a change in the number of deputies to city councils. The electoral system, based on a model of half majoritarian and half proportional representation, mandated paired candidates, and the required number of pairs rose in all councils. The pre-election changes were to have been explained to voters because the electoral model was new to them. Accordingly, an educational campaign in the form of distributed bulletins indicating both changes and the need for an election was ordered, but the initiative never materialized. Only on the day of elections, 31 October, did voters receive five or six bulletins in small print explaining the changes. This produced long lines at the polling stations as the electorate studied information about the candidates. The most determined voters stood in line for about three hours while others gradually drifted away. Problems reminiscent of Gerry Elbridge's "salamander"[23] also appeared in majoritarian districts when they were redistricted during the final stages of the municipal electoral process. Recalling the words of American political scientists Rein Taagepera and Matthew Soberg Shugart: "The electoral system is the most dynamic component of the political process, and a promising field for political engineering."[24] We were able to track this gerrymandering—manipulation of electoral districts to redefine their structures, size, and limits with the intent of creating more or less advantageous conditions for one party or another. Ukraine's ruling party also achieved significant results made possible by new legislative norms for registering candidates, forming committees, creating electoral funds, etc. Those who fashioned the new rules enjoyed the advantage of becoming acquainted with the changes in advance.

An argument in favor of the majoritarian system[25] took account of the fact that single-mandate candidates would be more electable than "listed" candidates, inasmuch as the former had name recognition, were experienced, authoritative, and knew how to promote voter interest in specific districts. Even when the new law was enforced, however, candidates still had to be nominated by a political party, and this presented another problem. An analysis of the lists of contenders for office testified to thoughtless selections of candidates. Perhaps the most notable example was found in the enormous influx of businessmen in this and other municipal elections. Of the 470 candidates for 50 positions in the Lutsk City Council, for instance, approximately 200 were businessmen. This suggested, among other things, a poor business environment motivating businessmen to protect their interests by running for office.

Inasmuch as the operational model of the new municipal elections has demonstrated its ineffectiveness, Ukrainians are already discussing potential changes and the introduction of corrections to the working norms, as well as changes to the electoral model itself. To date, only the public engages in genuine discussion. There is no evidence of a dialogue at the public-to-government level.

## Women's Rise to Government Office: Dangers and Possibilities

What truly matters in women's advancement to top-level government posts is the prevailing gender culture and positive reception of gender parity. In comparing models let us consider the leadership styles of female politicians like Margaret Thatcher and Madeleine Albright. Margaret Thatcher achieved her political position against the background of a male political culture. In her external politics she presented the image of a masculine politician, which flew in the face of the old adage that women love peace more than men. Thatcher did not seriously address the women's movement; in point of fact she assiduously distanced herself from it. On occasion she did exploit her feminine connection, but only when it enhanced her political image. Madeleine Albright, who headed the president's Interdepartmental Council on Women's Issues, also presented the impression of a ruthless politician. Unlike Thatcher, however, she actively advocated for women's equality.

And what about Ukraine and its virtual absence of prominent female political leaders? Yulia Tymoshenko is a rare case in point. A survey conducted by the Institute of Social Research in Kyiv led to the conclusion that older urban women sided with the communist leader Petro Symonenko, the middle generation threw its support behind Serhy Tyhypko, and only rural women backed Yulia Tymoshenko.[26] Tymoshenko benefited from their trust and endorsement because these women were not threatened by her power. They were accustomed to a greater measure of authority and influence than their urban counterparts because their physical labor was such a critical part of the village economy. Tymoshenko lost her opportunity to garner an even greater percentage of the female vote by not reaching out to the hundreds of community organizations sharing a concern for women's rights. In the end, after coming to office, she did emphasize the fact that more women must be brought into mainstream politics, but this would have been far more persuasive, and infinitely more productive, if she had done it earlier.

The question of female participation in mainstream politics frequently arises: Why do we need more women in the political process? What is in it for us? That women are in the majority, so their voice should count for more than it does, is a recurrent answer. And they are less prone to corruption, more inclined toward the harmony that is in such short supply in our politics.[27] Seeking a comparative perspective, Svetlana Taburova studied gender characteristics in the speech patterns of German parliamentarians. She concluded from this that women politicians are more inclined to harmonious communication, to emphasizing unity of viewpoints, manifesting solidarity in debates, and offering support where necessary. In a word, they adopt a more productive approach in politics. Their oral communication is direct and transparent, as it *should* be in a dialogue between two equals. As a rule, men personify political opposition; they move along a path of escalating conflict and inflamed enmity, impeding solutions to political issues.

The inevitable obstacles that women face in contemporary Ukraine can be characterized as a slippery slope that restricts most to the lower rungs of power, while a glass ceiling hovers above. Studies of the professional segregation of women show them beginning their careers as implementers on the lower levels, and there they generally are destined to remain.

One also hears: "Do you really want amateurs leading us"? What we have now is everybody's responsibility, but first and foremost its execution belongs to male leaders. "Have women shown themselves to be effective professionals?" they ask. "Must we suffer female cooks in the executive office again (invoking the Soviet practice of tokenism)?" "Where will you find professionals among women?" Despite the widely held opinion that the cost of an education is wasted on girls, we are aware that a greater number of advanced degrees are held by women, yet this does not translate to career advancement. Certain tenacious stereotypes are especially obstructionist. Note the comparison: "Not only is she enchanting, she is also a politician," versus "Not only is he a politician, but a fine father." Our society lives on stereotypes—in one way or another a woman must be beautiful. Something frequently heard from men during training sessions was that Angela Merkel could never become a national figure because she is so unattractive. I also recall the musings of a male acquaintance whose supervisor was a woman: "It is a fine thing to have an intelligent woman as supervisor," he ventured, "but I would never want a supervisor wife." Social norms consistently reinforce women's lack of self-realization and dependency by emphasizing their physical beauty and exploiting their decorative value as an enhancement of some man's status.

The world has changed. Physical strength is no longer needed in the way it was fifty years ago, and even wars can be conducted by pressing buttons. Nonetheless, the myth of a wife as Berehynia—guardian, mother, homemaker, and nurturer—lives on. The mass media are replete with reports about people who seek an expert opinion turning to men, but when it comes to a question of good taste in dress or food, women are consulted. In sum, we are facing a strategic task. How can we create favorable conditions for increasing the number of women in government with its decision-making authority, or form a governing body that would elevate women to the top of the ruling structure?

It is a truism that women in Ukraine have low self-esteem and do not fully understand the importance of political actions. A better understanding of politics is achievable only by introducing an effective educational policy. It might include seminar/training sessions, productive information campaigns, and appropriate public events.

## Establishing Gender Quotas

Worldwide, gender quotas have been recognized as an effective tool for achieving gender parity in the political sphere through an array of expedients such as constitutional, party, electoral, legislative, and voluntary establishment of quotas. They might be divided by percentages—30/70, 40/60, 50/50, etc.

In Ukraine Mykola Tomenko and Olena Bondarenko, deputies from the bloc of Yulia Tymoshenko, attempted to introduce a legislative mandate for improving gender parity. Its goal was to insure that women would be included in the electoral lists, but it failed to pass because no member of the ruling coalition voted for it. In order to move the process forward, early in 2007 a handbook listing nongovernmental organizations on women's and gender issues was published in Ukraine. Its contents included updated information on community organizations actively seeking solutions to women's and gender problems, and the elimination of all forms of sexual discrimination in economic and social life.

Contrary to the numerical preponderance of women's organizations, men's alliances do not come close to such numbers. Among the more prominent ones are: "Men against Force" in Kirovohrad and Kherson; "Single Fathers of Vinnytsia"; and a network of associations calling themselves "Oleh." One of the most active is the community association known as "Adaptive Men's Center," situated in Ternopil (western Ukraine). Its aim is to change the practice of stereotyping gender behavior by working to socialize men to a better understanding of their role in family and society, and raising public awareness of the current state of domestic violence. Meanwhile, the men have yet to become fully conscious of their own problems.[28] Paradoxically it is the women who lobby for solutions to their problems. Although this is still a relatively new phenomenon in Ukraine, the approach has the potential for creating a more harmonious society and improving the lives of both sexes.

## Conclusion

Gender politics should be a logical component of the mainstream political process. In tracing the dynamic of gender changes since the beginning of the new century we noted that the most impressive achievements were recorded between the years 2005 and 2009,[29] years which saw important advancements in the status of women. With the administration that rose to power in 2010 came stagnation and a reversal of many gains. The most positive legal development during the earlier administration was ratification of the law that normalized the term *gender*. With a sexist leadership coming to power in 2010, however, the chances for implementing this initiative stalled.

Ukrainian writer Maria Matios underscores the lack of significant progress with a quote from eminent writer Lina Kostenko, who theorizes that "our adaptive mind has been damaged by totalitarianism," and adds that this is much worse than imprisonment. Kostenko argues that an imprisoned mind will rouse itself and beat its wings against the bars, but an adaptive mind is incapable of breaking loose. It adjusts to everything without protest.[30] Sadly, most of contemporary society remains relatively apathetic when what is so urgently needed is outrage. As discouraging as all of this might sound the gains already achieved are a cautiously hopeful indicator of better things to come.[31]

**Oksana Yarosh** is a professor in the Department of Political Science and Public Administration at Lesya Ukrainka Eastern European National University and director of the Volyn NGO Gender Center. Her research interests extend to gender politics, electoral systems, and public relations. Among her publications are: *Gender Monitoring the Parliamentary Elections in 2012* (compiled by Maria Alekseienko and Yarosh, 2012) and *Gender Analysis of the Electoral Legislation of Ukraine* (with Ann Uimet, 2008). She is also the OSCE project coordinator in Kyiv.

## Notes

1. For the uninformed about Ukraine's pattern of voting, the excellent summary by Oleksandr Fisun 2012, "Electoral Laws" is recommended.

2. *Policy Memo* no. 229. Available online. http://nads.gov.ua/sub/hmelnitska/ua/publi cation/content/35525.htm?s398224032=caca24c5f8f25d7f0230dc2190a527d6.
3. A system in which the executive is answerable and responsible to the legislature—cabinet or parliamentary form of government.
4. Office for Democratic Institutions and Human Rights.
5. "International 2003". "International Experience of Governmental Guarantees of Equality for Men and Women," materials from an international conference in Kyiv, 30 June–1 July 2003. Kyiv: Lohos.
6. http://w1.c1.rada.gov.ua/pls/site/p_komitis.
7. *Materialy* 2003.These are materials from an international conference on gender equality held 2003.in Kyiv on 30 June to I July.
8. It is instructive that these are traditionally female issues.
9. The immediate likelihood of this happening does not inspire confidence in light of the misogynistic legacy of the governing body under Yanukovych.
10. http://gazeta.ua/index.php?id=313840.
11. Oksana Kysseliova and Natalia Musienko 2011.
12. "Al'ternatyvny" 2008. Kyiv: All-Ukrainian NUO "Women's consortium."
13. http://www.kmu.gov.ua/sport/control/uk/publish/article;jsessionid=169938F2 ACE624796DF4ADA308C1E8BA?art_id=124278&cat_id=45327.
14. Official offer tendered for acceptance.
15. Pyramid of Cheops, the largest and oldest of the Egyptian pyramids. There are three smaller ones nearby, together with the Sphinx. Cheops was an Egyptian pharaoh (Khufu in Egyptian Arabic).
16. Beveridge 2004.
17. Text available at http://zakon.rada.gov.ua/cgi-bin/laws/main.cgi?nreg=2866-15.
18. Half under party lists and half under constituencies.
19. Geraint and Moyser 2005.
20. Election Observation 2012.
21. http://www.washingtonpost.com/wp-yn/content/article/2011/01/13/AR201101 1300028.html.
22. In the 2012 general election, in multiple-mandate electoral counties the Central Electoral Commission registered twenty-two party electoral lists containing 2,643 candidates, plus 3,130 majoritarians (including 1,429 self-nominees). Women came up with 949 candidates, of which 528 ran according to the proportional list model (with only two heading the lists), and 421 candidates competed in single-mandate counties. Of the two hundred parties in Ukraine, eighty-seven ran at least one candidate in the election. Unlike the proportional representation system that provides for social representation of minorities such as women, in the majoritarian system people vote for a party. If a party gets the majority vote, it becomes the government.
23. In 1812 Governor Gerry Elbridge attempted to have a bill passed in the Massachusetts legislature that would have divided the state into special districts for election purposes. As the shape of one of the new districts had the appearance of a mythical animal, which some claimed looked something like a salamander, the news media named his proposal a "gerrymander."
24. Rein and Shugart 1989.
25. Commensurate with the new law, the latest model for municipal elections.
26. http://www.left.in.ua/?menu=info&id=1&idnew=64.

27. Taburova 1999.
28. The UN Population Fund and State Service for Family, Children, and Youth stress the fact that they live to an average sixty-two years. Old age or incurable diseases are not the most frequent causes of death. More often they die from alcohol-induced traumas or the abuse of narcotics. Ukrainian men have one of the highest rates of sickness in the world. There are twelve million active smokers among them. Only one in ten participates in any kind of sport. About a third of the men are unable to procreate. Almost every fifth man is infected with a sexual disease. About 80 percent of the suicides are men, and the majority of these have already had either a heart attack or a stroke. Each year eighty thousand men die in their prime.
29. Immediately following the Orange Revolution. In 2010 the Yanukovych regime came to power and Ukraine's social political environment began to take a serious step backward toward authoritarian control, with no concession to gender issues.
30. Quoted from Matios 2011.
31. The "Eurorevolution" that erupted in late November (2013) offered hope that change is not as hopeless as Kostenko's pessimistic note makes it sound. Subsequent events in Crimea, following an illegal plebiscite supported by a military takeover and illegal plebiscite leading to Russia's annexation of the peninsula reforms, once again became questionable.

# Bibliography

Al'ternatyvny zvit pro vykonannia Konventsiyi OON pro likvidatsiiu vsikh form dyskryminatsiyi proty zhinok. Vseukrainska NUO," *Zhinochy Kosortium* 2008. Kyiv.

Beveridge, Fiona, Sue Nott, and Stephen Kylie. 2004. "Mainstreaming and the engendering of policymaking: a means to an end?" *Gender and State Politics,* ed. Pauline L. Rankin. Kyiv: Osnovy.

Election Observation 2012. Mission, "Interim Report of the Draft Law on the Election of the People's Deputies of Ukraine," no. 1 (12–28 September).

Fisun, Oleksandr. 2012. "Electoral Laws and Patronage Politics in Ukraine," *PONARS Eurasian.*

*Gender Monitoryng Parlamentskykh Vyboriv 2012 r.* Compiled by Maria Alekseienko and Oksana Yarosh. Lutsk: TEREN.

*Genderni Aspekty Ustnoi Povedinky Parlameentariv. Vybory I Vybordebaty.* 1999. FPI/SOTSYS.

Geraint, Parry, and George Moyser. 2005. *More Involvement—More Democracy: Defining and Measuring Democracy* (2005), ed. David Beetham. Translated from English by Hanna Khomenko. *Bil'she Uchasti—Bil'she Demokratiyi, Vyznachennia i Vymiriuvannia,* ed. David Beetham. Lviv: Litopys.

Hadenius, Axel. 2005. "Tryvalist' demokratiyi: Instytutsiini chynnyky na protyvahu sotsioekonomichnym," in *Vyznachennia i Vymiriuvannia Demokratiyi,* ed., David Beetham. Translated from English by Hanna Khomchenko. Lviv: Litopys.

"International Experience of Governmental Guarantees of Equality for Men and Women," materials from an international conference in Kyiv, 30 June–1 July 2003. Kyiv: Lohos.

Kimmel, Michael S. 2003. *Genderovane Suspil'stvo*. Kyiv: Sphera.

Kysseliova, Oksana, and Natalia Musenko. 2011. *Finansova Kryza ta Antykryzovi Zakhody v Ukraini: Genderny Vymir.* Kyiv: Institute of Liberal Society.

Matios, Maria 2011. *Torn out Pages from an Autobiography*. Lviv: La Piramida.

Melnyk, Tamara. 2010. *Tvorennia Suspil'stva Gendernoi Rivnosti: Mizhnarodny Dosvid. Zakony Zarubizhnykh Krain z Gendernoi Rivnosti.* Kyiv: Stylos.

*Mizhnarodny Dosvid I Derzhavnoho Zabezpechennia Rivnosti Zhinok ta Cholovikiv. Materialy Mizhnarodnoi Konferentsiyi v Kyievi, 30 Chervnia–1 Lypnia. 2003.* Kyiv: Logos.

Nohlen, Dieter. 2004. *Prawo wyborcze i Systemy. Teoria Systemów w Wyborczych Tlumaczenie.* Translated by Robert Alberski, Jacek Sroka, and Wiktor Zbignew. Warsaw: Wydawnictwo naukowe SHOLAR.

Rankin, Pauline L., ed. 2004. *Gender I Derzhavna Polityka*. Translated from English by Ivan Yashchenko. Kyiv: Osnovy.

Rein, Taagepera, and Matthew S. Shugart. 1989. *Seats and Votes: The Effects and Determinants of Electoral Systems*. New Haven, CT: Yale University Press.

Schveda, Yuriy. 2010. *Vybory i Vyborchi Systemy. Evropeiski Standarty ta Dosvid Demokratiyi v Ukraini*. Lviv: Ivan Franko National University.

Suslova, Olena, et al. 2011. *Zakonotvorchist': Rozrobka Prohram Mistsevoho Rozvytku. Zakonodavstvo.* Kyiv: Program PDP II.

Taburova, Svetlana 1999. *Gendernyie aspekty rechevoho povedennia parlamentariv, na materialakh parlamentskykh debatov FRI,* 9: 84–91.

Zaitseva, Olena, and Anna Kononenko. 2007. *Neuriadovi Orhanizatsiyi, shcho Zaimaiut'sia Zhinochymy ta Gendernymy Pytanniamy*. Kyiv: Ukrainian Women's Fund.

# CHAPTER 3

# Theory to Practice

## *The Personal Becomes Political in the Post-Soviet Space*

### Tamara Zlobina

Is it possible to repoliticize the private lives of citizens in a post-Soviet country where sexuality appears to have been freed from all of its former constraints? Ukraine offers a good example of unbridled sexuality used for various purposes—the objectification of women's bodies for use as status symbols, their commercialization in advertising campaigns, and a thriving sex-for-hire industry. Indeed, it has become something of a tourist "Klondike"—purveyor of brides and prostitutes for the near and far abroad. In the most bizarre characterization of Ukrainian women, Victor Yanukovych proudly announced to the world in 2011: "In the springtime our women walk about undressed on the streets, their beauty shining through like some elemental force" for all the world to see and appreciate.[1] It seems that everybody—from consumers of the "goods-and-broads" style of ads (commercialization of women's bodies) to the highest officials in the land—relishes the sexuality of these "most gorgeous women in all of Europe."

Questions never asked in public include: How do women perceive their own sexuality? Does the public hype surrounding their sexuality bear any relationship to their private lives? Do they derive any pleasure from their sexuality? How often do they experience an orgasm? Do they discuss this with their girlfriends? How does the commercialization of a woman's body relate to its reproductive function? What role does sex play in the lives of young mothers exhausted from the daily demands of looking after small children? All such questions, in addition to those on abortion, teenage pregnancies, and rape, are far removed from public discourse. They emerge only during periods of moral panic to illustrate claims of the destruction of a traditional lifestyle and Ukrainian spirituality. We hear ad nauseam declarations from men in prominent positions of just how much they "love" us, but do we love ourselves? Do we love ourselves sufficiently to begin openly discussing our own bodies, not just to object to their commercialization and state control? Enough to demand genuine guarantees of our rights, inviolability of our person, and freedom of choice in sexual orientation as opposed to its denial and repression? The years 1956–1986 that witnessed medical interventions and moralization were followed in 1987 by the vulgarization and commercialization of private lives, in tandem with moral panic.

In post-Soviet Ukraine one cannot discuss the body without a reference to Soviet policy. The sexuality of our mothers was the backdrop against which our own sexuality was shaped, and it would be no exaggeration to point out that the basic axioms of my generation's sexual upbringing during the Soviet era was: "decent girls are not easy," and Soviet ideology continues to repeat itself with remarkable success, as does the commercialization of sexuality. As with any ideology, this is replicated through a complex balance of positive and negative acts—flirtation and offerings of flowers or expensive gifts. Viewed from a structural anthropological perspective, these rituals reveal vestiges of "bride price," except that in today's world the beneficiary is not the parents but the bride herself.

Returning for a moment to the Soviet era, Russian scholar Igor Kon identifies four ideological periods in its regulation of private life:

1917–1930: emancipation of women and sexuality; decline of traditional marriage norms

1930–1956: establishment of controls over sexuality through denial and repression

1956–1986: medicalization and moralization of sexuality

1987 and beyond: vulgarization and commercialization of the private in tandem with moral panic

Although Soviet policy and laws regulating the body were among the most progressive in the world in the 1920s (women's equal rights, state-sponsored children's institutions, community nutrition, legal abortions, and the absence of criminal persecution of homosexuals), by the mid-1930s this climate of tolerance had given way to a repressive punishment policy. Commenting on a new abortion ban, Lev Trotsky wrote in 1936: "Obviously, these gentlemen have forgotten that socialism needs to remove the causes that motivate women to seek abortions, instead of resorting to the despicable practice of police intrusion into the most intimate spheres of every woman's life in order to force her to embrace the joys of motherhood."[2] This same statement can be applied with equal validity to the current moralization in Ukraine.

A synchronized ban on abortions and criminalization of homosexuality evolved in conjunction with totalitarianism, which then led to an official antisex phobia. This sorry state of affairs continued until 1955 when pressure exerted by the medical community, alarmed over the unusually high incidence of illegal abortions, led to the lifting of criminal penalties for abortion This had no effect on the emerging conservatism in Soviet society, nor on the consignment of a monogamous family mythologem to the social primary cell.

In his analysis of the ideology of family evolving under capitalism, John D'Emilio suggested that along with the advance in relations of production, the patriarchal family lost its force as an autonomous economic unit whose members relied on each other for assistance. It discovered the previously unnoticed potential for personal autonomy and creation of alternative genders. The family as a basic reproductive unit did not go away in the modern era, however, because capitalism requires a workforce that is accountable to itself. Only the ideology changed; it became one that was based on romantic love that confers emotional and sexual gratification. What did not change with the altered economic configuration was the dominant principle of heterosexual monogamy within marriage. If we follow Alexander Tarasov's argument for examining the 1960s Soviet economic order of super-statism (super-etatism)[3] paired with capitalism as a system of economic control, we see that the synchronized development of the sexual sphere and the preservation of the monogamous family as society's primary cell—albeit with a modicum of democratized sexuality—lost its appearance as an accidental process.

As early as the late 1950s a majority of the Soviet people were city dwellers; by the end of the 1980s 75 percent of the population consisted of urbanites. Industrialization and new employment patterns destroyed the traditional patriarchal family (allowing for the modifications of individual [Asian] republics). This, in turn, created indispensable conditions for economic independence and with them a multiplication of gender models. Nevertheless, in its economic transactions the paternalistic state perpetuated the pattern of a citizen-employment pool, thereby foreclosing any possibility of individual freedom. Everybody was positioned as a supplicant and recipient of the state's material blessings, dependent upon their conformity to the image of a model Soviet citizen. This expanded the state's control over the most intimate spheres of private life. Open sexual conduct was limited by hypocritical public discourse purged of all references to sex. The limits of women's emancipation were well expressed in a popular film of the early 1980s, *Moscow Does Not Believe in Tears*.[4] Criminal prosecution foreclosed all evolution of Western-type homosexual subcultures, which were rooted in individual economic liberty.

Igor Kon expressed it well with his explanation that several generations of Soviet citizens grew up in an atmosphere of primal ignorance about sexuality, filled with worries and fears, not knowing how to articulate emotional or erotic longings. Women felt the impact most of all. As objects of vulgarized male desires, they found themselves in positions of demeaning passivity. In the 1970s–1980s a moralizing discourse evolved in the USSR, the essence of which consisted of a rhetoric of restraint and sublimation designed to shield the citizenry from sex, not to help people to understand the concept consciously, or to develop any freedom in sexual self-expression and mutual respect. It is not surprising that in the 1990s, when the chains of censorship weakened, and Soviet-style sex was cast off this was revealed as something uncivilized, primitive, and revolting in its vulgarity.

## Post-Soviet Gender Order

Insofar as the private women's space was secured in the USSR, construction of their bodies, their sexual orientation, and their social conduct offered a framework to be used in instituting policies regulating their private lives. In Ukraine during the 1990s two fundamental modes of rhetoric about the private sphere—simultaneously contradicting and fulfilling one another—evolved. On the one hand there was conservative discourse about returning to one's roots, national traditions, spirituality, and morality most compellingly portrayed in the Berehynia model,[5] and inscribed in nationalist state ideology. On the other there was the progressive commercialization and exploitation of women's bodies (a topic that Oksana Kis and Tetyana Bureychak also address in chapter 5) and sexuality against the backdrop of market reforms, following the Barbie model. The apparent "Berehynia-Barbie" binary (with Berehynia's sexuality reduced to her reproductive function while Barbie's forming the source of her glamorous identity) disappears as one examines these gender models through the feminist prism. The basis of both is serving men and attending to their needs through the performance of an array of services such as reproduction, nurture, rearing, and the pleasures of sex. Neither model confirms the woman as an independent, self-sufficient being.

Both varieties of rhetoric, as described by Kis (2002), are currently present in public discourse, creating a double standard for the socialization of young women. They must somehow reconcile these conflicting models when constructing their own identity as superwomen—mothers, guardians of the family hearth, beauties, and sources of material resources for the family, all rolled into one—without society legitimizing the process. Tetiana Zhurzhenko describes how in the 1990s, against the backdrop of a broken gender contract between working mothers and the state that was so characteristic of the USSR, economic penury, and mass unemployment, and the rhetoric of "returning women to the family" was touted as a progressive renewal of the natural state of affairs. Without state aid from the demonic Soviet regime, however, it merely served as a ploy to force women out of the highly competitive workplace. Few Ukrainian women could (or still can) afford the lifestyle of a homemaker supported by a husband, even if symbolically they are tirelessly categorized this way. On the discursive level, a woman's economic independence continues to be depicted as something undesirable, even demeaning, rendering it a disincentive in seeking employment and pursuing career advancement.

In the 1990s making a good "match" was viewed as a woman's ultimate achievement in life. Characteristic images of the good life, popularized by mass culture, acted as a carrot to induce young women to chase consumer goods, maintain an alluring appearance, wear sexually suggestive attire, and acquire "prestigious" skills—gourmet cooking, dancing, etc.—as opposed to cultivating her personal development or striving for professional growth. Poverty and gender discrimination in all spheres of life became the stick. One of the unhappy results of the so-called successful marriage ideologem was the high level of violence in the family as it built its "loving ties" on a foundation of an authoritative and economic imbalance. Contemporary romantic scenarios in Ukraine are now constructed on models of dependence, submissiveness, and domination, which cannot be eliminated as long as society looks upon the unmarried woman as an inferior being, a sexually active one as promiscuous, and an economically independent one as unhappy.

The successive elimination of professional achievement ideals and financial independence from the traditional paradigms of womanhood directly impacts access to economic resources (according to various estimates only 5–10 percent of the world's resources are controlled by women). Nonetheless, such resources are what form the basis of individual autonomy, enhanced protection against violence, and dependence. They also constitute the surest path to change in the symbolic discourse, called the absence of woman or nonexistence of woman in the Lacanian psychoanalytical tradition. In a word, the woman exists as an anomaly in the unmarked man-person norm.

The reproductive sphere in today's Ukraine is tightly connected to economic discrimination, and hence to potential dependence and the absence of individual protection. An emphasis on motherhood as a woman's fundamental role/mission uses its own chain of logic to justify women (as a social grouping) being paid less than men, but not because "that is how it has always been." Girls are discouraged from being competitive and standing up for their rights by a society that conforms to the notion that women have no need of high earnings, or even employment for that matter, because they have men to support them. When boys reach manhood, the argument goes, they will need the higher earnings in order to provide for their families.

Women are also hired less willingly and are only reluctantly promoted in the belief that they will be devoting their time to their children rather than to the work at hand. No such presupposition exists for men, who are considered always available to work longer hours. "Currently, government ministers tend to work fifteen hours a day, a regimen that should never be imposed upon any woman, especially one with children," Prime Minister Mykola Azarov once declared sanctimoniously.[6] As long as women are seen as the only ones able to effectively meet children's needs—and, paradoxically, even childless women fall into that category—the glass ceiling remains securely fixed for them in all spheres of public life offering admission to authority and material resources. They also remain doubly exploited in the capitalist economic system—selling their labor in the marketplace (at a reduced value) and performing without charge the vital (and symbolically devalued yet critical) reproductive and child-rearing duties. All of this in addition to providing essential care for the sick, disabled, and elderly. The ideology of the traditional family is promoted in order to cut the cost of creating the next generation of workers. This is why the connection between the intensified conservative attitudes in Ukraine's public space and the country's neoliberal deformation is so direct: returning women to their rightful place in the family and positioning motherhood as a natural and sacred mission is the ideal cover for dismantling a socialist state. All responsibility is transferred to the women, and compliments replace monetary compensation as expressions of appreciation for the performance of this honorable mission.

Such outlandish pronouncements by Ukrainian politicians are no accident—if the former Orange leadership (under Victor Yushchenko) could actively promote Berehynia, then arguably the blue-and-white administration (under Victor Yanukovych) might have felt justified in emphasizing as a preference the Barbie model, personified by "those diamond-adorned dollies who beautify the nights of exhausted gentlemen."[7] Some time ago the leader of the Regions political party, Oleksandr Yefremov, commented on this during a regular parliamentary session. Referring to President Yanukovych's gaffe about young women walking undressed on Kyiv's streets in the springtime he explained that such pronouncements are little more than light humor. Indeed, he noted that living in Ukraine is a joy if only because it allows us to understand and appreciate such sights. Adding insult to injury, he continued his sorry attempt at a justification with: "Ukraine has two types of beautiful women—those we meet on public streets, and those who are transported in private limousines!"[8]

As already observed, a systematic alienation of women from positions of authority and denial of access to economic resources construct the bases of their dependence—real and symbolic. Such measures deprive women of their rights, and forestall any possibility of their influencing post-Soviet social processes in Ukraine. Taken together, the paternalistic Soviet legacy of dependency, collective traumas of the twentieth century yet to be resolved, lawlessness, and economic instability all unite to create impediments to individual safety and autonomy, to a need for new gender policies and freedom of action. The private becomes political in the post-Soviet space, in defiance of the dominant discourse. That being said, it is also true that thanks to the economic base and professional engagement of some Ukrainian women, changes have become feasible. The new generation of women, born at the end of the 1980s and beginning of the 1990s, are now entering the public domain. They face two choices: either accede to the repressive rules of a patriarchal neoliberal economy, a conservative-minded state, and simulated democracy, or help to create, albeit by trial and error, an entirely new range of grassroots policies.

## Praxis and Politics

Ukrainians have a desperate need for new gender paradigms that are responsive to contemporary life experiences, as well as non-hypocritical guiding principles in the private space. At present young Ukrainian women are socialized to a simultaneous acceptance and a refusal of sexist stereotypes because they lack the symbolic resources with which to build their own identities, not to mention positive role models of alternative female types. Most of the publicly prominent women are variations on the theme of either Berehynia or Barbie, forced to flirt with patriarchal prejudices as the price to be paid for social acceptance in a "man's world."

Contradictions in the contemporary gender order have been brilliantly demonstrated by the women's group FEMEN, an active resistance force that emerged in 2008. The topless protests of these rebellious "Barbies" (who combined uninformed articulation of feminist ideas with a lack of decorum). They were perhaps the most dramatic embodiment of young women rejecting the socially prescribed pattern of dependent behavior and identity. These women constructed their own models by resorting to burlesque performances, taking patriarchal ideals to the point of absurdity, and a heteronormative objectification of the female body.

Forming a new tradition is a complex task for a post-Soviet society doubly excluded from social creativity by a protracted totalitarian experience, and the influence of commercialization in all aspects of life. Innovative methods, conceived and developed in the 2000s, lacked a sound theoretical underpinning and political articulation. Meanwhile, Ukraine experienced several waves of moral panicking as its reality leaned toward diversification and emancipation of the intimate sphere that entered into conflict with conservative doxas of traditional morals, family values, national character, etc. Against the backdrop of an economic crisis and concentration of authority in the hands of oligarchic groups, increased political naivté, and societal xenophobia, nonconformist rhetoric regarding the private sphere would have meant risking political suicide for contemporary parliamentarians. Lofty spiritual conversations and moralizing populism were cheaper and safer, but they placed the burden of reproductive activity, and ethical responsibility for abortions, without any accountability from the men. Declarations of support for traditional values did not preclude their enjoyment of cheap *devushka* style sexuality of Ukrainian girls.

Once Ukraine's public space began to undergo clericalization, actively supported by the political parties, the formation of emancipatory privacy policies became the task of the new generation of feminists and grassroots movements. From the early 1990s to the beginning 2000s the efforts of female educators and community activists were crowned by the introduction of gender equality rhetoric in state politics,[9] and expansion of gender studies in educational circles. Nevertheless, for this first wave of feminism in independent Ukraine a certain academic reticence remained characteristic. Against the backdrop of typical post-Soviet misogyny, in their desire to avoid direct conflict with the moral authorities (tradition, the church) academic and civic gender studies circles showed a tendency toward compromise. Women's rights were positioned in the same liberal channel as are human rights. There has been no analysis of the economic foundation of female inequality, and no explicit references to gender policy discrepancies within the ruling structure.

New grassroots movements activated in Ukraine at the beginning of 2010 recognized feminism as a necessary component of their own ideology. Although FEMEN is the most prominent example, it was not the only group to mount an activist campaign. New anarcho-feminist organizations also emerged—the group known as Gender Lviv, the student trade union Direct Action, a curator's collective *Khudrada* (Artists' Council), community organizations with political and educational orientations such as the Community Organization Insight, the expert gender platform *Krona,* and others. In the years of its existence the separatist women's activist initiative Feminist Offensive (now disbanded, ed.) radicalized and politicized feminism, while leveling its criticism at society's patriarchal practices as well as the androcentric tendencies within the country's emancipatory movements. The basic goals of the new initiatives include the creation of a space for grassroots politics and opposition to various forms of discrimination; accentuating the double exploitation of women within the post-Soviet environment of patriarchal capitalism; overcoming hetero-and monogamous normativity; expressing innovative ideas about the private by means of a symbolic division of sexual and reproductive behavior; postulating sexual rights and the values of diversity; promoting collective (shared by interested social agents) reproductive responsibility; and providing support for alternative forms of parenthood.

## Sexuality and Reproduction

Women's unique physiological attribute, the ability to give birth, still defines both their possibilities and their limitations in society. Nationalism always allocates responsibility for the physical and cultural reproduction of the nation, its values, and preservation of its language to women. In a word, it portrays women as guardians of all national traditions. That is why their actions are judged so differently from those of men, and their bodies and morals fall under more stringent social restraints. In a market economy the view of reproduction is paradoxical—it is indispensable for the formation of a new generation of workers and consumers, but in our globalized world it is cheaper to hire foreign workers than to assume the cost of reproducing a workforce. Without outside support children are a luxury for families existing under pressures created by capitalist demands—continuing development, mobility, and the need to adapt to new market requirements. Economic independence creates favorable conditions for the emergence of alternative genders and romantic relations, as a result of which the heterosexual monogamous family with children is no longer the only satisfactory model.

Insufficient information about new life situations that sanction cohabitation without marriage, or support alternative forms of parenthood such as same-sex marriages or polyamorous unions, conjures up fears that can be exploited by power brokers and economic hierarchies to divert attention from their own dubious activities. Negative gender stereotypes are routinely used to influence public opinion and inflame social animosities. Instead of genuine privacy policies, based upon public dialogue, sex education, and availability of contraceptives, Ukrainian women are offered newly elaborated traditions, puritanical controls, and prohibitions against abortions, but these things have no place in today's society because they do not conform to the realities of life experienced by most women. Instead, they mask important problems such as domestic and sexual violence, difficulties associated with single motherhood, complications in renewing professional qualifications following maternity leave, etc. The hypocrisy of the conservative rhetoric becomes even more apparent once we take into account the proposed return of women to the ideals of the nineteenth-century Ukrainian village, and the primordial respect they allegedly enjoyed—although not all scholars subscribe to this view. Some depict it as nothing more than a modern fabrication. Among the most recent such studies, ethnologist Oksana Kis points to a host of examples of inequality, and Maria Mayerchyk is one of the latest scholars to deconstruct the myth of chastity and Puritanism in traditional Ukrainian culture, the purportedly ancient origins of which she traces to the nineteenth century in Ukraine.[10]

The ethnographic studies of Kis and Mayerchyk are valuable for their demonstration of the existing ties between sexual and reproductive behavior, together with the nature of economic relations and household routines. Games during evening gatherings (*vechornytsi*) have a history reaching back to Ukraine's Middle Ages, when they were conspicuous by their uninhibited behavior, such as (multiple) choice(s) of sexual partners, and the use of contraceptive techniques, which provided erotic and emotional outlets for the youth. When it came to marriage, however, women would most likely be "promised" according to their parents' wishes, based on economic considerations. Children were an essential part of the nuclear family's workforce. They contributed to its survival, thereby making a close connection between sexual relations and reproduction essential. The desire for many children as a result came to engender a negative attitude toward all contraceptive techniques, especially because so many children failed to survive beyond early childhood owing to disease, inadequate care, and a much less caring attachment than today's parents exhibit. In the eyes of family and society the children's value was measured by their ability to contribute to domestic labor (beginning at ages of 6–8). Even more so if the parents decided to hire them out and appropriate their earnings, Kis reminds us.

Contemporary manipulation of information, and references to some idealized past, form the basis of a kind of moral hysteria that impedes open public discussions of issues relating to the private sphere. A typical example is found in the antiabortion frenzy, amid calls for the clericalization of society and rebirth of spirituality. The latter anticipates the hypocritical ethic of protecting youth from sex, prefaced by tropes such as "dirty," "undesirable," "indecent," and "something to be avoided whenever possible." This is the way that propositions to change sex education in the schools in the interest of abstinence until marriage sound. Conservatives postulate an unbroken connection between sex and reproduction, especially when it comes to women, forgetting that not every sexual act has pregnancy as its goal, and that erotic satisfaction is the same sort of bodily (hence natural) process as the sexual act aimed at bringing a new life into the world.

Must the politics of the private sphere be manipulated and publicly repressed when they impact women? Currently, alternative sexualities and gender identity, not directed exclusively toward reproduction, are being marginalized and demonized inasmuch as they go against the interests of dominant social agents. A society that aspires to self-regeneration, the state as manager of the interests of a social order requiring new taxpayers, employers as a class—all depend upon the reproductive process yet elect to circumvent all responsibility for its cost. In sum, the reproduction/sexuality connection, plus conservative moralizing, are rhetorical constructs used to divert the public's attention away from the negative material and social conditions of their private lives, to block all women's potential for solidarity in the struggle for equal rights and freedom, and in the process to shift the burden of reproductive activity onto private individuals, mostly women.

The practice of transferring responsibility (and satisfaction) for reproduction to the private realm is a prime example of a "false consciousness," inasmuch as the very possibility of giving birth, child rearing, and children's acculturation depend, in varying degrees, on a complex social, economic, and political environment. It is important to emphasize that the basic factor influencing the demographic situation is not so much the decision as to whether or not to have children, but the conditions that either facilitate or impede reproductive activity—the chances of survival; material circumstances; state of the ecology; quality control over consumer goods and foodstuffs; access to, level, and extent of social insurance; state, medical, and educational services (including preschool facilities); potential for combining career growth with responsible parenthood; etc.

To reiterate: a government-mandated reform of issues regarding the reproductive sphere, which should already be in place as a shared responsibility between parents and society, is rejected by the authorities. What we need is an effective program for the social, for paternity leave, and the rapid reintegration of women into their prebirthing professional function. This should replace the current practice of several years of isolation during the "mothering" process that, with few exceptions, is currently the norm. One way would be to fix an interval in maternity/paternity leave for each parent that is not interchangeable. A similar format works well in Sweden—the customary period is 480 days, with 60 reserved exclusively for each of the parents, and the remainder allocated according to mutual agreement. This suggestion usually produces a (male) panic, with jokes about feminists pushing for men to give birth and breast feed, while ignoring the work of rearing a child that lasts considerably longer and requires far more time and effort than the lying in and lactation periods.

The role of state and society in creating a child-friendly environment begins with effective reforms, making the birth of the nation's future citizens compatible with an active professional and social life for the mother. For instance, what is needed is decent reimbursement during maternity leave (funded by the state), together with legal norms according to which employers guarantee that the young parents will receive a shorter work day or a flexible schedule with no monetary sacrifice, that they will benefit from public sensitivity, and be able to take for granted society's responsiveness to the needs of parents with small children, as well as its provisions for quality and accessible children's facilities. Naturally, these must be consistent with Ukrainian customs, and with the cooperation of parents, employers, the state, and society in an equitable division of reproductive responsibility among all interested parties while constantly keeping in mind the urgent need to relieve women of a burden that they now bear alone.

A new standard of shared responsibility that provides for the involvement of social agents needs to replace our current repressive gender models. Society has long since ceased to depend on the patriarchal family for survival, for the right to cultivate an individual lifestyle, to enjoy unfettered romantic and sexual self-expression and creativity. The idea of shared reproductive responsibility must also be differentiated from state paternalism and its ability to foster dependence by means of monopolies in essential resources, allocated only to those willing to conform to a repressive normal lifestyle that lends itself to maximum control and exploitation by the governing apparatus.

This facilitates the reduction of care giving costs by shifting the obligation to the nuclear family so that funds can be used for other purposes. A policy of divided reproductive responsibility needs to be implemented with a view to public needs, such as adequately financed educational programs in municipal nursery schools that would replace draconian curricula restrictions. Funds should also be allocated to the financial support of children's institutions such as nonprofit community organizations, or collective supervision of children in places of employment and communal residences. This would stimulate public discussions on the ethical principles of child rearing and encourage state participation in the process. The very notion of child requires reconceptualization, inasmuch as the current upbringing focuses too closely on strict parental controls. Piercing the ears of female toddlers is a significant example of a thoughtless violation of the inviolability of the body. It ignores altogether the concept of indissoluble individual rights present from the moment of birth.

Individual lifestyles justifiably lay claim to democratic diversity, which must find its reflection in all symbolic and legal spheres. It is time to dispense with monogamy and heterosexuality as obligatory norms and change our options to provide for equally valued polyamorousness, diverse forms of sexuality, reproduction as individual choice, shared parenthood, same sex unions, etc. The moment has come to portray a new vision of private life, one that is fully valued, that comes with all-embracing rights that are legitimized by a society that considers a heterosexual lifestyle the unmarked paradigm, to abandon the notion that alternate lifestyles are deviant.

## Conclusion

Post-Soviet rhetoric in Ukraine's private sphere is replete with blind zones, which only serve to conceal crucial problems. Moral hysteria, induced by the incompatibility of real life and its symbolic representation, gets in the way of sober community discussions of new and effective ways of organizing the private sphere—sexual and reproductive to begin with, without the menacing tone that the motto "my body, my business" conveys.

Generally speaking, socially beneficial work conducted in the private sphere is not remunerated; as such, it lacks assigned value. Responsibility for it is not simply reducible to raising children and managing a household, it includes care giving to the sick, the elderly—all of which devolve on the backs of women. Young mothers (the very ones that are on a pedestal in Ukrainian society) find themselves in the most insecure, discriminatory position in light of their inadequate social guarantees, few opportunities in the employment market, absence of quality preschool facilities for their children (although few could afford them even if they were available), possibilities for an active social and professional life (a child in tow in a public library or a concert hall is regarded with disapproval), or even the lack of such basic amenities as facilities for parking a stroller or an infant's changing table in public restrooms.

Much remains to be done in our post-Soviet country to advance the cause of human rights. Because so much of the burden rests on the backs of women, we must pay special attention to gender equality as an essential first step toward building a democratic society in which there is no place for old prejudices, and outdated practices.

**Tamara Zlobina** is a feminist philosopher and art theorist who specializes in women's contemporary art in Ukraine, Belarus, and Moldova. She has coedited the social critique magazine *Commons,* where she is responsible for its feminist and contemporary art departments, was an invited editor and art critic for the magazine *Art Aktivist* (Minsk), and collaborates with several art journals *Krytyka, Gendernie Issledovania, Korydor, Art-Ukraine, Perekrestki* (Lithuania), *Public Preparation* (Estonia), *Vector* (Romania), *Khudozhestvenny Zhurnal* (Russia), and others. She exhibited in the New

European College Black Sea Link on a fellowship from Bucharest, and in Warsaw on a Poland Gaude Polonia scholarship.

## Notes

1. https://www.youtube.com/watch?v=zYxut3y5COE.
2. See Lev Trotsky (1937), *Revolution Betrayed: What is the USSR and Where is it Going?* http://www.marxists.org/russkij/trotsky/1936/betrayed/7.html.
3. According to Tarasov, super-etatism, also defined as state capitalism, is based on the combination of an industrialized mode of production with state (instead of civil) ownership of the means of production.
4. It contains the famous scene in which the male protagonist declares to the heroine, "from now on all the decisions in the family will be made by me because I'm the man."
5. Symbolic mother of the nation and model of empowered womanhood, especially in the domestic sphere.
6. http://maidanua.org/static/news/2011/1300110784.html.
7. http://maidanua.org/static/news/2011/1300110784.html.
8. http://www.pravda.com.ua/news/2011/01/31/5862849.
9. The law on "Guarantee of equal rights and opportunities for women and men" was passed in 2005 and ratified at the beginning of 2006. As for women's equality, an allegedly ancient (prehistoric) ritual placed the senior woman of a clan in a position of power owing to the fact that she presided over the family hearth. As such, she was present at all clan decisions, routinely taken around that hearth during clan councils. It is not known whether or not she had an actual voice in the decision making, but her presence during these all-important meetings gave rise to what morphed into a topos of empowered womanhood. More recently that topos has become a tongue-in-cheek expression frequently used by men to maintain that Ukraine has always been a "feminist" society owing to its "domestic dominance," obviating any need for such nonsense as Western feminism.
10. A long line of researchers has engaged this topic, many of whom take their studies all the way back to primordial times. Mayerchyk narrows the focus to the nineteenth century.

## Bibliography

Bohachevsky-Chomiak, Martha. 1988. *Feminists despite Themselves: Women in Ukrainian Community Life, 1884–1939.* Edmonton: Canadian Institute of Ukrainian Studies, University of Alberta.

D'Emilio, John. 1983. *Sexual Politics, Sexual Communities: The Making of a Homosexual Minority in the United States, 1940–1970.* Chicago, IL: University of Chicago Press.

Gapova, Elena. 2005. "On gender, nation, and communism," *Gender Research* 13: 101–118.

Kis, Oksana. 2002. "Modeli konstruiuvannia gendernoi identychnosty zhinky v suchasnii Ukraini." http://www.ji.lviv.ua/n27texts/kis.htm.

———. 2008. *Zhinka v Tradytsiinii Ukrainskii Kul'turi* (*XIX–Pochatok XX st*). Lviv: Instytut Etnolohiyi. Ukrainska Akademiia Nauk.

Kon, Igor. 1995. *Sexual Revolution in Russia: From the Age of the Czars to Today.* Translated by James Riordan. New York: Free Press.

Mayerchyk, Maria. 2010. "Doshliubni intymni stosunky sered molodi v selakh ta mistakh Skhidnoi ta Tsentral'noi Ukrainy na pochatku XX stolittia," *Moloda Ukraina* 6(17): 101–112.

Tarasov, Alexander. 1996. *Superetatyzm I Sotsiolohizm. K Postanovke Problemy.* http://scepsis.ru/library/id_102.html.

Trotsky, Lev. 1937. "Revolution Betrayed: What is the USSR and where is it going?" http://www.marxists.org/russkij/trotsky/1936/betrayed/7.html.

Yuval-Davis, Nira, and Marcel Stoetzler. 2002. "Imagined boundaries and borders: A gendered gaze," *European Journal of Women's Studies* 9(3): 329–344.

Zhurzhenko, Tatiana. 2008. *Gender Marketplaces in Ukraine: Political Economy of Nation Building.* Vilnius: European Humanities University.

# PART II

# Power of the Media

# CHAPTER 4

# Ukrainian Glamour as a Consequence of the Soviet Past

Tetiana Bulakh

The adjective *post-Soviet* is used to signify contemporary Ukrainian society with mounting frequency, with *post-* as a prefix seemingly implying that we have left behind all Soviet achievements. However, it cannot be shown that the massive legacy of this powerful state left the historical stage without a trace. The truth of the matter is that Soviet-constructed dominants of political, social, and cultural life continue to impact the value system of even the new generation, one that was born or came to maturity in an independent country. Ukrainian independence was achieved in 1991, but an attachment to all things Soviet continued to exist in the people's mindset, if only at the subconscious level.

We will attempt to trace the characteristics of the contemporary Ukrainian value system with an emphasis on its women by examining the phenomenon of glamour and its transmutation over the course of the past two decades. Questions to be asked are: What external appearance did this glamour assume in post-Soviet Ukraine, and how did it evolve as the country moved into the twenty-first century? In what ways did the realities of Ukrainian life and its values change as the post-Soviet generation trod its path to maturity in a country that was no longer directly impacted by an authoritarian system?

## Glamour as a Sociocultural Phenomenon

Various theories have been advanced to explain the etymological evolution of the word *glamour,* and its connection to concepts such as fascination, sorcery, bewitchment, and the present-day phenomenon of idealized reality. Based on his research on the genesis of the term, Stephen Gundle provides us with a useful hypothesis. He has concluded that its original connection might have stemmed from Sir Walter Scott's use of the word "glimbr" in his 1805 "Lay of the Last Minstrel" to indicate that glamour exhibits a public lifestyle that makes ordinary things appear better than they are, that it turns reality into a form of daydream (2008). Its etymological origins aside, glamour as a cultural expression of style imparts certain characteristics that evoke magical transformations, allure, an accent on outward appearance, and variability.

In its contemporary application, glamour correlates with the creation of an illusory reality, an enchanting world of magic, luxury, and perpetual leisure. This product of a particular myth-creation process, based on its own specific canons and rules, has acquired a special meaning in the post-Soviet Ukrainian space. It encompasses the tastes and the lifestyle of the new bourgeoisie—as reflected in fashion, glossy magazines, advertising, and show business. In analyzing post-Soviet discourse on glamour, the Russian sociologist Dmitrii Ivanov emphasized several key criteria for defining it in its post-Soviet manifestation of luxury, exoticism, naiveté, superficial optimism, and "blondinization" (2008). These are expressions of glamour that no longer connote genuine charm. In today's Ukraine such a depiction often presents a blend of simulated Western chic and the remnants of the Soviet vision of style.

Equally important is the fact that today glamour in Ukraine is indissolubly tied to the cult of what is perceived as the "sophisticated" woman, something that post-Soviet women have enthusiastically embraced. Research on its early twentieth-century manifestation has indicated that working women spent very little time on themselves; husbands and children were their first priority (Dyhouse 2011: 47). By the end of the century, however, women's expenditures on fashionable attire and cosmetics had risen exponentially. The earlier profile of a typical woman shifted from self-sacrificing homemaker to female shopaholic, fascinated by the perpetual exercise of following the latest fashions in order to appear alluring and seductive. Glamour as an objective continues to encourage women to enhance their appearance. Carol Dyhouse expressed it well when she observed: "Glamour is often linked to a dream of transformation, a desire for the exceptional, a form of aspiration, a fiction of female becoming" (2011: 47). It inspires one to imagine that exquisite femininity and uniqueness can be achieved through artificial means, through the use of cosmetics, plastic surgery, etc.

Beginning with the 1960s in the United States, and only during the past decade in Ukraine, the feminine profile has gone through some notable changes. Women have become more engaged, more independent, and they have arrived at an awareness of new perspectives, new possibilities—ranging from birth control to successful careers. An interesting offshoot of this is the altered focus of glamorous images in advertising. Once women became self-sufficient, advertisers began to target them directly, instead of resorting to male mediation. For instance, at the beginning of the twentieth century ads for fur coats were aimed at male customers. They were the ones with the purchasing power to afford such luxuries for their wives or mistresses, and the ones with the influence and resources to turn dreams of glamour into reality. During the course of the twentieth-century glamour became more universal. What is more, it also linked certain feminine attributes to men, and through the escalating actualization of their metrosexuality, glamour brought men closer to a socially constructed female essence. Discourse on glamour, the cult of a pampered body subjected to continual modification—from the simple use of perfume to surgical manipulation—is so general in scope that in many respects it now habitually embraces both men and women, to one degree or another.

As a phenomenon, glamour is quite complex and multifaceted. It is a lifestyle that integrated itself organically into the culture, first as an indivisible link to the elite, and subsequently as a component of mass culture. It has navigated its own unique life cycle—from genesis to flowering, to mass culture, and finally to self-irony. So-called classic glamour encompasses the time span between the thirties and the fifties of the twentieth century in the United States—the age of Hollywood's "dream factory." During the Great Depression escapist tendencies were intensified as they began laying down a secure foundation for this artificial, dream-like, luxury-loving, and, most important, ideally carefree lifestyle. Hollywood "divas" like Marlene Dietrich, Greta Garbo, and later Grace Kelly and Marilyn Monroe embodied it. In the second half of the twentieth century glamour lost some of its appeal; it transformed itself in tandem with newer cultural trends. Not least of all, popularized through women's magazines, the appearance of television, and a massive infusion of advertising and consumerism, it was democratized and acquired increasing significance as a guide to life's values. At the end of the twentieth century the shocking styles of celebrities like Madonna and Courtney Love became complicit in the process of glamour giving way to its antithesis—grunge. In the 2000s glamour morphed yet again; it became self-reflective, postmodern, and given to self-irony. Lady Gaga can be viewed as an icon in this new trend as she combined a fresh variety of sexuality, shock value, and manipulation of public space.

If the evolution of Western glamour can be described schematically as a genuine cultural expression, the same cannot be said of its Ukrainian imitation. During the twentieth century glamour existed only beyond the iron curtain, separating Western countries from the Soviet Union, where it was denounced on an ideological level as a manifestation of "decadent" bourgeois culture. It is also true that members of the Soviet elite able to shop abroad for goods and luxuries were in a position to approximate it. As for the masses in Ukraine, they gained access to glamour only after it had been evolving in the West for decades. The first wave of its expansion came to post-Soviet Ukraine during the nineties of the twentieth century, when a social phenomenon known as the New Ukrainians emerged. An informational expanse opened up in the early 1990s, and once it was launched its interaction with Western culture impacted the masses with alacrity.

The second wave of this trend came to prominence in a period of economic evolution during the temporary stabilization of the economy in the 2000s. Newly acquired purchasing power, backed by the availability of credit, gave Ukrainians access to heretofore unaccustomed luxuries. Naturally, both during the first and second waves of expansion it was mostly the business and political circles (basically identical categories in Ukraine) who rushed to embrace this lifestyle. In a word, these were the individuals with deep pockets for whom making an impression and establishing a prominent position in the social hierarchy were of paramount importance. Glamour's shift to irony, as happened elsewhere, bypassed Ukraine, although it did produce a penchant for anti-glamour as a form of protest against whatever issue was foremost at a given moment.

## Kitschisization of Glamour and Glamorization of Kitsch

When glamour finally appeared on Ukraine's cultural and social terrain, it became more than a part of bourgeois life. It paralleled the postmodern lifestyle, where boundaries between elites and masses were systematically erased, with the result that glamour was democratized and vulgarized. The new consumerist environment made it available to mass society, while demand for exclusivity accompanied by a craving to participate in the glamorous life gave birth to a paradoxical mishmash of exclusivity and access. Insofar as luxury was not available to most, while aspiration to glamour increased exponentially, one witnessed counterfeiting, adulteration, etc. This brought a semblance of glamour, or whatever passed for it in Ukraine, within reach of the masses, even as the genuine article strained the means of most people. Accordingly, excessive ornamentation, replication, and luxurious (if tasteless) immoderation became the new aesthetic that defined an emerging kitsch—a craze of Ukraine's consumer culture and its pseudo-artistic expressions with tendencies to vulgarism, and tasteless extravagance.

Kitsch and traditional American glamour are contradictory concepts. Kitsch anticipates an imitation of objects and experiments, as well as a mass cultural orientation, whereas glamour cultivates exclusivity and elitism. Following Jean Baudrillard on this dichotomy—the higher echelons of society attempted to distance themselves from the masses through the use of objects and labels issued in restricted quantities (high-end automobiles, limited editions of watches, etc.). Simultaneously, kitsch labored to imitate these exclusive items, producing thereby a special closed circle. Together, kitsch and the genuine articles fashioned their own consumer world (2006).

The Ukrainian variant of glamour is quite complex. On the one hand, it is a simulation of Western/American glamour that was not rooted in any specific cultural-historical or social substratum. By contrast, Ukrainian glamour has been kitsch from its very inception. Much of it is oriented toward a combination of the folk tradition and Western expressions of glamour. This can be traced, for instance, through the transformation of the national star of pop culture Verka (Vierka) Serdiuchka, a cross-dresser often referred to as "Lady Kitsch." Initially, "she" distorted the profile of a typical national leader by wearing a folk costume that eventually was replaced by a glamorous pink plush outfit. It is possible to perceive Ukrainian kitschisized glamour and glamorized kitsch as the creation of an ideology of conspicuous consumption, with external manifestations of opulence intimating elite status.

## Glamour in the Nineties: First Wave of Glamorization

The collapse of the USSR disrupted its value system and stimulated a gradual shift in models of consumption. Overcompensation for the deprivations of the Soviet past (Menzel 2008: 7) drew on Soviet consumption patterns but it shaped its own distinct characteristics. Everything Western assumed a superior hue, consumerism acquired more prestige than it was worth, and consumption of luxuries far exceeded the actual needs of social groups for whom conspicuous spending had become an indivisible part of their being.

A dichotomy of "ours" and "Western" had already emerged during the Soviet era. The propaganda system worked vigorously to generate support for the monotonously uniform Soviet-made products, but as the far more highly valued merchandise began trickling in from abroad, and was offered for sale on the black market, a day-by-day competition for the still-scarce goods developed. The insufficiency of these imported items gave rise to special types of social relationships, involving the pursuit of consumer goods through bribery and personal connections. This competition spawned speculation in American jeans, Japanese tape recorders, chewing gum, and the much-prized Coca-Cola (Filipov 2009); seemingly ordinary items assumed a highly symbolic value. They accentuated the owner's status and testified to his/her special possibilities. The symbolic aureole of goods from abroad had moved the Soviet people ever closer to some illusory better life. In the second half of the 1990s the influx of Western wares delivered a similar moment to Ukraine, and even when the once-forbidden fruit became widely available it did not lose its desirability.

Small wonder then that with the disintegration of the Soviet Union, the potential for a life of increasing consumption opened up for Ukrainians, and the psychology of the so-called *Homo sorbeos* (one who consumes) emerged. The very act of purchasing certain goods constituted a moment of self-affirmation, although, paradoxically, it also attested to the inferiority complex that had developed in Ukrainians living for so long under the repressive communist regime. For a people trapped behind the iron curtain for many decades the realities of a world outside were often idealized and aroused extraordinary interest as they first became available. To illustrate—when the first McDonalds opened in 1997 it produced an unmatched air of excitement. Here is how one newspaper described it:

> The launch of this first famous fast-food establishment in the Ukrainian capital attracted unprecedented stock-jobbing. Inside the restaurant the crush was so bad that a sheet of paper couldn't have passed between two people. A huge throng spilled out through the doorway onto the city sidewalk, its lines snaking as far as the eye could see, and parked cars jammed the walkways along Melnyk Street for blocks. (Panchenko and Ryapolov 2011)

The process of integrating aspects of a Western lifestyle to Ukraine following the collapse of the Soviet Union came closest to Fredric Jameson's description of consumerism (2000). It bordered on excess and ostentatious display, especially by those who not only relied on objects to satisfy their needs, but turned to them for a validation of their status. This tendency was most conspicuous in the subculture of the recently launched bourgeoisie—the New Ukrainians. Members of this social class became the self-styled bearers of glamour and the foremost "authorities" on luxury items. This brings to mind a paradoxical scene from the Soviet era: Mikhail Gorbachev, the communist leader who precipitated the demise of the USSR, was featured in a print ad for Louis Vuitton, one of the most glamorous, most popular fashion brands at the time, and contemporary symbol of status and wealth.[1]

The New Ukrainians seized upon the glamorous lifestyle and transformed it to conform to their own notion of luxury and social status. Initially glamour had been a feature of the upper class and its aristocratic traditions. Class disparity was built into its very foundation, in contrast to the demonstrable, demonstrative consumption patterns and games of the wider public as it tried to emulate the romanticized glamorous world of its "betters." With the advent of independence and absence of an aristocratic tradition, that position was usurped in large measure by the nouveau riches—the New Ukrainians—those who had formerly occupied high positions in the Communist Party. These were enterprising individuals capable of exploiting the newly opened possibilities for amassing wealth.

It can be argued quite convincingly that precisely at this moment the lack of intellectual talent and an upper class heritage became problematic for Ukrainians. The waves of murderous repressions during the Soviet era had ravaged the upper class base, and with it any potential for rebuilding one that might have established a basis for embracing glamour in a dignified environment. Instead, an ersatz elite was forged with neither an apposite upbringing nor an uncompromised cultural legacy. The Soviet system had removed the Ukrainian upper class from its own cultural roots and effectively cut it off from the cultural tradition of the West.

The process in Ukraine at the end of the twentieth century was somewhat reminiscent of the Industrial Revolution in nineteenth-century Britain. At that time in this aristocratic country a social layer of wealthy bourgeoisie had already formed. Although lacking an aristocratic tradition, owing to the technological progress of the time, its members accumulated wealth very rapidly. This upper bourgeoisie aspired to inclusion in a higher social order, and the scale of their assets facilitated access. For its part, the genuine aristocracy disdained these upstarts, citing vulgar manners and lack of pedigree, which gave rise to numerous secret societies with stringent membership requirements. In the Ukrainian contest, economic conditions facilitated the formation of that new social layer of New Ukrainians with its pretensions to elite status. There was, however, a difference separating them from their bourgeois counterparts in the West—they had no model to emulate and no one to reject them. In a word—they were on their own! From a sociological perspective they became extreme examples of vulgar conduct, crude individualism, and tasteless conspicuous consumption.

For the emerging elite the ostentatious visual display had a special significance. It introduced a consumer craze for Mercedes automobiles, cell phones, and gold chains, possessions that constituted for them the indispensable attributes of plenty and prosperity. As Roland Barthes described it, "For centuries the variety of styles coincided with social classes; apparel was a sign that responded to an established code" (2006).[2] In his characterization of fashion and dandyism, Barthes explained that over the course of several centuries apparel was a sign, a conventional code designating the social status of its wearer. Changing one's dress indicated an attempt to change one's class status, a practice that began during the postindustrial era. The emergence of the New Ukrainians was seen as its closest parallel. The coveted status-changing possessions included a substantial gold chain worn around the neck, and a Mercedes automobile. Somewhat later this vogue was extended to a huge (for the time) cell phone, but the most representative possession was a raspberry-colored jacket, with its ersatz gold buttons,[3] a gauche imitation of Western attire.

In the information age Ukrainians became beneficiaries of yet another mass-oriented product—the 1990s brought a boom in popularity of Latin American soap operas emulating the lifestyle of the rich (*Rich People Also Cry, Simply Maria, Wild Rose*), in which the simple subject is invalidated by on-screen visions of luxury estates and high-priced automobiles. As long as uncertainty reigned at home, this was a form of escapism for the masses, as well as a way to learn something about other cultures. Streets were suddenly emptied whenever a succeeding episode of serialized glamour was scheduled to appear on television. The mass popularity of heretofore unfamiliar objects dictated fashion in hair styles, apparel, etc. In a curious corollary during the 1990s the tiny household plots where the people grew fruit and vegetables for personal consumption in Ukraine were named *fazendames*. This was a borrowing from the first soap opera to be shown in Ukraine—*The Slave Izaura*. The broadcast originated in Brazil and the term signified Spanish *haciendas*. Since the nineteenth century in Brazil *fazendas* had applied to large landholdings—sites of large coffee plantations. Ukrainians' appropriation of the name stemmed from the popularity of the Brazilian soap operas. The impact of these "soaps" can be equated with the glamorous Hollywood images that became so popular in the United States during the Great Depression. Just as Americans dreamed of a better life through Hollywood films, Ukrainians found their solace in soap operas.

Also in the 1990s Ukrainians began to experience ideological freedom; it played a prominent role in promoting glamour. One of its earliest harbingers—the first glossy women's magazine, analogous to its American counterpart *Cosmopolitan*, made its appearance under the name *Natalie* in 1995. The new woman-oriented popular journals did not feature the customary practical advice for doing/making things—a significant departure from the popular Soviet-era *Burda*, with its practical aids such as patterns for women who made their own clothes. In a deviation from other earlier publications such as *Soviet Woman* (*Radianska Zhinka*, which morphed into *Zhinka*) or *Peasant Woman* (*Krestianka*) the sleek new formats crowned the magical world of glamour with their emphasis on sex, travel, and celebrity, and the glossy ads promoting glamour that appeared for the first time.

## Glamour in the Millennial Ukraine

The third millennium ushered in a renewed perception of glamour in Ukrainian society, and *glamorous* became a synonym for *stylish*. A stabilized economy and continued developments in the country instilled a feeling of confidence and a sense of financial security in the nation's population, all of which contributed to the formation and growth of a middle class. Naturally this affected the lifestyle of the young generation whose voyage of maturing was progressing in an independent Ukraine. The Orange Revolution in 2004 also played a part. On the one hand it introduced the hope for a life that might be differently understood and lived—a feeling of rising expectations—and helped to instill confidence in Ukraine's potential for a democratic society. On the other hand the betrayal of the revolution's promise of a better life confirmed Ukraine's uneven state-building progression. Against this background a return to power of oligarchic forces gave a new twist to the development of glamour—more costly, yet still stimulating. In the midst of this volatility, democratic tendencies revealed themselves in the form of an antiglamour protest.

At the end of the 1990s, divisions in the businessmen's spheres of influence moved to another level. If the initial years of independence included racketeering and banditry, by the dawn of the twenty-first century the most powerful representatives of business and governing circles had gone public. The term *oligarch* acquired a solid foothold in Ukrainian discourse, marking a new era and a new form in Ukraine's historical evolution. Privatization processes, corruption, firm ties between business and government—all breathed life into the Ukrainian circle of oligarchs, a cohort not unlike the narrow circle of Soviet power mongers.

An analysis of life under the Soviets will reveal two kinds of existence—real and unreal—but the portrayal of unreal life was so idealized and real life so hushed up that the actual division became increasingly diluted. Real life resembled a carnival—individuals were transformed into "enemies of the people," "stakhanovites" broke work records, everyone was encouraged to contribute to the creation of the myth of a worker state. By the beginning of the twenty-first century such idealization of life was no longer necessary, although it still needed to be concealed. In 2005, for the first time in history, *Forbes* annual billionaires list included three Ukrainians—Renat Akhmetov, Serhii Taruta, and Victor Pinchuk, accompanied by an explanation that a culture of secrecy had prevented an earlier listing. Wealthy Ukrainians began to feel more comfortable with a public display of their status. Gradually Western boutiques carrying luxury items—Louis Vuitton, Chanel, and Bally—made their débuts in Ukraine.

In Russia a similar process was linked to the Putin era—the IX Russian Economic Forum that took place in London in 2006 was colorfully christened by journalists "Luxury as a national idea." The editor-in-chief of *GQ*, Nikolai Uskov, noted during the proceedings that a "golden traders" class had materialized, for whom luxury had become a priority in life (Rudova 2008). Naturally, Russia, with its vast reserves of gas and further economic possibilities, had many more resources available for imitating luxury items associated with glamour, which is why fashion shows for millionaires, etc., found a home there.

Although we began by noting that Ukrainians imitated Western glamour, gradually the Ukrainian Beau Monde also started to emulate Russian glamour. Collective projects using show business stars, Russian television programs, and so on, became common occurrences. For a long time Ukraine did not have its own glamour-oriented periodicals, so Russian editions of Western women's magazines *Cosmopolitan, Elle,* and *Harper's Bazaar,* with localized advertising, were circulated instead. The scale of Ukrainian glamour was naturally smaller, but in the twenty-first century such idealization of life was no longer necessary, although it still needed to be concealed. In 2005, for the first time in history, *Forbes* annual billionaires list included three Ukrainians—Renat Akhmetov, Serhii Taruta, and Victor Pinchuk, accompanied by an explanation that a culture of secrecy had prevented an earlier listing. Wealthy Ukrainians began to feel more comfortable with a public display of their status. Gradually Western boutiques carrying luxury items—Louis Vuitton, Chanel, and Bally—made their débuts in Ukraine.

In Russia a similar process was linked to the Putin era—the IX Russian Economic Forum which took place in London in 2006 was colorfully christened by journalists "Luxury as a national idea." The editor-in-chief of *GQ,* Nikolai Uskov, noted during the proceedings that a "golden traders" class had materialized, for whom luxury had become a priority in life (Rudova 2008).

It is important to emphasize that the desire to copy glamour frequently exceeded all sane proportions. Eventually Ukraine's business and government elite found itself in the eye of public scandal connected to excessive wealth, and increasingly vociferous expressions of outrage. The son of Ukraine's former president Victor Yushchenko, for example, earned his place in yellow journalism when his ownership of items such as an expensive automobile and a Vertu cell phone were made public. And, while visiting Paris, the daughter of Kyiv's mayor Leonid Chernovetskyi was robbed of her handbag. Among its contents was jewelry valued at €4.5 million; powerful international reverberations followed. Scandals exposing the holdings of Ukrainian businessmen and politicians were routinely covered in the press, attesting to the fact that Beau Monde in Ukrainian society had not yet been securely assimilated by the elite, while the restrained tradition of the aristocracy remained alien to them.

Scandals surrounding businessmen and politicians whose assets were now routinely exposed in the press attested first and foremost to the inability of Beau Monde codes of conduct to gain a foothold in Ukraine. By the end of the twentieth century it was patently obvious that the capability for transforming glamour into an expression of irony was not indigenous to Ukrainian culture. Accordingly, the desire to emphasize one's status through the acquisition of luxury items remained central and defining.

By the beginning of the twenty-first century the tendency to spend money with abandon was no longer limited to the wealthy. Young people perceived the crisis and instability of the 1990s from a somewhat more detached perspective than their elders. To a large extent, the spending tendencies of the era were preserved through a kind of inertia, while the succeeding generation came to maturity in a cultural milieu in which glamour gradually became an organic component. With it came the increased desire to live for the moment and spend accordingly.

As noted by the International Center for Policy Studies, the rise in Ukrainian prosperity at the beginning of the new century arrived on a wave of heightened demand.[4] Research on consumer sentiment carried out by the center, together with the GfK (Growth for Knowledge) illustrated the huge potential of consumer demand in Ukraine. What is more, Ukrainian consumers manifested increasing optimism in future income expectations, allowing for more liberal spending in the present.[5]

Confidence in the future, and a modest stabilization of finances in Ukraine, together with the myth-creation capabilities of advertising, stimulated that spending. Access to credit played its part as well, especially the zero-interest offers. While in America this was a familiar economic model, for Ukrainians it was an unaccustomed phenomenon. The availability of credit encouraged purchases even if the means to pay for them were in question. Goods remained a cult, and purchases not limited to necessities continued.

In millennial Ukraine American telephones and other such gadgets represented an analogy to the prestigious American jeans during the Soviet era. Apple products enjoyed the highest status and greatest popularity. In 2012 it was impossible to purchase an iPhone legally in Ukraine because no seller had yet been certified. This automatically invested the phone with a cult of exclusivity embodied in expensive items. To make such a purchase possible the telephones were sent from the United States through various devious channels. Similar to the process during the Soviet era, acquisition depended upon contacts with dealers in contraband. It is symptomatic that Chinese knockoffs were, and still are, inordinately popular in Ukraine. Imitations of luxury items have remained stable among Ukrainian consumers, who actually poke fun at themselves as they ob-

serve: All we need to make an impression is to use a new telephone cost-
ing several thousand hryvnia, even when we have nothing in the bank. If
it can be attested that glamour creates a whole new reality, this is a unique
enhancement of such an imagined world.

Even those with the means to purchase expensive goods do not shun
fakes; all they care about is flaunting a show of their importance and status. The blog of the Italian merchant who trades in luxury items Maurizio
Asker makes for an interesting observation: "In Kyiv I have women as
clients from a certain social stratum who display ostentatiously their ugly
counterfeit goods, especially Hermes handbags. Their attitude is: 'If I am
wealthy and distinguished it will not occur to anyone to question the au-
thenticity of what I own, so why spend money on the real thing?'"[6]

Changes in consumer styles evolved in tandem with transformations s
in the information sphere. On the one hand, publications demonstrating
a luxurious existence, and simultaneously popularizing it, began to appear
(*Platinum, Luxury Watch and Diamond, Luxury Life*). On the other, ordinary people started to demonstrate an interest in the lifestyles of rich and
famous Ukrainians who had recently opened up their lives to the public
by holding their wealth up to scrutiny. This stimulated the inauguration of
new publications—issues devoted to the existence of the nouveau riches.
Biographies of film and television stars written in a creative, persuasive,
intimate style, accompanied by vivid photos and descriptions of sophisticated events, became the subjects of the first Ukrainian magazines featuring such stars as *Story, Viva, Ok!,* offering yet another avenue of escape
from reality. They printed the latest gossip, evoked an imaginary existence,
thrilled the reading public with stories of glorious destinies, and created a
unique vision of bliss.

Television also witnessed a new product on the market—*The Secular
Life with Kateryna Osadcha* (2000)—the first television program to deal
with the subject of leisure for wealthy Ukrainians. What is interesting is
that the program became a highly esteemed information resource that,
perhaps for the first time in the history of Ukrainian television, won the
opportunity to participate in such international events as the Cannes Film
Festival, the Viennese Ball, etc.

The 2008 financial crisis brought its own correctives, stemming from
severe cost-cutting measures. Not the least of these was the decline of the
middle class, accompanied by widening status differences. This process
scarcely touched wealthy Ukrainians, as one Ukrainian analyst pointed
out.[7] The government's inability to stabilize the economic and political
situation in the country against a backdrop of its own consumption of
luxuries increasingly generated negative reactions and skepticism among
ordinary people. It is no wonder that over the course of the past several
years glamour had acquired a negative connotation, becoming almost a

term of opprobrium. In this environment oppositional tendencies in the form of antiglamour increasingly reflected the negative reaction to imitation, to the artificial and unrefined nature of Ukrainian glamour.

In 2009 Ragu.li became the most popular Internet site in Ukraine. It is an informational resource known in its expanded title as a blog about the "aggressive tastelessness of the Ukrainian Beau Monde." Resorting to irony and sarcasm, its authors write about personalities, and events, and display photographs exposing and ridiculing the Ukrainian elite and members of show business. We have as an example the versified reaction to photo sessions of actress Olha Sumska: "This is a photo of her, scenes shot without a break, bewitching, sexy, and intelligent, especially with a dusting of powder, and needing to show off her tiny Chinese shaggy dog. She dresses in stylish frocks, topped by a hat covering a brain slug logo on her forehead. A blouse billowing like the azure sea is worn over a skirt of floral and fauna print."[8]

Among the most prominent authors who demonstrate their objections to glamour in their works are two brilliant personalities, Andrii (Kuzia) Kuzmenko and Irena Karpa. The latter is part of the imaginative youth, and an active participant in creative performances. She participates in part in the worldly life but positions the heroine of her novel as one who disparages it: "I detest both the pseudo-glamorous and glamorous hangouts. Actually, I detest and love them simultaneously. It gives me great pleasure to sneer at someone and I like to jot down descriptions of two or three different kinds of heroines for possible use in one or another of my future trash movies" (2005: 42). Karpa is an author of anti-glamour novels. To underscore her ideological stance, in 2005 she staged a creative public action known as *Starry Second-hand* by burning glossy magazines and stylish apparel.

Pop music, performed by various women's musical ensembles, also reflects the cultural glamour/antiglamour binary. The beginning of the twenty-first century represented a real boon for popular young singers. As was the case with glamour itself, the fundamental emphasis was on externals, on visual appeal, through erotic video clips and scantily clad performers. Generally speaking, the performers in these musical groups were either former models or beauty pageant contestants, but in no way might they be considered vocalists. Looking for any meaning in the lyrics also was an exercise in futility, but the public was quite content with undemanding rhymes and simple motifs. For example:

Spring has divulged its secrets about
hormones, meetings, dawns.
All conversations are about:
ladies that are naked

And I am a VIP, VIP.
I have a jeep, jeep.
I race everybody, I cut them off,
and they all go beep-beep.[9]

Commercial ventures such as this enjoyed and continue to take pleasure in unprecedented popularity. This particular format became popularly known as "The singing underpants." The name speaks for itself. Percolating through an emphasis on the Ukrainian/Russian vernacular blend of language (*surzhyk*) is sarcasm about Ukrainian show business imitating art and producing goods for mass consumption in trendy packaging. The parody on musical glamour is aggressive, provocative, and revealing. What is more, at any given moment it might represent Ukrainian culture—on such occasions as the international musical festival *New Wave—2010*, held in Jurmala (Latvia)—in conjunction with the glamorous Beau Monde of other post-Soviet countries.

Anti-glamour became an original assertion of freedom and protest—freedom because class polarization and the glamorous lifestyle of the governing bodies make open ridicule and parodied glamour possible. Protest also takes aim at Russian culture as the source of a powerful incoming wave of glamour, generated by its literary output, mass culture, television shows, etc. It is precisely this type of protest that exhibits the principle of Ukraine's self-affirmation by negating postcolonial culture. "In their current form the post-colonial cultures evolved from their experience of colonization and asserted themselves through their objections to the imperial government, and declarations of difference from the imperial center" (Zabuzhko 2007: 41).

## Glamour as Anti-Soviet Protest

Glamour in Ukraine is tantamount to a protest against Soviet ideals on various levels. Its transformation, in response to the newly emerged sociocultural space that followed the demise of the Soviet system, and its popularity within various strata of the population, exhibit Ukraine's new priorities. The New Ukrainians quickly grew their business enterprises by exploiting former connections, and through luck, corruption, and creating the impression that success is achievable not by dint of hard work, but by chance. The value of work was shaken; instead of self-fulfillment its reward became status, luxury, and glamour.

Having thus established themselves in the recently constructed "social register" the New Ukrainians constituted what Thorstein Veblen dubbed the leisure-class century (1984). In describing the leisure class, Veblen identified a woman's role as underscoring the status and potential of her "master." The respectability of a wealthy proprietor was always emphasized by the fact that those in his household also benefited from a uniquely privileged state. In the event that a woman occupied the position, she too was obligated to match the level of her husband's consumption, to create a luxurious lifestyle for him in order to reinforce his high status. This role left its stamp on the formation of the women's gender model of a "Barbie" as the "new Ukrainians" were coming into being. Such a woman must be a young and beautiful companion who spent her patron's money lavishly in order to transform herself into a suitable accessory akin to that of an expensive automobile or watch.

In the aftermath of the Soviet demise socioeconomic conditions catalyzed class polarization. Sociologists have frequently emphasized the absence of a middle class in Ukraine; they argued that as late as 2008 it was still in a stage of infancy, constituting less than 10 percent of the population. Meanwhile, conspicuous consumption was stimulated by the newly emerged information space and popularization of glamour, but it soon became obvious that ambitions for this level of consumption exceeded the income of average Ukrainians.

Sexuality and seductiveness as a component of glamour is yet another form of opposition to the asexual and traditional family-oriented ideology of the Soviet Union. The extravagant phrase "there is no sex in the Soviet Union" illustrates the state of sex education in the USSR, where intimacy was branded trivial and self-indulgent. This ideologically controlled information space left no room for eroticism. What is more, the "Twelve Sex Commandments of the Revolutionary Proletariat" condemned not simply eroticism, but flirtation and coquettishness (Zalkynd 1924). At that time the family epitomized the bedrock of society, in which capacity it was also traditional, a society in which a wife had no right to be seductive, in which her designated role in life was confined to that of worker-mother.

The 1990s in post-Soviet Ukraine brought erotic magazines and films, together with erotic advertising. Glasnost had already radically transformed the social/psychological climate of the country. Now, half-parted lips, partly bared shoulders—tantamount to light eroticism—legitimized itself in the information space, and hard porn became easily accessible. Glamorous advertising offered the new sexuality and temptation in accessible and exquisite ways. The information boom generated an over-saturation of sexual freedom, and in mass culture individualized intimate sexuality was de-romanticized and trivialized. After the puritanical Soviet years, the erotic nature of glamour was increasingly emphasized as something exotic and enticing. Representatives of the fashion industry, as *Play Fashion* designer Inna Huzenko explained, declared that in its Ukrainian variant the sexualization of glamour crosses all rational boundaries. "In the course of our lives glamour has been cheapened and debased. Instead of dressing for comfort, our culture demands that we dress sexually, even mega-sexually, audaciously. Glamour in Ukrainian society is tantamount to porno-chic" (*Open discussion* 2011).

With this emphasis on sexuality and attractiveness, the concept of family in any discourse on glamour recedes into the background. A glamorous diva cannot be a homemaker because according to the reality that discourse on glamour imposes she spends her time cultivating an enticing appearance, attending parties, and frequenting restaurants.

## Influence of Glamour in Transforming the Profile of Ukrainian Women

As mentioned earlier, in large measure consumer society has significantly influenced the new profile of women in Ukrainian society. The information highway has imposed a concept of what it means to be a woman that differs significantly from the previous Soviet ideal. The fashion industry, glossy magazines, television shows—indeed the entire system in the 1990s was responsible for the successful creation and promotion of the new glamorous profile of Ukrainian womanhood. According to Tatiana Zhurzhenko: "Advertisements that so forcefully promote unaccustomed goods and services for Ukrainian women have transformed consumption into a high art form, requiring certain routines, expertise, even talent" (2001: 40). Ukrainian women started from zero in familiarizing themselves with this art form and a Western way of life necessitating the appropriate behavioral change.

With a determined emphasis on external appearance, glamour advocated an array of new criteria for "body beautiful." A woman must maintain a perfect, attractive, youthful figure demonstrating the attributes of a true cult. Accordingly, a variety of measures were employed to achieve self-improvement and move toward the absolute ideal of glamour. A popular approach consisted of transforming the woman's appearance to conform to the images of Hollywood stars to the extent possible. This is why women's magazines routinely include a rubric on how to create such a celebrated image, or where designers dispense their advice on how to apply makeup in order to approximate the appearance of a Hollywood star. A television program titled *Victim of Fashion* had a relatively long run recently. It portrayed Ukrainian designer Andre Tan, who took a woman of "ordinary" appearance off the street, and with the help of makeup and a new wardrobe created a double of some prominent actress or singer—an image produced and packaged for public consumption.

Advertising now offered an alternate profile for the Ukrainian woman, one which diverged markedly from the standard mother-worker or traditional Berehynia (empowered keeper of the ancient hearth and, more recently, mother of the nation). This new image approximates more fairly the Ukrainian concept of glamour: "Barbie's lifestyle brings to mind the narcissistic existence of a beautiful, expensive doll" (Kis 2003).[10] Accordingly, the woman adopts extraordinary measures to maintain an outward appearance that conforms to her basic agenda—find and marry a rich entrepreneur. Naturally, owing to the exaggerated narcissism in Ukraine's glamorous space, the perception of such an alluring picture also exerted its influence elsewhere.

One of the newest fads to infiltrate Ukraine in recent years was plastic surgery, which promoted alterations to the face and body according to the latest standards of glamour. Even in this case Ukrainian women resorted to exaggeration. On his blog, Mauricio Askero, the director of a chain of elite boutiques in Kyiv, noted: "All over the world plastic surgeons change the shape of lips. I work in the fashion industry and all around me I am beset by the countenance of Donald Duck. Kyiv is full of such apparitions under women's noses; they resemble duck-shaped celluloid boats more than human lips" (2010).

In the 1990s, the distorted adaptation of elements of Western glamour might have been referred to as a vision from the Soviet past, but it is significant that the latest generation also maintains these traditions, albeit through inertia. One explanation for this might be that the young people came to maturity in an environment where glamour and its imitation were so pervasive that they became encoded into the worldview of the whole of society, forming an organic component of its culture. The values of its youth were transformed in conformance with this environment. For instance, according to the latest tendencies, a truly symbolic initiation of a young woman's rite of passage into adult life is not marriage, but the graduation party. The institution of family is steadily losing its traditional standing. Girls tend to have their first sexual encounters well before their wedding nights. Research has also shown that many tend to lose their virginity on the night of their graduation parties (*Kraina* 2011). The money spent on a graduation dress often costs as much as a wedding gown, frequently reaching the sum of several thousand hryvnia (*Korrespondent* 2011).[11] It was only a few short years ago that it was customary to hold such a party in the school lunchroom. Today, finances permitting, even in small provincial towns parents strive to rent space in a restaurant and stage a celebration, creating, at least for a day, the illusion of something akin to a Hollywood star's night at the Oscars.

The view of a woman's adult life also underwent a change in the early period of post-Soviet Ukrainian life. It became a widely held belief that a woman's future would be secured if she succeeded in marrying a foreigner. This "Cinderella" story is another popular model for a better life, except that Prince Charming has been replaced by the oligarch. The press routinely publishes lists of eligible bachelors, and women's magazines include practical advice on how to entice a rich suitor. During the past few months television channels have begun featuring highly rated shows for which carefully selected participants have been schooled in the art of imitating glamorous divas, and informing readers how to attract desirable marriage partners (*Bachelor, Miss,* etc.).

As an alternative to Cinderella, the image of a strong, independent, business woman, representing a type that emerged at the end of the twentieth century, is also promoted. Carol Dyhouse described such women as wearing business suits with broad shoulders, as portrayed in television commercials and supplemented in business publications, where they are also featured wearing plain spectacles and other typically male accessories. The glamorous woman combines femininity with the masculine image; in a word—glamour has been emancipated (2010). This portrayal also found a place in the Ukrainian variant, with one important exception: "The woman's adoption of the stereotypical gendered role of 'businessman' is viewed as one of a homemaker compelled by economic necessity to adopt the role of temporary breadwinner. As soon as circumstances permit, however, she would be able to return to her traditional feminine role" (Kis 2003).

A unique picture of a combined empowered leader and glamorous diva (in the finest sense of the word) is found in Yulia Tymoshenko. During the many years of political struggles, Tymoshenko created in the information highway the image of a tireless and powerful Ukrainian leader, who lost neither her femininity, nor her unique sense of a glamorous style. Yulia Tymoshenko is one of the most brilliant examples of the way glamour is joined to the conventional Ukrainian (Berehynia) profile. The blended image is signified by a braided halo encircling her head, offset by high-heeled shoes and Louis Vuitton suits. Thanks to this fortuitous combination, Yulia Tymoshenko graced the cover of a leading women's magazine, *Elle,* the first female politician to hold a place typically reserved for fashion models. Journalists studiously tracked and reported on her love of the glamour and wardrobe changes. On the one hand Yulia Tymoshenko reemphasized the extent to which the Ukrainian concept of glamour is assimilated to politics, and on the other she demonstrated how tastefully it can be done.

A worthy counterpoint to this political glamour is found in the activist organization FEMEN. Its members stage provocative demonstrations challenging nearly all social and political abuses, pushing one of the key elements of anti-glamour to the limit. In challenging responses to the eroticism and sexuality in the pervasive images of glamour, they seek to invalidate its exotic and luxurious nature by baring their breasts and donning such folk accessories as floral wreathes (a traditional component of folk costumes, and an ancient symbol of women's empowerment). Their deliberate kitsch became a trademark that placed a significant emphasis on protest over the new variety of glamorous womanhood. They pit glamour against itself. If a woman's body can be exploited to market consumer goods, they explain, it can also be employed for effective social and political protests. "If this method can be used to sell something, why not utilize it to advance social and political causes. I see nothing wrong in this," was the sentiment voiced in an interview with the founder of FEMEN, Anna Hutsol (Mayerchyk and Plakhotnik 2011).

## Conclusion

Glamour and its adaptation to the Ukrainian terrain illustrate both the ties to a Soviet past, and a unique denunciation of it. After years of shortages and compulsory values in the Soviet Union it seemed only natural for Ukrainians to indulge in excessive and demonstrative consumption, both in the name of consumption itself, and as an assertion of their social standing. The disintegration of the Soviet Union and new economic opportunities that it opened up made possible the emergence of a new bourgeoisie. The New Ukrainians gradually transformed themselves into an elite body whose members hypertrophied the glamorizing process, and converted luxury to a cult in the process. The fact that they metamorphosed into an economic elite, as opposed to a cultural one, bore the marks of their Soviet past, during which the Ukrainian cultural elite was systematically annihilated. All of this played its part in the fact that the Ukrainian style of glamour became a failed attempt at a strict emulation of the Western model. Influenced by their Soviet legacy, only the external Western likenesses were imitated, which Ukrainians then reinterpreted in their own special way, transformed into caricature.

The other aspect of this borrowing was its politicization. The new elite represented politicized business circles, whose self-realization consisted of luxurious living that, in turn, perpetuated their new ideology. In sum, severely impacted by their Soviet past, they were incapable of a genuinely glamorous way of life. Only the externals of Western-style glamour were borrowed and adapted to the Ukrainian reality. Thus it can convincingly be claimed that a distinctive interpretation of glamour emerged from the ruins of Soviet ideology. Just as communist ideology was distorted during the Soviet era, however, so too was glamour deformed in the post-Soviet Ukrainian environment. The fact, however, that Ukrainian society still finds itself at a crossroads, in a continuing period of transition, seeking new ways to evolve, offers hope that one day the value system will right itself.

**Tetiana Bulakh** is a Fulbright scholar and graduate student in socio-cultural anthropology at Indiana University, Bloomington. She obtained an MA in Theory of Literature and Comparative Studies from the National University of "Kyiv-Mohyla Academy" (Ukraine), and received a scholarship from the Zavtra.ua foundation in 2007 for research on contemporary Ukrainian poetry. Currently she is conducting ethnographic research on the introduction of a Western consumer culture in post-Soviet Ukraine.

## Notes

1. The advertisement was published on 5 June 2007. It shows Gorbachev sitting in a limousine as it drives by the remains of the Berlin Wall. Next to him is a Louis Vuitton travel bag.
2. Initially published between 1956 and 1969, it was translated by Andy Stafford and published in 2006.
3. The blazer resembles a men's sport coat, although the cut is somewhat different— akin to a military-style jacket.
4. International Center for Policy Studies. Examines democratic social processes in Ukraine.
5. Informational Bulletin of the International Center for policy studies (2000).
6. Askero 2010.
7. Varenyk 2011.
8. http://raguli.sumno.com/post/litso-koljektsyi/.
9. Hot Chocolate is the rock group. The group known as Dress Code sings "VIP."
10. In the mid-1990s Solomea Pavlychko was the first to introduce the juxtaposition between Berehynia and Barbie with: "there is an invasion of mass culture from the West. Barbie dolls ... The two utopias (Barbie and Berehynia) have similar double standards and a similar misogynistic message." The concept was then left for ethnologist Oksana Kis 2005 to develop more fully.
11. In 2012 the hryvnia equaled approximately eight to the dollar. Today it hovers around twenty.

## Bibliography

Askero, Mauricio. 2010. *Jetsetter,* 14, 06. http://jetsetter.ua/ru/Blogi/Blog-.

Barthes, Roland. 2005. "Dandyism and Fashion," originally published in *United States Lines Paris Review,* special number on Dandyism, July 1962; *Oeuvres Completes,* vol. 1, 963. Translated from the French into Ukrainian by Myroslav Lemyk for *Yi* 38. http://www.azh.com.ua/lib/dendysm-i-moda.

———. 2006. *The Language of Fashion.* Oxford: Berg Publisher.

Baudrillard, Jean. 2006. *The Consumer Society: Its Myths and Structures.* Moscow: Cultural Revolution Republic.

Brazhnikova, Iana. 2006. "The decline of glamour," *The Right View* (18 November). http://www.pravaya.ru/look/10208.

Dyhouse, Carol. 2011. *Glamour: Women, History, Feminism.* London and New York: Zed Books.

Filipov, Evhen. 2009. "The deficit as a lifestyle component of Soviet Ukrainian society," in *Scientific Notebooks of the History Faculty at Lviv University: Collected Scientific Works,* no. 10: 227–238.

Gundle, Stephen. 2008. *Glamour: A History.* New York: Oxford University Press.

*Information Bulletin of the International Center for Policy Studies.* No. 75.

Ivanov, Dmitrii. 2008. *Glam-kapitalism.* St. Petersburg: Petersburgha Vostokovedeniee.

Jameson, Fredric. 2000. *Postmodernism and the Consumer Society.* Logos (April). First published in 1988 in *Postmodernism and its Discontents: Theories and Practices,* ed. E. Ann Kaplan. London: Verso, 192–204.

Karpa, Irena. 2005. *Perlamutrove Porno Supermarket Samotnosti.* Kyiv: Duliby.

Kis, Oksana. 2003. "Modeli konstriiuvannia gendernoi identychnosty zhinky v suchasnii Ukraini," *Yi.* 27: 38–58. http://www.ji.lviv.ua/n27texts/kis.htm.

———. 2005. "Choosing without choice: Predominant models of femininity in contemporary Ukraine," *Gender Transitions in Russia and Eastern Europe,* eds. Madeleine Hurd, Helen Carlback, and Sara Rastback. Stockholm: Gondolin Publishers, 105–136.

"Koly Vtrachaty Tsnotu." 2011. *Kraina.* 20 April: 12–17.

"Luxury lifestyle awards." 2010. http://luxuryawards.net/press/news/news12.htm. 1New.

Mayerchyk, Maria, and Olha Plakhotnik. 2010. "Radykal'ny 'Femen' I novyi zhinochyi aktyvizm," *Krytyka* 11–12: 7–9.

Menzel, Brigit. 2008. "Russian discourse of glamour," *Kultura* (June): 4–8.

"Open discussion: Has glamour outlived itself?" 2011. http://weekend.odua/exclu_full.plp?id=1172.

Panchenko, Aleksandr, and Konstantin Ryapolov. 2011. "20 let strane." http://www.segodnya.ua/ukraine_20_years/14248110.html.

Rudova, Larissa. 2008. "Uniting Russia in glamour." *Kul'tura.*

Varenyk, Nataliia. 2011.*Gumer* 17, 13 May. http://www.gumer.info/bibliotek_Buks/History/Article/_12SexZap.php.

Zabuzhko, Oksana. 2007. *Notre Dame d'Ukraine: Ukrainka v Konflikti Mitolohiyi.* Kyiv: Fakt.

Zalkynd, Aaron. 1924. "Dvenadtsat polovykh zapovedei revolutsionnogu proletariatu," *Revolutsia i Molodezh.* Moscow: Sverdlov Communist University Press. http://www.gumer.info/bibliotek_Buks/History/Article/_12SexZap.php.

Zhurzhenko, Tetiana. 2001. "Free market ideology and new women's identities in post-socialist Ukraine," *The European Journal of Women's Studies* (February), 29–49.

CHAPTER 5

# Gender Dreams or Sexism?

## *Advertising in Post-Soviet Ukraine*

Oksana Kis and Tetyana Bureychak

Academic and public discussions about the gender aspects of advertising have a long history in the West. The Second Wave of Feminism triggered them in the mid-twentieth century, and since then a number of prominent feminist scholars have probed various dimensions of the issue. Analysis and criticism of advertising, which actively exploits existing gender stereotypes thereby reinforcing and legitimizing the dominant patriarchal gender ideology, constitute the core of the classical works on the subject by Betty Friedan (1965), Trevor Millum (1975), Erving Goffman (1979), Judith Williamson (1978), Naomi Wolf (1991), and others. Their Western theories of gender and advertising, however, need to be tested in a non-Western cultural context. Post-Soviet Ukraine represents an interesting case study for examining the relevance and meaning of certain key concepts—sexism, among others—of this feminist scholarship. The main aim of this chapter is to provide a critical analysis of gender representations reproduced in Ukrainian advertising, along with paying particular attention to the mechanisms of reproduction of gender stereotypes and sexist practices.

## Gender and Sexuality in the Distorted Mirror of Post-Soviet Advertising

Commercial advertising is a relatively recent phenomenon in Ukraine. During the Soviet period this industry was underdeveloped. Indeed, in the context of a centralized planned economy, the state monopoly on virtually all production and distribution of goods and services, and permanent shortage of a host of essentials, advertising scarcely made sense. Unlike Western countries, where commercials are generally aimed at increasing mass consumption, Soviet advertising served mainly propaganda purposes. It was designed to boost communist ideas and values, praise socialism, and promote the Soviet way of life (Savelyeva 2006).

With the collapse of the USSR dramatic changes occurred in all spheres of life in the previously Soviet republics, including Ukraine. The new economic realities of a free market introduced former Soviet citizens to advertising—a cultural phenomenon they were scarcely familiar with. Initially it attracted and intrigued people with its novelty; for many it was a sign of a highly admirable "Western" lifestyle with all its wealth and glamour. By the mid-1990s commercials had invaded and conquered the media and public spaces. Their omnipresence, obtrusiveness, and aggressiveness started to irritate people, so in the late 1990s activists and scholars began to voice their concerns. It became clear that advertising not only affected consumer behavior, but because its content is rarely gender neutral it also worked as a powerful agent of gender socialization. Women's rights advocates and feminist scholars pointed to the prevalence of patriarchal stereotypes in all kinds of commercials, with the growing usage of an eroticized female body as the most popular marketing tool (Radulova 2005). An excessively sexualized portrayal of women became the norm in the post-Soviet media, and the very boundary between erotic and pornographic was blurred (Goscilo 1995: 164–194; Voronina 2000: 87–107). At the same time, advertising of household merchandise, food, and medicine persistently promoted the most traditional woman's roles of mother and housewife, as opposed to a man's self-fulfillment in the public sphere (Sinelnikov 1999: 83–97; Groshev 2000: 172–187; Yurchak 2000: 65–77; Belikova 2004: 409–412; Bureychak 2008b: 227–242; Kis 2010: 50–69).

The period of transition from a socialist economy to a free market and from totalitarianism to democracy has been marked by profound ideological transformations. In Ukraine the ideology of Marxism-Leninism was challenged and defeated by nationalism and consumerism. Consequently the former canon of femininity—the Soviet Super Woman—lost its monopoly and was replaced by new ones, namely Berehynia and Barbie, produced in the framework of corresponding nationalist and consumerist ideologies (Kis 2005: 105–136). In its modern interpretation, the Berehynia model constructs the ideal woman in the traditional gender order, primarily as a self-sacrificial mother and guardian of the family hearth.[1] The Barbie model implies a different gender script, according to which the erotic and aesthetic potentials of a female body are to be developed and highly valued. In both cases, however, a woman is imagined to achieve her life successes exclusively through her relationship with a man—either as his devoted housewife or sexy mistress.

These ideological transformations overlapped with major trends in advertising and reinforced the sexist tendencies. Beginning with the late

1980s the liberalization of sexuality has become a distinct trend in the post-Soviet space. The opportunity to articulate and refer to sex and sexuality in the public space and discourse that opened up after decades of silence and censorship symbolizes not only sexual, but also social and political liberation. This has resulted in a massive informational wave of materials with erotic and pornographic content. Coverage of intimate relations and eroticized nude female bodies is presented as a revolutionary breakthrough and indicator of progressiveness in the mass media, lifting the veil from formerly forbidden topics. Due to the population's low level of sexual culture, however, this was often shocking and caused a moral panic, especially among the older generation. The absence of any regulation also promoted the vulgarization, trivialization, and commercialization of sex and sexuality. Advertising plays a key role in these processes.

The issue of prevailing gender stereotypes in advertising has attracted the attention of many scholars in postsocialist countries, including Ukraine. Initial attempts to analyze the gender aspects of advertising were based on a theoretical framework offered by Western scholars (Kravchenko 1993: 117–131; Alchuk 1998: 255–261). The rapidly growing number of publications and quality of research on this subject in the years beginning with 2000 testify to a certain maturity of post-Soviet gender studies (Tartakovskaya 2000: 168–187; Azhgikhina 2000: 261–273). The research of Russian scholar Igor Groshev stands out by its methodological coherence, relevant theoretical framework, and well-grounded interpretations (2000: 4:172–187, 6:38–49). Other researchers also pay attention to the gender aspect of women's visual representations in the media and advertising. In Ukraine this process was slightly delayed; initial publications were quite descriptive, with authors raising ethical questions and blaming the advertising industry for abusing and degrading women, but they did not offer any specific research strategies, nor did they apply a feminist analysis of gender discourses in advertising (Sukovata 1999: 91–109; Taran 2001: 151–160; Shpaner 2002: 152–161; Marushevska and Sharova 2001: 220–225). Recent years, however, have been marked by a series of publications exhibiting a thorough sociological and culturological analysis of advertising gender messages and their social-psychological effects (Bureychak 2007: 149–161, 2008a: 375–383; Kis 2010: 50–70, 2007: 221)·
Authors of these studies were unanimous in their findings that sexism is characteristic of most Ukrainian advertising.

Sexism can be defined as the ideology and practice of discrimination and/or hatred against people based on their sex rather than their individual merits (Gamble 2001; Tuttle 1986). Sexism, like racism, claims one part of humankind (men) to be physically, intellectually, emotionally, and otherwise superior to another part (women). If racism is defined as any attitude, action, or institutional structure that systematically subordinates a person or group because of color, sexism is about any attitude, action, or institutional structure that systematically subordinates a person or group because of their sex (Russell). Sexism comes in explicit forms (sex-based limitation of rights and opportunities, or provision of privileges) and implicit forms (double moral standards, "glass ceiling," etc.), all leading to systematic gender-based devaluation, marginalization, subordination, and exploitation of people on the basis of their sex. In patriarchal societies, of which Ukraine is no exception, sexism against women prevails.

## Gender Censorship of Advertising: Ukrainian Legislation and Public Initiative

Local feminist scholars and activists, alarmed over the situation, have repeatedly called upon the government to impose limitations on advertising practices that abuse and degrade women. In Ukraine the first attempts to establish some rules and regulations for the media aimed at the protection of basic human and civil rights of citizens took place as early as 1992–1993. The Law of Ukraine "On the print media in Ukraine" (December 1992) stated: "The print media in Ukraine cannot be used for ... fomentation of racial, national, religious enmity; distribution of pornography ... interference in the private lives of citizens, infringement of their honor and dignity" (chap. 3). In a similar manner the Law of Ukraine "On television and radio broadcasting" (January 1993) pronounced illegal the following:

> Propaganda of exclusivity, superiority or inferiority of persons because of their religious persuasions, political views, nationality, race, physical condition, property status, or social background; broadcasting of shows or video which could hurt the physical, emotional or moral development of children and teenagers watching it ... dissemination of information encroaching on the legitimate rights and interests of physical or juridical persons, infringing a person's honor and dignity. (chapter 6)

None of the laws, however, mentions the inadmissibility of publishing gender discriminatory information, while claims of protecting "a person's honor and dignity" are too broad and equivocal to be legally enforced.

The second attempt to restrain the unbridled advertising practices was made twelve years later, in 2004, when the Law of Ukraine "On Protection of Public Morality" came into force. One of its goals again was to protect the honor and dignity of Ukraine's population by rigorously limiting the circulation of objects of an erotic nature. Such objects are defined as: "material objects, items, and printed, audio or video products, *including advertisments,* information and materials, media products, together with the electronic media, containing any information of an erotic nature aiming at an aesthetic effect, which addresses the adult population and are insulting by nature" (chap. 1, emphasis added). Another article in the same law regulates the circulation of objects of a sexual and erotic nature, stating that those "could be distributed provided they are not accessible to minors and not foisted off on customers" (chap. 8). The following year (January 2005) the special Law of Ukraine "On Advertising" was adopted to establish general rules in this sphere. Despite the fact that "gender discrimination" finally did appear on the list of prohibited content, this legal norm was very difficult (if even possible) to enforce because it lacked a clear definition of what might be considered discriminatory. The concepts of "human honor and dignity" applied to the two laws are too vague and general to be used in legal practices.

Women's rights advocates placed their primary hopes on the Law of Ukraine "On Ensuring Equal Rights and Opportunities for Men and Women in Ukraine" (September 2005)—generally known as "the bill on gender equality."[2] Its aim was to establish gender equality in all spheres of society by eliminating sex-based discrimination. The law provides a clear-cut definition of gender discrimination: "Sex-based discrimination is an action or a lack of thereof leading to a distinction, exclusion, or privilege based on sex, if intent exists to restrict or render impossible any acknowledgement, use, or exercise of human rights and liberties of men and women on an equal footing" (chap. 1). Accordingly, sex-based discrimination is prohibited (chap. 6), and state policy requires that any information with a sexist content must be elaborated (chap. 3).

Despite its enormous significance and obvious progressiveness (not to forget, this is the only special law in existence on gender equality in all of the FSU-NIS countries), the law is not perfect. The main problem lies in its rather declaratory nature, with no efficient mechanism provided for its implementation, nor as yet any control or enforcement methods elaborated. In addition, it was not accompanied by any by-law or other normative documents to provide precise criteria or markers according to which certain acts, attitudes, content, behavior, etc., could be identified as gender discriminatory. Although Ukrainian legislation aims to regulate media content and media circulation as to its public appropriateness and protection from discriminatory messages, leaving room for various readings and interpretations of media content Ukrainian legislation on gender equality renders it impossible to prosecute and penalize violators of the principle of gender equality, especially in the media and advertising spheres. Such impunity leaves advertising agencies and media owners free to use, reproduce, and disseminate sexist texts and images in commercials as long as this remains profitable for their business. In short, state efforts to take control of gendered content in advertising have yielded virtually no positive results, and sexist commercials continue to proliferate throughout Ukraine.

Realizing the omnipresence and normalization of sexism in advertising, many Ukrainian scholars and women's rights activist have chosen a different approach to this problem. The central idea is to develop a critical attitude and public intolerance toward sexist advertising through mass awareness raising and educational campaigns. A series of events identified by the slogan "Stop sexism!" took place throughout Ukraine during 2006–2010.[3] The process was initiated by the Lviv Research center "Women and Society" (NGO) in March 2006, and later replicated by women's organizations, scholars, and educators for other audiences. The organizers used numerous examples of sexist commercials to exemplify the sexist mechanism, to explain its explicit and implicit manifestations, to discuss the detrimental effects of sexist portrayals of women's gender identity. Participants also had the opportunity to familiarize themselves with Ukrainian legislation on gender equality, and to learn about the true situation of gender discrimination in Ukraine. Those taking part in the "Stop sexism!" actions confirmed that after attending this event their perception of gendered advertising changed forever; they have become more critical of the stereotypes imposed by it. The effect of this action may be legitimately compared to immunization, as people learn to resist the advertising industry's manipulative technologies to frame a worldview according to the principles of consumerist ideology, one that reduces the endless variety of individuals to a few limited templates of "ideal" men and women.

## Gender Messages of Advertising in Quantitative Perspective

Advertising as a mechanism for promoting a consumer culture constructs symbolic relationships between products and their cultural connotations. Most advertising integrates gender messages, representing particular images of masculinity and femininity. It addresses the audience with a male or female voice through TV or radio commercials, often orienting an advertised product or service toward male or female consumption. Advertising defines normal and ideal femininity and masculinity and makes available to the viewer or reader consumer tools for comprehending the concept. Although advertising depicts a plurality of gender images, most are unrealistic and stereotypical (Bretl and Cantor 1998). Gender stereotypes reflect the dominant gender ideology, prioritize the patriarchal gender regime, and legitimize gender hierarchies in relations between men and women. Advertising is dynamic in nature and responds to social transformations, thus its gender messages reflect the changes in the understanding of normative and desirable masculinity and femininity.

To explore the gender messages of post-Soviet Ukrainian advertising this chapter provides quantitative and qualitative perspectives. In particular, it presents a content analysis of video advertising, broadcast by one of the central Ukrainian TV channels, "1 + 1," during 2006 (n = 1046),[4] and a semiotic analysis of outdoor advertisements (billboards, city lights, shop windows, etc.) posted throughout Ukraine in 2005–2011.

Content analysis is a research technique that is grounded on systematic and quantitative data analysis (Berelson 1952; Kostenko 2005). It is based upon examining the frequencies of key characteristics in manifest data. The rate of appearances of these categories indicates the social significance of the ideas they represent. Application of content analysis to the study of gender messages in advertising allows identification of the most frequent and thus most socially accepted and desirable gender representations, relations, and norms. It provides an opportunity to illustrate the production of gender inequality and stereotypes through a detailed empirical study.

The present study explores dominant representations of femininity and masculinity in relation to the types of advertised products, as well as the audio and visual characteristics of commercials and portrayals of male and female advertising models. It reveals dissimilar and, in most cases, contradictory ways of constructing femininity and masculinity, which tend to exaggerate gender differences and perpetuate gender stereotypes and inequalities. Appearance of models, their positioning in relation to private and public spheres, and opinions by male and female experts are the key points through which gender differences are emphasized in Ukrainian TV commercials. In particular, the study reveals that female characters tend to prevail in the visual advertising mode, whereas male voiceovers take the lead in its audio mode. Men as main characters appear in 10.2 percent of the TV commercials, whereas women in such roles constitute 27.4 percent of the cases. The representation of men and women together is the most common (41 percent). Children as the main characters in advertising appear infrequently (1.2 percent). In most cases, when they do appear they are portrayed with both parents (13 percent), which appeals to traditional family values. When depicted with only one parent, children appear more often with their mothers (5.3 percent) and less frequently with their fathers (2 percent). This reflects the gender stereotypical idea of unequal parental responsibility distribution, with mothering of greater importance. Before proceeding to any conclusions about the prevalence of women over men in the visual mode of advertising, it is important to consider the ways in which they appear according to another category analyzed (Bureychak 2007).

Although the majority of models featured in advertising are young (between ages 17 and 35), young women are shown more frequently than

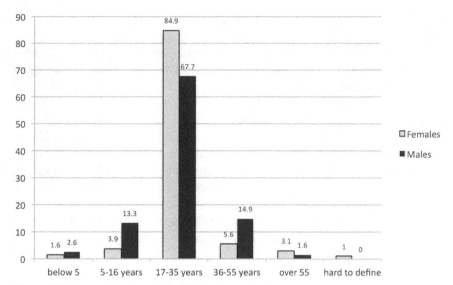

**Figure 5.1.** *Ages of male and female characters in TV commercials.*

young men in TV commercials: 84.9 percent of the female characters and 67.7 percent of their male counterparts are depicted as young people. Advertising emphasizes greater age variations for men, while youth is more important for women. Males prevail in the representations of characters up to the ages of 16 and 36–55 (Bureychak 2007).

Although advertising suggests a narrow age frame for female characters, it broadens simultaneously the parameters of their attractiveness (wider spectrum of variability in hair styles and clothes compared to those of men), and higher expectations for women to be involved in appearance and body-care practices (e.g., more body-care commercials targeting women). Advertising offers an opportunity for women to be different and free in the construction of their unique appearance. Normally this freedom is limited, however, by the specific conception of a woman's beauty, which is in most cases associated with youth, slimness, and sexual attractiveness. Advertising often encourages women to think of their body as a project, which requires continuing perfection. Compared to men, women receive considerably higher numbers of messages that accentuate the importance of systematic efforts in the support and improvement of their appearance. This is evidenced in the greater incidence of commercials for cosmetics, body products, and services targeting the female audience (Bureychak 2007). In the Foucauldian sense, control over one's own body and aspirations toward its ideal parameters become expressions of the internalized disciplinary power that women reproduce in their everyday practices. Although the market for men's grooming products has significantly expanded in recent years, social expectations toward their appearance and attractiveness remain lower than for women.

Clothes on models shown in commercials can be seen as indicators of social roles and status. Although male and female characters are most commonly presented in casual wear (59.4 percent and 57.3 percent respectively) men are depicted twice as often in clothes that reveal their professional engagement. Men in business suits and uniforms are presented in 16.9 percent and 7.4 percent of the cases. Women in TV commercials are featured wearing such clothes in 7.1 percent and 2.9 percent of the cases. As opposed to men, women are more often portrayed in formal evening dress—9.7 percent, whereas only 0.5 percent of the men are seen wearing formal evening attire. Although formal wear and business suits both signify high social status, there is greater emphasis on physical attractiveness than on professional achievement, and this is accentuated more in women than in men. Physical attractiveness and sexuality can also be emphasized through the clothes that expose the body to the public gaze. Our study demonstrates that in this case there are no considerable gender differences. Men in underwear (5.8 percent) appear in advertising more often than women (3.4 percent), which may well indicate a rising public acceptance of revealed male corporeality. Women and men appear in swimwear in roughly equal numbers (2.7 percent for women, 2.1 percent for men) and sleep wear (2.1 percent for women, 2.3 percent for men). At the same time, it is more common for TV commercials to portray naked women (2.6 percent) than men (1.4 percent). The study also reveals that female models change clothes during a commercial more often than male models (3.1 percent vs. 1.4 percent). This might imply higher social acceptance and normalization of variability in women's appearance.

Positioning of advertising models in relation to private and public spheres is another way to trace the construction of normative femininity and masculinity in popular culture. To some extent this is possible to detect by exploring the location of male and female characters. Portrayals of men and women in private settings prevail over all other venues where models are featured. Women tend to be represented in the private sphere more often than men: 43.2 percent women and 34.4 percent men appear in private settings. In contrast, men are more commonly depicted in public (indoor) settings (29.4 percent men and 23.7 women). Men also prevail among those pictured outside, and their location looks more dynamic. Although our findings demonstrate a higher association of male characters with the public sphere and female characters with the private sphere, the actual location of the models does not explicitly indicate their gender roles and statuses. Location of female characters in the public sphere as well as portrayals of male characters in private settings would not necessarily function as clear markers of their equality in both spheres.

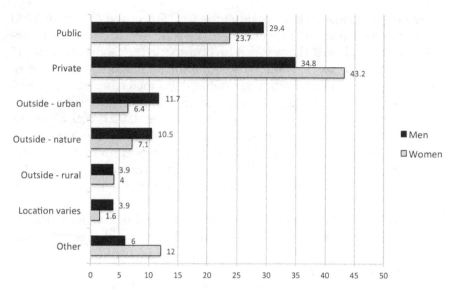

**Figure 5.2.** *Venues for male and female characters.*

An analysis of the roles performed by male and female characters in commercials provides more explicit indicators of men's and women's social status, as well as appropriate activities for each. Women most often appear in TV commercials as product demonstrators (51.1 percent), housewives (22.3 percent), women in love (17.6 percent), wives (16.4 percent), and mothers (15.9 percent). These roles position women as objects of gaze and stress family and household responsibilities. An examination of the roles of women in commercials of particular types of products allows us to see a more nuanced picture. As product demonstrators women most commonly appear in commercials for beauty products (73.3 percent). Women as housewives dominate in advertisements for household appliances (76 percent). Wives (60.6 percent) and mothers (30.3 percent) are most often presented in commercials for health products and medicine. Women in love prevail in commercials for entertainment (44.4 percent) (Bureychak 2007). In most cases, the women's roles and advertised products do correspond to the conventional understanding of femininity as rooted in bodily beauty and family duties.

A spectrum of men's roles in advertisements demonstrates a different pattern. Males appear in the role of product demonstrators (25.9 percent), men in love (21 percent), experts (19.4 percent), children and teenagers (18.7 percent), and husbands (16.6 percent). Men as product demonstrators prevail in commercials for electronic equipment (40.9 percent). And like women, men in love prevail in advertisements for entertainment (66.7 percent), but with an important difference. They most commonly appear as experts in commercials for beauty products (50 percent) and household essentials (37.3 percent). In such cases, they are depicted as knowledgeable individuals instructing women on how to use the products. Boys and male teenagers prevail in commercials for food. Men as husbands are most often represented in ads of health products and medicine (62.2 percent) (Bureychak 2007). Mostly, they are depicted with illnesses being treated by women. A comparison of these sets of gender-based roles allows us to trace their typical distribution. It also permits us to recognize roles in which models are not represented; this too reflects traditional understandings of femininity and masculinity. In particular, women are considerably less often featured as experts and children, and men are rarely portrayed as housekeepers.

In contrast to the prevalence of women in visual representations, voiceovers remain overwhelmingly in the male domain, with men constituting 56.5 percent of the off-screen narrations. Voiceover is an important element of a commercial, offering as it does comments, summary, action encouragement, and expert opinions. It is a measure of symbolic power distribution in popular cultural representations. As this study shows, an unequal gender pattern in symbolic control over definitions of social reality manifests itself in the prevalence of men in the audio field of commercials. Male voiceovers dominated in commercials of all types of products including those in which the main characters are female.

The prevalence of women in the visual field of advertising emphasizes the importance of their self-representation, physical attractiveness, and

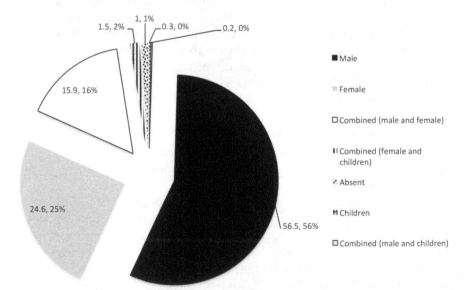

**Figure 5.3.** *Distribution of voiceovers in TV commercials.*

positioning as an object of gaze. By contrast, the prevalence of men in voiceovers normalizes their right to define social reality, a claim supported by further findings in this study. As already suggested, they include the dominance of female characters in commercials promoting body products and a higher representation of women as models and product demonstrators.

The current quantitative study of Ukrainian TV reveals a prevalence of traditional understandings of gender, expressed and reinforced in a variety of ways. At the same time, decontextualization and fragmentation of images does not allow an exploration of the social and cultural connotations of the holistic gender messages in commercials. In order to integrate this aspect, we suggest an analysis of gender symbolism, subtexts, and associations promoted by the advertisements.

## Plural Strategies of Commercialized Sexism

There are some features of commercials that contribute more than others to creating an inferior image of a woman. In what follows, the outdoor commercials will be scrutinized for the latent sexism inherent in their portrayals of women. As noted earlier, socially approved desirable images of femininity and masculinity, as well as patterns of gender interaction, are drawn in part from the media, including advertising. Taking into account the fact that outdoor commercials have literally flooded the cityscape in Ukraine it is impossible to ignore the powerful gendered messages they convey affecting the youth directly.

> In attempting to appeal to consumers, the majority of commercial imagery reproduces heterosexual hegemony and generates images privileging the stereotypical feminine women and masculine men. These ideal gender images are often extreme in their expression, and unattainable in the real world. Nevertheless, commercial imagery is not a homogeneous visual world. It allows for various ways of encoding (through copywriting, directing and photographing) and decoding (interpreting, reading and re-writing) multiple and proliferating significations of genders to make them intelligible. (Rossi 2000).

Studying video commercials broadcast on TV and published in magazines is important because of their massive and intense influence over wide audiences. One must note, however, that in both cases the viewers/readers have choices—they can turn off a TV or put aside a magazine—but passersby can scarcely avoid outdoor advertising (billboards, city lights, shop windows, etc.). These assault the senses of city dwellers at every step with their bright colors, artistic designs, and witty slogans. Such motionless images, seen perhaps for only a few seconds, are particularly intense, as their messages are condensed and easy to comprehend. This kind of advertising leaves little opportunity for avoiding or ignoring it. It silently suggests to viewers certain gendered norms, values, and behavioral patterns, thus constructing normative models of gender identities, and affecting gender relations in contemporary Ukrainian society.

The following markers of sexism have been identified as a result of our visual and verbal analysis of Ukrainian advertising:

- aestheticization: excessive emphasis on the decorative function of a woman's body
- eroticization: abuse of erotic effects of a woman's naked body or its parts
- nature-binding: representing a woman as belonging to the realm of nature
- commodification: direct or indirect equating of a woman with a commodity
- face-ism: prevalence of faceless/headless women's portrayals
- machismo: cult of dominant masculinity
- domestication: representation of women as belonging to the domestic sphere

## Aestheticization

Women's beauty is perhaps the feature emphasized most in advertising, although excessive aestheticization of a woman's body and obsession with her appearance were not invented by the advertising industry. In commercials, however, the peculiarity of this one-dimensional patriarchal perception of womanhood reaches its apotheosis in the guise of beauty used as a basis for constructing and maintaining gender differences (Melosik 1996). Women pictured in advertising are designed to satisfy the aesthetic demands of those who are subjects of a gaze, evaluation, purchase, ownership, etc.—that is, of men. They become art objects, designed and decorated (with bijous, accessories, tatoos, body art, etc.) to strengthen the effect of exclusivity and refinement, and thus to satisfy the aesthetic expectations of a hard-to-please male viewer. For instance, one popular Japanese brand of electronics in advertising a new telephone featured it side by side with a half-naked woman sporting the hairstyle of a Japanese geisha whose back was covered with tattoos; the caption reads: "Elegant design."

Serving beauty and fashion industry interests, advertising is permanently stirring up the mass psychosis around a completely fictional, unrealistic ideal of a woman's body. Commercials have established a cult of "perfect beauty" and developed efficient strategies to make women buy into it. First women are frightened by exaggerated real or imaginary problems (bad hair, wrinkles, cellulite, small breasts, etc.), after which they are

**Figure 5.4.** *"Elegant design. New model series 2007."*

exposed to artificial and scarcely attainable standards of beauty, and finally are offered the means and instructions for making that (just implanted) dream come true.

Ukrainian advertising steadily constructs the image of a woman totally obsessed with her body and appearance: pretty models tirelessly enhance and polish their beauty. This mass trend is also typical of many other post-socialist countries.[5] It has a normalization effect in that it provides women with powerful role models. Ultimately it affects the gender identity and self-perception of most ordinary women. Scholars repeatedly warn of the negative impact of this kind of advertising on the women's psyche and physical health: low self-esteem and self-confidence, frustration, alienation from one's own body, all kinds of mental disorders, and related health problems stemming from the interiorization of such unrealistic standards of beauty, systematically imposed by advertising.

Assessing the traumatizing effect of imposing these idealistic beauty standards on young women, some scholars use the metaphor of the iron maiden, an ancient torture device in the form of an iron anthropomorphic box, shaped and painted as a young girl on the outside but covered with sharp thorns inside to maim anyone whose body does not fit (Jacobson and Mazur 1995).

The impact of sexist advertising on teenagers is especially harmful as their youthful psyche is unprotected from advertising mechanisms. The destructive effect of advertising has been conceptualized in the objectification theory, which suggests that patriarchal culture socializes girls and women to internalize an observer's perspective on their own bodies. When young girls and women do this, they live much of their life in the third person (phenomenon of self-objectification). In other words, females learn to be more concerned with observable body attributes rather than focusing on non-observable attributes such as emotions and internal bodily states (Fredrickson 1998). An extreme preoccupation with one's appearance can result in psychological problems. The study conducted among American students found that self-objectification leads to self-surveillance, and that, in turn, leads to body shame and appearance anxiety, with greater disordered eating and a more depressed mood in both (Tiggeman and Kuring 2004). In a study on the media, sex, and adolescence, Jane Brown maintained that the main problem is in the systematic substitution taking place in the female teens' value system, when the emphasis shifts from intellectual development to bodily perfection, from creativity to sexuality, causing serious distortions in women's personalities (1993: 366).

That is why one can claim arguably that advertising, which prioritizes female appearance and sexuality as key factors in the life success of women, is harmful for women's self-perception, and therefore sexist in nature. Indeed, if young women interiorize this idea they will perceive their bodies as their main asset, and invest in it at the outset in order to reap the interest later.

## Eroticization

Eroticization means deliberate exposure of and excessive emphasis on erotically charged parts of a female body. The mechanism of such eroticized images is simple: attractive female bodies aim to capture the attention of male consumers and stimulate their sexual desires, ultimately to be transformed into a willingness to purchase specific goods/services (Jacobson and Mazur 1995). Exhibiting a nude body or its intimate parts (hips, breasts, stomach, etc.) in the public space suggests to the audience that it is normal, even desirable, for women to expose the greatest part of their bodies to general viewing (normalization of nudity). This brings additional attention to the appearance (shape) of the body, although many studies demonstrate that the consumer of advertising does not automatically mimic its models. The advertising imagery facilitates acceptance of particular forms of social and gender arrangements, rendering it responsible for the messages and ideas that it articulates. The prevalence of red and red-derivative colors increases the sexualized effect of women's naked or half-naked portrayals. It is well known that in European cultures the color red is usually associated with sexuality, passion, and aggression.

Outdoor advertising must deliver certain messages to its audience in a very limited time/space frame, therefore it uses the most meaningful and lucid signs and symbols in an extremely condensed, outspoken, and intelligible way. The static format of this kind of commercial does not normally allow for development of a plot or dialogue. The entire message has to be squeezed into one brief moment to attract viewer attention. That is why in oudoor advertisements verbal elements are of exceptional importance. A viewer can interpret a picture in many ways, but with an inscription the author can control and manipulate this process so as to suggest the "correct" meaning of its visual component. This is the method of presupposition—using well-known and easily recognizable statements (truisms, idioms, popular jokes, proverbs, metaphors, paradoxical comparisons, etc.) associated with certain popular beliefs and dominant values (including gender stereotypes) to be instantly understood and taken for granted by viewers (Yurchak 2000). For instance, the slogan "She will lie down like a good girl" set underneath the image of a pretty woman against a stock of ceramic tiles, while invoking the ease of laying tiles, will at the same time evoke erotic fantasies in a male viewer looking at an attractive woman. Another example of verbal manipulation in advertising is the playing with associations: the constant use of erotically invested words (pleasure, desire, passion, enjoyment, etc.) alongside a female character contributes to a normalized perception of woman as sexual beings.

This seemingly innocent play on words in fact strengthens the popular perception of a woman through the prism of her sexuality. Once a woman interiorizes this self-image, she is more likely to pay attention to enhancing her attractiveness and sensuality. Since the alternative models of femininity (businesswoman, female politician, women professionals,

**Figure 5.5.** *"She will lie down like a good girl."*

etc.) are barely represented in popular discourse, the prevailing sexualized images of women channel young girls' energy into development of their appearance and sexuality, which they view as the most essential elements of genuine femininity.

Remarkably, some commercials clearly reflect the male fantasy of sharing a bed with two women. For instance, different companies have chosen to advertise their goods and services (ventilators, casino, vodka, cell phones, etc.) by featuring two attractive young women—a blond and a brunette—in such an intimate situation.[6] Time and again, these images aim to stir up sexual fantasies and desires in male viewers, so that they can be translated into a desirable consumer behavior—a wish to purchase the advertised goods.

Advertising produced by local companies can be striking for its indecency, yet the manner in which women are portrayed is often beyond criticism. In advertisements for local restaurants or meat-processing plants women are literally equated with meat products (mouthwatering ham or sausage), while elsewhere (car services, casinos) they are pictured in extremely suggestive postures or dressed like prostitutes promising (male) customers especially "delightful" services.

## Nature-Binding

Clothing is semiotically one of the key markers of humanity, a distinctive feature to distinguish human beings from animals, the civilized world of culture from the wild world of nature. When exposed in the nude, a woman's body lacks the essential symbolic markers of culture. It is excluded from the domain of cultural norms, so women are perceived as being subjects of the rules of nature; in fact, they are equated with animals governed by instinct.

The same idea is intrinsic to commercial portrayals of women as cat-like—wild female panthers and trots are to be hunted, domesticated, pacified, and/or civilized by men. Advertisements for Shustov vodka is perhaps exemplary in this sense; they depict a group of young women wearing furs and makeup to look like wild cats, and making aggressive moves as if they are going to scratch and bite. The caption reads "Shustov Premium. Traditional royal hunt."

Opposition of a woman to a man as representative of the culture/civilization dichotomy is one of the cross-cultural universals (Ortner 1974), and commercials actively exploit this stereotype, portraying women as a being essentially natural, ruled by nature and requiring treatment accordingly. Typically, a naturally beautiful female is embedded into a landscape (field, forest, river, garden, etc.) along with a slogan supporting the visual message attesting to advantages of things natural.

**Figure 5.6.** *"Landscape design—the true pleasure."*

Another noticeable gendered difference in portraying men and women in commercials is their clothing: men's apparel and accessories (business suits, designer shoes, watches, suitcases, electronics, etc.) aim to stress their professional and social standing, while women's attire and accessories do not reflect or suggest their social status or occupation, yet they do emphasize their sexuality and body features (Groshev 1999).

Sexualized portrayals of women in advertising condition a woman to look at herself through the male gaze, to imagine herself an object of his desire, and encourages her to attain this patriarchal ideal. After all, permanent public demonstration of a woman's nudity ultimately becomes perceived as a norm, so both men and women will tolerate, expect, or even require women to expose the intimate parts of their bodies to general viewing.

## Commodification

Representation of a woman as part of advertised goods/services is generally intended for male consumption. A woman's portrayal is used as an attractive label (bait) or promised as a bonus (symbolic reward) for the right customer choice. The concept was coined by a radical feminist group Women Against Pornography, based out of New York City—an influential force in the antipornography movement of the late 1970s and the 1980s (Gamble 2001: 286–287). The activists were concerned with the tendency to women as objects or commodities for the satisfaction of men. Picturing a woman side by side with an advertised product (especially if it had scant relevance to women's experiences) symbolically equated her

with an object for purchase. In Ukrainian advertising it is quite common
to equate a woman with a commodity that suggests participation in an
exclusive lifestyle, or constitutes a marker of a man's high social status
(pictured along with an expensive car, extravagant liquors, prestigious
entertainment, etc.). The most exemplary in this sense is an advertisement
for an expensive car—a Lexus. Foregrounded is a sexy young woman
whose long blonde hair waves provocatively in the breeze. The gaze of
the targeted viewer—a rich man seeking pleasure and prestige—is drawn
immediately to the woman's huge breasts. Like sex with such a woman,
the Lexus symbolizes the opulence and power he craves. A powerful car is
a sexy car. Here she is actually turned into another attribute of the lifestyle
of a rich man who can afford a premium-class vehicle, VIP leisure, and a
gorgeous girlfriend. This emphasizes yet again that the woman is deprived
of her humanity; she turns into an object to be purchased and used. This
is one of the most blatant manifestations of sexism in advertising (Shpaner
2002: 156; Yarskaya-Smirnova 2001: 70).

Another way to objectify a woman in commercials is to offer her as a
kind of bonus or promise her as a prize for the right consumer choice. In
advertising modeled after the principle "Buy the beer, get the girl!" the
girl represents a symbolic, objectified reward (Jacobson and Mazur 1995).
This phenomenon is most often used for the advertising of drinks intended primarily for male consumers: picturing a bottle of alcohol alongside a naked woman is pandemic in Ukraine.

An obvious manifestation of the commodification of women is a special
kind of advertising making them to look like objects. In many instances

**Figure 5.7.** *"Once you try it you won't be able to leave it alone"*

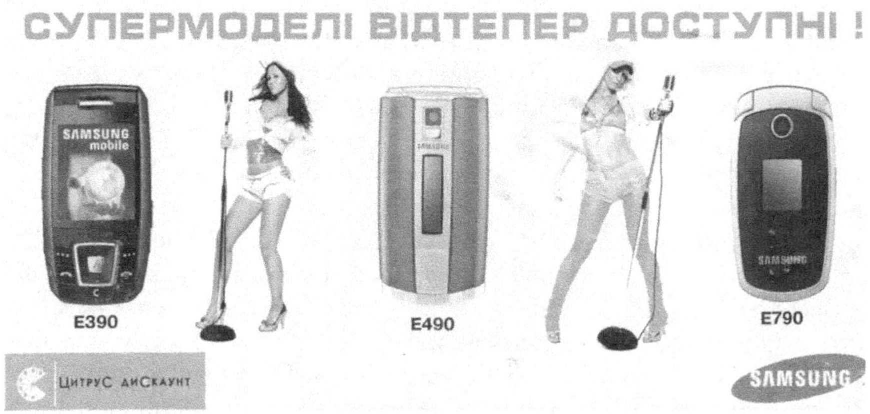

**СУПЕРМОДЕЛІ ВІДТЕПЕР ДОСТУПНІ !**

E390    E490    E790

ЦитруС диСкаунт    SAMSUNG

**Figure 5.8.** *"Super models are now accessible."*

women are portrayed in the same size as the advertised merchandise. The effect of such portrayals is quite predictable: women are equated with goods to be purchased, so they have to be handy, pocket-size, well designed, tasty, stylish, and reasonably priced.

In the most extreme cases women are not only given the same symbolic status as merchandise, they are literally named as objects. For instance, the advertising campaign of Perlova vodka, with a label designed in black and white, used the slogan "The *best things* are made in black and white." Commercials consistently pictured a bottle of vodka together with the following set of items: a black limousine and a blond woman in a sexy white dress; a black woman lying on white bed sheets; two girls—one black, another white—lying on black and white bed sheets. All of the women pictured in those commercials appeared nearly naked (with intimate body parts barely covered).

ВІДМОВИШСЯ
ВІД
ЧОРНО-БІЛОЇ ?

PERLOVA
VODKA

**Figure 5.9.** *"Can you refuse her black and white?"*

Thus a sexualized woman is included in the semantic package of men's belongings; she is transformed into an attribute of the man's subculture (just like alcohol or a car), something signifying the owner's status and prestige. Another vivid example is the advertising of a new brand of cell phone: it is pictured alongside a naked woman, body completely covered with body art (red flowers) and a caption that reads: "It's impossible to judge *some things* by appearance—the truth is inside."

But the most frequent portrayal of a woman is that of her playing the role of a bright label: women are featured in advertising of goods and services having little (if any) relevance to them as consumers (construction materials and tools, plumbing, car service, etc.). This lure is meant to attract a male customer, a sexist practice because it reproduces the patriarchal hierarchy: men are imagined as active subjects of gaze, evaluation, purchase, and action, whereas women are seen as passive objects to be viewed, evaluated, desired, obtained, consumed.

Objectification and commodification of women in ads suggest that they should be bright and attractive in order to draw attention to themselves, and develop all the features of useful merchandise to meet the buyers' expectations/needs (popular size, color, handy, easy to use, reliable, stylish, recyclable, etc.) If women are good enough they might become a component of a luxurious lifestyle, along with an expensive car, pricey drinks, and elitist entertainment. And again: body/appearance is the key to such success.

## Face-ism

There is a cross-culturally observed difference in picturing men and women as public images: "face-ism" refers to the relative prominence of the face in depicting a person (Archer et al. 1983). Scholars revealed gender asymmetry in portrayals of persons depending on their sex: there is a tendency to highlight men's faces and heads, while women are represented mainly by their bodies. The authors' conclusion is alarming:

> Anatomic differences in sex images may have important effects. If the unique qualities of men are associated with the face, these qualities are likely to be conceptualized in terms of intellect, personality, character, wit, and other dimensions of mental life. If the unique qualities of women are associated ... more with the body, these qualities are likely to be conceptualized in non-intellectual terms like weight, physique, attractiveness, or emotion. (Archer 1983)

In Ukrainian advertising this phenomenon is widespread. People are accustomed to seeing a half-naked headless woman's body as a background in commercials for expensive liquors, construction tools, restaurants, etc.

Indeed, because a head is perceived as the locus of one's personality, soul, will, intelligence, etc., a headless body turns into a depersonalized limp object, easy to possess and to manipulate. A faceless woman is similar to a doll, because she cannot think, speak, express her needs, act, or feel; at the same time the female body shape is stressed yet again, promoting a women's bodily self-absorption.

Face-ism is typical in media representations of women. A study of hundreds of illustrated periodicals in post-Soviet countries proved that they do not focus on women's issues, but tend to feature the women's bodies instead (Yampolsky 1995). Dismemberment is a tendency in advertising to focus on or highlight specific parts of the body (hips, breasts, stomach, legs, etc.; typical of pornography).

**Figure 5.10.** *Advertisement for* Kaktus *restaurant.*

Typically, fragmentation ads employ female body parts for the purpose of drawing the viewers' attention to a certain product on sale. Fragmentation has a detrimental effect on women because it promotes the idea of their being composed of separate entities existing independently and having different values (Kilbourne 2002; Mazur and Jacobson 1995). In a word, the woman is being dehumanized. These ads overtly and covertly encourage a woman to view her body as many individual pieces, so that her self-image is not holistic, and the integrity of her personality is undermined. In Ukrainian advertising women's breasts, lips, hips, legs, stomachs, etc., are exposed to the public as items for sale, for mass consumption; the ads are exclusively designed for straight people and lovers of the exotic, for the (male) taste and buying power. In any case, "in advertising a woman's body works as an appeal to male customers, what they should do—buy and possess" (Groshev 1999). One has to think hard about how a woman, trying to emulate this model, must think, as well as what can happen to her self-image, gender identity, and relationship with society.

## Machismo

Many commercials are marked by machismo. Its primary meaning includes a strong sense of masculine pride, exaggerated masculinity, and an exhilarating sense of power or strength. A macho man is proud of his physical strength, virility, and courage; he praises everything associated with masculinity and devalues whatever he considers as belonging to the realm of women. For him a woman represents a sexual object that is required to prove his manhood. Constructing an image of a macho man, advertising promotes a holistic worldview and corresponding lifestyle based on hegemonic masculinity, with men enjoying all the rights and opportunities, and women being devalued and positioned as inferior human beings.

An eloquent example of this attitude is an advertisement from Liga-Nova, a company producing office furniture. It features a middle-aged man in a business suit sitting in a luxurious leather office chair, a beatific smile on his face, with a caption that reads: "In a chair from Liga-Nova I enjoy the taste of life: I am Bonapart, I am Casanova—I feel like a winner!" On the one hand, references to two famous men do not allow women to self-identify with the status of a top executive sitting in that chair; the image suggests that women are not suitable for executive work. On the other hand, for men the same set of references imply that to be a winner, they must defeat other men on the battlefield and conquer women in bed—that would be a tasteful life.

Winner rhetoric permeates macho-style advertising, invariably stressing the sexual vigor of a male character. For example, advertisements for Altsest, a construction tools warehouse, feature a half-naked brawny man on a beach holding a power drill at the level of his genitals, with three surrounding women vying for his attention. The caption reads: "This is the tool for your success." Another advertisement for the same warehouse featured a woman's hands against her bare stomach (the rest of her body is beyond the frame), and the caption translates her thoughts to: "Faster, deeper, stronger!" The suggestive content of these commercials instructs audiences on what is to be most appreciated in a man.

**Figure 5.11.** *"Faster, deeper, stronger!"*

Through nonverbal messages ("body language"—postures, gestures, facial expressions, and context—details of the interior, props, attributes, etc.) commercials work to consolidate and promote the idea of women's subordination, passivity, receptivity, emotionality, and domesticity.[7] Women are often pictured lying down (on an expensive car, a casino table, a hardwood floor, bathroom tiles, or grassland, etc.) in order to advertise goods and services targeting male customers. Women's postures—legs spread apart, upside down, bottom up, etc.—signify their defenselessness, submissiveness, passivity, sexual accessibility, and inferiority. Sexually appealing women featured in advertisements for liquors, cigarettes, construction materials, and tools, etc., are meant specifically for the male gaze; advertisers cater to the expectations and tastes of their intended audience of solvent male consumers.

Another aspect of a macho lifestyle—hedonism—is omnipresent in this kind of advertising, in which sexual pleasure is equated or compared to gourmet enjoyment. Indeed, time and again men are encouraged to *taste* the life full of delicious meals, expensive drinks, and gorgeous women. It is remarkable how often two or more women are pictured with one man. In a billboard advertisement for Pal Mal cigarettes that states, "Two filters—one pleasure," beautiful female twins are featured. A poster advertising Sarmat beer features a regular man wearing blue jeans and a t-shirt, sitting comfortably on a sofa, sipping beer and smiling; four dressed-up beauties (evening gowns, jewelry, and hair styles) surround him trying to catch his gaze. This is the "taste of life" the caption suggests.

The idea of free choice as an inalienable right of a true man persists in machismo-style advertising. A macho man regards women as sexual objects, necessary for his masculine self-assertion. His virility is beyond question, but he also needs a choice of women to satisfy his sexual appetite. He is the one to decide who will serve his desires, and when. The advertising campaign of Shustov vodka (TV, video, and billboards) tells the story of a fallen angel who lost his wings (symbolizing his lost sanctity) when he decided to come down from the heavens to enjoy sexual relations with two attractive women. The caption reads: "Traditional freedom of choice"—choosing between a pure world of male brotherhood and a sinful world inhabited by women, or choosing between the two women; in any case he is the one to decide.

Advertising for Gazbank goes even further: it shows an ordinary young men standing between two women dressed like brides; the women stare at each other with hostility as if they are going to fight for that man. The slogan, "Flexibility of decisions, more options," is not only a slogan of this campaign, but actually the life credo of a macho man who is always in control. Women remain in a passive role, competing for attention, waiting to be chosen, and dreaming of a good owner. As Alexei Yurchak correctly

**Figure 5.12.** *"Taste life."*

remarks, "In such advertising messages a woman is always secondary to a man, she exists only as an indicator of his phallic power.... A man becomes a true man in the social realm when he acquires a set of symbolic goods, including a woman" (2000).

## Domestication

One of the most noticeable gender differences in portraying men and women in commercials is the strong association of women in the household. They are represented as though bound to the domestic space. Their core interests, needs, activities, and pleasures are rooted in their homes and they are happy living this life. The context in which advertising locates the women strengthens the conservative gender stereotypes of separate spheres and different ways of self-fulfillment for men and women. Too often women are portrayed performing family roles and household chores (as housewives and mothers, tirelessly cleaning, cooking, nurturing children, and healing sick family members—that is, as caregivers, etc.), whereas men appear in roles signifying their professional achievements, financial success, political activities, or social status. Remarkably, only men are pictured in contexts of leisure time and entertainment, having fun with friends, or enjoying vacations.

Commercials suggest that the home is a woman's only universe; in it she applies her talents and finds happiness. In advertising, kitchens, bathrooms, and living rooms become bigger, full of light, equipped with luxurious furniture and housewares. The home is in fact presented as a modern version of a fairy tale palace of which each woman can only dream. But somehow she must fit in, so she turns from Cinderella into a princess, wearing stylish dresses, makeup, and jewelry. All of these magical transformations encourage women to believe that being a happy housewife is all they ever wanted in the first place.

Women's essential attachment to the domestic sphere is also suggested through the milieu into which she is inserted. A woman is often pictured inside (most often at home) and immobile (lying down, sitting, or standing), while men tend to be portrayed in the open air, riding in transportation, or in dynamic roles (walking, running, etc.). Appearing outdoors, a female character is most likely to be accompanied by her family members (children, husband, or parents). This type of advertising is peculiar to commercials offering loans for families. Thus the stereotypical perception of travels and trips as inappropriate activities for lonely women is promoted. Restricting women to the domestic sphere only creates the impression that their self-fulfillment rests within a very limited spectrum of roles, as if they are incapable or unsuitable for public life, professional careers, creativity, intellectual achievements, political activity, etc. The idea of separate spheres for women and men is based on the principle of women's economic dependency on men; women perform certain services (cleaning, cooking, laundry, and sexual) in exchange for financial support—that is, women are socialized to live at men's expense, not to develop their own personalities, talents, and potential.

## Conclusion

The peculiarities of women's representations in outdoor advertising discussed in this chapter are sexist and as such contribute to the reproduction of a stereotypical image of a woman as an inferior being and defective member of the society. Women in advertising are denied most of their human features and rights. Commercials misrepresent and narrow the variety of the contemporary women's life experiences, degrading them to the level of objects of male aesthetic pleasure and erotic desire, or reducing their social roles to caregivers and housekeepers. Sexist advertising promotes the ideas and values that contradict such a basic principle of modern democracy as gender equality.

As a democratic country, Ukraine declared its commitment to ensuring the principle of gender equality in all spheres of Ukrainian life. The media would seem to be the logical instrument of gender-equality dissemination, but due to the inconsistencies in and vagueness of Ukrainian legislation, and almost total absence of law enforcement mechanisms, it is virtually impossible to eliminate sexist advertisements from print, TV, and the streets, so these negative, limiting, and discriminatory stereotypes are destined to continue.

**Oksana Kis** is a senior research fellow at the Institute of Ethnology, Ukrainian Academy of Sciences in Lviv. Her areas of expertise include women's history, feminist anthropology, oral history, and the gender transformations in postsocialist countries. Her book *Women in Traditional Women's Culture in the Second Half of the 19th and early 20th Centuries* (2008) has gone into a second edition (2012). Since 2010 she serves as president of the Ukrainian Association for Research in Women's History. Her current research focuses on women's everyday lives and experiences within the extraordinary historical circumstances of post-Soviet Ukraine.

**Tetyana Bureychak** holds a Kandydat Nauk degree in sociology. In 2012 she was appointed open position fellow at the Department of Gender Studies at Linköping University, Sweden. Prior to that she was an assistant professor in the Department of Sociology, Ivan Franko National University in Lviv. Her research interests lie in critical studies on men and masculinities, nationalism, postsocialism, gender politics, consumerism, and visual culture. She has published more than thirty articles in Ukrainian and international academic journals, and a book, *Sotsiologia Maskulinnosti* (Sociology of Masculinity).

# Notes

1. For an alternative interpretation of the meaning of Berehynia, see Rubchak 2001.
2. The Law of Ukraine "On Ensuring Equal Rights and Opportunities of Men and Women in Ukraine" is published on the official website of the Verkhovna Rada (parliament) of Ukraine, http://zakon2.rada.gov.ua/laws/show/2866-15.
3. For a more detailed report on this initiative, see Kis 2007: 235–238.
4. This study drew upon Tetyana Bureychak's doctoral research (2007).
5. Scholars in Ukraine, Russia, and Poland came to identical conclusions on this matter. See works by Shpaner (2002), Azhgikhina (2000), Olczyk-Twardowska, and others.
6. Remarkably, over twenty homosexual women who participated in the seminar "Stop sexism" after viewing and discussing these pictures refused to identify the

portrayals as representative of lesbian experiences. The event was organized by
*Zhinocha merezha* in Kyiv in April 2006.
7. For a more detailed discussion on this aspect of advertising, see Groshev 1999.

# Bibliography

Alchuk, Anna. 1998. "Metamorphozy obraza zhenshchiny v Russkoi reklame," *Gendernie Issledovaniia* 1: 255–261.
———. ed. 2002. *Zhenshchina i Vizual'ny Znak.* Moscow: Idea-Press.
Archer, Dane, et al. 1983. "Face-isms: Five studies of sex differences. Facial promi-
nence," *Journal of Personality and Social Psychology* 45(4): 725–735.
Azhgikhina. Nadezhda. 2000. "Gendernie stereotipy v sovremennykh mass media,"
*Gendernie Issledovaniia* 5: 261–273.
Belikova, Yulia. 2004. "Modeli gendernykh identichnostei v reklame: Kontent-analiz,"
in *Metodolohiia, Teoriia, ta Praktyka v Sociolohichnomu Doslidzhenni Ukrainskoho
Suspil'stva.* Kharkiv: Karazin National University, 409–412.
Berelson, Bernard. 1952. *Content Analysis in Communication Research.* New York: Free
Press.
Brown, Jane D., et al., eds. 1992. *Media, Sex and Adolescence.* Ed. Cresskill, NJ:
Hampton Press.
Bureychak, Tetyana. 2007. "Kommodyfikovane tilo: Dyskursy tilesnosti v Ukrainskii
reklami," *Visnyk Lvivskoho Natsional'noho Universytetu: Seriia Sociolohichna* 1:
149–161.
———. 2007. *Konstruiuvannia Gendernyh Identychnostei v Dyskursakh Reklamy.* Synop-
sis of doctoral thesis. Kyiv: Institute of Sociology, National Academy of Sciences.
http://www.nbuv.gov.ua/ard/2007/07btsidr.zip.
———. 2008a. "Genderni vymiry reklamy v sotsiolohichnii perspektyvi (druha polo-
vyna—xpochatok XXI stolittia," *Visnyk National'noho Universytetu Odessy. Seriia
Sotsiolohichna* 3(5): 375–383.
———. 2008b. "Reklamni stratehiyi konstruiuvannia normatyvnykh gendernykh dys-
kursiv (Na prykladi suchasnoi televiziinoi reklamy)," *Visnyk Lvivskoho Natsional'noho Universytetu: Seriia Sociolohichna* 2: 227–242.
Fredrickson, Barbara L. 1998. "That swimsuit becomes you: Sex differences in self-
objectification, restrained eating, and math performance," *Journal of Personality
and Social Psychology* 75: 269–284.
Friedan, Betty. 1965 (c. 1963). *The Feminine Mystique.* Harmondsworth: Penguin.
Gamble, Sarah, ed. 2001 (c. 1998). *The Routledge Companion to Feminism and Post-
Feminism.* London and New York: Routledge.
Goffman, Erving. 1979. *Gender Advertisements.* London: Macmillan.
Goscilo, Helena. 1995. "New members and organs: The politics of porn," in *Post-Com-
munism and the Body Politic,* ed. Ellen E. Berry. New York: New York University
Press, 164–194.
Greening, Kacey D. 2006. "The objectification and dismemberment of women in the
media," *Undergraduate Research Journal for the Human Sciences,* vol. 5. http://
www.kon.org/urc/v5/greening.html.

Groshev, Igor. 1999. "Gendernaia neverbal'naia kommunikatsiia v reklame," *Sotsis* 4: 71–77

———. 2000. "Reklamnie tekhnologiyi gendera," *Obshchestvennie Nauki i Sovremennost'* 4: 172–187.

Jacobson, Michael F., and Laurie Anne Mazur 1995. "Sexism and sexuality in advertising," in *Marketing Madness: A Survival Guide for a Consumer Society,* eds. Michael F. Jacobson, and Laurie Anne Mazur. Boulder, CO: Westview Press, 74–87.

Kilbourne, Jean. 2002. *Beauty and the Beast of Advertising.* http://www.medialit.org/reading_room/article40.html.

———. 2012. *Sexism, Racism, and the Image of Women in the Media.* http://www.jeankilbourne.com/resources-for-change/sexism-racism-the-image-of-women-in-the-media/.

Kis, Oksana. 2007. "Seksyzm u ZMI: Protydiiuchy komunikatyvnomu potokovi," *Zbirnyk Naukovykh Prats' Donetskoho Derzhavnoho Universytetu Upravlinnia* vol. 8, issue 3(80): 221–241.

———. 2010. "Genderni aspekty reklamy: Seksyzm iak negatyvny chynnyk. Formuvannia gendernykh vidnosyn v Ukraini," in *Praktychni Aspekty Vprovadzhennia Pryntsypu Rivnykh Prav ta Mozhlyvostei Zhinok ta Cholovikiv v Ukrainskomu Parlamenti.* Kyiv: Parliamentary Development Project II, 50–70.

Kostenko, Natalia, and Vladimir Ivanov. 2005. *Dosvid Kontent-analiz: Modeli i Praktyky.* Kyiv: Evrika.

Kravchenko, Elena. 1993. "Muzhchina i zhenshchina: Vzgliad skvoz' reklamy," *Sotsis* 2: 117–131.

Marushevska, Olena, and Ksenia Sharova. 2001. "Obraz zhinky v Ukrainskii presi na materialakh gazety *Fakty i Komentari*," in *Filosofsko-antropolohichni Studiyi. Spetsvypusk.* Kyiv: Stylos, 220–225.

Melosik, Zbyszko. ed. 1996. *Identity, Body, and Power: Cultural texts as pedagogical (Con)texts.* Poznan: Torun.

Millum, Trevor. 1975. *Images of Woman: Advertising in Women's Magazines.* London: Chatto and Windus.

Olczyk, Eliza, and Anna Twardowska. 2000. "Women in the media," in *Polish Women in the 90's. The Report by the Women's Rights Center,* ed. Urszula Nowakowska. Warsaw: Women's Rights Center, 249–269.

Ortner, Sherri B. 1974. "Is female to male as nature is to culture?" in *Women, Culture and Society,* eds. Michelle Zimbalist Rosaldo and Louise Lamphere. Stanford, CA: Stanford University Press, 67–87.

Pomazan, Olena. 1999. "Genderni problemy i mass media," in *Genderny Analiz Ukrainskoho Suspil'stva.* Kyiv: UNDP, 91–109.

Radulova, Natalia. 2005. "Obyknovenny seksyzm. Tovar+ baba. Vot skhema po kotoroi stroitsa bol'shaia chast' reklamnykh obiavlenii," *Ogoniok.* http://www.ogoniok.com/win/200508/08-22-23.html.

Rossi, Leena. 2000. "Masculine women–viable forms of media representation? Options for gender transitivity in Finnish television commercials." Paper delivered at the Fourth European Feminist Research Conference. http://www.women.it/quarta/workshops/spectacles2/leenamrossi.htm.

Rubchak Marian J. 2001. "Evolution of a feminist consciousness in Ukraine and Russia," *The European Journal of Women's Studies* 8(2): 149 160.

Russell, Valerie. 1997. *Racism and sexism—a collective struggle: A minority woman's point of view.* http://scriptorium.lib.duke.edu/wlm/racesex/.

Savelieva, Olga. 2006. "Sovetskaia reklama 1920h godov kak sredstvo agitatsiyi i propagandy," *Chelovek* 2–3. http://vivovoco.rsl.ru/vv/papers/men/soviet_20/soviet_20.htm.

Shpaner, Lyudmyla. 2002. "Obraz zhinky v telereklami: Pohliad psykholoha," in *Ukrainsky Zhinochy Rukh: Zdobutky i Problemy,* vol. 1. Drohobych: Kolo, 152–161.

Sinelnikov, Andrei. 1999. "Vozhydanii referenta: maskulinnost', feminnost', i polytiky gendernykh reprezentatsiiakh," in *Zhenshchina, Gender, I Kul'tura.* Moscow: MTsGI, 83–97.

Sukovata, Viktoria. 2000. "Genderny analiz reklamy," *Sociologia: Teoriia, Metody, Marketyng. Sociology* 2: 176–182.

Taran, Liudmyla. 2001. "Genderni problemy i zasoby masovoi informatsiyi," in *Gender i Kultura,* eds. Vira Aheeva and Svitlana Oksamytna. Kyiv: Fakt, 151–160.

Tartakovskaya, Irina. 2000. "Muzhchina i zhenshchina na stranitsakh sovremennykh Rosiiskykh gazet: Diskursivny analiz," *Rubezh* 15: 168–187.

Tiggeman, Marika, and Julia K. Kuring. 2004. "The role of objectification in disordered eating and depressed mood," *British Journal of Clinical Psychology* 43: 299–311.

Tuttle, Lisa. 1986. *Encyclopedia of Feminism.* New York: Oxford: Longman.

Vinogradova, Svetlana, ed. 1998. *Zhenshchina v massovoi kommunikatstiyi: Shtrikhi k portretu.* Saint-Petersburg: SPbGU.

Voronina, Olga. 2000. "Problemy erotiky i pornografiyi v SMI," in *Zhenshchina i vizual'nie znaki,* ed. Anna Alchuk. Moscow: Idea-Press, 87–107.

Williamson, Judith. 1978. *Decoding Advertisements: Ideology and Meaning in Advertising.* London: Boyars.

Wolf, Naomi. 1991. *The Beauty Myth: How Images of Beauty are Used against Women.* London: Vintage.

Yampolskaia, R. M. 1995. "Tendentsiyi razvitiia tipologicheskoi zhenskoi prozy," *Vestnik MGU Journalism* 10(6): 3–11.

Yarskaya-Smirnova, Elena. 2001. *Odezhda dlia Adama i Evy.* Moscow: INION RAN.

Yurchak, Alexei. 2000. "Po delam zhenskgovo obraza: Simvolicheskaia rabota novogo reklamnogo diskursa," in *Zhenshchina i Vizual'nyie Znaki,* ed. Anna Alchuk. Moscow: Idea-Press, 65–77.

Zakon Ukrainy. 1993. "Pro drukovani zasoby masovoi informatsiyi (presu) v Ukraini," *Vidomosti Verkhovnoi Rady* 1. http://zakon2.rada.gov.ua/laws/show/2782-12.

———. 1996. "Pro reklamu," *Vidomosti Verkhovnoi Rady* 39: 181. http://zakon1.rada.gov.ua/laws/show/270/96-вр.

———. 1994. "Pro telebachennia ta radiomovlennia." *Vidomosti Verkhovnoi Rady* 10: 43. http://zakon2.rada.gov.ua/laws/show/3759-12.

———. 2004. "Pro zakhyst suspil'noi morali." *Vidomosti Verkhovnoi Rady* 14: 192. atthttp://zakon2.rada.gov.ua/laws/show/1296-15?test=XX7MfyrCSgkyb.XIZif 4hk97HI40Ms80msh8Ie6

# CHAPTER 6

# Masquerading as Womanliness

## Female Subjectivity in Ukrainian Contemporary Art

Tamara Zlobina

In December 2012 I viewed a photo exhibition of works by two women.[1] It documented the private lives of Ukrainian women who were born in the 1980s and hence had little to no experience of life under the Soviets. These women posed in domestic settings wearing only their underwear; short texts explained their personal lives, their dreams, and their aspirations. The photos were torn into fragments and reassembled into a collage with wide gaps between parts of the main image. In these gaps the white background became the structural part of the artwork; it conveyed the meaning of something trying to go beyond the surface of a typical woman's life centered on marriage, beauty, domestic work, and children. This was something unknowable and yet so powerful in its veracity and transcendence that it obliterated the customary reality. Such disturbing whiteness can be interpreted as the undiscovered potential of true female desire, desire that disrupts the stability of "woman as sign" in the patriarchal symbolic order.

What is plain for the post-Soviet generation to see in these pictures is that womanliness as masquerade is a concept that no longer works. It is about the unsatisfying, hypocritical, and destructive cultural construct of "femininity that is handed to us and obliges us to replicate it instead of allowing us to go through the self-exploratory processes leading to an independent creation of self-identity." The shortest description of that experience is "woman's adoption and adaptation of femininity by means of "a mimetic process in which women convey through masquerade that which they are required to be" (Robinson 2006: 36).

So precisely what are Ukrainian women required to be? Our generation grew up between two gender models—on the one hand, it was the artificial discourse of national traditions, spirituality, and morality, most

**Figure 6.1.** *Photo from the exhibition,* Construction Set of Assemble a Woman.
*Images by Elmira Sidyak, texts by Olena Vorobiova, Lviv gallery "Ch/B.5×5." Courtesy
of the artists.*

compellingly portrayed in the Berehynia paradigm and inscribed in nationalist state ideology (Berehynia's sexuality was reduced to her reproductive,
protective, and nurturing functions). On the other, there was the ongoing commercialization and exploitation of women's bodies and sexuality
against a backdrop of market reforms (the Barbie paradigm). The basis of
both was waiting on men and attending to their needs through the performance of an array of services such as reproduction, nurture, child rearing,
and the pleasures of sex. Both varieties of rhetoric, as described by Oksana
Kis (2002), are currently present in public discourse, creating thereby a
double standard for the socialization of young women. "To be a woman"
in Ukraine means to unite somehow these conflicting models in constructing a woman's personal identity as "superwoman"—mother, guardian of
the family hearth, beauty, and source of material resources for her family—

with the latter role taking center stage. Very few Ukrainian women can afford the relatively carefree existence of a homemaker, supported by a husband, although symbolically they are persistently categorized this way.

There is no alternative gender model presenting women as a self-sufficient beings. The most prominent female public figures show variations of the Berehynia and Barbie models, with their corresponding rhetoric and appearance. Attempts to create an active and powerful female subjectivity through such a gender model as the former Prime Minister Yulia Tymoshenko à la Berehynia, and the women's group FEMEN à la Barbie, are opposed by such devices as mockery, physical abuse, and imprisonment.[2] In this context young women are trained to expect a man/husband to be of the utmost value in their lives. He is the primary provider of material resources. Conversely, a woman's successful career is portrayed as undesirable, and financial independence as not womanish. The male is also depicted as a defender against other men (the level of violence and sexual harassment is extremely high), while society stigmatizes sexually active women as promiscuous. The way for a woman to achieve ontological self-actualization is to become a wife and mother. Only then is she able reach the apogee of a "realized," or "genuine woman." To quote from the American movie *All About Eve*: "All [her] previous achievements are insignificant. … And in the last analysis, nothing's any good unless you can look up just before dinner or turn around in bed, and there he is. Without that, you're not a woman."[3] Social pressure on young women in Ukraine is so intense that even sex-tourists are known to comment on it.[4] Students themselves, usually the most broadminded of all social categories, prefer to conform silently to the ugliest forms of sexism in their universities.[5]

Small wonder, then, that feminine subjectivity and desire are impossible to construct. The public sphere does not allow for multiple gender models and life paths. Instead it confuses young women by advocating gender equality (without acting to implement it) while endorsing the veiled patriarchal demands. Young women are socialized to assurances that they are the equals of men but simply have different roles to play, that their husbands will be tender protectors and caring providers, that feminism is thus redundant. That point of view was destined to change after the birth of their first child, however, as they experienced the negative attitude of society toward dependent woman. In addition, often finding themselves in unsatisfactory marriages, filled with the prospect of emotional, economic, and even physical and sexual violence, many women finally turned away from their former "I'm not a feminist, but …"[6] position themselves to declare instead: "I'm a feminist, therefore …" and are now going through separation or divorce proceedings.

This is not the case of the protagonists in the photo project. None is yet contemplating divorce, although a few did express dissatisfaction in their relationships. Notwithstanding, the subtle increase in the feminist consciousness it is becoming ever more self-evident in the disappointment and disillusionment of woman who earlier had embodied their socially approved role of "femininity." The authorial strategies of combining texts and images in their artworks underline this unconscious confusion. The real female body is almost absent in the photos. It is presented in its naked form, often up close and built into a domestic environment (surrounded by kitchen cabinets, for instance), so as to make it virtually impossible to symbolically distinguish it from the adjacent objects. The faces are shadowed (partly for reasons of privacy), and eyes (subjectivity) are unrepresented. A persistent emphasis on subjectivity shows through the white lacuna cut from each photo in the shape of a vagina. Thus the project reflects the impossibility of discussing the womanliness ensconced behind the patriarchal symbolic order, yet it urgently needs to do so. This does not depict intelligible impossibility, as theoretical studies have shown, but rather the incapacity to imagine/describe/create the initial self.[7]

The female self or feminine subjectivity is structurally absent in the patriarchal symbolic order where "femininity itself … is constructed as mask—as the decorative layer which conceals a non-identity" (Doane 1990: 48). The features of the mask are defined by the female's relation to the male (mother, wife, lover, sister), and her ontological function of the "other" in the interest of masculine "similitude." In such a context (particularly in the patriarchal regime that was reshaped in contemporary Ukraine in 1990s and 2000s), female subjectivity is seeking a way to invent itself by using all possible expedients. It deceives the enemy by feigning conformance to social demands—wearing the mask of femininity as a shield to secure an autonomous space for itself.

In the variable public sphere shaken by tremors of imprisoned female subjectivity the art of women creates a site where this new subjectivity might emerge. Art in post-Soviet Ukraine constitutes a milieu marked by a dramatic conflict between innovatory art practices and atavisms of the "social realist" style (an excellent example of the "New Imaginaries" paradigm). During the 1990s the latter was appropriated by nationalist ideology and transformed into the patriotic sentimentalism of official state-supported art. The new ideologies of a (neo)liberal economy and consumerism transformed the very idea of "artist"—he/she became a private entrepreneur fully responsible for his/her own survival while the possibilities for public funding for contemporary art projects and their sales in the art market were constricted. This situation placed multiple burdens on women artists—they are now required to defend freedom of artistic expression, seek funding, and resist sexism in their professional and private lives.[8] Simultaneously, feminine/feminist topics are marginalized in art discourse,[9] even as female artists of the 1990s and 2000s have created and continue to create a space for advancing female subjectivity.

Ukrainian women use mimesis and masquerade to reflect the patriarchal ideal of femininity. They create thereby a layer around the unknown, inaccessible potential for female subjectivity, for emancipation, all concealed behind a socially sanctioned wall. According to French philosopher Luce Irigaray, however, mimesis and masquerade can be overplayed, turned into instruments of withdrawal of one's own self from the exploiting social and symbolic systems. A few recent projects by Ukrainian woman artists (Alina Kopytsia, Masha Shubina, Alevtina Kakhidze) provide vivid examples of such withdrawal. All of these artists use their bodies and private experiences as sources for their creative work, but the critical and emancipating potential of their statements differs. A close analysis of selected projects makes it possible to see more clearly the working of mimesis and masquerade when deprived of their patriarchal function and used as stratagems to establish personal autonomy. This enables us to understand both their productivity and their limitations in creating female subjectivity.

## Productive Mimesis in Alina Kopytsia's Works

Mimesis and masquerade are closely intertwined in individual performances of femininity. Hilary Robinson draws attention to the cluster of terms implying some form of repetition—mime, masquerade, mask, mimicry, hysterical mimeticism, mimesis, reproduction, representation, etc. (2006: 17)—in Luce Irigaray's writings on creating the female gender. Such repetition/reproduction is crucial for adaptation to society's normative demands, but it also implies the structural impossibility of individual identity based on free choice.

In her rewriting of Plato, Irigaray describes two types of mimesis: "there is the *mimesis* as production, which would lie more in the realm of music, and there is the *mimesis* that would already be caught up in a process of *imitation, specularization, adequation,* and *reproduction*" (1985: 131). Irigaray describes the second process as privileged throughout the history of philosophy, and names among its consequences the suffering and paralysis of desire. This "maintenance mimesis" or "non-productive mimesis" a là Robinson supports a given cultural system; it produces female identities assimilated to a patriarchal society, and it produces women's identities as they are assimilated to patriarchy at the cost of enormous repression (2006: 28). Mimesis contains aspects of pantomime—"*already miming* the femininity of our culture," voiceless representation, manipulation of absent objects (love and happiness are the first to be mentioned)—while the audience pretends to see them, and mimicry when "the subject compromises, represses or adapts its perspective on its own identity in favor of an *apparent* ... assimilation to its environment—in this case, assimilation to the virtual world of 'femininity' as erected by the structures of patriarchy" (Robinson 2006: 31).

The first type of mimesis has been somewhat obscured, although it constituted the very possibility of women's writing. Robinson uses music to continue Irigaray's analogy—musicians simultaneously read the piece of music they play and give their own interpretation of it, so there is limited freedom embedded in this type of productive mimesis (2006: 26). Productive mimesis can also create a new phenomenon, and in addition to providing a script it ensures its individual performance under a unique set of spatial-temporal circumstances. Although the speechlessness of a mimetic pantomime is an obstacle to the articulation of one's own desire, the necessity for reinterpreting the script also provides the possibility of turning away from it. In some cases this can create a wide gap between patriarchal demands and an actual mimetic performance of the circumstances in which the origins of female subjectivity become possible.

Brilliant examples of both varieties of mimesis can be found in the art of Ukrainian women. Maintenance mimesis can be seen in paintings by Evgenia Gapchinska, a prominent artist who produces kitsch variations on doll and angel themes. The stunning success of her works can be explained by the dominant views on the feminine as domestically inclined, sweet and carefree, as well as infantile and harmless. Numerous female painters work in this style, supporting societal demands for traditional femininity. Miming the femininity of our culture can also be done in a much bolder way. Alina Kopytsia's performative works demonstrate the strategies of productive mimesis executed with a high degree of irony.

The *Personal Space* artist traveled by a variety of urban transportation systems in Kyiv during the height of the morning rush hour (18 August 2008).[10] She wore a long old-fashioned dress with a huge crinoline. It guaranteed a meter of personal space for her—something otherwise impossible in a transportation jam. The action was connected to issues of personal space, privacy, and respect for the individual, especially women. Kopytsia's work focuses on the ease with which the limits of female personal space are transgressed in everyday life by physical and verbal abuse and sexual harassment. In the absence of other means of defense the artist used the exaggerated femininity (long princess-style dress) that appeals to the patriarchal tropes of a weak woman-to-be-cared-for, woman-to-be-saved, and man-as-protector. In this long dress with its wide skirt, and sporting high heels, she was obviously incapable of protecting herself or running in the event of danger, but she captured the attention of her fellow passengers. Although her presence in the subway was an undisguised inconvenience for others (she highlighted it by her behavior) they were unable to react negatively because she was such a perfect embodiment of ideal femininity. Her wide crinoline guaranteed the surrounding personal space she desired; otherwise she would have had to fight aggressively for it. From that space she was able to interact safely with the other passengers, even to impede their walking, to read extracts from classical feminist texts (I see here a slight allusion to Virginia Woolf's *A Room of One's Own*, emphasizing the fact that in order to write/talk a woman must have a space of her own).

A superficial reading of Kopytsia's oeuvre might also imply an element of antifeminism—be properly feminine and everything in your life will be fine. In her action, however, Alina is *not* properly feminine; she exemplifies the ideal of weak and deliberately overdressed femininity. She reproduces a camouflaged façade in which the dress becomes a substitute for identity, and she wears the princess-style dress in an inappropriate place and time (with no possibility of finding her prince). Still, that is not her purpose. Her resistance strategy is to do something that is not directed toward men (looking for a man, pleasing a man) while staying within the limits of femininity (projected onto men).

The cultural construct of femininity is impressed onto women's bodies leaving no space for personal choice. Mimesis is performative; it is not just about how a body should look, it is also about what a body

**Figure 6.2.** *Alina Kopytsia,* The Personal Space. *Courtesy of the artist.*

should feel and desire. Great courage and recklessness are required to go beyond mimetic femininity toward the place where only the magma of bare potentiality pulses. Moreover, one needs to invent some new means of identity production beyond the patriarchal symbolic order in which femininity works only to reflect back to men their "sameness" by being their "other."[11]

In the action portrayed, the artist performed the Otherness that was demanded—but through its exaggeration she gained an extended personal space and the opportunity to behave and talk independently. In a second work Kopytsia mimed female submission in such a way as to make it undeniably obvious. For the *Woman's Factory* exhibition, held in March 2011 in Kyiv, she created a stock, the medieval instrument of punishment consisting of a heavy wooden frame with holes into which the hands and head of an offender were locked. She painted the heavy stock in shades of light brown, surrounded by small roses, consciously applying this decoupage technique as a decorative device. This constitutes one of the most popular crafts for housewives insofar as it does not require any special skills.[12] Without knowing the function of the object the stock seemed to be some charming interior decorative piece, yet its true purpose was to limit freedom, to immobilize the woman, to put her in her place. This instrument of torture was presented as a beautiful and desirable object, deceptive and hiding its own essence behind an attractive facade in the same way as the patriarchal ideal attempts to hide its requirements for femininity. In this case, the tension between surface and function was evident, but recognizing the obvious truth would be terrifying.

When the time came for artists to bring their exhibits to the gallery, Kopytsia decided to wear hers and use public transportation. It was a voluntarily masochistic performance—the stock was heavy, causing the artist to suffer pain in her spine and hands. Nevertheless, while in the stock, as

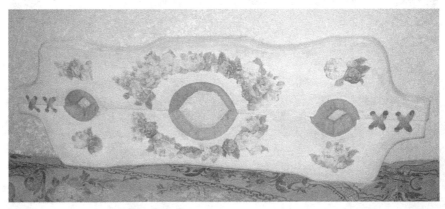

**Figure 6.3.** *Alina Kopytsia,* The Stock.

she reported, the artist experienced great enjoyment and an exhilarating sense of freedom.[13]

The pleasure that comes from turning away from the patriarchal norm is crucial. Women are not permitted to have any desire other than serving men's needs. These are the pleasures derived from being the object of love, pleasing to someone's gaze, caring about someone, being protected, and financially secure (it also means being controlled and forfeiting all responsibility for one's life). Inventing and performing a person's own means of enjoyment is forbidden; indeed this very possibility is withheld from women. Thus the consequences of Kopytsia's action are twofold: she literally performed femininity as a submissive function making visible all the inconveniences of this role with its delusive facade. By wearing her stock consciously as an act of free will she created an autonomous space in the public transportation system, enjoying the extraordinary circumstances it provided and the passengers' astonishment. In addition, it was possible for her to assess critically her fellow passengers because she too embodied their everyday suffering. Their stereotypically prescribed roles gave them no more freedom than her stock permitted.

In the analyzed works we see Alina Kopytsia using productive mimesis in order to establish her personal path of deflection from the specified script of femininity. Wearing the representational "feminine" objects that immobilize physically and symbolically in an unpredictable setting (the subway) she secured a space for her subjectivity to advance in accordance with her original desires and independent action.

## Masha Shubina: Masquerade and Narcissistic Desire

The notion of the "masquerade" with which I am dealing was introduced into cultural theory by psychoanalyst Joan Riviere in her famous essay "Womanliness as Masquerade" as early as 1929. Riviere begins her article with a description of the new women of her time who conducted themselves like "superwomen." They are excellent wives and mothers, capable housewives, maintain a social life and assist culture, have no lack of feminine interests (e.g., personal appearance), and at the same time are successful professionally (1929: 304). In this context Riviere analyzed a case study about professional women who seek reassurance from elderly men (father figures) through flirtation following some successful public performance. She portrays a perfect feminine look, accompanied by traditional domestic and family duties. Riviere's hypothesis attempts to show that a woman aspiring to "masculinity" might don a mask of womanliness in order to avert anxiety and the dreaded male retribution (1929: 303). By *masculinity* she means appropriation of a subject position through activity in professional and public (masculine) life. Riviere then proceeds to describe rivalry with the father and the feeling of anxiety regarding her success. In the following frequently quoted passage she concludes:

> Therefore womanliness might be something assumed and worn as a mask, both to hide her possession of masculinity and to avert the reprisals expected if she were to be found in possession of it.... The reader may now ask how I define womanliness or where I draw the line between genuine womanliness and the "masquerade." My suggestion is not, however, that there is any such difference; whether radical or superficial, they are the same thing. The capacity of womanliness was already there in this woman—and one might even say it exists in the most completely homosexual woman—but owing to her conflicts it did not represent her main development, and was used far more as a device for avoiding anxiety, than as a primary mode of enjoyment. (1929: 306–307).

The interconnection between masquerade and femininity was also conceptualized by Luce Irigaray (1985) and Judith Butler (1990), with the concept appearing in various studies related to literature, film, the visual arts, psychoanalysis, and gender (Rose 1982; Heath 1986; Fletcher 1988; Woodward 1988–1999; Doane 1990; Craft Fairchild 1993; Tseëlon 2001; Robinson 2006). Commenting on Riviere's text, Butler notes that rivalry with the father was not over the desire of the mother, but over the father's place in public discourse as a speaker, "as a user of signs rather than a sign-object, an item of exchange ... the desire to relinquish the status of woman-as-sign in order to appear as a subject within language" (1990: 51). In her other line of investigation Butler connects Lacan's notion of masquerade with the essential function of women in patriarchy (the heterosexual comedy consists of the masculine subject "having" a Phallus and woman "appearing to be the Phallus"): "In order to 'be' that Phallus, (in the sense of maintaining a posture as if they actually are) women establish the essential function of men" (1990: 45). This "masquerade suggests that there is a 'being' or ontological specification of femininity *prior to* the masquerade, a feminine desire or demand that is masked yet capable of disclosure, that indeed might promise an eventual disruption and displacement of the phallogocentric signifying economy" (1990: 47). Such an understanding of masquerade provides a space for the appearance of the female subject through feminine desire, regularly unrepresented by patriarchy. Feminist strategies should be aimed at unmasking, releasing, or inventing it. The art of women plays a crucial role in this process. Language as such itself is inseparable from the patriarchal symbolic order inasmuch as the Symbolic is also a cultural order indirectly influenced by language. The notions of visual signs are more fluid. Contemporary art as a visual and often bodily performative practice contains the possibility of deviation and invention of new spaces for independent feminine desire and subjectivity.

Riviere's insight regarding womanliness as identical to the masquerade correlates with Irigaray's definition of the masquerade of femininity as "to act like"—the value recognized by/for the male. In order to become a "normal woman" she "has to enter into the *masquerade of femininity*" which means entering into a "system of values that is not hers, and in which she can 'appear' and circulate only when enveloped in the needs/desires/fantasies of others, namely, men" (1985: 134). The "normal" woman will always be acting out the masquerade of femininity while simultaneously staying elsewhere without her own space, body, and desire. Masquerade follows a script of femininity provided by a man (Robinson 2006: 34), and therefore it is difficult to distinguish it from maintenance mimesis. But, as Riviere pointed out, it has the potential to reduce anxiety caused by the seizure of the subject position of an active agent (mimetic script does not contain the possibility for such a position). The masquerade of femininity played out as a tool, as a protective shield gains a new meaning. It shows that it is possible to proceed with one's independent agenda while appearing to be "enveloped in the needs/desires/fantasies of men." Productive mimesis makes possible a deflection from the patriarchal scenario of femininity, and the masquerade can render the gap between demanded and performed even wider.

Let us look into the way that the masquerade becomes a guerilla strategy for young Ukrainian female artists through the example of Masha Shubina, who uses it in order to create an autonomous space for narcissistic and autoerotic desire, depriving the masculine gaze of its hegemony. Although the artist does not declare a feminist position, or profess any interest in gender issues, a woman's self-writing is present in her oeuvre. From 2005 all of her projects are based on a self-portrait.[14] In *Self-Portrait* (Moscow gallery Fine Art, 2005), *My Dear Curator,* (London's Matthew Bown Gallery, 2006), *Fancies. From Dreams* (Fine Art, 2007), and *Digital Narcissism* (from the exhibition *Generations UsA*, Kyiv's Pinchuk Art Centre, 2007) she used almost the same material for each—self-portraits painted from photographs, then digitized and displayed on online dating sites. Shubina used these sites to inform viewers that she was seeking a curator prepared to promote her career. She communicated with the visitors to her site, and displayed the conversations, together with her art, in the gallery spaces.

The self-representation strategies that the artist uses exhibit mimicry of the specific style of online dating sites that feature corporeal reality embellished by ornate makeup and stylish clothing. These appear first, then eroticized poses are added, and together they produce a portrait of a glamorous young woman. Objectification of the female body is an old story in the world of painting. Shubina (who seemingly adapts her self-image to patriarchal stereotypes) creates an interesting ambiguity. Although she

**Figure 6.4.** *Masha Shubina,* Digital Narcissism, *installation view on the exhibition* Generations UsA *(Kyiv: Pinchuk Art Centre, 2007).*

masquerades in the guise of a particular kind of femininity, in back of this apparent surrender to the masculine gaze she conceals her personal interest. The various trappings that highlight Shubina's status of a bohemian woman constitute the key to the real meaning of her masquerade. They reveal the purpose of her self-portraits as self-admiration and self-glorification, not seduction.

Subsequently she turned to Indian themes, painting herself in different exotic settings or portraying herself as a pagan goddess. In *Masha's Time* (Collection Gallery, Kyiv Fine Art Gallery, 2008) she assembled visual fragments of her everyday life in India, and supplemented them with short itinerary-style notes. The artist continued her survey in *The Face of Surface* (Bereznitsky Gallery, Kyiv, 2010), presenting hyper-realistic still lifes painted on a plastic tablecloth instead of a canvas, with her self-portraits embellished by heavy makeup. Shubina is the center of the universe in her own paintings. The bodies she represents are too glamorous to provoke men's desire. The images are more like fashion photographs (targeting women) than a photo shoot for an erotic magazine. Although she seeks approval on dating sites in *My Dear Curator* and *Digital Narcissism,* and continuously adorns her own body, Shubina produces a certain space of autonomy behind her masquerade of femininity. She creates this image of herself in order to prevent giving visual pleasure to men, and achieves, instead, her own autoerotic enjoyment from being looked at. Albeit crucial, the difference is almost imperceptible; it constitutes a paradox to be commented upon later.

Shubina remains inside the mimesis of femininity. In the patriarchal culture the difference in the structural roles of men and women lies in the acting/being object of the action dichotomy. John Berger (1972) explains that a man's presence suggests what he is capable of doing to or for someone. By contrast, a woman's presence defines what can and cannot be done to her. Her appearance is of crucial importance here—in order to be the "Other" for the masculine "sameness" she needs to exemplify this "otherness" perfectly. That is why, "from earliest childhood she has been taught and persuaded to scrutinize herself continually ... because how she appears to men is of crucial importance for what is normally thought of as the success of her life" (1972: 45). Gaze is a moment of action. The very act of watching is a process of objectification and consumption, and this gaze is culturally assigned to men. It is as though Shubina's paintings exemplify Berger's classical quote: "Men look at women. Women watch themselves being looked at. This determines not only most relations between men and women but also the relation of women to themselves. The surveyor of woman in herself is male, the surveyed female. Thus she turns herself into an object—and most particularly an object of vision, a sight" (1972: 47).

As an artist Shubina acts from the male position inside herself. Laura Mulvey (1981). Mary Ann Doan (1990) describe this "masculinization" of spectatorship as a transsexual identification that became a habit for women from early childhood. When she wants to associate herself with some active hero the woman transgresses her own gender; otherwise she identifies with a female character and must adopt a passive or masochistic position. The latter can be overcome by assuming the image in the most radical way, through "the narcissism entailed in becoming one's own object of desire" (1990: 48, 54). This is the limited liberating potential of an unconscious guerrilla masquerade. Shubina does not look strategically for ways to invent female subjectivity and dismantle the patriarchal symbolic order, but by producing countless self-portraits she appropriates the subject position of both producer and consumer of images prescribed for males.

The *Face Control* project featured naked self-portraits (Bereznitsky Gallery, Kyiv, 2006; Berlin, 2007)—one view from the back with different hairstyles, the other an undisguised nude composition wearing a crown painted casually in pink, with shining vaginal labia executed in the childlike style. Despite the nudity, the body is dressed in the culturally constructed image of a seductive woman, and her playful crown emphasizes the desire to correspond to the ideal of femininity (to be a queen). The labia painted in the same manner establish a connection between the

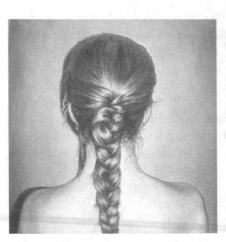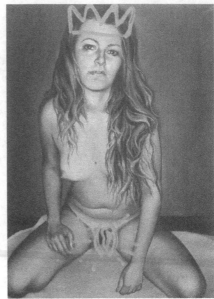

**Figure 6.5.** *Masha Shubina,* Face Control *(Kyiv: Bereznitsky Gallery, 2006; Berlin, 2007).*

crown and the female essence. Being a woman means to be the best of the best, continuously improving one's own surface. Casual strokes of bright pink hiding the obscene body part disclose the fear of reality behind the masquerade of femininity. But the symbolic labia are blurting out the very existence of that reality while the crown (signifier of power) implies the strengths of female desire. The body in this self-portrait is relaxed, with small imperfections like belly folds (in any glamorous magazine they would be photoshopped for deletion); it presents itself, affirms its own existence and disguised power, but it issues no seductive invitation to do something to it. The shining vaginal labia work as guardians, as a barrier between this naked woman's body and the viewer. It resembles an eye and so eradicates the traditional dichotomy between the female as an object of gaze and the male possessing that gaze.

A casual reading of these paintings will produce an instant diagnosis—narcissism. Indeed, the author is often accused of being "too narcissistic." Femininity itself contains elements of narcissism, an obligation to check oneself constantly, to verify that one's body fits patriarchal demands, to feel pleasure in conformism. The nude self-portrait was accompanied by views from the back with different hairstyles. Long hair signifies feminine allure (and women's empowerment in age-old Ukrainian culture), one of the core elements of womanliness (subsequently the artist adds portraits in national headscarves to the series, but the hair remains visible). The protagonist is hugging a grey wall, not absorbed by looking at something but merely striking the pose of a facade presenting itself. Shubina's narcissism comes from hysterical mimetism: "Hysteria is a strategic redoubling of that mime, taking it to the nth degree in order to attempt to wrest back some control over destiny, identity and sexuality" (Robinson 2006: 36). A viewer can easily conceive of the protagonist in these paintings saying something like: "You wanted me/woman to be a beautiful surface? Here you are! And I will enjoy my being, not you!" The slightly tragic facial expression on the crowned self-portrait tells us about the inner drama of masquerade, its limitations in pursuit of the true self.

Luce Irigaray reveals the essence of this position: a masquerade is what women do in order to participate in the men's desire, but at the cost of their own. Through masquerade they obey the dominant economy of desire in an attempt to stay in the market no matter what, but they are the objects of sexual enjoyment, not those who enjoy (1985: 133–134). Shubina identifies with the masculine gaze, and through this transsexual identification she bravely seizes the masculine desire and attempts to enjoy it. Her masquerade generates a distance—femininity is something worn, so theoretically it can be removed (although this means leaving behind the patriarchal economy of desire). Such a masquerade "constitutes transgressive doubleness, an inscription of alternative wishes, a critical distance from the mythemes of femininity—passivity, responsiveness, deference, flattery" (Fletcher 1988: 55). It carries a hidden threat to patriarchy disarticulating male systems of viewing; it can also be used successfully to conceal an inner refusal to obey and serve.

In a series of paintings called *Girl's Game,* signifying the participation of Ukraine's national football team in the World Cup (Gallery "Regina," Moscow, 2006) Shubina represents the femme fatale character. A ball, held at stomach level, produces an association with pregnancy (physical and cultural reproduction). The protagonist in high heels displays her "belly" in a nightgown, as she defiantly stares at the viewer. She goes far beyond the limits of prescribed feminine behavior; the girl is not affectionate, she is not fulfilling her natural "mission"—she is blackmailing. Mastering the ball, a symbol of one of the most masculine of sports, she declares herself the participant, not the prize. The furniture itself (a chair, a floor lamp) is featureless. Nothing suggests domestic comfort, happiness, fulfillment in maternity. The heroine refuses to serve either man or nation through the reproductive capacities of her body, or to feel any joy from such a process. Instead, she demands to be rewarded. She "takes" rather than "waiting to be cared for," but she does not take from life, she takes from men.[15]

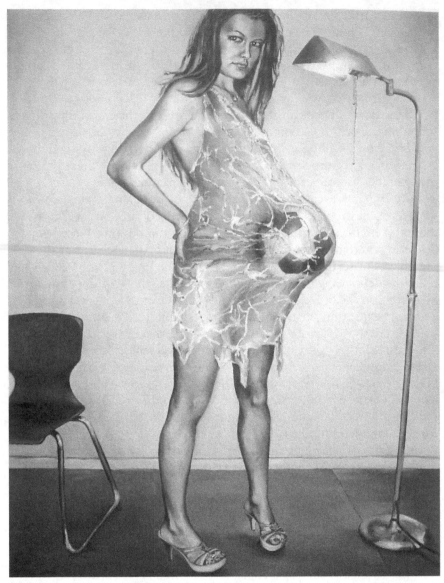

**Figure 6.6.** *Masha Shubina,* Girl's Game *(2006).*

The apotheosis of Shubina's method is her prize-winning installation *Maria. I Am My Own Religion* (Pinchuk Art Center, Kyiv, 2009). Shubina placed third in the Award for Young Ukrainian Artists category for this work, which consisted of a cross constructed from a neon light frame to which twenty-two of her portraits were attached, supplemented by a makeshift television set that translated a video shot of lighted church

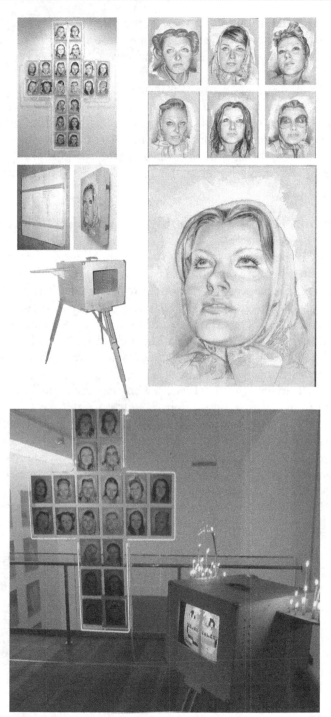

**Figure 6.7.** *Masha Shubina,* Maria. I Am My Own Religion *(2009).*

candles. This is the only photograph in the form of an enlarged portrait. The others are all the same size. The protagonist appears in a headscarf or fancy hairstyle looking upward with a faraway look in her eyes. Using the "hysterical" logic of exaggeration, overplaying what is demanded of her as a woman Shubina builds a small autonomous space within the patriarchal symbolic order. From that position she can securely attack even the most powerful of patriarchal institutions—like religion, for example—replacing the sole masculine god by multiple incarnations of herself. Instead of serving the Man-God though, in her reproductive and sexual capacities she asserts her agency and compels men to serve her with their gaze.

## Alevtina Kakhidze: Groping for Female Subjectivity

Alevtina Kakhidze uses masquerade consciously, as one of the main tools of her artistic method. She repeatedly returns to her identity of woman-artist and wife, using her body and personal experiences for the production of art. As stated above, the most emancipating feature of masquerade is its ability to engender a certain distance between a woman and her appearance. Kakhidze is a virtuoso in creating such distance, and manipulating her own image and other cultural symbols within the symbolic structures that she creates in her works.

In the performance *For Men Only, or Dear Promised Husband Show Yourself to Me in the Mirror* (curator Jerzy Onuch, Center for Contemporary Art, Kyiv, 2006) she used the old Slavic tradition of fortunetelling. On certain holidays girls assembled and performed various rituals to foretell their future. One of the most popular divinations involved looking into a mirror while holding a burning candle. A girl's fantasy is guessed at from among the shadows formed suggesting, for example, a figure resembling a man. Who will he be? Will he be old or young, rich or poor, kind or cruel? In traditional culture marriage was the pivotal moment in one's life. It defined a person's destiny, especially that of a woman. Such divinations are still amazingly popular. Only girls perform these rituals, whereas boys execute other rites prescribed for the same holidays consisting mostly in physical activity.[16] Kakhidze reenacted one in public. She installed a large mirror in the gallery space. Dressed in all white she sat in a chair in front of the mirror for a few hours in complete silence throughout the performance. The room was accessible only to men. The space was organized in such a way that all of the men were reflected in the mirror as the artist sat watching them. By this simple gesture Kakhidze turned all patriarchal logic on its head.

Kakhidze's statement was aimed at the latent male hostility toward working women in any professional environment, including seemingly

**Figure 6.8.** *Alevtina Kakhidze,* For Men Only, or Dear Promised Husband Show Yourself to Me in the Mirror *(2006). Photo by Evgeniy Chernyi.*

emancipated and democratic art discourse. She observed that all the key figures in contemporary Ukrainian art were men—curators, gallery owners, collectors, artists. Their male attitudes toward art and culture in general defined the main agendas in cultural production, and influenced the selection of topics and their further representation in critical texts and journal reviews. The patriarchal demands of art discourse were unspoken, showing themselves in the privileging of the universal approach and "big" philosophical issues, in the cherishing of myth about a talented artist as the Creator influenced by the Divine, and ignorance in the particular circumstances of art production.[17] Women's concentration on private life and specific cases (according to "personal is political" logic) was devaluated by the main discourse. Female artists often felt uneasy in turning to women's, and especially feminist, themes. Their statements lacked any substantial support in the attendant critical environment.

Kakhidze felt keenly the absence of adequate critical interpretations of her works. In 2005 she initiated the *True Alevtina* project where she interpreted her own works. In the lines dedicated to the *For Men Only* performance she wrote: "There was not a single critical article about this performance, only announcements with excerpts from my press release. That is why I take full responsibility for this interpretation of my project:

It was not about my personal problems (during the action I was married and satisfied in my marriage), and not about Slavic folklore, it was not more than 5 percent of my work, the remaining 95 percent was pure irony in the name of feminist discourse."[18]

Her feminist statement was so courageous and so radical that it left the Ukrainian art community at a loss for words. Masquerading as the girl in a fortunetelling process, Kakhidze pointed out how difficult it is for a woman to avoid "her areas" of beauty, private life, and love, even if she is a professional woman working in a public space. She fulfilled the unspoken patriarchal demand for concentration on the domestic sphere, but in doing so in a gallery, and in an ironical manner, she made the very demand visible.

It would be useful to compare Shubina's and Kakhidze's respective attitudes toward masquerade. Shubina creates her own autonomy of narcissistic enjoyment, but she identifies herself/subject with the masculine desire toward herself/object, and male gazes are structurally necessary for her satisfaction. Kakhidze's performance looks like an appeal to men although it is not. By masquerading she creates a completely independent structure through which she speaks about patriarchy, criticizes it, distorts and deforms the patriarchal logic, and manipulates the men who have fallen into her trap. In the meantime she remains protected by the mask of an appealing woman in a fortunetelling ritual. The mirror is crucial in this case: by putting it into a gallery space the artist liberated herself from the patriarchal role of woman-mirror reflecting masculine sameness. Visitors saw her face in the mirror—but they were visible there as well. According to the plot of this divination, all of them were possible "husbands" for Kakhidze; she possessed the power to choose. Moreover, in the mirror they turned out to be mere shades, ghosts of a promising future, alienated from any activity and forced to be a passive mob, while the artist achieved the status of active subject gazing at them and selecting from among them. Doan notes: "There is always a certain excessiveness, a difficulty associated with women who appropriate the gaze, who insist upon looking at, as well as usurping the gaze they pose a threat to an entire system of representation" (1990: 50).

Presenting herself as a proper object (she sits silently, dressed well, smiling), Kakhidze is far from being objectified. The artist is gazing into the mirror not to compare her image to the ideal of femininity; she is looking through it at men and laughs at their helplessness in the situation she has created. Men look at her but they cannot consume her image in the usual way; they are neither active agents nor voyeurs in her performance. Symbolically Kakhidze exposes their privileges in social life and culture; moreover, inside her work men are deprived of their exclusive ontological subject position. She cunningly uses patriarchal stereotypes, but behind the masquerade one finds a woman who has the power to assign meanings and provide scenarios. As a creator of the situation she pretends to rewrite the symbolic order.

Kakhidze is deeply concerned about her role as a woman-artist. This is revealed in her work *My Husband has Eyes like Jeanne Samary* (for the *Tenderness* project, curator Olesya Ostrovska, Center for Contemporary Art, Kyiv, 2003). The famous portrait by Pierre Auguste Renoir and an old photo of the artist's husband were projected onto opposite walls. Between them the two pairs of eyes were compared on the video projection. For the conservative observer the irony of the project and its critical subtle message would not be obvious. The woman exposes her private life and makes sentimental comments about her beloved, comparing his eyes to a certain well-known picture. Hence the artist is placed into the proper patriarchal setting relating to a man and concerned with love and partnership. But for the audience, fully aware of the positioning of woman as a passive object in a patriarchal society, Kakhidze's dramatic gesture assumes a different meaning. In her *True Alevtina* texts[19] she asks: "how many portraits of men by famous women-artists do we know?" In the meantime the history of world painting is filled with famous portraits of wives, lovers, prostitutes, and courtesans, as well as countless nudes and unknown models. The relationship between the artist and his model is one of the most common themes. Almost any picture of the female body was eroticized by the masculine gaze of the artist for voyeuristic consumption by other males. The painting Kakhidze uses for comparison points directly to this collision. Renoir was well known for his genre scenes and portraits of women. In the portrait of Jeanne Samary the traditional gender relation man/subject–woman/object is doubled; it is the relation between a male creator and viewer, and a female model and singer. Exposing the photo of her husband Kakhidze asks the question: is it only the man who has a right to gaze, to be inspired, to have a muse?[20] The whole installation denaturalizes the patriarchal gender order—both protagonists look somewhat awkward in their poses; it is as if they feel uncomfortable in their gender roles. Kakhidze deliberately takes the masculine position of creator and presents her husband as the desired object. She views the well-known masterpiece and a modest photo from the family archive side by side. The obvious nonequivalence of the images points to the inequality the working woman feels in her sphere of expertise.

Unlike male artists who do not hesitate to use the domestic services of their nameless wives, Kakhidze makes very visible the existence of her own husband, yet does not use her marital status to confirm her self-actualization according to patriarchal logic. On the contrary, she examines his role in their private and professional lives, and makes their marriage the subject of her artistic research. In the *Contract* (for the *New Ukrainian Language* project, curator Group R.E.P., Karas Gallery, Kyiv, 2008) the artist codifies spousal relationships.

**Figure 6.9.** *Alevtina Kakhidze,* Contract *(2008).*

Kakhidze hung up the marital agreement between her and her husband, according to which the husband possesses certain objects of material value like a house, shares of equities, etc., whereas her capital consists of her drawings.[21] In the event of divorce, their properties are evaluated and the first (richer) party is ordered to pay half the difference to the second party. By doing so, the artist symbolically equalizes the difference in financial wealth between them. Kakhidze maintained that her artistically stated symbolic values were equal to the price of the material objects he creates as an architect. Performance of *Marital Agreements* became the continuation of this theme (Warsaw, 2008). The artist invited her husband, Volodymyr Babiuk, to come to Warsaw (she paid his fare from the project budget) and join her in a haircut at a famous salon. Then they had dinner in an upscale restaurant during which they were interviewed by Wojtek Ziemilski about their marriage. Everyone in the restaurant was able to listen to the Polish translation of their conversation through headphones. By this action the artist extended the masquerade to her husband. She also convinced him to color and cut his hair, to use professional makeup, and they dressed in jeans and matching shirts. In the symbolic structure of her project we do not observe a woman who serves her husband and reflects his sameness by her "unimportant" feminine art activities while he is earning money. We confront a professional woman concentrated on her career in a constant dialog with her partner, one who values her critical feminist approaches. He agreed to show himself in the unconventional status of a husband to a woman-artist, to declare his identity publicly through his private life, not his professional achievements. With the same haircuts and shirts, but with different jobs and experiences, the spouses embodied

**Figure 6.10.** *Alevtina Kakhidze,* Marital Agreements *(2008).*

the possibility of equal subjectivities. Kakhidze used patriarchal tropes of the "feminine" interest in appearance and romance, but in doing so she smashed traditional gender roles.

For her art Kakhidze resorts to masquerade to represent her different personae. By altering her own image she creates complicated symbolic structures with the potential to explore and rearrange different phenomena in social life and culture. The artist is always aware of her female position in a patriarchal society and incorporates feminist critique into her polysemantic art works. In a two-minute video titled *I Can Be a Girl with Blue Eyes* (2005)[22] she commented on the instability of changing national and gender clichés, along with Ukrainian society. In *I'm Late for the Plane That Can't Be Missed* (2010) she questioned the broad problematic of gender, class, and creative work. Kakhidze endeavors to dismantle social expectations by consciously overplaying them. While masquerading she creates a "queer" space where a female subject position is made possible, and harshly criticizes society from that position. She recalls one episode: It was early spring, the weather was sunny, and many young girls could be seen in extremely high-heeled boots, wearing party-style outfits, looked ridiculous as they walked along the muddy country streets. In *I'm Late* Kakhidze masqueraded in the mundane outfit of an artist—she had a nice "bohemian" costume, a tube for her artworks, etc.[23] In the configuration of the artwork her masquerade was visible as a tool consciously used to point to some stereotypical societal expectation. But how does this masquerade work in daily life, in the ordinary rhythm of the reality of Alevtina's village neighbors? These girls are not protected by their outfits, as Alina Kopytsia was; rather, they are endangered by associating themselves with the masquerade, performing the maintenance mimesis of femininity. Riviere's case study shows us that there can always be a hidden agenda behind an overplayed feminine exterior, a secret unknown even to the woman herself. This is crucial knowledge for understanding a society in times of a patriarchal backlash, when direct resistance is scarcely plausible and guerilla strategies become a site of emancipation. Productive mimesis and small deviations, narcissistic desire, protective or ironical masquerade all appear as what their female fellow-citizens apply in everyday life.

## Conclusion

Normative monogamy and heterosexuality are deeply connected to the reproductive scenarios in today's Ukrainian society. As everywhere in the neoliberal capitalist world, the traditional family is promoted as the site of reproduction. As a result the full responsibility for raising children shifts from social agents to private citizens, and ultimately devolves upon the women.[24] Contemporary Ukrainian patriarchy demonstrates the sophisticated interweaving of related social processes in which female responsibility for reproduction is closely connected to limited access to financial recourses and political power, effectively forcing women away from the position of active agents into the world of beautiful but passive reflective surfaces. And vice versa—the basic psychotic processes of identity creation center women's energy on replication of the passive ideal of femininity.

Finally, changing expressions of love (polyamory, for example) and queer sexualities require more flexible politics, more privacy for the individual than currently exist. Unlike the domestic challenges, these reject state intrusion. In all of this the voices of leftist and feminist groups in Ukraine are challenging the stubbornness of a conservative state, and its Soviet legacy.[25]

The new generation of female citizens, born at the end of the 1980s and beginning of the 1990s, are just now entering the Ukrainian public ambit. Young Ukrainian women are socialized to a simultaneous acceptance and refusal of sexist stereotypes because they lack the symbolic resources with which to build their own identities, and positive examples of alternative female types. They face a choice: consenting to the repressive rules of a patriarchal neoliberal economy, a conservative state, and simulated democracy, or creating—through continual experimentation—an entirely new range of grassroots policies in the private and public spheres. After Luce Irigaray— the establishment of female subjectivity is a task for constant emancipation, experimentation, and creativity for the women of the world. Women's art shows how crucial to this process even small deflections can be.

**Tamara Zlobina** is a feminist philosopher and art theorist who specializes in women's contemporary art in Ukraine, Belarus, and Moldova. She has co-edited the social critique magazine *Commons,* where she is responsible for its feminist and contemporary art departments, was an invited editor and art critic for the magazine *Art Aktivist* (Minsk), and collaborates with several art journals, *Krytyka, Gendernie Issledovania, Korydor, Art-Ukraine, Perekrestki* (Lithuania), *Public Preparation* (Estonia), *Vector* (Romania), *Khudozhestvenny Zhurnal* (Russia), and others. Zlobina exhibited in the New European College Black Sea Link on a fellowship from Bucharest, and in Warsaw on a Poland Gaude Polonia scholarship.

# Notes

1. Construction set of Assemble a Woman, photos by Elmira Sidyak, texts by Olena Vorobiova, Lviv gallery. "Ch/B.5×5."

2. Currently, FEMEN organizers have become targets of vicious physical attacks that leave them in fear for their lives.

3. Elmira Sidyak and Olena Vorobiova used this quote to supplement their project.

4. The professional sex-tourist V. Roosh wrote in a guide to Ukraine that after the age of 25 Ukrainian women suddenly become diffident and are prepared to marry any man. The main reason for this is unremitting pressure from the family. http://life.pravda.com.ua/society/2013/01/17/119166/.

5. Sociologist Taras Salamaniuk described student reactions to a gender studies course offered in his university as aggressive and sexist among males and timid and reticent among females. Girls who ventured any emancipated views during seminars were ostracized. Taras Salamaniuk, "Sex in our village (diagnosis of 'radical' consciousness)." http://commons.com.ua/?p=13925.

6. Feminism generally remains a much misunderstood and maligned concept in Ukraine.

7. On New Year's Eve we played a game with my friends; everyone had to represent his or her vision of the "human body in 2023" with a three-minute bodily performance. I tried to signify the future unlimited freedom and fluidity of appearance, sex, and gender by showing the transformations of my own body from female to male, and later to a cat. I was struck by my inability to represent the male or female gender by means other than stereotypical markers. Instead of some free and fluid future body I unintentionally showed it as kitsch buffoonery by exaggerating each of my characteristics.

8. I can identify a few gendered professional strategies of Ukrainian women artists: the symbolic refusal of one's own gender; denial of sexism and discrimination in the world of art and society in general; attempts to compete with men "on equal terms" with sequential selections of themes and strategies, patrilineage (Schor 1997); appealing to male art works as sources of inspiration; acceptance and re-translation of popular stereotypes of femininity; serving social and state demand on womanliness and women's art as domestic, infantile, pleasant, beautiful, traditional, caring, and crafty; conscious articulation of feminist problematic; creation of autonomic spaces and critical discourse.

9. Recent retrospective exhibitions of Ukrainian art in 1990s and 2000s—Red Forest, Kyiv: Pinchuk Art Centre (2009); Ukrainian New Wave, Kyiv: National Art Museum (2009); Independent, Kyiv: Art Arsenal (2011)—provided an opportunity to observe "on the spot" strategies of omitting female artists from the historical canon. The number of female participants was considerably lower than their male counterparts; the works of the former were rarely discussed in curatorial texts; no attention was afforded the feminist agenda; and the critical potential of feminist messages was often hidden in revealing and describing art works.

10. Available on video from http://www.youtube.com/watch?feature=player_embedded&v=of_M6Bt_jZc.

11. "She cannot be 'the same as'; nor, in a particular culture, can she securely identify with a genealogy of women. Her function in patriarchy is that of the mirror, as a result of her 'otherness' reflecting back to man his 'sameness'. She has to adapt—and assimilate to femininity. The almost fatal nature of this move is therefore twofold: first, it requires her adaptation and assimilation to a homosexual culture; and second, as the necessary corollary (because she is not 'the same as'), it requires her to replicate 'femininity' that is not of her making. This is 'femininity' erected

by 'the same' to be its 'other'—an 'other' that is needed in order to recognize sameness" (Robinson 2006: 28).

12. The artist's explanation: "The second object can easily decorate a family hearth. The stocks were decorated by a decoupage technique, chosen deliberately. Also, decoupage is a common activity for bored housewives. It is an easy way to embellish the family nest or to renew the shine on the rods of the golden cage. Stocks keep in check any resistance to punishment and endearment. But is resistance worthwhile."

13. Available on video at http://www.youtube.com/watch?v=4zfwtgo3E1E&feat ure=youtu.be.

14. From the artist's personal webpage, http://www.shubinamasha.com.

15. The Internet forum http://matriarchat.ru/ (and various others) features a variety of advice for women on how to behave with men in order to get as many benefits as possible (attention, romantic dinners, vacations, expensive presents) without serving them emotionally, or by domestic work. Women-visitors share techniques of disguised demands for gifts and pragmatically discuss their relations with multiple partners. Such behavior might be considered one means of achieving emancipation in the oppressive milieu of feminist agenda marginalization, and as a redirection from the patriarchal scenario of serving and responsive womanliness.

16. This phenomenon represents restoration as opposed to continuation. Divinations are described in educational courses dedicated to national culture. Pupils and students are urged to replicate them in their extracurricular activities.

17. The hidden patriarchal agenda of Ukrainian contemporary art correlates to a great extent with the sexist logic of the art history as described by Linda Nochlin in "Why Have There Been No Great Women Artists?" (1971).

18. Available at http://truealevtina.livejournal.com/22244.html.

19. Available at http://truealevtina.livejournal.com/21881.html.

20. Demonstration of intimate details (the associations that my husband's eyes invoke in me) is not the purpose of my project. It is to be like Renoir—to create ideals of beauty as he did, to have muses like he had. Accessed as a paraphrase from http://truealevtina.livejournal.com/21881.html.

21. These are drawings from The Most Commercial Project (http://www.alevtinaka khidze.com/topic_01.html) in which Kakhidze painted different goods (from clothes to antiques) and declared the prices of her works to be equal to the prices of the depicted merchandise.

22. Available on video from http://www.goethe.de/ins/ru/lp/prj/bew/kue/kak/ruin dex.htm.

23. The project was a continuation of Alevtina's symbolic appeal to Ukrainian oligarchs—she asked them to draw Earth in the way they see it from the windows of their own planes (Earth from The Private Plane, for Endless Sphere project, curator Tomas Trummer, Center for Contemporary Art, Kyiv, 2008). In I'm Late for the Plane that Can't Be Missed she was given access to a plane rented by the Renat Akhmetov Foundation Development of Ukraine, and her journey was shown in the mass media. The main fascination of the event was what she would draw while in a plane. Kakhidze played with the common understanding of art as some skillful realistic painting or drawing. She masqueraded in an "artist" costume; traveled by different means of public transport to the airport; and drew nothing in the plane, ignoring demands from journalists to give them a good picture for

shooting. She structured her work in order to comment on the class division of society, the status of creative work, and the meaning of art as such.

24. In Marxist terms, the redistribution of reproductive work is a crucial strategy for changing society on the fundamental level. On the level of superstructure gender ontology becomes a battleground.

25. Among the basic goals of the new initiatives ("Gender Lviv," the student trade union "Direct Action," a curator's collective "Khudrada," Community Organization Insight, the expert gender platform "Krona," the separatist women's activist group "Feminist Offensive") we have: the creation of a space for grassroots politics and opposition to various forms of discrimination; accentuating the double exploitation of women within the system of patriarchal capitalism; overcoming hetero—and monogamous normativity; articulating innovative rhetoric of the private through a symbolic division of sexual and reproductive behavior; postulation of sexual rights and values of diversity; and mutual (shared by interested social agents) reproductive responsibility; as well as support for alternative forms of parenthood.

# Bibliography

Berger, John. 1972. *Ways of Seeing.* London: British Broadcasting Corporation.

Butler, Judith. 1990. *Gender Trouble: Feminism and the Subversion of Identity.* London and New York: Routledge.

Chowaniec, Urszula, Ursula Phillips, and Marja Rytkönen. 2008. "Introduction: Masquerade and Femininity," in *Masquerade and Femininity: Essays on Russian and Polish Women Writers,* eds. Ursula Phillips and Marja Rytkönen. Newcastle: Cambridge Scholars Publishing, 1–8.

Craft-Fairchild, Catherine. 1993. *Masquerade and Gender: Disguise and Female Identity in Eighteenth-Century Fictions by Women.* University Park, PA: Pennsylvania State University Press.

Doane, Mary Ann. 1990. "Film and the masquerade: Theorizing the female spectator," in *Issues in Feminist Film Criticism,* ed. Patricia Erens. Bloomington: Indiana University Press, 41–58.

Irigaray, Luce. 1985. *This Sex Which Is Not One.* Ithaca, NY: Cornell University Press.

Fletcher, John. 1988. "Versions of Masquerade," *Melodrama and Transgression, Screen* 29(3): 43–71.

Heath, Stephen. 1986. "Joan Riviere and the Masquerade," in *Formations of Fantasy,* eds. Victor Burgin, James Donald, and Cora Kaplan. London: Methuen, 45–61.

Kis, Oksana. 2002. "Modeli konstriiuvannia gendernoi identychnosty zhinky v suchasnii Ukraini." http://www.ji.lviv.ua/n27texts/kis.htm.

Mulvey, Laura. 1981. "Afterthoughts on 'Visual Pleasure and Narrative Cinema' inspired by *Duel in the Sun.*" *Framework* 6: 15–17.

Nochlin, Linda. 1971. "Why Have There Been No Great Women Artists?" *ARTnews,* January, 22–39.

Riviere, Joan. 1929. "Womanliness as Masquerade," *International Journal of Psychoanalysis* 10: 303–313.

Robinson, Hilary. 2006. *Reading Art, Reading Irigaray: The Polititcs of Art by Women.* London: I. B. Tauris & Co Ltd.

Rose, Jacqueline. 1982. "Introduction II," in *Feminine Sexuality: Jacques Lacan and the Ecole Freudienne,* eds. Juliet Mitchell and Jacqueline Rose. New York: W.W. Norton & Co, 27 –57.

Schor, Mira. 1997. *Wet: On Painting, Feminism, and Art Culture.* Durham, NC, and London: Duke University Press.

Tseëlon, Efrat. 2001. *Masquerade and Identities: Essays on Gender, Sexuality, and Marginality.* London and New York: Routledge.

———. 1995. *The Masque of Femininity: The Presentation of Woman in Everyday Life.* London: Sage.

Woodward, Kathleen. 1988–1989. "Youthfulness as a Masquerade." *Discourse* 11(1): 119–142.

# CHAPTER 7

# Women's Voices in Contemporary Ukrainian Literary Journalism

Mariya Tytarenko

The Literary Journalism, or New Journalism,[1] that appeared in the United States over half a century ago in 1960 has only recently emerged in Ukraine, but is not being taught as part of any curriculum of Ukrainian media studies, so Ukrainian journalists and readers have not had the opportunity to learn about it. Not a single anthology of Literary Journalism has been translated into Ukrainian thus far, and no individual volumes of the most famous practitioners of New Journalism such as Tom Wolfe, Truman Capote, Norman Mailer, Hunter Thompson, Robert Christgau, Joan Didion, Barbara Goldsmith, and others are available in Ukrainian.[2]

In American Creative Nonfiction the number of women's voices has been increasing constantly since the 1960s, although only two female journalists were included in Wolfe's anthology—Barbara Goldsmith and Joan Didion. A later anthology by Kevin Kerrane and Ben Yagoda[3] contained seven women: Lillian Ross, Marvel Cooke, Rosemary Mahoney, Martha Gellhorn, Rebecca West, Joan Didion, and the Belarusian writer Svetlana Alexievich, the only woman representing a Slavic voice. The Polish journalist Ryszard Kapuscinski is the only man being represented.

Currently American nonfiction has a large-scale and sophisticated typology (based on time period, theme, genre, gender, etc.), with numerous collections of female nonfiction writers,[4] but no Ukrainian voices. Women comprised the majority of the speakers at the prestigious Nieman Conference on Narrative Journalism in Boston on 20–22 March 2009,[5] indicating that in world culture the feminization of journalism has become an important and intrinsic tendency in Literary Journalism.[6]

Although the field of creative nonfiction remains relatively unknown in Ukraine, there are brilliant female and male voices not yet linked to New Journalism. Some of them have appeared in traditional mass media outlets, such as Klara Gudzyk's voice in her weekly column in Kyiv's daily bilingual newspaper *Den'* (The Day), Maria Matios's in various national and local print media sources, including the newspapers *Bukovyna, 24ua, Ukraina Moloda,* and the weekly magazine *Kraina.*

Other nonfiction writers have published in the blogosphere on the Internet, either on their own web portals, or in mass media publications such as *Ukrainska Pravda* (Ukrainian Truth),[7] *Telekrytyka,*[8] etc.; these include Oksana Zabuzhko, Larysa Denysenko, Svitlana Pyrkalo, and Irena Karpa, among many others. In rare cases an author's (male or female) weblog notes might result in a book, as was the case with *An Adventure, or the Practical Realia of the Traveler on a Shoestring Budget (An Erotic and Political Documentary Kaleidoscope),* written by the young Ukrainian journalist Artem Chapeye.[9] His subsequent nonfiction book[10] was published by Nora-Druk Publishing House in its recently launched series *Mandry* (Travels), represented thus far by new nonfiction writers such as Iren Rozdobudko,[11] Lesia Voronina,[12] and Maksym Kidruk.[13]

One might also find several nonfiction stories in contemporary literary anthologies such as: *An Anthology of Authors from Foreign Countries,* compiled by Mariya Shun and Vasyl Gabor (2010); and the three-volume *A Handful of Incidents,* compiled by Yury Kokh (2004, 2005, 2010), etc.

Finally, there are the collected works containing nonfiction: *Let My People Go,* and *Piatnadtsiat tekstiv pro Ukrains'ku revoliutsiiu* (Fifteen Texts on the Ukrainian Revolution), by Oksana Zabuzhko; *Apokryfy Klary Gudzyk,* by Klara Gudzyk; *Vyrvani storinky z avtobiohrafii* (Pages Torn Out of My Autobiography), by Maria Matios; a nonfiction diary *Wormwood Forest: A Natural History of Chernobyl,* by Mary Mycio (first published in English by Joseph Henry Press, Washington, DC, in 2005, then republished in Ukrainian in the Independent Cultural Journal *Yi* in 2006), and others.

Some of these voices juxtapose traditional Ukrainian *publitsystyka* (essayistic/analytical journalism) with a new journalistic style, demonstrating the shift away from an old analytical tradition to modern literary reporting. There are, however, many more essayists than literary journalists among Ukrainian writers. Female authors include Oksana Pakhliovska, Lina Kostenko, Larysa Ivshyna, Julia Mostova, Natalia Ligacheva, Natalka Bilotserkivets, Liudmyla Taran, the late Mykhailyna Kotsiubynska, and others.

The turning point for the development of the Ukrainian nonfiction sphere was a recent contest titled *Samovydets* (Eyewitness) conducted by Tempora Publishing House. As a result a collection of ten nonfiction stories, under the umbrella title *Veni, Vedi, Scripsi: The World in a Scale of Ukrainian Reportage,* was published (*Samovydets*). It was initiated by a young Ukrainian poet, essayist, and translator, Les Beley. In his introduction he claimed: "A genre of literary reportage in Ukraine is almost nonexistent. There a are few authors who write popular travelogues but unfortunately their texts do not match the quality of literary nonfiction.

In 2012 Tempora Publishing House Literary Reportage tried to change this situation by announcing a contest for the best literary reportage. ... We hope that such a phenomenon as a School of Ukrainian Literary Reportage will soon appear in our country."

It is worth noting that there were no restrictions or a thematic focus for the contest. The only requirement was that the text should be in Ukrainian. Authors of any age, profession, or writing experience were eligible. The main criteria for the jury were several basic principles postulated by Tom Wolfe in his anthology, among which were vivid voices and dialogue, original description of details, personal experiences, etc. The fact that forty-four reportages were submitted suggests that this particular genre was in high demand in Ukraine, both in the media and within the literary landscape, a collection of ten reportages featured three female and seven male voices.

The reportage that received first prize was published as a separate volume under the title *Ukraine. Schale one-to-one,* by prominent Ukrainian journalist and writer Oleg Kryshtopa from the Ivano-Frankivsk region (2013). His narrative is characterized by vivid dynamism, change of focus, and precise descriptions of Ukrainian landscapes, people's behavior, their food, and clothing. Oleg possesses a unique sense of humor that at times merges with black humor. His travelogues are deeply philosophical and map the story of a lost human being who exists in poverty.

The present work will explore several Ukrainian female voices from the perspective of Literary Journalism as well as their impact on sociocultural life. In the process of identifying the features of New Journalism in Ukrainian female narratives I will delve into the peculiarities of their idiosyncratic styles, featuring styles such as mixed genres and the use of metaphors/dialect/slang/neologisms, etc. I will also compare female voices within the framework of Ukrainian and world literary and media discourse, and analyze the Ukrainian peculiarity of the phenomenon and its background.

## Maria Matios: Reconstructing Historical Truth and Memory through Literary Journalism

"With this book in outline form I want to leave a truthful profile of an epoch in which my first half century passed," Maria Matios, a famous Ukrainian writer, poet, and journalist, claims in her recent nonfiction "The fixing of a time, the conservation of an epoch through real names, dates and actions, comprise genuine witnesses of history."[14] It was, in fact, the main idea for the writers of Literary Journalism in the United States, who aimed to present a verbal picture of the revolutionary 1960s–1970s.

According to Matios, her bilingual (Ukrainian and Russian) book is "an uneven, 'hilly' digest like my life up to now, like the mountain peaks where I was born. One will stumble upon names, actions and dates, because *life* is here. Because these pages were written in different times ... in varied moods, in copybooks, in newspapers, on receipts for communal apartment service 'payments,' in letters, but most of all—preserved through and in memory. Here there is much of my own and alien" (2011: 3).

The volume consists of nonfictional stories, media articles, letters, speeches, interviews, publicistic essays, poems, archival sources, theoretical insertions, even telegrams. It has an intentionally unfinished form and therefore contains some drafts for future projects and some incomplete articles. Still, its main idea is the reconstruction of historical memory and a search for the truth that was not welcomed by the recent Ukrainian government. It is likely the reason why the book had such great resonance in Ukrainian sociocultural life, generating a real scandal. Matios was persecuted by the Ukrainian Special Services and Ministry of Internal Affairs of Ukraine. On 12 January 2011 she published an open letter to the Ministry representatives entitled: "Chomu strazhi poriadku vzhe misiats vlashtovuiut na mene lovy?" (Why have the guardians of peace been hunting me for an entire month?). She put that letter along with other documents into her story *"Khronika Ukrainskoho Samashestviia. Pysmennytske Rozsliduvannia"*. (Chronicle of Ukrainian Self-Madness.[15] A Writer's Investigation).[16]

"During the Soviet era people were afraid to talk about such a time," Maria adds, "many people are afraid to talk even today" (2010: 85). Under the circumstances, she sometimes changes the names of her narrators, like the Belarusian (and half-Ukrainian) nonfiction writer Svetlana Alexievich did in her *Zinky Boys* (1989) or *Chernobyl' Prayer* (1997). It bears mentioning that Alexievich was also brought to trial for her book *Tsynkovie malchiki* (published in translation as *Zinky Boys*).[17] The title refers to the zinc caskets in which young soldiers were shipped back home after being killed in the Soviet war with Afghanistan. In the 2007 edition of *Zinky Boys* she included a new 27-page chapter under the title "Zinky Boys on Trial (History in Documents)," compiled from court chronicles, media abstracts, letters, shorthand records, speeches, interviews, and voices from the court, along with the results of independent literary expertise.[18] Obviously, this twenty-year-old chronicle of her court case is reminiscent of Matios's real life situation.

Both women aim to uncover truth. "Who besides artists can tell people the truth about themselves bloodlessly, about what volcanically is dozing at the bottom of their souls, or what has nestled along the dust of oblivion?!" Maria asks (2010: 28). This is the reason why, she thinks, the writer should "live carefully and carefully listen to life," and that is why she claims herself to be "a sapper of history." "A Ukrainian writer is a *just person*. Perhaps other nations do not need such people, but Ukraine does need *gata* (in Romanian), *fertyk* (in Czech), *kapets* (in Ukrainian), and *konets* (in Russian), and *the end* "wimp" (in English)!" (95). She is confident of the fact that the demand for our own history will never disappear, even within a frayed contemporary society.

Born in Bukovyna (southern Ukraine on the border of Romania), Matios focuses primarily on the history of western Ukraine (the frontier), about which "Ukrainians themselves know less than the history of Ancient Rome or Greece." Maria retells that history while enduring the tragedy of what she calls "a border person"[19] who suffered cruelly at the hands of each new occupational regime. That "border person" has embraced characteristics of individuals whose stories Matios takes either from her family and neighbors' lives, or from other sources, including archives— even epitaphs on burial mounds become a valuable source of information. She writes about *real events,* personally witnessed or taken from conversations and documents. A factual basis is a fundamental practice of Literary Journalism. In fact, young journalists often ask Matios where she finds the plots for her stories; she always answers that they come from real life, which is both cruel and wonderful at the same time.

In her *Autobiography,* Matios uses all four devices of New Journalism postulated by Tom Wolfe in 1973. The first is a scene-by-scene construction creating a dynamic "cinematographic" narrative. Matios's text is easy to visualize, it reminds one of a movie where stories appear out of chronological order as she draws together various fragments of people within one ideological framework. The second device is the use of characters' dialogues, in which Matios preserves all the peculiarities of language, its dialectal features, vulgar words, sound imitations, etc.[20]

The next device Wolfe mentions is the third-person point of view. In Matios's book this principle is often supplanted by that of her own, according to the genre of autobiography. The last device is recording details, including gestures, habits, manners, customs, furniture style, clothing, decoration, etc.[21] Her writing technique is marked by an emotional vocabulary, folklore, idioms, metaphors, a brilliant female sense of humor and irony, all of which alleviate the narrator's pain.

The dramatic territory of human pain is important for Matios: "Sometimes it seems to me that my word bleeds from longing and sadness because we—Ukrainians—are not recognized by ourselves and not recognized by the world. Or we are so distortedly recognized, so biased, that a single writer's life is scarcely sufficient to overcome this sorrow" (2010: 335). This very sorrow forces one to "press the most painful points of history and persons, forces you to make your way into the absolute borderlines, whatever they might be—zones of conditions, of the psyche—

that exist beyond the surface of an average person's understanding." She herself seems to be "a mole, a detective, a surgeon, a diagnostician, an expert in resuscitation, a healer, a confessor for all who were born under 'the mouse' of her computer" (335). Matios's literary nonfiction as well as her fiction writing are both trauma-oriented and deeply traumatic.

## Klara Gudzyk: Reporting for *The Day* and Eternity

One might also find reconstruction of historical memory in the nonfiction stories written by Klara Gudzyk.[22] Among her newspaper columns in *The Day* there is a story entitled "Memorial na balkoni" (Memorial on a Balcony).[23] It is the confession of an 80-year-old woman about WWII and her life of deprivation. The voice of a journalist appears only in the first paragraph, where she explains how she met the narrator, while the rest of the story is told by the heroine. Alexievich employs a similar method of writing nonfiction in her book *U voiny ne zhenskoie litso* (War Doesn't Have a Woman's Face).[24] There, there are no journalistic interruptions except for some information read from a tape recorder. In Gudzyk's other story "Slidy viiny" (War Tracks),[25] she retells her father's memories about a tragic and almost forgotten "Kharkiv Boiler" battle during WWII. In the story "Sviato vichnoho voskresinnia" (Holiday of Eternal Resurrection),[26] Gudzyk merely rewrites an incredible nonfiction story by an anonymous author from the samizdat underground about how prisoners celebrated Easter in the Solovki concentration camp in the 1920s. Similarly to Maria Matios, Klara Gudzyk constantly seeks truth in her nonfiction.

"I spent the majority of my life under the Soviets, that created a dislike for the official news, views, and prognoses by Soviet people for our so called 'society,' which included me," Klara writes in her book. "True information came to people via totally different channels at that time" (Gudzyk 2005: 5). This might explain Gudzyk's wish to uncover the unofficial truth in her reporting, interviews, and sketches.

In the Ukrainian media and literary discourse, so-called reconstruction reportage is another medium used to reveal history. It is a genre that imitates reportage, through the utilization of archival sources.[27] Gudzyk's story "Shchob ne zaznavavsia" (So That He Doesn't Put on Airs (2005),[28] a retelling of Hetman Petro Sahaidachny's election in the Zaporozhian Cossack encampment (*Sich*) in such a way as though it was happening today, is a brilliant example of reporting of this kind. A Ukrainian writer Halyna Pahutiak also makes use of this genre. Her story "Avantiurnyk z Urozha" (Adventurer from Urizh)[29] opens with her own memories and experiences of the present day, and segues smoothly into the seventeenth century.

Not only did Gudzyk experiment with this particular genre, she also wrote fictional interviews with classic and famous heroes such as Winston Churchill, Thomas More, and Pontius Pilate. She wrote dozens of fictional pamphlets and feuilletons à la Jonathan Swift and assembled them in her book in the chapter titled "Fairy Stories of The Day." First and foremost, however, she experimented with nonfiction journalism—reporting on daily life.

Most of Gudzyk's nonfictional stories appear in her *Apocrypha of Klara Gudzyk,* in the chapters entitled "Social Mosaic" and "The Wind from Journeys Far Away and Close," while most analytical writing and essays are found in the other five chapters, including "Church Affairs," "Portrait Sketches," and "Seasons of the Year." Interestingly, Gudzyk often inserts New Journalism fragments into her analytical articles to make them more vital and dynamic, usually putting them at the beginning of a story as a precedent for further reflections.[30]

Gudzyk had a curious personality, which might explain why in her nonfiction there are so many interviews with people she accidently met on a street or elsewhere; for instance a former engineer Vitaly, who became a shoemaker in order to survive (2005: 289–291); a beggar Eduard who was wasting his life in jails and garbage containers,[31] an "old-old" Hutsul on Mt. Hoverla in the Carpathians, who was losing his sight[32]; Mrs. Malgozhata, ex-wife of a former Soviet official who sang loudly "The International" in a square in Poland[33]; a Crimean musician who was playing the bandura, the Ukrainian national instrument, in Krakow, and who recognized Gudzyk by her picture from her newspaper column[34]; a Ukrainian student, a fellow traveler, monks, and many others. Klara Gudzyk also wrote about retired spouses who lived next door to each other and their almost Shakespearian passions;[35] about her old friend who emigrated to the United States but never changed his Soviet way of thinking;[36] Crimean "Apocalyptic" levels of pollution and decay (153–155); an overheard conversation of admiration for the Führer between two young intellectuals at the trolleybus station (159–160); a woman carrying an old stool in a crammed trolley;[37] a chaotic and absurd communist rally on Red Square in Moscow;[38] the cruelty of people who did not pay any attention to an old drunken man lying in the snow;[39] and numerous other things meriting journalistic consideration.

Gudzyk wrote all these stories in a literary journalistic manner; she made use of strange language, detailed descriptions, dialogs, third- and first-person points of view, and several publicistic features such as allusions, citations, reflections, and didacticism. All her stories are characterized by her witticisms: "The return of our history, the inclusion of Ukrainian culture in a broader European context—these are the features that made Klara Gudzyk well recognized by and a favorite for Ukrainian and foreign readers," wrote to the editor-in-chief of *The Day,* Larysa Ivshyna. "At the basis of all that she has written is her true interest in what is happening all around her" (2005: 4).

## The Orange Revolution in Nonfiction: Oksana Zabuzhko, Olena Suslova

There were probably no journalists in all of Ukraine who did not write about the Orange Revolution of 2004–2005. Not only did an abundance of articles appear on the subject, but numerous books have also been published ever since. Among the authors of these either fiction or nonfiction works, however, there were many fewer women than men,[40] and the reason still needs to be examined.

If we compare the nonfiction hypertext of the Orange Revolution with an iceberg, the larger "underwater" part of it would remain on the Internet, in witnesses' diaries, emails, and text messages. Texts in the mass media were often written in nonclassical genres, first and foremost, in the style of literary journalism that allows the author to investigate the event through his/her own experience while using all the atypical literary techniques in the media arsenal. The revolutionary era in Ukraine, as well as the rebellious times in the United States in the 1960s, required a new formulation, new wording, and new textual rhythms. This is why Oksana Zabuzhko,[41] unlike many journalists, wrote about Maidan (Freedom Square) as the locus of the revolution in the hearts of the people, not a stage for popular art (2006: 14).

Zabuzhko's nonfiction book *Let My People Go, and Piatnadtsiat tekstiv pro Ukrainsku revoliutsiiu* (Fifteen Texts on the Ukrainian Revolution, 2005) became, according to the author, not her personal chronicle about the Revolution, but "an attempt to answer the main question that tormented me at the time, how simultaneously to *experience* history and to *write* about it. How, being 'inside' it, to derive some *sense* form it—the kind that in the end is stored in the arsenal of the nation's cultural memory" (2005: 8–9). It was, in fact, the main device that the American new journalists of the 1960–1970s used to recreate and reinterpret history through their literary reporting.

Zabuzhko's book consists of interviews, articles, letters, speeches, a fictional story "An Album for Gustav," and her diary notes (from 1 December 2003 to 6 January 2005). The latter exhibits essential features of Literary Journalism, Gonzo journalism in particular. Here, one can find various voices, dynamic scenes, detailed images, play with languages (Ukrainian, Russian, Polish, and English) as well as with slang, surzhyk (a mishmash of Ukrainian and Russian), and curse words, Zabuzhko's original metaphors, irony and sarcasm, insertions of poetry and dreams, anecdotes, reflections, first-person narration, and with that a subjective angle in a laconic, almost draft form.[42] Still, according to New Journalism standards, accounts of witnessed events, details, and facts are lacking.

Zabuzhko herself confesses that "I am still sure that I needed then to clamber through the Maidan, and not meet with western correspondents.... And the details, which I regret and it seems to me I irretrievably missed" (2005: 179). She draws the conclusion that "the proper reaction to such an event as the Orange Revolution can be a diary, journalistic reporting, a chronicle; but the reality of the revolution is always immeasurably greater than the resources of one person." In her last diary note, Zabuzhko states that current culture has failed to capture that "spiritual burst," just as Tolstoy failed to do it in his *War and Peace,* where he "narrates using too many words instead of showing, picturing" (181).

While writing about the Orange Revolution, Klara Gudzyk urged others "to walk the streets of Kyiv, to listen to conversations of concierges, streets cleaners, and old spinsters near their houses and in their yards!" (2005: 98).

Oksana Pakhliovska, a well-known Ukrainian writer and essayist now living in Italy,[43] has also appealed to the reader:

> One needed to listen to miners, villagers, workers, drivers. Those people, who, when the tanks were moving toward Kyiv, stepped out on the streets and lay down before oncoming vehicles. One had only to listen to the taxi drivers who refused to ride through the city when called, and instead closed a tight circle around the people, defending them from armored weaponry. The bus drivers, who drove away from their routes in order to warm up the people. The truck drivers, who defended the entrances to the presidential residence on Bankova Street.[44]

She strolled along the Maidan, talking to people, some from western Ukraine, students and the intelligentsia, whose views she judged to be obvious.

Pakhliovska does not report the stories she heard on the Maidan in the style of Literary Journalism; rather, she builds her own publicistic narrative around them. However, there are some nonfiction insertions that make her narrative more dynamic, intimate, and vivid, for example: "Oh, at times on the Maidan people argued. Two people from Ternopil got into an argument. ... They defended their right to go first. A man said: people, they're going to start shooting. Then I'll go first. I've already done everything in my life, I've given my daughter in marriage, I can go. Eh, no, a woman from his village took exception, let me go first. You still have a son, I'm older than you, and I have no one" (2008: 283). In another piece, she recalls events in Rome, including "orange" marches of students in various Italian cities, and Ukrainian women's worried eyes and their anxiety roused by the threatening situation in Kyiv.

Olena Suslova, a Gender Activity coordinator, and founder and chairperson of the board of Women's Information Consultative Center in Ukraine (from 1995 to date),[45] talked primarily to women on the Maidan. She published a book, *Liudy, iaki nas zdyvuvaly, v kraini, iaku my ne znaly* (People Who Surprised Us in a Country We Did Not Know), in 2005 that was translated into English and Russian.[46] The main part of the book[47] consists of fifteen interviews with Ukrainian women of different ages, professions, and regions, which she transcribed either on the "barricades" during the Revolution in December 2004, or during the next three post-revolutionary months. The author published these interviews in the form of monologues, similarly to the way Alexievich did this in her books.

According to Suslova, she used a biographical method that she called "oral/verbal stories." This particular method is based on recording and analyzing verbal testimonies for two purposes: first, to reconstruct the past from the point of view of a person who "dropped out" of history; second, to show and understand the way people interpret the past. "Oral sources give us evidence not only of what people were doing at that time," she claims, "but also of what they saw, their feelings, thoughts, beliefs, aspirations, what they wanted to do but failed, and what they never wanted to do" (2005: 69).

Similar to Matios, Gudzyk, Zabuzhko, and Alexievich, Suslova tries to render these voices as close to real life as possible: her heroines use authentic dialectal features and colloquialisms, different vocabulary, language, and syntax; each and every one of them shares their extraordinary experiences in their individual voices. This often results in a narrative full of grammatical mistakes and inconsistencies. Nevertheless, every story reveals a personal truth about each character; and taken together they produce an impressive mosaic of an historic epoch. In her introduction, Suslova explains why she chose exclusively female voices: "Women's view of history has rarely been taken into account, or considered … something peculiar. Therefore, it is either totally ignored, or it occupies a specific secondary 'female' space" (2005: 6). Her statement suggests an answer to a question I raised earlier: Why are there fewer female than male voices in the nonfiction texts about the Orange Revolution?

## Travelogues: Lesia Voronina, Iren Rozdobudko, Maria Mycio

Another large segment of Ukrainian nonfiction is based on travel experiences. The first book I will focus on was written by a famous children's author, Lesia Voronina, and is entitled *U poshukakh Ogopogo.* [*Notatky navkolosvitnioyi mandrivnytsi*] (In Search of Ogopogo [Notes of a Female World Traveler], 2010). It won a prize in the *Koronatsiia Slova* (Corona-tion of the Word) contest in 2010. According to Yuri Logush, the initiator of the contest, *Koronatsiia Slova* has produced a new wave of Ukrainian literature—"bright, exciting, and of diverse genres; it acts as a mirror, reflecting the present, and is a treasure for future generations" (Voronina 2010: 3). The work represents a New Journalistic style registered as a "travelogue" by the publishing house.

Lesia Voronina describes her travels in Ukraine, Russia, Poland, Egypt, Canada, the United States, Greece, Estonia, Hungary, and Austria in a laconic—yet in its own way also dynamic—and at the same time dense manner, saturated with facts, events, dialogues, and personal thoughts. In her travel notes she is determined "to write the solemn truth (to the extent that this is possible)" (2010: 8). She "was just travelling, and did not in-tend to come to any political or economic conclusions" (12). Nonetheless, some of her conclusions did find their way into the text, especially as far as the comparison of the Ukrainian and foreign mentality is concerned.

Voronina paid particular attention to the details that would later help her "recreate moods, sounds and smells" (2010: 170). She always car-ried a pocket tape recorder and a camera.[48] The author prefers the dialog form in writing about places or her own experiences, and she often does it by intentionally avoiding clarification. "I have no idea what Northern Palmyra means," she claimed on her way to St. Petersburg. Although, it can be looked up easily enough on the Internet, she leaves it to the reader to figure out the meaning. Voronina fills her narrative with Ukrainian proverbs, songs, and names, with pieces of advice, with memories from her childhood, dreams, anecdotes, and endless optimism, along with an extraordinary sense of humor.[49]

Another book in the same nonfiction *Mandry* series is *Mandrivky bez sensu i morali* (Travels Without Sense or Morals, 2011), written by one of today's most popular Ukrainian writers, Iren Rozdobudko. As a pro-fessional journalist, Rozdobudko fills her texts with much informational background material; every story about a country she travels through ends with a recipe for local cuisine, together with a recommended list of famous national writers and their books.

In her book, Rozdobudko experiments with different genres. While Voronina's narrative is quite homogeneous, Rozdobudko's journeys to Finland, Sweden, Croatia, Egypt, Malaysia, Greece, the Czech Repub-lic, the United States, Israel, and Malta are written in different styles. A travel story about Malaysia, for example, is organized as a series of responses that intend to counteract some stereotypes from her friend's text messages. The author's travel to Malta is narrated through correspondence with an addressee nicknamed Michael who remains unknown to the reader. A reportage of her travel to the United States becomes a deep analytical story about the problem of trafficking in women. In this story, Rozdobudko switches to a third-person narrative and gives seven specific pieces of advice on how to avoid such enslavement.

Similarly to Voronina, Rozdobudko pays particular attention to "the majesty of details" that help her to "put together all these puzzles" (2011: 136): "If we perceive this world in detail," she states, "the major things become more understandable" (7). To make her texts more visual, Rozdobudko coins vivid metaphors,[50] uses verbal "freeze-frames," describes colorful scenes, etc. The author also plays with various voices and languages, inscribes her husband's poetry into the text; expands it with P.S. and P.P.S. just like Matios, and peppers all this with humor and irony. Despite the book's title, *Traveling without Sense and Morals,* Rozdobudko does make numerous moral remarks in her book, although her travel story published in Yuriy Kokh's collection of anecdotes[51] has none of this.

A third book that deserves a brief analysis is the nonfictional diary *Wormwood Forest: A Natural History of Chernobyl,* written by Mary Mycio in 2005. Drawing on her articles published in the *Los Angeles Times,*[52] it comprises an interesting mixture of literary travel nonfiction with a scholarly paper, a diary, a documentary, a report, and reportage. Her book consists of eight parts and an introduction.[53]

On the one hand, Mycio's narrative is dynamic; it contains action, dialogue, anecdotes, black humor, vivid portraits, metaphors, dreams, and switched scenes. On the other, it might appear static, abundant with specific terminology, data, statistics, schemes, numbers, long meticulous descriptions and explanations of different phenomena, constant measurement of the radiation, etc. Mycio the journalist used a tape recorder while Mycio the scholar carried her binoculars with her. Once, when she was forced to choose, she opted for the latter. As a responsible author, she always makes notes, like Rozdobudko, sometimes not even "in a less sober but still legible hand" (82).[54]

Interestingly, at times it appears in Mycio's narrative that her inner nature somehow resists her journalistic task. "One of the things I dislike most about journalism is playing tourist in other people's lives," she confesses, "especially, when those lives are so difficult compared to mine. I feel stupid and intrusive even asking them questions".[55] It seems to me, that I annoy people with my questions." (2005). Probably, it is a feature of the Ukrainian mentality that raises the dilemma "to ask or not to ask?" Mycio would not ask why in one house the portrait of Lenin hangs beside an icon: "Their ideologically eclectic décor was their own business" (210).[56] Nevertheless, Mycio's book, being an original fusion of nonfiction and natural science, represents a developing Ukrainian tradition of New Journalism.

# Conclusions: The Ukrainian Paradigm
## of Literary Journalism

Although there are many more female voices in Ukrainian Literary Journalism, the present chapter has focused on the most recognizable and influential ones. In addition to them, numerous young voices have appeared either on the web or in the various media. The editorial policy of the weekly magazine *Kraina* (The Country),[57] for example, is oriented toward experiments with journalistic narrative. Thus, one can find many articles there with features of nonfiction, such as a recent (2011) interview with Sviatoslav Shevchuk, the Major Archbishop of the Ukrainian Greek Catholic Church, conducted by the young journalist Olha Bartysh-Kolomak.[58] The author goes beyond the frame of the interview genre, creating a new nonfiction story. Bartysh-Kolomak, in fact, uses the same interview technique that an American new journalist Barbara Goldsmith used when she wrote about the social environment of a hero and accompanied him/her at all times in order not to miss a thing. In that way the interview became a story.

Another brilliant example of nonfiction reportage is entitled "I Mii batko Mykhailo na tantsi khodyv bosy" (And My Father Mykhailo Went Dancing Barefoot). It was written by Khrystyna Shevchuk-Staretska for a magazine's web portal in 2007.[59] It tells the story of a visit by the Ukrainian-American astronaut Heidemarie Stefanyshyn-Piper to her father's village in the Lviv region.[60] It is a dynamic and expressive narrative with a continuous switching of scenes, third-person narrative, dialogue, and local color that includes numerous details and voices. Seemingly, the author used all seven secrets to wicked good prose articulated by Constance Hale, Director of the Nieman Program on Narrative Journalism at Harvard (2001),[61] or all twelve tips on "hunting and gathering while reporting the story" by Tom French, a famous American journalist and professor of journalism.[62]

Hence, while Ukrainian theory of Literary Journalism has yet to be fully developed, this new genre has been spreading in the Ukrainian media and in literature. Although the Ukrainian paradigm of New Journalism has many similarities to its American counterpart, it is also characterized by certain unique features that have emerged in the context of Ukrainian history, culture, and mentality. Among the basic problems that the female authors raise in their nonfiction are: reconstruction of Ukrainian historical truth and memory; human pain and death; life of the post-Soviet/post-Chernobyl/postcolonial generation; personal stories of people who "dropped out" of history, including WWII witnesses, members of Ukrainian national organizations, the "Orange" revolutionaries; the problem of poverty and trafficking of women; challenges and achievements of everyday life; and others. Ukrainian nonfiction has its roots in the journalistic tradition of publicistics, which explains the authors' use of reflections, philosophical synopses, allusions, moral conclusions, etc.

On another, comparative, note in the Slavic monograph on Literary Journalism in Slovenia (published in 2008), its author Sonja Merljak Zdovc claims that there has been no literary nonfiction in Slovenia except for essays/publicistics (2008). In Ukraine the genre exists in all its typological varieties, as indicated by John Warnock. This includes Literary Journalism, and Literary Documentary, Travelogues, Biography, Autobiography, as well as narratives about culture, nature, and history.

Ukrainian Literary Journalism, written by either women or men, does not yield to global patterns of the genre. It is hoped that it will soon appear on its own merits representing the original Ukrainian paradigm.

**Mariya Tytarenko** is the founder and director of the Master's Degree Program in Media Communications at the Ukrainian Catholic University in Lviv, Ukraine. She is also an associate professor of journalism and media communications, a candidate of social communication sciences at UCU, and a Fulbright Faculty Development Program Fellow (2008–2009) at Pennsylvania State University. She is a columnist, poet, freelance reporter for *ONE Magazine* (CNEWA). In 2012 she won the Catholic Press Award for the best print and web combination, and in 2013 received the Best Ukrainian short novel award from the Ukrainian magazine *Kraina*.

# Notes

1. New Journalism, sometimes defined as literary journalism, creative nonfiction, neojournalism, prose of plain fact, subjective prose, the nonfictional novel, or the literature of ideas, was the name given to a style of news writing and journalism in the 1960s and 1970s. It used literary techniques that were unconventional for the time. The movement was an outgrowth of the nineteenth- and twentieth-century realistic novel tradition including authors such as Mark Twain, Charles Dickens, William Thackeray, Jack London, Ernest Hemingway, and others. The term was codified in its current meaning by Tom Wolfe in a 1973 collection of articles: *The New Journalism [by] Tom Wolfe* 1973.
2. The only Russian translation of the first Anthology of New Journalism, compiled by Tom Wolfe in 1973, was produced in St. Petersburg in 2008. It bears mentioning that the genre of the book has been designated as "publicistic" (i.e., essays).
3. Kevin Kerrane and Ben Yagoda, eds. 1998.
4. One example is an annual edition of *The Best Women's Travel Writing: True Stories from around the World*, which has been published since 2005. In the recent 2011

issue, edited by Lavinia Spalding, there is a story about Russia written by American journalist Marcia DeSanctis.

5. There were two women among the three keynote speakers: Gwen Ifill and Connie Schultz, a 2005 Pulitzer Prize winner. More detailed information about the conference is available at http://nieman.harvard.edu/Microsites/2009NiemanConfer enceOnNarrativeJournalismTellingTrueStoriesInTurbulentTimes/Home.aspx.

6. I recorded my investigation of feminized journalism within the broader context of the discipline in my recent article "Feminizing journalism" 2011.

7. http://blogs.pravda.com.ua/.

8. http://blogs.telekritika.ua/.

9. Chapeye's (whose real name is Anton Vodiany) *Live Journal* weblog notes about his travels in North and Central America, entitled *Down-and-out with a Laptop,* along with thirteen articles published in Ukrainian periodicals, served as the basis for his nonfiction novel published in 2008. It can be accessed at http://zhurnal .lib.ru/c/chapaj_a/avantura.shtml. In a paper on this book that I presented at the Fourth International Conference for Literary Journalism Studies (IALJS) at Northwestern University on 14–16 May 2009, I claimed that Chapeye's book comprises the most vivid example of contemporary Ukrainian Gonzo journalism as it has all the features of Gonzo style such as: subjectivity, including the reporter as part of the story via a first person narrative; mixing factual and fictional elements to emphasize an underlying message and engaging the reader; favoring style over accuracy; using personal experiences and emotions to provide context for the topic or event being covered; as well as using exaggeration, quotations, dialogues, sarcasm, humor, curse words, etc.

10. Artem Chapeye 2011.

11. Rozdobudko 2011.

12. Lesia Voronina 2010.

13. Maksym Kidruk, *Podorozh na Pup Zemli* (Journey to the Nub of the Earth), in two volumes. Kyiv: Nora-Druk 2010.

14. Maria Matios 2011. She claims that her book is "a book 100% about contemporary reality."

15. The word *samashedsviie* in Matios's story refers to Lina Kostenko's recent novel *Zapysky Ukraiins'koho Samashedsheho* 2011. Here I am using Professor Michael Naydan's translation of the word *play* in the title.

16. The *Chronicle* is available at http://www.istpravda.com.ua/articles/2011/03/14/ 31194/view_print/.

17. According to the Belarusian Court verdict in 1993, one claimant was denied his petition, while another petition was recognized for the plaintiff. Svetlana refused to admit her guilt in "the distortion of the truth." Eventually, she emigrated from her homeland.

18. Based on the expertise that was actually not taken under consideration by the judge, the genre of Alexievich's book was identified as "documentary literature," and therefore was considered to be associated with fiction rather than with journalism. As for American New Journalism theory, this book is considered nonfiction journalism, and it appears in anthologies of Literary Journalism.

19. Interestingly, having interviewed hundreds of officers and soldiers who served in Afghanistan, and their relatives, Alexievich intends to draw a type of a *post-*

*Afghanistan lost generation*; similarly, she constructs *a Chernobyl* or *post-Chernobyl* being based on hundreds of interviews taken after the Chernobyl disaster.

20. She uses broadly the Bukovyna vocabulary (e.g., усе-усіське, на холєру, замаціцькана); sound imitation (e.g., very, 191); numerous punctuation marks (e.g., twelve question marks at once, 298).

21. Matios can impress the reader with many details she remembers from her past, for example prices on some products and salaries (70); word-for-word rendering of numerous dialogues, as if she had her inner tape recorder turned on every minute of her life (e.g., her dialogue with a KGB agent on 155–156).

22. Klara Gudzyk died in 2011 in the age of 81. She became a journalist when she was 60 and started writing for *The Day* in 1996. She was writing a popular weekly column on religion that later became the basis for her book *Apokryfy Klary Gudzyk* 2005.

23. The story is available at http://www.day.kiev.ua/57142/.

24. This is a collection of women's stories about WWII, about their own truth from a female perspective that no men told.

25. The story is available at http://www.day.kiev.ua/136679.

26. The story is available at http://www.day.kiev.ua/290619?idsource=57089& mainlang=ukr.

27. It is oxymoronic, since reportage has to be the work of a witness. The concept is taken from the *Modern Vocabulary of Literature and Journalism*, compiled by M. Hetmanets and I. Mykhailyn in 2009.

28. The story is available at http://www.day.kiev.ua/130892.

29. Halyna Pahutiak is a famous Ukrainian writer, a laureate of the prestigious Shevchenko Prize in 2010. Her story "Avantiurnyk z Urozha" was published in the second *Coral* volume of *Handful of Incidents*, compiled by Yuriy Koks, 2005, 211–227.

30. Apokryfy Klary Gudzyk 2005, 149–151. The story is also available at http:// www.day.kiev.ua/112761/, 151–153; http://www.day.kiev.ua/60547, 356–358; http://www.day.kiev.ua/71661/, etc.) Usually these stories begin with "Yesterday I became a witness of. ..." Gudzyk wrote a popular weekly column on religion that later became the basis for her book *Apokryfy Klary Gudzyk* 2005.

31. Ibid., 155–156, http://www.day.kiev.ua/284867.

32. Ibid., 310, http://www.day.kiev.ua/35962/.

33. Ibid., 338–340, http://www.day.kiev.ua/3707/.

34. Ibid., 346–347, http://www.day.kiev.ua/61934.

35. Ibid., 147–149, http://www.day.kiev.ua/285936/.

36. Ibid., 157–159, http://www.day.kiev.ua/119340.

37. Ibid., 110, http://www.day.kiev.ua/66962.

38. Ibid., 358–359, http://www.day.kiev.ua/58553/.

39. Ibid., 145–147, http://www.day.kiev.ua/10961.

40. Books about the Orange Revolution written by male Ukrainian authors include: Slaboshpytsky's *Peisazh* 2005; two books by Danylo Yanevsky, *Khronika Pomaranchevoii revolutsii* 2005a, and *Oblychchia Pomaranchevoi revolutsii* 2005b; Stanislav Kulchytsky's *Pomarancheva revolutsiia* (Kyiv, 2005); etc.

41. Oksana Zabuzhko is one of Ukraine's leading prose writers as well as a poet, essayist, and scholar of philosophy.

42. Such drafts written by Thompson built up his Gonzo journalism and became a book in 1970.
43. Oksana Pakhliovska is also director of the Ukrainian Studies Department at Sapienza University of Rome. She had been working toward the creation of a Ukrainian department since 1991 and finally managed to make her dream a reality in 2000. Today, it is one of the leading centers of Ukrainian Studies in the world. She is also a prominent poet, essayist, translator, art critic, literary scholar, and daughter of Lina Kostenko, one of the most famous of the living Ukrainian poets.
44. It is the abstract from Pakhliovska's essay, "Maidan, Prostir Maibutnioho," first published in Rome in 2005, then republished in *Suchasnist* (no. 1) in 2006; and now is available in her recent collections of essays on Ukraine's relations with Europe—*Ave, Europa!* (2008), 279–286. Although this particular essay is characterized by features of Literary Journalism, they appear in a publicistic narrative form.
45. A web site of the organization is located here: http://empedu.org.ua/index .php?option=com_content&view=frontpage&Itemid=28. The main goal of the center is to gather, summarize, and spread information on women's organizations activities and women's initiatives in Ukraine and abroad. The organization also contributes to discourse on gender problems in the political and social life of Ukraine, and conducts various educational programs.
46. The book in Ukrainian is available at http://empedu.org.ua/index.php?option= com_content&view=article&id=104:2010-01-28-05-17-15&catid=48:2010- 01-13-23-22-32&Itemid=54.
47. In a 7-page epilogue to the 75-page book based on these interviews, Suslova explores the distribution of gender roles during the Revolution, the treatment of women, female and male behavior, female values, and moral principles; she analyzes such key notions as Motherland, responsibility, violation, singing, smiling, and others. The author concludes that Ukraine has presented itself as a female culture.
48. Numerous photos illustrate the text. It is, in fact, a common feature for all books published by Nora-Druk Publishing House in its new series called *Mandry*.
49. There are even some "shameful limericks" written by the author about an Austrian nudist in a women's sauna that became popular after she had uploaded them to the Internet.
50. She compares for instance the color of Lake Plitvytsky with water in a bath with two drops of brilliant green added (49); she also compares golden fish in the sea in Egypt with a box of lemons spilled out over the water (62), etc.
51. Iren Rozdobudko 2004.
52. The book in Ukrainian is available at http://www.ji.lviv.ua/ji-library/mycio/my cio-knyha.htm. I am taking this female voice into consideration since Mycio is American of Ukrainian heritage, and the story was published in Ukrainian.
53. In the seventh part of the book titled *Homo Chernobylus*, Mycio, like Alexievich, wanted to research this particular type of human being. In Voronina's story "Bosoiu nizhkoiu" (Bare Foot) the author also explores the post-Chernobyl generation. Thus, this particular topos becomes crucial in Ukrainian discourse.
54. Mycio 2005.
55. Ibid., 2005.

56. Ibid., http://www.ji.lviv.ua/ji-library/mycio/chapt7.htm.
57. The first issue of the magazine was published in 2009. Its target audience is 20- to 30-year-old readers with a higher education, according to the editors of the magazine. There are numerous original columns written by Yuri Andrukhovych, Andry Bondar, Yaroslav Hrytsak, Evhen Holovakha, Maria Matios, and others. An electronic version is available at: http://gazeta.ua/kraina.
58. The interview may be accessed at http://gazeta.ua/articles/opinions-journal/_zh inkamae-poednuvati-v-sobi-dvi-protilezhnosti-glava-ugkc-svyatoslav-shevch uk/410959.
59. The article may be accessed at http://gazeta.ua/post/148469.
60. I usually open my New Journalism course in the Department of Journalism in Lviv's Ivan Franko National University by reading and discussing this particular reportage with my students who then describe the main features of the nonfiction genre. Exercises that I use in my class can be found in my recent article "American New Journalism: Terra Incognita," available at http://www.mediakrytyka .info/za-scho-krytykuyut-media/amerykanskyy-novyy-zhurnalizm-terra-incognita .html.
61. Excerpts may be accessed at http://www.sinandsyntax.com/.
62. Tom French's notes are available at http://www.nieman.harvard.edu/assets/pdf/co nferences/narrative/handouts09/HUNTING%20AND%20GATHERING.pdf.

# Bibliography

Chapeye, Artem. 2011. *Podorozh iz Mamaiotoiu v Poshukakh Ukrainy.* Kyiv: Nora-Druk. *Literary Journalism.* New York: Touchstone.

Cox, Yury. 2004. *Smarahdovy Zhmutok Kazusiv vid Vel'my Tsikavykh Liudei,* vol. 1. Lviv: La Piramida.

———. 2005. *Koralovy Zhmutok Kazusiv vid Vel'my Tsikavykh Liudei,* vol. 2. Lviv: La Piramida.

Gudzyk, Klara. 2005. *Apokryfy Klary Gudzyk.* Kyiv: ZAT "Ukr. pres-grupa."

Hale, Constance. 2001. *Sin and Syntax: How to Craft Wickedly Effective Prose.* New York: Broadway Books.

Hetmanets, Mykhailo, and Ihor Mykhailyn. 2009. *Suchasny Slovnyk Literatury I Zhurnalistyky.* Kharkiv: Prapor.

Kerrane, Kevin, and Ben Yagoda, eds. 1998 (1997). *The Art of Fact: A Historical Anthology of Literary Journalism.* New York: Touchstone.

Kidruk, Maksym. 2010. *Podorozh na Pup Zemli,* in two volumes. Kyiv: Nora-Druk.

Kostenko, Lina. 2011. *Zapysky Ukrainskoho Samashedsheho.* Kyiv: A-ba-ba-a-la-ma-ha Publishers.

Kulchytsky, Stanislav. 2005. *Pomarancheva Revolutsiia.* Kyiv: Geneza.

Kryshtopa, Oleg. 2013. *Ukraina: Masshtab,* 1:1. Kyiv: Tempora.

Matios, Maria. 2011. *Vyrvani Storinky z Avtobiohrafiyi.* Lviv: Piramida.

Mycio, Mary. 2005. *Wormwood Forest: A Natural History of Chernobyl.* Washington, DC: Joseph Henry Press.

Pahutiak, Halyna. 2005. "Avantiurnyk z Urozha," vol. 2, *Koralovy Zhmutok Kazusiv vid Vel'my Tsikavykh Liudei.* Compiled by Yuriy Kokh, 211–227. Lviv: La Piramida

Pakhliovska, Oksana. 2008. "Maidan, Prostir Maibutnioho," in *Ave Europa!* Kyiv: Pulsary, 279–286.

Rozdobudko, Iren. 2004. *Nevyhadani Istoriyi pro Podorozh do Prybaltyky,* vol. 1, *A Handful of Incidents.* Compiled by Yuriy Kokh. Lviv: La Piramida.

———. 2011. *Mandrivky bez Sensu i Morali.* Kyiv: Nora-Druk.

Samovydets. *Veni, Vidi, Scripsi: Svit u Masshtabi Ukrainskoho Reportazhu.* 2013. Kyiv: Tempora.

Slaboshpytsky, Mykhailo. 2005. *Peisazh dlia Pomaranchevoyi revolutsiyi.* Kyiv: Yaroslaviv Val.

Spalding, Lavinia, ed. 2011. *The Best Women's Travel Writing: True Stories from around the World.* New York: Solas House, Inc.

Suslova, Olena. 2005. *People Who Surprised Us in The Country We Did Not Know.* With Financial support provided by Mama Cash (Agreement OEM 402543 / PJ-2127). http://empedu.org.ua/eng/sites/default/files/attached-files/publications/people-eng.doc. Also published in Ukrainian.

Thompson, Hunter S. 1970. "The Kentucky Derby is decadent and depraved," *Scanlan's Monthly.*

Tytarenko, Maria. 2011. "Feminizing journalism in Ukraine: Changing the paradigm," in *Mapping Difference: The Many Faces of Women in Contemporary Ukraine,* ed. Marian J. Rubchak. New York and Oxford: Berghahn Books, 145–161.

Voronina, Lesia. 2010. *U Poshukakh Ogopogo. Notatky Navkolo Svitnoyi Mandrivnytsi.* Kyiv: Nora-Druk.

Wolfe, Tom. 1973. *The New Journalism, an Anthology,* ed. Tom Wolfe and E. W. Johnson. New York: Harper & Row.

Yanevsky, Danylo. 2005a. *Khronika Pomaranchevoii Revolutsiyi.* Kharkiv: Folio.

———. 2005b. *Oblychchia Pomaranchevoi revolutsiyi.* Kharkiv: Folio.

Zabuzhko, Oksana. 2006. *Let My People Go.* Kyiv: Fakt, 14. Published in Ukrainian under the title *15 tekstiv pro Ukrainsku Revoliutsiiu.*

Zdovc, Sonja Merljak. 2008. *Literary Journalism in the United States of America and Slovenia.* Lanham, MD: University Press of America.

# PART III

# Changing Demographics

# CHAPTER 8

# Homemaker and Breadwinner Roles in the Eyes of Female Labor Migrants

## Viktoriya V. Volodko

The disintegration of the Soviet Union became one of the seminal causes of intensified migrations throughout the world. For Ukraine, migratory movements are no new phenomenon, given that throughout the past century alone Ukrainians relocated to various parts of the globe on both a voluntary and a compulsory basis. After 1991 the Ukrainian labor migration abroad increased statistically—fluctuating between 1.5–7 million—than any other migratory movement that had gone before, and it inheres in all regions of the country (Sylina 2008).

The overwhelming majority of labor migrants hail from regions in western Ukraine, comprising 12.9 percent of the entire working-age population (External 2009: 34). A number of factors account for such a high proportion of this migratory activity: there is a virtual absence of heavy industry in western Ukraine; the territory shares borders with many Western European countries; it has a substantial labor surplus; and the people possess deep historical labor migration patterns going back to the nineteenth and early twentieth century (Konechna 2005; Kacharaba 2003).

An additional feature of the current migratory process is the active participation of women (especially from the western region) who, until recently, were not categorized as independent migration subjects. Their latest migrations have prompted countless public debates on the transformation of family relations, and alarm over the fate of migrant families in general.[1] In the wider context, these debates should be regarded as unsettling because of the changes the women's migrations have prompted governing the conventional structure of the family. The conventional model specifies the husband as breadwinner and household head making all-important decisions. His wife is cast in the role of homemaker and mother who renders the daily decisions on domestic affairs (Parreñas 2005: 34). The politics of gender parity and inclusion of women in social production during the Soviet era resulted in certain modifications to the traditional model. Today's nuclear family continues to regard the husband as the breadwinner and household head, but it is typically a two-earner family. The wife combines her professional life with a woman's traditional household duties, including child care (Amadzhadin 2007).

Ukrainians in general subscribe to the traditional views of family labor divisions (Novytska 2005: 279, 282). At the same time, researchers underscore the emergence of rising innovative components in the established family configurations. According to research titled "Gender stereotypes and public attitudes toward gender problems in Ukrainian society,"[2] the dominant view of men and women is that both partners should participate in preserving all family functions (carrying out domestic duties and child care), although the level of commitment to these convictions differs between the sexes. Women are far more committed than men to the concept of sharing domestic obligations (Amadzhadin 2007: 68). A majority of the men spend one to fifteen hours a week on household chores, while most women devote five to thirty hours a week on these tasks. Such an unequal division of labor has led to escalating tensions within the family, yet 50.3 percent of the men and 54 percent of the women continue to support the concept of the man as breadwinner, while 24 percent of the men compared to 19.4 percent of the women are in partial accord (Amadzhadin 2007: 68).

The aim of this chapter is to illuminate some of the changing approaches to the accepted homemaker and breadwinner roles, together with suitable responsibilities for women with experience as labor migrants. The accumulated experience of migrant workers is a vital new component because, to begin with, it permits us to structure the women's role from a temporal perspective—pre-, during, and postmigration; and secondly to trace the impact of that labor experience on the reconfiguration of conventional familial roles.

## Survey of the Literature

To date Ukrainian researchers of gender, family, and labor migrations have generated a relatively modest literature owing to the newness of the subject. It began to attract attention only at the end of the 1990s, and large-scale Ukrainian studies on the family life of labor migrants are nowhere to be seen. The greater part of Ukrainian research focuses on other areas, while information on migrant labor family life is considered secondary in importance. Scattered references to those families can be found in the work of Iryna Prybytkova (2002, 2003), Olena Malynovska (2005), Nikolai Shulha (2002), Marta Chumalo (2005), Victor Sysak (2002), Myroslava Keryk (2004), and Olena Fediuk (2006, 2009); in two monographs based on sociological research conducted in the cities of Kyiv, Chernivtsi, and the village of Prylbychi (Pirozhkov, Malynovska, and Marchenko 1997); and in Sergey Pirozhkov, Malynovska, and Aleksandr Homra (2003); as well as in conference materials devoted to studies of migratory processes (Boiko 2009, 2010). Such researchers as Victoria Riul (2010), Halyna Katolyk (2005), Olha Sydorenko (2005), and Liudmyla Kovalchuk (2008) work at the intersection of social psychology and social pedagogy, investigating mostly issues of labor migrants' children. A Ukrainian-wide sociological monitoring regularly conducted by the Institute of Sociology, National Academy of Sciences of Ukraine includes questions about the scale of migratory processes in the country. Access to such data provides information about certain characteristics of the families involved (Holovakha and Panina 2008). In addition to illuminating the social and demographic characteristics of migrants, and the migratory impact on the well-being of households left behind, the latest, most extensive, research on Ukrainian labor migrations is devoted to the effect of a stay abroad on family relationships (Report 2009).

One such publication, titled *The Problems of Labor Migrants' Children: Analysis of the Situation,* is devoted exclusively to a single aspect of migrant family life. Using a semi-structured interview model, the authors studied the impact of parental absence on the psycho-emotional state and conduct of children left behind, including deviant behavior (Levchenko 2006: 4–5). The monograph in question would have portrayed the multifaceted nature of the problems even better, however, had it also taken into account the sex of migrating parents and the intervals between their respective migrations.

Among the small number of publications dedicated to migrant family relationships, the works of Olha Yarova and Alissa Tolstokorova deserve special attention. Yarova carried out a qualitative research project interviewing women working in Italy. In addition she conducted interviews in Ukraine with men whose wives work in Italy, as well as with their children. Her research confirmed the negative effects of absent mothers on their offspring, who often experience emotional distress brought on by the separation, an absence of love, and oversight of their behavior (2006: 38–40). Tolstokorova's publications are based on an analysis of secondary sources, in combination with her primary research. Her goal is to project a panorama of Ukrainian migrant family life, and the changes in individual behavior as those left behind go about their day-to-day living (2008, 2009, and 2010).

Among the foreign authors who write fully or partially on Ukrainian migrant families we find Francesca Vianello, Marta Kindler, Cinzia Solari, Bettina Haidinger, Agata Górny and Ewa Kępińska, Martina Cvajner, and Jennifer Dickinson. Vianello emphasizes the significance of motherhood for Ukrainian female migrants working in Italy, who justify their absence by claims of self-sacrifice, yet this rhetoric also serves as a defense mechanism masking their emancipation in Italy (2009). Basing herself upon the experiences of Ukrainian women, Kindler studies migrant strategies in overcoming the risks of working in Poland (2005, 2009, and 2012). Solari examines gender, nation, and migration intersections. She has authored a pioneering study of two migration concepts by means of which two key models were constructed during the post-Soviet era. They have generated various accounts of migrant practices and life experiences. These models function in different ways in the process of Ukrainian nation-building. They also produce a host of consequences for women migrants as well as specificities in the interpretation of their experiences in Ukraine's public spaces (2010: 231). Haidinger studies transnational housekeeping practices of Ukrainian women working in Austria from the perspective of three interrelated sectors: the Austrian households where they work, transformed households in Ukraine, and newly constructed international households which they create together with other migrant workers (2009). Cvajner researches the sexuality of women migrants from Eastern Europe, including Ukraine, living in Italy. She does this in an attempt to explain certain changes in their sexual activities, norms, and modifications while living in the new social environment of the receiving country (2007). Applying both qualitative and quantitative methods, Górny and Kępińska examine the experience of contemporary Polish-Ukrainian families (2005). Using one Transcarpathian village as her example, Dickinson has authored some interesting studies on the interrelation of gender, work, and economic reconstruction. Her focus is the gendered division of household labor and the professional activities of men and women. She also examines the effect of labor migrations on the family relationships of individuals (2005).

## Theoretical Basis of the Research

The central concepts of this chapter are the functions of homemaker and breadwinner studied from a structural/activity perspective. The social processes within this framework are viewed as open, dynamic, and incomplete. They are marked by human choices and decisions, within historically engendered configurations and institutions. By their deeds or, more accurately, as a result of either deliberate or inadvertent occurrences, people create or alter existing social orders. The transformative potential is intrinsic not only to activity-oriented changes in elites and popular movements, but to the daily practices of ordinary people who are often far removed from reformist ideas (Babenko 2004: 255). As Anthony Giddens argues, society is the product of active, reflexive actors, who in executing social practices within given historical parameters produce and reproduce themselves and society alike. These actors function within historically set frameworks. The structures represent specific organizational expedients and reproductions of social space, produced and reproduced through daily practices. The rules and resources that constitute the formation of these structures facilitate the reproduction and construction of social institutions during the course of the actors' activities (2003). Structure and deed are mutually complementary (dual) rather than mutually opposite (dualistic) phenomena. "The duality of structure" anticipates the fact that structures call forth the practices and impressions of individuals, yet the practices in which actors engage produce or change those structures. In a word, the structure exists only in the action, and the action can be apprehended only as it applies to structures.

The basis for determining the part that homemakers play is domestic work or, more to the point, its requisite execution. Certain difficulties exist in ascertaining the tasks involved owing to the variety and multiplicity of what constitutes domestic work. As a rule, it necessitates physical exertion and frequently requires domestic multitasking (Anderson 2000: 11–22). It also involves nurture and care giving, be it raising children or caring for the elderly or sick. Within the margins of a patriarchal order such tasks are considered the responsibility of women. In this work the role of homemaker is deemed to constitute a unified personality of internalized thinking and activity components associated with her domestic duties.

The role of breadwinner signifies responsibility for the family's material security. In today's world, this role is no longer exclusive to men. Rather, it anticipates a two-earner family (Warren 2007: 320). What is more, whether by necessity or design, more and more women are becoming breadwinners (Drago et al. 2005; Gribich 1994). Today's breadwinner is defined as the principal earner and contributor to the family budget, something that is taken into consideration in the workplace.

The internalized contemplative component causes, organizes, and supports the reciprocal activity of actors in space and time, which, in the wider sense, implies structuring social space. The social role denotes the positions and functions of individuals in various societal systems.[3] Thus the structure acts as the basis for the thinking constituent that is exhibited in the individual's role fulfillment. As a consequence, it takes on the characteristics of the structure itself, indicating that the thinking and active constituents are merely "two sides of a single coin," although the first of these is primary. It establishes the parameters of performance while continuously reconstituting itself through reciprocity (duality of structure). The active constituent of family roles is viewed as role activity (performance) based on the thinking component. Its key focus is role practices—

an aggregate of routinely repetitive and situational social and reciprocal individual actions localized in space and time, and organized around familial roles. Any societal practice counts as role fulfillment, hence whatever societal activity the individual performs, it is always from the position of some established role, whether or not the individual is in fact aware of it. Localization in time and space anticipates not only reciprocal actions of individuals in the "here and now," but their performance in the interest of expanding spatial and temporal interstices.

The family functions as a repository of familial roles through which it positions itself as a family unit. The sociocultural system establishes the key parameters of family functioning by means of which, in the course of performing such roles, they can be reassessed. Family roles ensure that the family functions as a small social group through the existence of similar social practices along the parameters of rule formation in the course of reciprocal actions by actors within the family, and relative to other social groups and institutions. In this work such family formations can be identified as follows: the complete or nuclear family consisting of two parents and their children all living together; the extended family with various relatives added to the nuclear unit; the incomplete family with one absent parent; or the extended family that can also be partially constituted.

Gender penetrates, and in a specific way organizes, all human life. Family roles exist in and of themselves as an analytical construct. In societal life particular actors regularly assign, anticipate, and implement the established functions. These actors might have various levels of blood ties, and occupy diverse social positions, etc., with all of the characteristics intrinsic to, and running throughout the gender prism.

Traditional models of homemaker and breadwinner roles are designed to reproduce the existing structure of society, defined as patriarchal. For example, the dominant gender order of most, if not all, societies possess patriarchal characteristics (Tartakovskaia 2007). They require a precise ordering of the contrasting roles assigned to women as homemakers and men as breadwinners.

Innovative interpretations of the above-mentioned roles are alternatives to traditional concepts. The idea is to treat what is established in ways that counteract these time-honored interpretations. In this instance two family roles emerge which do not exhibit conventional characteristics. Innovative ones are much less prevalent compared to ambivalent and traditional roles, but thanks to a redefinition of male and female positioning in the family they hold considerably more deconstructive potential.

Ambivalent models of homemaker and breadwinner roles are a blend of innovative and traditional components in the role structure and are the most prevalent in contemporary societies. Sociologists offer diverse explanations for the influence on family roles of labor migration. Research findings testify to noticeable changes in family relationships indicating a move away from tradition to innovation, at least in some spheres of family life. Evidence points to receiving societies allowing women greater freedom than they enjoyed in sending societies (Alicea 2006: 600), as well as increased authority thanks to the women's breadwinner status (Salazar Parreñas 2005: 5), greater male participation in domestic duties, and the subsequently lessened domestic burden for women. The majority of researchers also concur that the migrant experience does not necessarily present a serious challenge to the supremacy of patriarchal values (Alicea 2006: 600), so the reconfiguration of the relevant duties does not lead inevitably to innovative role practices.

In assessing the potential influence of labor migrants on family roles, researchers frequently analyze them from the perspective of the migrant experience alone. This oversimplifies that experience insofar as it does not take account of the importance of the pre-migrant experiences, even though, as Alice Szczepanikova correctly observes: "Migrant lives do not normally start with migration. There are complex histories and legacies behind migration processes" (2006). Well before the move, stories and experiences accumulate to exert a decisive influence on immigrant practices and imaginations. Post-migration life also falls very infrequently into the scholarly purview, although this period is crucial to understanding the full extent of the migrant labor influence on the family.

The transnational perspective in research on contemporary migratory processes is also important. Within this framework both sending and receiving societies open up a single field of research, and the labor migrant exists simultaneously in a relationship with both (Levitt and Sørensen 2004). New forms of social interactions unfold, involving change between physical presence and social space within the confines of the latest transnational social expanse. Following Giddens, it can be asserted that in this case societal integration is noticeably breached or is absent altogether (Klimov 2000). A new form of interaction among transnational migrants allows for coordinating social action beyond the focus on a customary concrete space and local context of activity. Residing abroad, the labor migrant is able to carry out (or not) certain transnational practices, which can be very diverse and vary by frequency of performance and intensity. They might be permanent, sporadic, or accidental, and performed in a variety of venues—political, economic, social, cultural, or domestic—simultaneously or separately (Waldinger 2008: 5).

Transnational migrant family practices demonstrate new forms of relationships and contacts extrinsic to families sharing a single geographical and temporal space. In and of themselves transnational families whose members live in two or more societies are not a totally new phenomenon tied to global processes. Nevertheless, it has only been since the end of the twentieth and beginning of the twenty-first century that this subject has captured the attention of researchers, because the number of such families has grown and those in which the role of breadwinner has passed from male to female has risen. The new status of women as breadwinners has given rise to serious changes in family roles. Transference of biological mothers and homemakers beyond their own domestic space, together with the growth in their leadership roles as their income potential expands, have produced significant alterations in family routines (Parreñas 2005: 5), and challenges to the dominant patriarchal order.

## Research Design

Ukrainian labor migrants are among the most numerous of such groups in Europe (Kindler 2005). They secure employment in the Southern European tier (Italy, Spain, and Greece), as well as in Central European countries (Poland, Hungary, and the Czech Republic), the United States, Israel, Russia, and others.

Poland is a leading destination in Central Europe (Grzymała-Kazłowska 2008), with Ukrainians comprising its most numerous labor migrants, estimated at 450,000. As for gender, according to the latest research, female migration to Poland either dominates (Markov 2009: 23), or constitutes half the total migrant population in the country (External 2009: 33). The critical mass (60 percent) of immigrants is concentrated in Warsaw and its environs (Markov 2009: 24). Women work in agricultural enterprises, trade, construction, and the domestic sector (External 2009: 41; Iglitska 2003). Only a limited number secure employment in Poland consistent with their education and training (teachers, nurses). Some retrain for different professions and find employment in new sectors. The attraction of Poland for Ukrainians is not only based on its geographical and cultural proximity, but also a flexible policy regarding visa requirements and employment. Geographical proximity facilitates relatively easy distance supervision of the family, which is especially important for women. The presence of family in Poland, or even Polish roots, not to mention knowledge of the language and traditions, frequently act as mediating stimuli for migration to that country (Volodko 2007: 684). Relatively low wages and unanticipated difficulties with visa requirements, however, can present serious problems for some migrant laborers in Poland.

According to the 2001 census conducted in Greece, a country in the southern tier of Europe to which migrants gravitate, there were 13,616 Ukrainians (1.78 percent of the total number of migrant laborers), constituting one of the top ten groups of non-Greeks living there (Triandafyllidou and Maraoufof 2008: 3). Women represent over 70 percent of overall migrant labor (Baldwin-Edwards 2004). By 2008, 17,456 (4.04 percent) Ukrainians had become legal residents of Greece (Triandafyllidou and Maroufof 2008: 3). Various sources place Ukrainians living in Greece at 20,000 to 80,000 (Rovenchak and Volodko 2010; Markov 2009: 29). It is one of the countries in which Ukrainian female migrants clearly dominate. Of the total number of Ukrainians working in Greece, two-thirds are women (Baldwin-Edwards 2004). The largest segment (80 percent) hails from western Ukraine and settles primarily in Athens (Markov 2009: 30), with most (60 percent) engaged in domestic work, caring for the elderly and children, or doing housework. Women also find job opportunities in the tourist sector, agriculture, and manufacturing.

The peak years of Ukrainian emigration to Greece were the mid-1990s to 2000. Today that number has decreased substantially owing to the economic crisis which became apparent in Greece well before it surfaced as a global predicament—as evidenced by wage cuts and the reduction of employment opportunities. One of the negatives of working in Greece is the women's fear of falling victim to the sex industry (Rovenchak and Volodko 2010). Additional disincentives include the substantial monetary outlay or "seed money"—for the cost of a visa, airline ticket, etc., required to launch the migration process, geographical distance, unfamiliar cultural conventions, and a language barrier. On a more positive note, the attraction of Greece, true of other Southern European and Western European countries as well, lies in the substantially higher wages than those in Central Europe.

During the years 2008–2010 a total of 103 half-structured interviews were conducted with female migrant laborers who have worked in Poland[4] or Greece. The snowball method was applied to the search for respondents. Interviews were conducted in Poland (Warsaw), Greece (Athens), and Ukraine, primarily in the towns and villages of Lviv Oblast (region). The dominant group of respondents was born in the 1950s, 1960s, and 1970s; as for education, secondary vocational training predominated. The majority of female respondents came from western Ukraine, especially Lviv Oblast. Most respondents were married, sometimes more than once, or divorced with one or two children. While working abroad, most were employed in the domestic sector, caring for children and the elderly, or as domestic help.

## Role of Homemaker

To repeat, respondents agreed that the woman is the "proper" person to take on the housekeeping role. They justified this position in biological terms (nature made it that way), custom (it has always been thus), or simply treated it as self-evident. As the respondents thought more about the question during the interview, however, most began to express doubts as to whether domestic obligations should fall exclusively upon women. They argued that in the past, or in the village today, such a distribution might have made/makes sense, but when the family lives in the city the division of labor into male and female spheres of domestic labor becomes more complex.[5] "When one lives in a village, in each household it is natural for the woman to assume all housekeeping duties while the man takes care of the farm. When it comes to city life, I can see no so-called men's work, except in the professions" (M. IP19).[6] The women did suggest that it would be a good thing if men were to assume a more active domestic role. None of the female respondents indicated that men might assume the entire burden (a concept that women evaluated in negative terms), they merely stressed the husband's help. In other words women should function as the principal homemakers (traditional model) or as mostly homemakers, with active male assistance insofar as the ambivalent model exhibits no clear-cut division of labor into male and female. Meanwhile, as the women thought more about it most were prepared to rethink the assimilated models of gendered domestic duties, and the need for the greater involvement of men. Ultimately, most demonstrated ambivalent feelings regarding the main actor in the role or, somewhat more rarely, traditional beliefs.

## Premigration Period

The first-hand family experience of respondents is more varied. All women interviewed fell into the category of homemaker. Only the emphases differed. We will begin by examining the status of married women. In the problematic families,[7] found among female migrants with experience of work in Poland or Greece, where one might frequently discern a blend of traditional role practices and an occasional innovative thinking component. This model was characterized by the fact that all, or nearly all, domestic obligations fell upon the women, who were unhappy about this but acceded to its seeming inevitability: "What was I to do?" or "There was no way out." Women continued to perform their customary domestic obligations, although they would have preferred greater male involvement. The most prevalent model combined traditional thinking with some innovative practices. Although women were the basic traditional labor force here, contrary to the first model, their husbands did share in some of the domestic duties. Men occupied themselves primarily with traditionally male tasks, and only occasionally performed "women's" domestic work. Women valued male help, something that might have motivated their reflections on the primary responsibility for domestic duties. The dynamic of men's participation in household obligations during the premigratory period often differed in accordance with the various stages of family life. On the whole it fluctuated between total avoidance and partial engagement. Young and older couples tended to live with one or the other set of parents in expanded households. Parental participation in domestic functions represented the standard division of labor model: the mother-in-law performed the customary women's tasks, and the father-in-law was engaged in typical men's undertakings.

The situation differed in incomplete families. In the absence of a man, the woman was expected to perform all or nearly all domestic duties. Here, the presence of parents (less frequently other family members) was extremely important. Mothers of divorced respondents provided essential assistance in household duties, and at times assumed the entire burden. It is worth mentioning that inasmuch as such work was universally considered the women's responsibility, respondents from incomplete families evinced no discomfort over the absence of male help. In many families children played an important part in the household routine, daughters especially provided substantial assistance, particularly in incomplete families. In exceptional circumstances, such as a household consisting of a mother and two sons, it was customary for the mother to perform all domestic tasks.

## Migration Period

Women's labor migration gave rise to various forms of transnational families, with wives heading for Poland or Greece while, as a rule, the rest of the family remained in Ukraine. According to the interviewees, the role of homemaker then assumed new dimensions. Employed in the domestic sector, migrant women tended to perform many of the same kinds of tasks that they had carried out at home, only now they received remuneration for their efforts. At the same time, telephones made it possible for them to continue exercising their control over the household operations in the homeland. These practices were at once innovative and traditional—traditional because women retained responsibility for and control over the domestic sphere, and innovative by virtue of the fact that control was now being exercised from a distance. Such transformations were more distinctive to women working in Poland than in Greece for several reasons. Geography played an important role because labor migrants in Poland were able to make more frequent visits to Ukraine and maintain thereby closer scrutiny over the family: "I have to look after everything, be it hoeing the garden, harvesting radishes, or banking potatoes—everything that needs doing. What can I do, it is all on my shoulders? I must be aware of every-thing, think about everything" (O. IP14).

Gendered division of household labor models in fully formed nuclear or extended Ukrainian families can differ depending on whether they apply to the pre- or postmigration period. An example of an ambivalent reconfiguration, which assumes relatively greater male participation in domestic duties following a period of female labor migration is M's experience (M. IP6): "It seems to me that he has changed. Since I left he has been obliged to assume many more responsibilities." Naturally not every man takes on these duties; some avoid them altogether, as the next interview attests (O. IP4): "Vegetable rows are overgrown with weeds and wolves have been sighted there, but they say they have no time; my husband goes drinking with his buddies, or to football games.... When my daughter gets after him he might help a little."

The traditional reconfiguration of household roles applies often enough, although not as often as the ambivalent one, so the basic domestic duties continue to fall upon the women (daughters, sisters, grandmothers) in migrant families. "Basically, my daughter does the cooking and takes care of the household. I left her when she was seventeen years old with the entire household burden. Naturally, this was very hard on her" (D. IG4). More than a hundred interviews contained evidence of only a few partially innovative reconfigurations of the homemaker role. The experience of N (IP3) conforms to this model. Her husband lives with his elementary school-age son in Ukraine. "He has been with this child since his birth.... Performs all of the traditionally women's jobs." As we see, in this instance the husband voluntarily assumed the entire domestic responsibilities, including child care, during N's absence, yet she continues to reinforce her conviction that the role properly belongs to the woman.

In incomplete families the fundamental domestic burden tends to shift to the children, especially girls, or upon other family members (usually the respondent's mother) in the case of an extended incomplete family. This is a compulsory reconfiguration of the homemaker role in the absence of the husband. An example of a partially innovative reconfiguration of family roles is that of M (IP19), who, following her divorce, almost immediately left to work in Poland. During her absence her former husband lived with the couple's children in Ukraine and looked after them—a son somewhere between 10 and 12 years old, and an 18-year-old daughter: "They cooked together and did some shopping.... I was at peace with the arrangement. There were no unfair divisions of food or clothing." This model is considered a partial innovation for two reasons. First of all, even though the couple was divorced, while the wife was absent the former husband remained with the children. Secondly, he did not merely live in the home, but was fully engaged in its domestic routine.

# Postmigration Period

Temporary visits home by female migrants also illustrate the erratic nature of reconfigurations in the homemaker role. This is particularly apparent in the case of women migrants working in Poland, who come home more frequently and remain for longer periods than those who work in Greece. "Polish" female migrants return and immediately behave like engaged members of the family, assuming fully or in large part the traditional duties of homemaker. As N (IP3), in whose family a partially innovative reconfiguration of the domestic role had already been established, relates: "In my absence my husband takes on all domestic obligations, yet as soon as I return they automatically become mine." Migrant laborers who work in Greece are more likely to behave like guests during their one- or two-month stays in Ukraine. They relax, visit friends, and determine which domestic obligations they are prepared to assume. "I don't really know what I want to do first when I'm in Ukraine. There is so much work, but really I am not interested, I prefer to go out and see things. I like to attend the theater. In fact, my vacation works out very well because I come home for Christmas. It's cold outside, there is no garden to tend, no windows to wash. So I go to the theater" (O. IG20). Every one of the respondents named the man as breadwinner. To validate their position they referred to the public-private dichotomy: "it is right—the wife should stay at home and the husband should earn the money" (O. IG3). As for the woman's place in the context of this arrangement, three areas were identified.

The first was traditional: women belong in the home looking after children and the house while the husband works, although in reality few respondents endorsed such a radical idea, even though most had worked in Greece where they frequently encountered these traditional models and were intrigued by them. From the perspective of their family status, unlike their married counterparts, the majority of women who were either divorced or widowed, without any possibility of changing their roles, were the breadwinners by default. Whether they came from incomplete families or not, the traditional model fascinated them owing to its prospect of relief from the responsibility for the family's material well-being.

The second, ambivalent, was the most prevalent view; it allowed for the wife working outside the home with the proviso that employment must make it possible for a woman to maintain her domestic responsibilities as well. At issue here is family self-realization; the possibility of professional self-improvement or career advancement was not addressed. A more radical version of this second view was that the woman should work outside the home in the interest of interaction with other people, to earn money (at least sufficient for her own needs), and to expand her circle of interests, etc. Migrant women from complete families, whether they worked in Poland or Greece, favored this model.

Finally, the innovative view presented itself in only a few instances. Its advocates were younger women, from complete or complete extended families, with work experience either in Poland or Greece, who argued that each partner should be a wage earner. Alternatively, the role should fall to the one with the most marketable skills. Although such instances were few, they were no less important, representing as they did increasing reflexivity, and changes in role images that are seemingly resistant to transformation. Nonetheless, the male continued to represent the dominant model of optimal achiever and primary breadwinner.

The predominance of Ukrainian women's positive attitude toward professional engagement, although without any special enthusiasm for excelling, began with their participation in manufacture going back to the Soviet era. Professional engagement without any substantial possibilities for career growth was, in its own way, the optimal model that permitted most Soviet women to successfully combine their professional activity and domestic lives, a pattern that continued into the post-Soviet period. It would be most accurate to refer to the prevalence of two-breadwinner families, but where equivalent earning power seldom existed. For this reason, the Ukrainian experience tended to diverge somewhat from a strict adherence to the patriarchal model, even though it was espoused.

One woman said it well: "He provides for the family financially so he should be considered the breadwinner, but what about my contribution? I earn less, to be sure, but I have always worked" (M. IP19). And in another case, even when the wife's earnings were actually higher she did not self-identify as the breadwinner. Demonstrating an internalized conventional model, she explained: "I was employed in a factory on piece work and my finished article determined remuneration. My husband worked as an electrician. His wages were stable, but I brought home more money than he did" (Z. IG21). Her omission might have suggested a preference for a sole- or higher-earning husband. Yet another model combined the two variants operating at different stages of family life, when the primary breadwinners might change roles: "My husband worked at 'Electron' at the time and earned a good salary. Meanwhile, nurses' salaries were so-so; I earned less than he did—that is until I left for Poland" (O. IP9).

In incomplete families the situation was different. As Ia. explained after her husband died: "I had thirty-five rubles and two small children on my hands" (IP7). In 1998 a third child was born. The father was a man with whom she cohabited after her husband died, but they separated when the child was born and he did not contribute anything. In other cases of such extended incomplete families parents might assume almost the entire domestic burden, while the daughter was fully engaged in her professional life and supported the family.

As already indicated, working status was nothing new to Ukrainian women at the point of their migration, but migrant life changed things. Regardless of the composition of the family, and its role distribution, in the final analysis most judged their migrant situation in negative terms. Two kinds of explanations can be extrapolated—objective and declarative. In the first instance female migrants described their circumstances as compulsory and temporary. What they really wished for was to give up their role of breadwinner, to pass it along to someone else (preferably a husband). They tended to be poorly integrated in the host society and, generally speaking, derived little pleasure from living abroad. These respondents also suffered because of the separation from their families (especially those with minor children). All of this prompted a negative assessment of the breadwinner role: "What can I like about this role of breadwinner?" The declarative explanation was more common to those who worked in more distant countries like Greece. Sheer distance made visits home difficult, although adaptation to the receiving country was easier. This, higher wages, and breadwinner status provided a greater measure of satisfaction in working abroad, notwithstanding the doubt as to whether the rewards could outweigh separation from their loved ones.

A small cohort of respondents demonstrated a positive attitude, although they too tended to feel that the role of primary breadwinner properly belonged to men. Those who were more or less freed from family obligations, such as divorced respondents with adult children, and married women with adult children in problematical families were naturally more positive in their assessment of migrant life. For them, a journey to Poland or Greece was more likely to be transformed from a temporary stay to a permanent lifestyle.

Finally, return from abroad ended the breadwinner status for women who chose to stay. Their subsequent public employment (or lack of it) at home depended upon a variety of factors. Age was especially important, as was the presence of dependent family members and needs of the family itself, etc. Regardless of family structure the younger cohort of returning women generally attempted to secure employment in the homeland, even if it meant working at something outside their expertise. Older women did this less frequently. They were able to live on the money earned abroad that at times might be supplemented by additional earnings at home, by their children's financial help (A. IUG6; H. IUP2), or their pension (V. IUG7).

## Conclusion

Relocation abroad signified a spatial and temporal distancing between migrant laborer and family, leading to a reconfiguration of customary family practices. To one extent or another both the migrant and the family members continued to fulfill their assigned homemaking and breadwinning functions regardless of the transnational experience, but these were now likely to come with modifications. The women's monetary remittances and transfer of goods to the sending country changed perceptions about the value of domestic duties. Women from partially formed families tended to favor traditional models of family roles to a greater extent than those from fully formed families, although their responses suggested ambivalence and innovation. This can be explained in part by the fact that these women enjoyed less flexibility in defining traditional family roles, so the male breadwinner model might have appeared more attractive because it was imposed. In sum, whatever the modifications in practice, on the most general level the premigration pattern in the distribution of domestic responsibilities was reestablished in most families upon a migrant's return.

**Viktoriya V. Volodko** holds a Kandydat degree in sociology, and is a coworker at the Monitoring Center, Ivan Franko National University in Lviv. She is currently (2014) a visiting researcher at Humboldt University in Berlin. Her research interests include the impact on familial roles of the Ukrainian women's labor migration to Poland and Greece, and their reemigration to these countries, and they extend to the sociology of migration, the sociology of family, and gender studies.

# Notes

1. Most labor migrants, men or women, are married with children. According to the *Report* (2009: 28), Ukraine's married women labor migrants constituted 51.3 percent of the respondents, 22.2 percent were divorced, and 3.9 percent were widowed. Another survey demonstrated that married men and women were in the majority in this labor migrant category. Divorcees represented the highest proportion of this group; women especially found themselves unable to support their children on their earnings alone (Levchenko 2006: 9).
2. Research was conducted by the Center of Social Expertise Institute of Sociology, Ukrainian Academy of Sciences in five regions (Lviv, Donetsk, Kyiv, Zhytomyr, Odessa), the Autonomous Republic of Crimea, and the city of Kyiv in 2006. The survey sample consisted of 1784 persons, representing the adult population of Ukraine according to sex, age, education, and type of settlement. Also included are interviews with experts, plus content analyses of assorted media publications (Amadzhadin 2007: 68).
3. Family roles are variants of social roles.
4. Research work in Poland was supported by the International Visegrad Foundation.
5. According to the respondents domestic duties are divided into men's work, requiring greater physical strength, and women's less strenuous household tasks.
6. The chapter draws upon 103 interviews that, depending upon the respondent's country of origin, are designated as follows: IP—interviews taken in Poland;

IUP—interviews originated in Ukraine, and respondents' experience in Poland; IG—interviews in Greece; IUG—interviews originated in Ukraine, and included respondents' experience in Greece. Numbers preceded by an initial indicate its position in the interview series. The name of the woman is designated by the first initial of her name.

7. Problematic families are those that experience various forms of violence (physical, psychological, economic, etc.) or other forms of unacceptable deviations from the expected norms of behavior among family members.

# Bibliography

Alicea, Marixca. 1997. "A chambered nautilus: The contradictory nature of Puerto Rican women's role in the social construction of a transnational community." *Gender and Society* 11(5): 597–626.

Amadzhadin, Lidia. 2007. "Transformational changes in the institution of marriage and family in Ukrainian society. Gender-based analysis," *Sociology: Theory, Methodology, and Marketing*, 3: 60–75.

Anderson, Bridget. 2000. *Doing the Dirty Work? The Global Politics of Domestic Labour,* vol VII. London and New York: Zed Books.

Babenko, Svetlana. 2004. "Sotsial'ny mechanism post-Sovietskoi transformatsiyi deiatel'nostno-strukturny podkhod," in *Postkommunisticheskiie Transformatsiyi: Vektory, Napravleniia, soderzhaniie,* ed. Olha Kutsenko. Kharkiv: V. N. Karazin National University, 251–274.

Baldwin-Edwards, Martin. 2004. "Immigration into Greece, 1990–2003: A Southern European paradigm?" Presentation on "International migration: Promoting, management and integration," *European Population Forum,* Geneva (12–14 January). www.unece.org/pau/_docs/pau/2004/PAU_2004_EPF_Sess4PresnBaldwinEdwards.pdf.

Boiko, Evheniy, ed. 2009. *Sotsial'no-ekonomichni Problemy Suchasnoho Periodu Ukrainy. Mihratsiini Protsesy v Umovakh Poli-etnichnoho Seredovyscha Regionu: Zbirnyk Naukovykh Prats.* Lviv: Institute of Regional Research, Ukrainian Academy of Sciences.

———. 2010. "Migratory processes in Europe," in *Socio-Economic Problems of Contemporary Ukraine. Regional Peculiarities in Labor Organization during a Systemic Crisis. Collection of Scholarly Works).* Lviv: Institute of Regional Research, Ukrainian Academy of Sciences; 4: 84, 480.

Chumalo, Marta. 2005. "Ukrainski zhinky na zarobitkakh v Italiyi," in *Ukrainska Trudova Mihratsiia v Konteksti Zmin v Suchasnomu Sviti,* ed. Ihor Markov. Lviv: Lviv Manuscript Company, 78–89.

Cvajner, Martina. 2007. "Migrating Sexualities, Migration Romances," *First Global Conference, Salzburg* (27–29 March). http://www.inter-disciplinary.net/probing-the-boundaries/persons/persons-intimacy-and-love/project-archives/1st/session-4b-intimate-space-intimate-geographies/.

Dickinson, Jennifer A. 2005. "Gender, work and economic restructuring in a Transcarpathian (Ukraine) village," *Nationalities Papers,* Special issue: Identity Formation and Social Problems in Estonia, Ukraine and Uzbekistan, guided by J. A. Dickinson and O. Malanchuk. 33(3): 387–401.

Drago, Robert, David Black, and Mark Wooden. 2005. "Female breadwinner families: Their existence, persistence and sources," *Journal of Sociology* 41(4): 343–362.

Fediuk, Olena. 2006. "Ukrainian labour migrants: Visibility through stereotypes," *Multicultural Centre of Prague*. http://aa.ecn.cz/img_upload/3bfc4ddc48d13ae 0415c78ceae108bf5/OFeduyk_Ukrainian_Labour_Migrants_1.pdf.

———. 2009. "Death in the life of Ukrainian labor migrants in Italy," *Multicultural Centre of Prague*. http://www.migrationonline.cz/e-library/?x=2162690.

Giddens, Anthony. 2003. *Ustroienie Obshchestva: Ocherk Teoriyi Structuratsiyi* (The Constitution of Society: Outline of the Theory of Structuration). Moscow: Academic Project.

Górny, Agata, and Ewa Kępmińska. 2005. "Life between two countries: The case of Polish–Ukrainian marriages," in *International Migration: A Multidimensional Analysis*, ed. Krystyna Slany. Cracow: AGN (Akademia Górniczo-Hutnicza) University of Science and Technology Press, 155–187.

———. 2005. "Małżeństwa mieszane w migracji z Ukrainy do Polski," *Przegląnd Połoniiny. Quarterly* 3(117): 59–75.

Gribich, Carol. 1994. "Women as primary breadwinners in families where men are primary caregivers," *Journal of Sociology* 30(2): 105–118.

Grzymała-Kazłowska, Aleksandra, ed. 2008. *Między jednością a wielością. Integracija odmiennych grup i kategorii imigrantów w Polsce*. Warsaw: OBM (Osrodek Badan nad Migracjami), ZWP (Zaklad Wydawnicho-Poligraficzny) MPiPS (Ministerstwo Pracy i Polityki Spoleczney.

Holovakha, Evhen, and Nataliya Panina. 2008. *Ukrainske Suspil'stvo 1992, 2008. Sotsiolohichny Monitoryng*. Kyiv: Institute of Sociology, Ukrainian Academy of Sciences.

Haidinger, Bettina. 2009. "Contingencies among households: gendered division of labour and transnational household organization: The case of Ukrainians in Austria," in *Migration and Domestic Work: A European Perspective on a Global Theme*, ed. Helma Lutz. Padstow, Cornwall: Ashgate, 127–142.

Iglitska, Krystyna, ed. 2003. *Migration and Labour Markets in Poland and Ukraine*. Warsaw: Institute of Public Affairs.

Kacharaba, Stepan. 2003. *Emihratsiia z Zakhidnoi Ukrainy* (1919–1939). Lviv: Ivan Franko National University.

Katolyk, Halyna. 2005. "Z dosvidu psykhoperopavtychnoi roboty z dit'my trudovykh emihrantiv," in *Ukrainska Trudova Mihratsiia v Konteksti Zmin Suchasnoho Svitu*, ed. Ihor Markov. Lviv: Manuscript Company, 179–181.

Keryk, Myroslava. 2004. "Labour migrant: Our savior or betrayer? Ukrainian discussion concerning labour migration," *Multicultural Centre of Prague*. http://www .migrationonline.cz/article_f.shtml?x=200479.

Kindler, Marta. 2005. "Irregular migration in Central and Eastern Europe: the case of Ukrainian workers in Poland," paper presented at the *Conference on Irregular Migration: Research, Policy and Practice*, Oxford (7–8 July).

———. 2009. "Risk and risk strategies in migration: Ukrainian domestic workers in Poland," in *Migration and Domestic Work: A European Perspective On a Global Theme*, ed. Helma Lutz. Padstow, Cornwall: Ashgate, 145–159.

———. 2012. *A Risky Business? Ukrainian Migrant Women in Warsaw's Domestic Work Sector*. Amsterdam: Amsterdam University Press.

Klimov, Ivan. 2000. "Sociological conception of Anthony Giddens," *Sociological Journal* 1–2. www.nir.ru/socio/scipubl/sj/sj1-2-00klim.html.

Konechna, Joanna. 2005. "Ishly na Zakhid ... 'Pro mihratsiini pliany Ukraintsiv,'" in *Ukrainska Trudova Mihratsiia u Konteksti Zmin Suchasnoho Svitu*, ed. Ihor Markov. L'viv: Manuscript Company, 126–138.

Kovalchuk, Liudmyla. 2008. "Children of labour migrants," *Sotsial'ny Pedahoh* 3(15): 56–59.

Levchenko, Kateryna, ed. 2006. "Problemy Ditei Trudovykh Mihrantiv," *Analiza Situatsiyi*. Kyiv TOB (Association of Limited Responsibility). Agenstvo Ukraina.

Levitt, Peggy, and Ninna Sørensen. 2004. "The transnational turn in migration studies," *Global Migration Perspective* 6. http://www.gcim.org/gmp/Global%20Migration%20Perspectives%20No%206.pdf.

Malynovska, Olena. 2005. "Trudova mihratsiia z Ukrainy za danymy doslidzhen' 1994 i 2002 u mistsi Kyievi, m. Chernivtsi ta s. Prylbychi Yiavorivskoho Raionu Lvivskoi Oblasti," in *Trudova Mihratsiia u Konteksti Zmin Suchasnoho Svitu*, ed. Ihor Markov. Lviv: Manuscript Company, 21–86.

Markov, Ihor. 2009. "Ukrainska trudova mihratsiia sotsiolohichno-statystychny portret," in *Na Rozdorizhzhi. Analitychni Materialy Kompleksnoho Doslidzhennia*, ed. Ihor Markov. Lviv: Karitas, 21–86.

*Migratory Processes in Europe: Evolution of the Migratory Interactions of the EU and Central and Eastern European Countries*. 2010. Brochure of abstracts of conference participants, Odessa.

Novytska, Valentyna. 2005. "Sotsial'no-roliovy obraz zhinky ta cholovika u suchasnomu Ukrainskomu suspil'stvi," in *Sotsial'ni vymiry Suspil'stva*. Kyiv: Institute of Sociology, National Academy of Sciences, 277–286.

Parreñas, Rhacel Salazar. 2005. *Children of Global Migration: Transnational Families and Gendered Woes*, vol. XI. Stanford, CA: Stanford University Press.

Pirozhkov, Sergey, Aleksandr Homra, and Elena Malinovskaya. 2003. *Foreign Labour Migration in Ukraine: Socio-Economic Aspect*. Kyiv: NISC (National Institute of International Security Challenges).

Pirozhkov, Sergey, Olena Malynovska, and Nina Marchenko. 1997. *Zovnishna mihratsiia v Ukraini: prychyny, naslidky, stratehiyi*. Kyiv: Academpress.

Prybytkova, Iryna. 2002a. "Trudovi mihranty u sotsial'nii iierarkhiyi Ukrainskoho suspil'stva. Statusni pozytsiyi, tsinnosti, zhytievi stratehiyi, styl', I sposib zhyttia," *Sotsiolohiia, teoriia, metody, marketyng* 4: 156–167.

———. 2002b. "Trudovi migranty v Ukrainskom Obshchestve," *Metodolohiia, Teoriia, ta Praktyka Sotsiolohichnoho Analizu Suchasnoho Suspil'stva: Zbirnyk Naukovykh Prats'*. Kharkiv: Karazin Natsional'ny Universytet, 363–370.

———. 2003. "Trudovi mihranty u sotsial'nii iierarkhiyi Ukrainskoho suspil'stva. Statusni pozytsiyi, tsinnosti, zhytievi stratehiyi, styl', I sposib zhyttia," *Sotsiolohiia, teoriia, metody, marketyng* 1: 109–124.

Riul Victoria. 2010. "Zhyttievi trudnoshchi iak mechanism hal'muvannia sotsializatsiyi ditei transkordonnykh trudovykh mihrantiv (na prykladi Zakarpats'koi oblasti)," *Sotsial'na Psykholohiia* 1: 142-151.

Rovenchak, Ol'ha, and Viktoriya Volodko. 2010. "Ukrainian labor migration to Greece (gender aspect)," *Western Analytical Group*. http://www.zgroup.com.ua/article.php?articleid=3491.

Shulha, Nikolai. 2002. *Velikoie Pereselenie. Repatrianty, Bezhentsy, Trudovyie migranty*. Kyiv: Institute of Sociology, Ukrainian Academy of Sciences.

Solari, Cinzia. 2010. "Resource drain vs. constitutive circularity: Comparing the gendered effects of post-Soviet migration patterns in Ukraine," *Anthropology of East Europe Review* 28(1): 215–238.

Sydorenko, Ol'ha. 2005. "Do pytannia pro Tsinu za identychnist'," *Ukrainska Trudova Mihratsiia v Konteksti Zmin Suchasnoho Svitu.* Ed. Ihor Markov. Lviv: Manuscript Company, 67–71.

Sylina, Tetiana. 2008. "Na rikakh Vavylonskykh," *Dzerkalo Tyzhnia.* (December 20). Available at http://www.dt.ua/newspaper/articles/55766#article.

Sysak, Victor. 2002. "Ukrainski hostiovi robitnyky ta imihranty v Portuhaliyi (1997–2002)," in *Ukraintsi v Suchasnomu Sviti. Konferentsiia Ukrainskykh Vypusnykiv Prohram Naukovoho stazhuvannia u SSH, Yalta, 12–15 Veresnia* (1997–2002). Kyiv: Stylos, 194–207.

Szczepanikova, Alice. 2006. "Migration as gendered and gendering process: A brief overview of the state of art and suggestions for a future direction in migration research," *Multicultural Centre of Prague.* http://www.migrationonline.cz/e-library/?x=1963604.

Tartakovskaya, Irina. 2007. "Gendernaia teoriia kak teoriia praktyk. Podkhod Roberta Konnela," *Sotsiologicheskii Zhurnal* 2: 5–23.

Tolstokorova, Alissa. 2008. "Locally neglected, globally engaged: Ukrainian women on the move," *Technologies of Globalization.* International Conference in Darmstadt, Germany, 30–31 October, 44–61.

———. 2009. "Costs and benefits of labour migration for Ukrainian transnational families: Connection or consumption?" *Circulation Migratoire et Insertions Èconomiques prècaires en Europe*: 12. http://urmis.revues.org/index868.html.

———. 2010. "Where have all the mothers gone? The gendered effect of labour migration and transnationalism on the institution of parenthood in Ukraine," *Anthropology of East Europe Review* 28(1): 184–214.

Triandafyllidou, Anna, and Michaela Maroufof. 2008. "Immigration towards Greece on the eve of the 21st century," *IDEA newsletter* 5: 1–6.

Vianello, Francesca Alice. 2009. Conference paper on "Suspended migrants: Return migration to [the] sic! Ukraine," *Central and Eastern European Sociology Workshop: Social Inequalities and Migration in Post-communist Societies,* Poznań (20–21 September).

UN Human Development Report 2009 *hdr.undp.org/.../human-develo.*

Volodko, Viktoriya. 2007. "Vybir krainy mihratsiyi ta zhyttievi traiektory Ukrainskykh trudovykh mihrantiv (regional'ny aspekt)," in *Visnykk Odeskoho Natsional'noho Universytetu. Sotsiolohiia i Politychni Nauky: Zbirnyk Naukovykh Prats'* 12(6). Odesa: Odesa Mechnilkov National University, 679–686.

Waldinger, Roger. 2008. "Between 'here' and 'here': Immigrants cross-border activities and loyalties," *International Migration Review* 42(1): 3–29.

Warren, Tracey. 2007. "Conceptualizing breadwinning work," *Work, Employment & Society* 21: 317–336.

Yarova, Olha. 2006. "The migration of Ukrainian women to Italy and the impact on their family in Ukraine," in *Migration Processes in Central and Eastern Europe: Unpacking the Diversity,* ed. Alice Szczepanikova et al. Prague: Multicultural Centre of Prague, 38–40.

*Zovnishna Trudova Mihratsiia naselennia Ukrainy. Zvit Red Ukrainsky Tsenter Sotsial'nykh Reform. Derzhavny Komitet Statystyky Ukrainy.* 2009. Kyiv. http://www.openukraine.org/ua/programs/migration/research-program/.

# CHAPTER 9

# Some Peculiarities of Ukrainian Female Migration to Spain

## Galyna Gorodetska

"I think that no one will say 'I regret that I came'—to the interviewer. I am very happy to be here ... misery ate away at me ... however, washing those toilets—five to seven a day—did upset me."

—Woman, age 56, foreman at a Ukrainian plant

At the beginning of the 1990s Ukraine was ranked forty-fifth in the UN Human Development Index (UNDP 1990–2011). A middle class, the basis of any market economy, was a reality but the transition from a planned to a market economy would soon bring undesirable changes. The shift to a market economy, together with a host of ineffective social and economic policies, impoverished millions of Ukrainians. The internal market was disrupted, factories were unable to pay their workers, and massive inflation rapidly wiped out savings, all of which produced severe financial distress for the Ukrainian population. In 2004 only 16 percent of the people recognized themselves as belonging to a middle class, 32 percent considered themselves poor, and 46 percent indicated that they were in the "not well-off" category. A mere 0.6 percent identified as rich or very rich (Chernyshev 2006).

The vagaries of Ukraine's post-Soviet period of transition generated a severe crisis in the country. To begin with, reform of the Ukrainian economy was dictated by a structural reconstruction of production that produced significant inflation (Libanova 2009). New labor market conditions resulted in a decline in real wages and payment delays. Between 1990 and 1996, the mean income in the country fell dramatically as funds earmarked for social transfers and public assistance, formerly sent from what was once the center of the USSR, dried up, forcing Ukrainians to look for support elsewhere. Private households had little choice but to pick up the slack, even as their expenditure for food almost doubled, causing outlays for nonperishable goods to fall by half, and savings to drop to negative values (Libanova 2009).

During the decade 1990–2000 the unemployment figure rose by 20 percent, or 5.2 million, forcing many Ukrainians to look for alternative means of survival. Hardest hit were the rural areas, with fewer opportunities and a high degree of employment insecurity. By 2009 more than 67 percent of the rural population was making a living in the informal sector of the economy. This meant exclusion from any type of social security and lack of protection under the existing labor laws. Low salaries and unpaid or partially paid wages added to the people's overall poverty and distress even among the employed (Libanova 2009). During the period of hyperinflation in 1992–1994, real wages fell three times. Administrative leave, affecting 43 percent of those still working in 1993, exacerbated this grim picture. As late as 2004 approximately one-quarter of the population lived below the poverty line, with 16 percent of the workers earning less than US $2 a day (Chernyshev 2006). By 2005 this figure had risen to 27.1 percent, while 50.8 percent of the working population earned less than a minimum wage. Poverty impacted both the employed and the unemployed (UNDP 2006: 2–3).

## The Role of Migrant Labor

Under these conditions it is scarcely surprising that emigration increasingly presented itself as a solution for large numbers of people, although an exact figure is virtually impossible to ascertain—large gaps exist in the data provided by different scholars. Based on the numbers of the World Bank and a report provided by Agnieszka Kubal (2012: 4–5), an estimated 6.5 million Ukrainians, or 14 percent of the total population of the country, now reside and work abroad. Franck Düvell (2006) argues that the number of Ukrainians involved in the foreign labor market is closer to seven million. He calls Ukraine "Europe's Mexico" since it is one of the biggest suppliers of irregular labor migrants to Europe. For her part, Olena Malynovska (2007) refutes these statistics, and argues that incomplete statistics amount to unreliable data. This kind of information, she insists, yields many fables about migration flows from and through Ukraine. To support her position she offers examples from parliamentary hearings where the Ministry of Labor and Social Policy estimated the Ukrainian labor migration at up to 3 million, while the International Labor Organization placed this number at 2.3–2.7 million. This involved not only Ukrainians who have worked abroad for many years, but seasonal workers and frontier migrants as well (2007: 76).

The first Ukrainian migration experience dates to the beginning of the 1990s, with petty and shuttle trading inaugurating the process. Purchases of low-cost goods in countries such as Poland, Hungary, Turkey, and China were sold in Ukraine at modest prices. Longer-term labor migration of large numbers of people to countries such as Russia, Italy, the

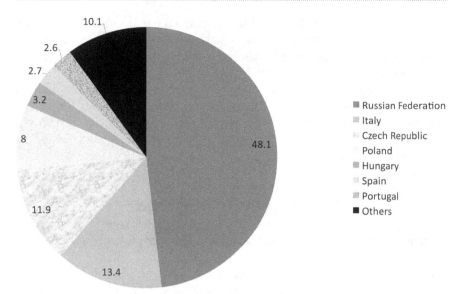

**Figure 9.1.** *Main countries of destination for Ukrainian labor migrants. Source: Geyets 2009: 219.*

Czech Republic, Poland, Hungary, Spain, and Portugal followed in the late 1990s (Geyets 2009). The World Bank estimated that remittances of US $829,000 by 2006, $4.503 million in 2007, and $5 billion in 2008 flowed into the Ukrainian economy (Vollmer et al. 2010), and Malynovska (2007) speculates that the estimated number of remittances might have reached $6–7 billion. That is almost commensurate with the direct foreign investments in Ukraine in 2006. The majority of Ukrainian labor migrants, 7.9 percent, come from rural areas, with only 4 percent migrating from the cities (Malynovska 2011; Libanova 2009). This is explained by fewer employment opportunities, and a higher poverty level in the countryside.

Currently, the largest concentration of migrant workers are those aged 20 to 49. Men tend to reduce their migration activity by age 50, while women continue into their retirement years. Ukrainians working in neighboring countries prefer short stays, with regular returns to the homeland, whereas those finding employment in the southern tier of Europe, in countries such as Spain and Portugal, are likely to remain for much longer periods (Libanova 2009).

## Methodology

Although Ukrainian labor migrants travel to many different countries, this chapter concentrates on those working in Spain, particularly in the

Basque Country. In-depth interviews provided the main source of research data. Using the "snowball or chain sampling" principle—a non-probability method relying on referrals from the first respondents to recruit Ukrainian migrants for research purposes. Respondents, twenty-three in all, were sought out in places where they congregate, such as "Russian shops" (selling items from countries of the former Socialist Bloc), the Ukrainian church, or sites where clusters of migrants meet to dispatch parcels to Ukraine; a chance meeting on a public street also yielded an occasional interviewee.

## Characteristics of Respondents

Female labor migrants in Spain outnumber the men; they comprise a total of 47,674 workers, or 55 percent of the labor pool, while men number 38,642 workers, or 45 percent (Instituto Nacional de Estadística [INE]). My respondents constituted a cohort of 20–64 year olds. According to information from the National Institute of Statistics in Spain (INE), the most significant age group of Ukrainian women migrants falls into the 20- to 34-year-old category, or 43 percent; the second largest group is the 35- to 49-year-old cohort, or 37 percent, and the smallest group is in the immediate retirement age category of 50–64, or 20 percent. This means that 80 percent of the female migrants fall into the 20- to 49-year-old cohort.

The presence of family members in the host country also acts as a significant draw. Relatives can assist with housing, or contribute to the earnings that hasten a return to the home country, but fewer than half of the respondents indicated that they live with family members. Every third female migrant worker lives in Spain with her husband, while the children stay behind in Ukraine (usually in the care of a female relative such as a grandmother), and a quarter reside in Spain alone.

One of the most compelling aspects of migrant life in the receiving country is the issue of official status—regular or irregular. Regular status permits migrants to participate openly in the host society; this can lead to better employment, accommodation, health care, etc. Irregular migrants are in a precarious situation, and are therefore more likely to accept any job offer even if it pays only minimum wage or below, with few or no benefits (health insurance, pensions). Employment is often only part-time or seasonal, and not infrequently obliges migrants to work at several jobs simultaneously in order to support their families (Creticos et al. 2006). Apart from the absence of benefits enjoyed by those living openly in the mainstream, even more important is the illegal migrant's permanent fear of discovery and deportation (Rubio-Marín 2000). The majority of the research participants indicated that they enjoy regular status in Spain, while one in five lives precariously under irregular conditions.

> If I had possessed legal documents at the time I might have found something better. My friends with documents worked as waitresses in restaurants and bars and earned twice as much. When I finally found work in a bar I earned 250 EU for handling the desk, serving customers, relieving the cook, and cleaning tables. The salary was only half of what I might have earned if I had papers but I was happy because, as you know, unregistered workers are forced to accept any job offer. (Woman, age 38, ten years in Spain).

Education is valuable migrant capital. According to Olympia Bover and Pilar Velilla (2005), as a rule people who elect to migrate tend to have a higher education. They are often looking for professional advancement and a higher standard of living, and this makes them most open to a migration challenge. Alejandro Portes (1998) argues further that people with some resources, such as small rural proprietors, skilled workers, and urban artisans are among the first to consider migrating. Statistically, more than half the respondents are university graduates. Every four of five interviewees indicated that they have had some professional training, and only a tenth had not proceeded beyond a secondary education.

## What Influences Labor Migration

Whatever other factors might have motivated their migration, the majority emphasized financial need to meet such obligations as, for instance, supporting a family as a primary inducement in their decision to migrate. Others indicated that a breakdown in the family structure placed the responsibility of breadwinner, normally the man's role, on the woman. Still others listed the impossibility of repaying accumulated debts under the current economic circumstance in Ukraine as a cause. A smaller number indicated that the existence of an acquaintance(s) provided the incentive to choose Spain as their country of destination, with many of these declaring that without such contacts they would not have considered leaving their homeland.

Three categories of the respondents were among those who were either unemployed or underemployed. The search for a decent standard of living drove the resolve of many to leave the homeland for a foreign country such as Spain. The final cohort consists of three groups—those to whom Spain appealed most as a host country, individuals with a desire to live abroad, or those seeking reunification with family members already living in the country of their proposed destination. In sum, although financial incentives headed the list of motives for migrating abroad, it is plain to see that other considerations also had a role to play.

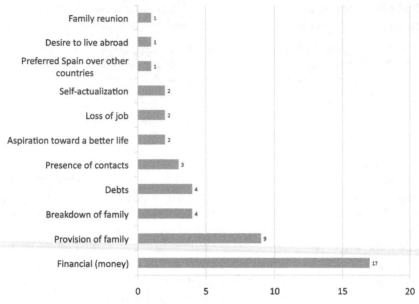

**Figure 9.2.** *Women's incentives to migrate in search of work*

## Migrant Women's Occupation in Spain

More than a half of the migrant Ukrainian women work in Spain's cleaning sector. Another large cohort (almost a fifth of the participants) is concentrated in the food industry. Equal numbers (approximately 10 percent in each of three groups) are proprietors of their own businesses, are employed as domestics, or are among the unemployed. One-quarter of the migrants interviewed specified that they began working as domestics. Almost every tenth respondent was employed in the hotel industry, and another tenth worked in bars. Three women indicated that they worked as caregivers to the elderly, and one found employment in a factory. The largest group, or four of every ten interviewees, worked in the cleaning sector. New contacts and a broadened social network act as limited sources of opportunity for improvement, but upward mobility of any consequence, while possible, is rare.

A survey of the female workers' professional qualifications indicated that every third one has trained in economics, and another third are pedagogues. Others have medical backgrounds, and four of them said that they had been trained in fields such as metal working, mining, construction, etc. The remaining tenth or so are those with a secondary education who appear to have come out of some type of factory work. How well the prior education, training, and experience of these workers coincides with their employment patterns in the host country will be examined in the next segment.

In a comparative study of the career paths between women in the home country and those in the host countries one difference stands out. According to Anthony Heath and Yaojun Li (2008), although migrants are disadvantaged upon arrival in the receiving country, after a time they begin to improve their position. They learn the language, start to understand recruitment rules and work practices, acquire work experience and new skills, and their integration proceeds to one degree or another. Barry Chiswick (2005) takes this a step further. He has developed a U-shaped model of professional attainment to demonstrate that after the initial downward social and professional spiral immigrants with the proper qualifications and drive are capable of rising to the same professional level that they enjoyed in the home country (2005; Chiswick, Lee, and Miller 2005). To help in determining if any real improvement could be found in the professional position of migrants, respondents were queried about the after effects of their first job. Responses indicated no significant upward mobility.

Women who commenced their labor history in the receiving country with domestic work insisted that the most important move for them was not professional advancement, but rather relocation from internal to external (not live-in) work. Such a transfer required some proficiency in the Spanish language, and an ability to negotiate the social network, thereby increasing the prospects for locating new employment, securing more desirable living accommodations, and an altered way of life. Many women described the time of their live-in experiences as a most difficult period of adjustment not only because it meant living in their employer's household, but also pointed to the overall control that this entailed, the lack of free time, large workloads, and discrimination; these were all likened to penal servitude: "I worked as a live-in employee, and it was like penal servitude; we worked like slaves from the moment the alarm rang till late at night" (woman, age 59, nine years in Spain). This internal occupation did have its own reward, however. For one, it offered a less challenging entry into the labor market. Without a command of the Spanish language women had few employment options. Once their language proficiency had improved, however, they were able to leave their "internal" positions for the coveted "external" occupations, even if such a move might have precluded upward mobility.

## The Informal Economy and Migrant Self-Employment

The competitive advantage of the small Spanish business economy, which absorbs a large share of the migrant population, is based upon the cheap labor concentrated in particular sectors and industries, all of which tend to the segmentation of the labor market (Bernardi, Garrido, and Miyar 2011). At the same time it must be recognized that migrants are not the only ones engaged in such sectors. Spanish citizens are also known to participate in the irregular market (Maroukis, Iglicka, and Gmaj 2011). In 1999–2007 Spain's shadow economy was estimated at 22–23 percent of GDP (Schneider, Buehn, and Montenegro 2010). In 2009 it fell to 19.5 percent (Schneider 2010). To quote Portes (1998: 29): "The informal economy is defined as the sum total of income-earning activities that are unregulated by legal codes in an environment where similar activities are so regulated. Informal activities are distinguished from criminal ones in that they encompass goods and services that are legal, but whose production and marketing is unregulated."

Portes (1998) relates immigrant overrepresentation in informal activities to a close relationship with their dominant numbers in small entrepreneurship. For many it is a way to survive in a new social setting; for others it might be the path to rapid economic advancement. The migrant labor force is also segmented by gender: men are mostly employed in agriculture and construction while women work in the domestic sector, or in the service industry. The autochthonal population has not traditionally been overly attracted to these occupations, owing to their substandard environment: they are dirty, noisy, dangerous, and sometimes located in hazardous surroundings. The migrants who work there often encounter abusive and exploitative situations—low wages, poor working conditions, the absence of social protection, restriction of freedom of association and denial of union rights, discrimination, and social exclusion (Froy 2006). Jobs are frequently temporary—a dominant characteristic in countries like Spain, Portugal, and Finland (Corcoran 2006; Froy 2006). As far as earning power is concerned, in their interviews many Ukrainian migrants stipulated that they preferred to be paid by the hour in the hope of improving their wage-earning capacity, although this tended to limit certain other advantages:

> Generally speaking, although I have been working for seven years, but I have a documented service record for only three years and six months. ... Let us suppose that I work ten hours: each day is different ... today I work six hours, tomorrow—six hours, and then—five hours. In total I log forty-five hours, but am registered for only thirty-six. What I earn ... is ready cash with a little extra in the pay envelope. I am neither the first nor the only one. ... Many people work this way. For example, waitresses are registered for half-time, resulting in half a service record; this is no novelty ... everywhere it is the same. (Woman, age 52, eight years in Spain).

And:

I have a friend who lives pretty well in Ukraine, but now there is a crisis there. Several times she has indicated: "I will come, find me a job." My advice to her is to stay where she is. She will not improve her situation by coming here. There, she has her own apartment. Here, the problems are never ending.… Nobody will come from the village to bring you eggs and milk. As for employment—earlier it was possible for migrants to find it more readily; now locals are also seeking it. When these workers advertise their services they specify nationals. Why? Because in the current unemployment environment now even the Spaniards are willing to take the menial jobs [and native status provides an advantage]. (Woman, age 38, ten years in Spain).

As already suggested, migrants often enter the shadow economy market through an established social network. Being involved in the chain migration scheme, Ukrainians rely on the main pillars of this migration pattern—on familism and patronage (Macdonald and Macdonald 1970). Generally speaking, the same networks will tend to channel the new arrivals into the labor niches in which other migrants are already engaged. "I came to Spain because a friend of my mother-in-law lived and worked here and I went directly to her. In Madrid, a woman from Ternopil helped me to find a job, and in San Sebastian another friend helped me" (woman, age 35, thirteen years in Spain).

On a somewhat different employment note, almost one-tenth of the respondents have opened their own business, although, as Aleksandra Ålund (2003) argues, immigrants are not too keen on establishing businesses. High levels of unemployment often oblige them to resort to more creative expedients. Ålund also calls attention to the discrimination in the labor market, and the marginalization of even educated migrants. Self-employment serves as a way out of exclusion and discrimination. Migrant entrepreneurs are shown to be creative and resourceful enough to find new commercial niches to fill. They have built a tangible segment of the economy and have even taken control of certain economic niches thanks to the support of the well-organized "ethnic enclave economies." One of the outstanding examples of this phenomenon is the Russian shop system, catering to recent Russian-speaking arrivals and offering the special merchandise that migrants seek.

To reiterate, it is a truism that migrant workers in the irregular shadow economy often become victims of intolerance. As an example, more than a half of the female migrant workers in Spain reported enduring discrimination. In large measure these are domestic workers; they complained of insufficient food, sexual harassment, discriminatory attitudes, and insults. Pablo Angulo Bárcena (2008) offers an alternative explanation: the main culprit is not discrimination but the informality of the market. Let us consider this: a lack of a contract can result in wage discrimination, unenforced safe working conditions, working over the required norm of hours, etc. All are examples of the conversion of human beings into a cheap and exploitable workforce dependent upon the good will of employers who are generally disinclined to show workers any respect. "Discrimination? In my first job, seven months as an internal [domestic] worker, I never had enough to eat … not even the food that was left over. … They buy a small piece of bread and never offer me what is left.… I was always hungry" (woman, age 34, ten years in Spain).

> There are families with which you can feel comfortable, on their level. They treat you with respect. But there are also those who think that you are from the third world, that you cannot even use a vacuum cleaner. They show you how to dust a picture. It is humiliating because you look at such a person and realize that your education and culture exceeds hers. And then—I worked for a family for a month and a half and the husband hinted at sexual relations—a grandfather of seventy-four, without shame, who suggested: "I'm horny, my wife is sick, but I am still young. I want sex." I looked at him and thought, What do you think that I am, stupid? I said that I couldn't help him." (Woman, age 27, two years in Spain).

## Future Plans

Although female migrants might complain of poor working conditions, lack of labor safeguards, discrimination, and bureaucratic hurdles dealing with the validation of their working papers, they seldom make an attempt to find employment commensurate with their training and experience. Instead, these migrants choose to work at menial jobs in the interest of earning the money needed to build a secure and comfortable future in the homeland as rapidly as possible. The experience of one serves to illustrate:

> I rush from house to house in order to earn more money [respondent works in the cleaning sector]. This way, I can earn more than my Spanish counterpart. For example, if I worked in a store or a shop, I would earn 800 EUR. But I would also have more expenses. Should I decide to live here permanently, I would need to think about an education, better language skills, etc.… but since I plan to return home, I feel no need to improve my working conditions, just as long as I can earn enough money to build a secure future. (Woman, age 41, ten years in Spain).

Research shows that four of every five respondents indicated their intention to return to the homeland, while the remainder contemplate a permanent arrangement in the new country. If a respondent has a family in Spain and its members decide to remain, the choice is relatively clear-cut. These labor migrants become involved in the life of both the home and the host societies. They follow the news in each country and try to analyze the changes. They stay in touch with their family members and friends at home through mobile phones and the Internet, and send back remittances, etc. At the same time they begin to recognize certain nascent changes within themselves, to experience a growing attachment to the receiving country. As one respondent put it: "I'm still in Ukraine psychologically. I grew up there, but I do live in this country and it is impossible for me not to feel that I am a part of its society. Still, I have ties to my homeland, I agonize for its fate, and I would like my children to live there" (woman, age 52, eight years in Spain).

The following demonstrates this state of in-betweenness—being torn between home and host country, being involved in the life of both, and developing a growing attachment to the receiving society:

> I like the way of life in this country although there is really nothing of real significance to bind me to this place. At the same time life is impossible in the homeland. In the unlikely event that the situation normalizes and it becomes feasible to open a business in Ukraine in a way that is possible here ... but then there is the European culture, a way of life to consider ... if only Ukraine had a little of that we would be living there now. How often we have talked about this, dreamed about it. Meanwhile, I have adapted to Spain, and at least I have a job here. (Woman, age 51, five years in Spain).

Migrants often postponed their final decision to undertake that return journey. In choosing to prolong their stay in Spain they knowingly contribute to a greater measure of prosperity for their families left behind (Fakiolas 2003). On a less persuasive note, however, highly skilled migrants occupying inferior positions continued to experience frustration and feelings of inferiority (Froy 2003), all of which lowered their self-esteem and might have strengthened the decision of some to consider a return (Sánchez Urios 2008). The choice was not an easy one: "Upon our arrival in Spain we immediately felt the language deficiency, the lack of money, the feeling that nobody needs us. Everybody smiles, but nobody helps us ... people seem very considerate, civilized, but they lie" (woman, age 52, eight years in Spain).

## Conclusion

Two considerations come to the fore as migrant workers struggle to resolve the dilemma of return: they need to weigh the options of a relatively good income and their ability to continue helping financially those left behind (Fakiolas 2003) against the aggravations of spending their most productive years in dead-end, psychologically unrewarding work leading to low self-esteem (Sánchez Urios 2008). Then there is the reality of the return—however attractive it can appear, reentry might not be as gratifying or as straightforward as one might hope, especially for women.

As we have observed, the majority of Ukrainian women labor migrants are married and most live in the Basque country with family members, or at least with a spouse. However, one-third of the interviewees are either single, divorced, separated, or they live without family members. Although some researchers believe that with time, learning the host language, and achieving greater familiarity with the labor market would enhance the migrant situation, evidence gathered in the Basque country runs to the contrary. This is not to say that upward mobility is impossible, but to achieve any level of advancement migrants need a reasonable degree of proficiency in the Spanish language, a sound knowledge of labor market intricacies, an appreciation of the value of social capital among the locals, motivation, etc. Temporary "inferior" employment can provide a bridge for overcoming handicaps, especially through the daily use of the Spanish language, which is perhaps the most reliable way to enter the mainstream labor market in Spain. When all is said and done, however, each individual must make the most of her/his skills and energy, and apply them to their personal advancement, should that become a goal—all of this in a labor market that relies upon unskilled foreign labor to fill certain gaps, to perform the work that locals shun, a reliance that works against such mobility.

An additional factor impacting upward mobility is the initial expectation on the part of the first generation of migrant workers of a speedy return to the home country. Living this dream, they hope to accumulate enough money in a relatively short period of time to facilitate that return, but as the weeks and months (even years) pass they begin to understand that realization of that rosy dream might take much longer than anticipated. As a result, the migrants gradually become involved, to one extent or another, in the life of the host society. At the same time they continue to maintain close ties with the homeland, the consequence of which is that they begin to live a bifurcated cultural existence. Meanwhile, they are becoming accustomed to the benefits of the higher standard of living in Spain, and their decision to leave the host country can conceivably lead to one postponement after another. The potential for an indefinite stay begins to assume a new meaning. As the possibility of a return home starts to recede it can be argued that upward mobility, whatever route it is destined to take, takes on an unanticipated urgency.

No matter what combination of elements came into play to impact that decision, however, the presence of family members in the receiving country must also not be underestimated. Women who live and work in Spain without family around them to provide support might be less inclined to remain permanently. They work hard to accumulate enough money for a return as quickly as possible, and that objective plays an important part in inhibiting incentives for improving one's employment situation, in striving for upward mobility.

That said, whatever the ultimate choice, most Ukrainian migrants look upon their stay in Spain as a largely positive experience. In the end, the loss of prestige and the frustrations that invariably accompany their employment situation can come to seem like a modest price to pay for the improvement in their standard of living (even if only a temporary one), not to mention the rewards of a brighter future that their accumulated earnings are expected to provide wherever they might choose to settle in the end.

**Galyna Gorodetska** earned her graduate degree at the National University of Kyiv Mohyla Academy and soon thereafter became the deputy head of their International Office. Inspired by her work experience she went on to study International Relations at the Estonian School of Diplomacy, after which she returned to her former studies, this time in pursuit of a doctoral degree with a concentration on the integration of Ukrainian labor migrants in Spain, which she completed at the University of Duesto, Spain. Her contribution to the present collection reflects this focus.

# Bibliography

Angulo Bárcena, Pablo. 2006. "Immigration and Labour Market: Reality and Future Perspectives," in *Immigration: Views and Reflections. Histories, Identities and Keys of Social Intervention,* eds. Rosa Santibáñez and Concepción Maiztegui. Bilbao: University of Deusto Press, 207–224.

Ålund, Aleksandra. 2003. "Self-employment of Non-privileged Groups as Integration Strategy: Ethnic Entrepreneurs and Other Migrants in the Wake of Globalization," *International Review of Sociology* 13(1): 77–87.

Bagnoli, Anna. 2004. "Constructing the hybrid identities of Europeans," in *Resituating Culture,* ed. Gavan Titley Strasbourg: Directorate of Youth and Sport, Council of Europe Publishing, 57–67.

Bernardi, Fabrizio, Luis Garrido, and Maria Miyar. 2011. "The Recent Fast Upsurge of Immigrants in Spain and Their Employment Patterns and Occupational Attainment," *International Migration* 49(1): 148–187.

Bover, Olympia, and Pilar Velilla. 2005. "Migrations in Spain: Historical Background and Current Trends," in *European Migration: What Do We Know?* ed. Klaus F. Zimmermann. Oxford: Oxford University Press, 389–414.

Chernyshev, Igor. 2006. *Socio-economic security and decent work in Ukraine: A comparative view and statistical findings.* Policy Integration Department, Statistical Development and Analysis Group, International Labour Office Geneva. http://www.ilo.org/wcmsp5/groups/public/—-dgreports/—-integration/documents/publication/wcms_079176.pdf.

Chiswick, Barry R., Yew Liang Lee, and Paul W. Miller. 2005. "Immigrant earnings: A Longitudinal Analysis," *Review of Income and Wealth* 51(4): 485–503.

Chiswick, Barry R. 2005. *The Economics of Immigration: Selected Papers of Barry R. Chiswick.* Northampton, MA: Edward Edgar Publishing.

Corcoran, Mary P. 2006. "Local Responses to a New Issue: Integrating Immigrants in Spain," in *From Immigration to Integration: Local Solutions to a Global Challenge,* OECD, 239–823.

Creticos, Peter A., et al. 2006. *The Integration of Immigrants in the Workplace.* Naperville, IL: Institute for Work and the Economy.

Düvell, Franck. 2006. *Ukraine—Europe's Mexico?* Research resource report 1. Oxford: COMPAS. http://www.compas.ox.ac.uk/fileadmin/files/Publications/Research_ projects/Flows_dynamic_s/Transit_migration_Ukraine/Ukraine_Country%20 Report_1of3.pdf

Fakiolas, Rossetos. 2003. "Regularising undocumented immigrants in Greece: Procedures and effects," *Journal of Ethnic and Migration Studies* 29(3): 535–561.

Froy, Francesca. 2006. "From Immigration to Integration: Comparing Local Practices," in *From Immigration to Integration: Local Solutions to a Global Challenge,* OECD, 31–100.

Geyets, Valery, et al., eds. 2009. *Sotsial'no-ekonomichny Stan Ukrainy: Naslidky dlia Narodu Ta Derzhavy. Natsional'na Dopovid'.* Kyiv: NASU. http://www.idss.org.ua/ monografii/nandop1.pdf.

Heath, Anthony, and Yaojun Li. 2008. "Period, Life-Cycle and Generational Effects on Ethnic Minority Success in the British Labour Market," in *Migration und Integration,* ed. F. Kalter. Wiesbaden: \\GWV Fachverlage GmbH, 277–306.

Instituto Nacional de Estadística (INE). www.ine.es.

Kubal, Agnieszka. 2012. *Facts and Fabrications: Experiences of law and Legality among Return Migrants in Ukraine.* Working Papers, Paper 59. Oxford: International Migration Institute, Oxford University. http://www.imi.ox.ac.uk/news/pdfs/ imi-working-papers/wp-59-2012-facts-and-fabrications.

Libanova, Ella, ed. 2009. *Bidnist' ta nerivni mozhlyvostri ditei v Ukraini.* Kyiv: Institute of Demographya and Social Research Institute, Ukrainian Academy of Sciences. Children's Fund UN (UNICEGF), Ukrainian Center for Social Reforms. http:// www.unicef.org/socialpolicy/files/Ukraine_Ukrainian.pdf

Macdonald, J. S., and L. D Macdonald. 1970. "Italian Migration to Australia: Manifest Functions of Bureaucracy Versus Latent Functions of Informal Networks," *Journal of Social History* 3(3): 249–275.

Malynovska, Olena. 2007. "Migration in Ukraine: Challenge or Chance?" *European View* 5(Spring 2007): 71–78. http://www.migrocenter.ru/science/book5 .pdf#page=72.

―――. 2011. *Trudova migratsiia: Sotsial'ni naslidky ta Shliakhy reahuvannia.* Kyiv: National Institute of Strategic Research. http://www.niss.gov.ua/content/articles/ files/Malin_migraziya-dace3.pdf.

Maroukis, Thanos, Krystyna Iglicka, and Katarzyna Gmaj. 2011. "Irregular migration and informal economy in Southern and Central-Eastern Europe: Breaking the vicious cycle," *International Migration* 49(5): 129–156.

Portes, Alejandro, ed. 1998. *The Economic Sociology of Migration: Essays on Networks, Ethnicity, and Entrepreneurship.* New York: Russel Sage Foundation.

Rubio-Marín, Ruth. 2000. *Immigration as a Democratic Challenge: Citizenship and Inclusion in Germany and Unites States.* Cambridge: Cambridge University Press.

Sánchez Urios, Antonia. 2008. "Los Ucranianos Residentes en España en los Procesos de Inserción/Integración: Necesidades, Diferentes Fases del Proyecto Migratorio," *Migraciones* 24: 135–162.

Schneider, Friedrich, Andreas Buehn, and Claudio E. Montenegro. 2010. *Shadow Economies All over the World: New Estimates for 162 Countries from 1999 to 2007.* The World Bank Development Research Group, Poverty and Inequality Team & Europe and Central Asia Region, Human Development Economics Unit. http://www-wds.worldbank.org/external/default/WDSContentServer/IW3P/IB/2010/10/14/000158349_20101014160704/Rendered/PDF/WPS5356.pdf.

Schneider, Friedrich. 2010. *The Shadow Economy in Europe: Using electronic payment systems to combat the shadow economy.* Johannes Kepler University of Linz. http://media.hotnews.ro/media_server1/document-2011-05-8-8602544-0-shadow.pdf.

United Nations Development Program (UNDP). 1990–2011. *Human Development Reports*, New York. http://hdr.undp.org/en/reports/global/hdr2011/.

United Nations Development Program (UNDP) Ukraine. 2006. *Ukraine: Poverty Alleviation*, Kyiv. http://www.undp.org.ua/files/en_24267mdgp.pdf.

Vollmer, Bastian, et al. 2010. *Ukraine: Country and Research Areas Report.* COMPAS and CSR. http://www.eumagine.org/outputs/PP3%20-%20Ukraine%20Country%20and%20Research%20Areas%20Report.pdf.

# CHAPTER 10

# Changes in the Lives of Post-Soviet Women in Lviv Oblast

Halyna Labinska

Lviv Oblast, a region in the westernmost part of Ukraine, boasts the most balanced male/female distribution in the country. It also tends to mirror the prevalent failings of the entire country and as such will serve as a microcosm of the nation for purposes of this study. Apart from its gender balance, Ukraine is a country with significant male/female disparities—in serious illnesses, suicides, and untimely male mortality. These factors offer valuable insights into the reasons for the nation's inability to reproduce itself at the present time. The aim of this piece is to examine in some detail some of the causes of the current catastrophic population decline.

## Demographic Changes

On 1 January 2010 female residents in Lviv Oblast (region) numbered 1.34 million, constituting 53 percent of the region's entire population. Males predominated up to the age of 45, only to be overtaken in their numbers by women in the 40–49 age group. Cities draw inhabitants by offering more attractive employment opportunities, greater potential for self-realization, and access to education, leisure, medical, and other social services. Women comprise 61 percent of the urban population in Lviv Oblast, up from 59.6 percent in 2005. This includes an invisible population of peasant women who, for a variety of reasons, are unable to adapt to urban life. For one, surveys indicate that their insufficient purchasing power compels women to grow much of their own food, leaving them little time or energy for personal growth, career advancement, or participation in mainstream politics.

Responding to the catastrophic decline in Ukraine's birth rate, state payments to women in post-Soviet Ukraine designed to stimulate their reproductive activity helped to slow demographic decline, but by 2010 the stimulus was yielding diminishing returns. Not surprisingly, researchers concluded that such expedients would continue to have only a temporary effect, roughly two years, before the situation returned to its former regressive state. That is why in March 2011 the parliament (*Verkhovna Rada*) voted for a periodic increase in the stimulus.

Currently, the death rate in the Lviv region has almost reached the 1939 level. Researchers link this elevated mortality to several factors: diminished material circumstances; an inhospitable ecological environment; a seriously deteriorating public health system; and social-psychological stress with the people's inability to cope. Male death rates continue to exceed those of women, which scholars explain by the women's chromosomal structure and greater resistance to stress. In 2010 the average age of women in Lviv Oblast was 41, and that of men 36. In urban areas the median age for women was 40, and 36 for men. The lifespan of women had risen steadily since 1989, when it reached 37.1; in 2001 it rose to 39.6; then 40.4 in 2005, and finally it stood at 41.2 in 2010 owing to such factors as advances in medicine, increased attention to hygiene, and decrease in deaths during childbirth.

Although couples are increasingly postponing marriage, early marriages are still the norm in the region, and traditional church weddings continue to prevail. Ninety percent of all children are born in such unions. Common-law marriages are on the rise, however, attesting to the poor material environment and the lure of government subsidies for single mothers. Meanwhile, divorce rates are escalating, especially in the villages. The number of women who travel abroad as labor migrants correlates with the divorce rate. In the 40–49 cohort (most active in labor migration) extended separations have contributed substantially to the most elevated divorce rate to date among couples married for twenty years or more.

The average household in the Lviv region now consists of three persons; three-fifths of these are found in urban areas. Most village households still consist of extended families—three generations of relatives and in-laws. Meanwhile, the number of orphans is mounting owing to the men's rising death rate, children abandoned by their fathers, and those whose mothers are working abroad. One-child families are also on the rise and the number of single adults, especially among women of middle or advanced age, is greater than ever.

Finally, a redistribution of assets and exchanges of services between kin and families has become a complex feature of life in Lviv Oblast. Young mothers, especially, rely on significant assistance from parents in raising, feeding, and educating their children, and later for the grandchildren.

Insufficient earnings make it impossible for working mothers to avail themselves of any professional services even assuming that these are available. Such a depressed living standard will continue to favor the process of women's labor migrations abroad. Working-age women comprise 50 percent of these migrants. Generally speaking, they have a secondary education, and are married with children. Their basic motivation for seeking employment in a foreign country is the need for money to pay off debt, purchase real estate, renovate homes, and pay for their children's education. Only 10 percent of the female migrants make any attempt to start any sort of a business upon their return (Labinska 2006).

Receiving countries of Ukrainian labor include Russia, Poland, the Czech Republic, Belarus, Hungary, Italy, Spain, and Portugal. Gender differences in choice of destination countries are clearly delineated, however: women migrants head primarily for the Western-tier countries. For instance, Italy hosts 86 percent of the long-term female workers and 94 percent of the short-term women migrants from border regions such as Lviv, Ternopil, and Ivano-Frankivsk. Geography is a vital factor in women's decisions to migrate.

The primary areas of employment for Ukrainian women during their stay abroad include: agriculture (26 percent), the service industry (15 percent), manufacture (10–11 percent), construction, the food industry, and trade. In Russia one-third of the women migrant laborers work in petty trade, out of trucks and at markets, and another quarter are employed in construction. In the Czech Republic 46 percent are engaged in the public food service sector (restaurants, cafes, bars, and dining halls). Bakers and wood carvers make up 32 percent. Two-thirds of the women working in Poland make their living in agriculture, and one-third in the service sector. In Italy, Ukrainian women work predominantly as caregivers. Another category of women encompasses those who choose to work in places like Turkey and Japan, knowing that they are being recruited for prostitution, although in today's circumstances the recruitment process has assumed more cautious forms because both internationally and domestically the issue is receiving greater attention.[1] One problem, however, remains acute--trafficking. Illegal status, no competence in legal matters, and no language skills create a rich breeding ground for white slavery.

Once European countries have declared an end to the recession and the demand for labor from the European labor market exceeds supply, we will witness an even more sizeable, more diverse, Ukrainian labor migration. According to UN labor experts the potential for a growing need for workers in the European Union will precipitate an accelerated exodus of intellectuals from Ukraine, brought on by the continuing lack of opportunities and inadequate pay scales at home. In light of this, at the end of 2010 the Ukrainian administration signed a General Agreement effective for 2010–2012 announcing that the budget office would authorize an increase in salaries, but only to keep pace with inflation.

Insofar as internal migration is concerned, indicators show that since 2000 there has been a tendency for young women to return to the village after completing their studies in the city, but they do so more out of necessity than any real desire. Between 1989 and 2000 nearly 70 percent of the young village women, having concluded their secondary education in the city, elected to remain, but then the situation changed. Difficulties in finding employment and securing housing provided persuasive incentives for living and working in the village.

## Changes in the National, Linguistic, and Religious Composition of Women in Lviv Oblast

According to the 2001 census 91 percent of the women in the region lived in cities and 9 percent resided in rural areas. Russian women constituted the most prevalent national minority. They settled primarily in urban areas where their numbers are twenty-seven times higher than in rural communities, especially in cities like Lviv, which are under oblast jurisdiction. Elsewhere in Ukraine the highest density of Russian women relative to the total female population is found in the Brody and Mykolaiv sectors. The southwestern region holds the most compact settlements of Poles. This is especially true of the Mostyska (7.5 percent), Sambir (2.7 percent), and Starosambir (1.3 percent) regions. The most compelling indicator of a population's self-identification is language. Ninety-eight percent of the women living in Lviv Oblast consider the language of their nationality their native tongue. For 95 percent Ukrainian is that language, while 4 percent regard Russian their native language. Territorial demarcations of residence—village/city—most clearly delineate divided linguistic identities. Besides a knowledge of the native tongue, 1 percent of the women are proficient as well in the language of their nationality, 4.2 percent speak Ukrainian, and 17 percent communicate in Russian.

Designation of one's native language is closely structured according to geography. In Ukraine as a whole, where the linguistic picture differs from that of Lviv Oblast alone, immigrants from the former Soviet bloc comprise a sizeable number of speakers who consider Russian their native language on the same level as the language of their nationality. A large percentage of Bulgarians, Greeks, and Jews also consider Russian their native language, but among Americans, Arabs, Italians, Canadians, Germans, Poles, Romanians, Slovaks, Czechs, and Gypsies this label holds little meaning; instead they assign equal status to their own native language, and Ukrainian.

Throughout history, along with national identity religion has played an important role in the life of a society. Researchers characterize religion as a social process of religious rehabilitation that strengthens its role, together with that of the church, in all spheres of social being. In Ukraine as a whole, globalization makes itself felt in the growing influence of Catholicism, the evolution of Protestant religious institutions, as well as a consolidation of non-Christian, neo-Oriental streams and movements.

In excess of fifty confessions exist within the boundaries of the region, three times the number that were identified at the beginning of the 1990s. In recent years, the number of confessions, religious communities, and monasteries has stabilized, and their canonical dependence has been regulated. Overall, traditional churches are in the strongest position—the Ukrainian Greek Catholic Church; the Ukrainian Autocephalous Church; and the Ukrainian Orthodox Church, Kyiv Patriarchate, all of which have a clearly defined national and cultural Ukrainian profile and block any intrusion of new cults and movements. In its liturgy, the Ukrainian Orthodox Church avails itself of the Russian variant of Church Slavonic, whereas in the sermons, educational institutions, and church literature contemporary Russian generally prevails. The Roman Catholic Church functions in Polish. Forty-seven orders and communities have registered their statutes in the region (12 percent of the total in all of Ukraine), with most under the jurisdiction of the Ukrainian Greek Catholic Church. In this respect, western Ukraine diverges from the total picture of Ukraine, in which the Orthodox Church prevails.

Women's monasteries hold a special place within the structure of religious organizations. They too are under the jurisdiction of the Ukrainian Greek Catholic Church in western Ukraine, and are distributed throughout the Lviv Oblast Archeparchies of Sokal, Stryi, Sambir, and Drohobych. Half of the monasteries are concentrated in the oblast center where the governing and educational links are situated. Women's monasteries under the Ukrainian Greek Catholic Church have a much wider range of Orders and Communities than do men's, but both display a tendency to expand their networks. The Roman Catholic Church in Lviv's diocese unites six women's monasteries, although it is difficult to determine with any degree of accuracy the proportion of the women's population concentrated in these monasteries, their median age, level of education, and motives for their decisions to enter monastic life. Available data suggest that monasteries account for 1 percent of the total female population in the oblast. Their median age is thought to be approximately 39. Roughly one in three have a basic higher education, and one in four a special secondary education. Their excellent record of learning has been designed to serve secular interests, especially in education, and to renew the material base of the monasteries.[2]

# Changes in Educational and Qualification Levels of Women Working in the Region

The educational level of women in Lviv Oblast is relatively high (paralleling the all-Ukrainian picture). Based on the 2001 census, a total of 47 percent of the general population possessed a secondary education, and 53 percent had completed a program in higher education. Distribution of women by education and age allows us to establish a tight connection between the two. The high proportion of women in a region with a secondary education is accounted for in direct proportion to the total number of people with the same educational qualifications in the region today.

Grouping the women according to age and education permits us to establish a firm connection between the two. Unquestionably, sociopolitical conditions and the role of women's education in a given historical period make a significant impact upon the educational level of the population at large. The dominance of men with a full secondary education is explained by their greater numbers in any given age group. Naturally, only a certain segment of young people acquire a secondary education, and their numbers shift periodically. Nonetheless, the prestige of a higher education among women in the region does determine to a significant degree the correlation between their educational level and employment, social status, level of prosperity, and potential for career advancement.

**Table 10.1.** *Literacy Level of Entire Population 1979–2001*

| | Permanent population fifteen years and older. The following numbers indicate those with an education | | | | | |
| | fully educated | | | Full secondary education | | |
| Indicators | 1979 | 1989 | 2001 | 1979 | 1989 | 2001 |
|---|---|---|---|---|---|---|
| General population | 148094 | 234712 | 314344 | 483244 | 671638 | 861889 |
| relative weight of women in general population with an education, % | 48.3 | 50.6 | 52.8 | 49.5 | 47.1 | 46.9 |
| *Urban population* | 131587 | 207816 | 264082 | 320760 | 410721 | 507825 |
| relative weight of women in general population with an education, % | 47.8 | 50.1 | 52.7 | 50.8 | 49.0 | 48.6 |
| *Rural population* | 16507 | 26896 | 50262 | 162484 | 260917 | 354064 |
| relative weight of women in general population with education, % | 52.0 | 54.3 | 53.5 | 49.6 | 44.0 | 44.4 |

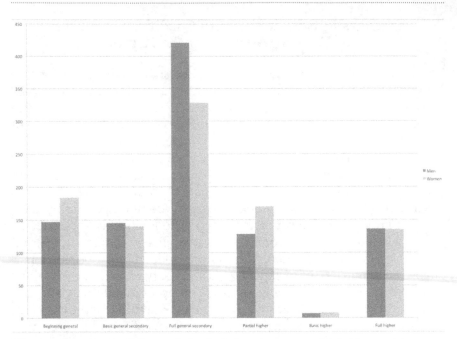

**Figure 10.1.** *Gender differences in levels of education among all inhabitants with an education (2001 census figures).*

In the Lviv region the greatest number of women with a higher education is concentrated in the city of Lviv as well as Drohobych and the Striysky district. Graduates of polytechnic institutions lead in securing employment (94 percent), and graduates of pedagogical institutions are at the bottom, where women dominate (68 percent). Insufficient opportunities in specialized positions have become available to absorb the educated populace since Ukraine's transition to a market economy began, which accounts for the high rate of unemployment. Women's unsuccessful job searches have resulted in one segment moving from the official to the nonofficial sector of the economy, while another has stopped looking altogether. For 29 percent of the women pensions have become their primary source of income, whereas 26 percent work at lower end jobs in various enterprises.

A new tendency has made itself felt of late in Lviv Oblast as well as all of Ukraine—the feminization of education, with female graduates on the rise because men have moved on to other, more lucrative, employment sectors. Additional disciplines in which women dominate (where women constitute half or more of the student cadres) include pharmacy, psychology, architecture, chemistry, and medicine. Men are concentrated in the philosophy, political science, physics, and mathematics departments.[3]

**Table 10.2.** *Population Distribution in Lviv Oblast According to Basic Modes of Income, 2001 Census*

| Indicators | Weighted value of the overall number of people of a given sex | |
| --- | --- | --- |
| | men | women |
| | percentages | |
| Employed in an enterprise, organization, institution, or agriculture | 28.9 | 25.7 |
| Working for individual entrepreneurs | 0.3 | 0.3 |
| Self-employed | 0.5 | 0.2 |
| Working as individual entrepreneurs | 0.7 | 0.4 |
| Working in one's own agricultural enterprise | 0.1 | 0.0 |
| Working in personally owned subsidiary enterprises | 6.7 | 4.6 |
| Income from asset ownership | 0.1 | 0.0 |
| Pension | 17.8 | 28.6 |
| Grants | 0.3 | 0.2 |
| Assistance, including government sources except unemployment insurance or other government assistance | 2.0 | 1.4 |
| Unemployment insurance | 1.7 | 2.0 |
| Compensation for dependents | 35.8 | 33.7 |
| Additional sources of cost-of-living allowances and unknown sources | 5.1 | 2.9 |
| Total sources of income | 100 | 100 |

Irrespective of the existing problems in the educational sector, overall interest in learning, especially on the part of women, remains relatively high. Forty percent of the female population, age 15 and up, have a complete secondary education, 26 percent a partial higher education, and 25 percent have completed a tertiary education. For every one thousand women age 15 and up, 646 have completed a general secondary education; for men the figure is 719.

Education in preparation for one of the professions facilitates the adaptation of qualified individuals in the workplace, especially when it comes to performance and salary negotiation. A higher education lessens the risk of poverty by 2.3 times, and raises projected earnings by an average of 1.6 times. The same cohort of people tends to have savings, they are more likely to spend substantially for their children's education, and own their own homes. As for women's career advancement, only a higher education can guarantee this.

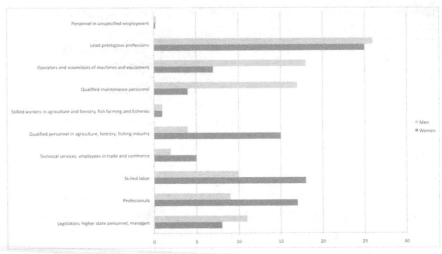

**Figure 10.2.** *Distribution of women engaged in economic ventures, grouped by nature of employment (2002 census figures).*

Employment data suggest that women leaving their positions, voluntarily or otherwise, is a characteristic feature in the traditionally female branches of the economy, where women find employment upon completion of their studies. Together with this, a new trend has become evident lately—the pool of pregnant women electing to take a leave of absence due to pregnancy or childbirth is shrinking. Also on the decline is the number of women who stay at home to care for children until the age established by the existing law. In the past, during periods of mass female layoffs, such leaves acted as a rescue mechanism by preserving for women with children of an appropriate age at least minimal social guarantees and benefits. Today's reduction in the number of women taking advantage of maternity leaves, as well as the growing demand for preschool services testify to the women's depressed economic activity.

The changing economic environment has intensified the already extreme prejudice against women in the workplace. Employers are also ignoring labor laws guaranteeing special benefits for them, and the expression "feminization of poverty" translates to their limited access to resources such as land, credit, professional training or requalification, decision-making circles, international institutions of collaboration, various funds, etc. The work regimen for women has also changed, especially in rural areas where the exhausting nature of physical work and low remuneration have resulted in the progressive attrition of women in the workplace.

The rural women's workload is manifestly greater than that of their urban counterparts (most notably for those between the ages of 60 and

70), leaving them little time to access essential services, visit health clinics, and participate in the social infrastructure. This information is based upon the results of the Ukrainian sociological study: *Social Standing of Rural Woman in Ukraine,* 1998, which, for all practical purposes, has remained steady. A summary of work time budgeted for women in a 24-hour period is 25.7 hours, not counting sleep, evidence that rural women are engaged in a number of overlapping occupations, and have less time to spend on subsidiary domestic tasks and childcare.

Time spent by women on household tasks during the week has gone from 14 to 23 percent, constituting 2.1 times over that expended by men. Meanwhile, their leisure time has fallen from 10 to 4 percent. They spend eighty hours a week on socially useful work (including time spent traveling to and from work), whereas men spend sixty-seven hours; domestic duties take up thirty-nine and nineteen hours each week respectively (Stashenko 2001).

## Changes in Women's Public/Political Activity

Active public service and political engagement of women in the oblast have been established by tradition (Labinska 2002), but in the Lviv region they have their own specificity, conditioned by a host of different factors from those generally obtaining elsewhere in Ukraine. In women's public organizations (POs), as sociological inquiries attest, the following dominate: public unions—77 percent; charitable funds—11 percent; auxilliaries and separate centers of all-Ukrainian (international) POs—10 percent; associations of juridical personnel—2 percent; credit unions—5 percent. The lion's share in Lviv Oblast falls to centers of all-Ukrainian organizations, but their public associations are relatively few. Those registering fewer than one hundred members comprise 53 percent of the total, and only 36 percent pay their dues. To fully comprehend the situation, we must also consider the willingness of Ukrainian women to join POs, to understand their role, and exhibit commitment to them. From among the various sources of financing for such organizations most important are donor contributions, grants from international sources, and miscellaneous funds.

We have grouped the public women's organizations according to the nature of their activities: charitable, commercially oriented, scholarly research, health/wellness and sports/physical fitness, politically oriented, educational, socially oriented, and specialized. Most representative in the oblast are those that focus on educational activities. Interterritorial divisions of women's public organizations demonstrate bipolarity: on the one hand, they are concentrated in the cities, especially Lviv (60 percent of all women's community organizations), yet are totally absent in some districts, particularly in rural areas. An interesting fact is that most of those organizations labeled *educational* are what Antonina Kolodii (2002) calls umbrella types, whose activities are supported by various grants from the West. These offer counseling, organize forums and seminars, publish manuals and periodicals, analyze activity, take inventory, and classify the separate organizations in existence. Every fifth women's association is socially oriented toward charitable organizations.

Commercially oriented POs are fewer in number (7 percent), as are scholarly research POs (5 percent). Health and physical fitness and narrowly specialized POs each comprise 4 percent. Charitable organizations with programs such as women's rights and violence prevention, women's employment abroad, and promotion of women's enterprises are even lower on the scale. The most active expansion of public union networks in the oblast derives from centers of political parties, with the largest number located in Lviv and, to a lesser degree, in towns under oblast jurisdiction. Among them are: the Women's Community, affiliated with the Christian Democratic Party; the All-Ukrainian League of Women, allied with the Congress of Ukrainian Nationalists; and the All-Ukrainian Peoples' Democratic Women's Union Act, with ties to the Peoples' Democratic Party. Three women's parties—the All-Ukrainian Political Union "Women for the Future"; All-Ukrainian Women's Party of Initiatives; and Women of Ukraine—all maintain oblast and urban centers located in the city of Lviv. One of the reasons for the low level of electoral support for women's parties might be attributed to the fact that professional women, who operate on the highest rungs of the social ladder, focus on business and professional matters rather than gender-specific goals. Politically oriented women's POs constitute 11 percent of the whole. Political participation is variously distinguished, however: voting; activity in political parties, urban governments, and social organizations; petitioning state officials; and political activists for solutions to social problems. Voting in elections for national and city government offices is judged to be the most important political activity.

Women in Lviv constitute more than 50 percent of the electorate. Demographic differences among village populations will determine the impact of gender on the way women's political will is expressed, using as our guide the high electoral activity of residents in the Lviv district. Political participation of the general electorate is expressed through the ballot box, but a sample of relevant articles demonstrates that these statistics are not readily available. We can offer only approximate figures, based upon exit polls, and the type of general information released in each region.

An indicator of the gender balance worldwide is the 30 percent quotas set for the female electorate. The percentage of female parliamentary deputies in the latest Ukrainian legislature has fallen by more than one-third. Most illustrative are the pre-election lists of candidates for office in Lviv's oblast council (2006 and 2010).

The clearest indicator of this trend is found in Lviv's Oblast legislature, which demonstrates that the higher the level, the lower the number of women. Gender disproportion is also evident in the executive organs, especially village council chairs. There are no women among these in oblast or rayon (district) councils, and no women are found among oblast council executives, despite the fact that women comprise 40 percent of the membership.

Experts confirm that qualitative changes in the political life of regions and districts are made possible by the application of certain legal measures such as preferential quotas, which remove obstacles to women's entry into social institutions on the same bases as men. In Ukraine, however, such a quota is perceived differently from the one established worldwide,

**Table 10.3.** *Gender Analysis of Electoral Lists of the Election Process in the Lviv Regional Council in 2006 and 2010 Census*

| 2006 | | 2010 | |
|---|---|---|---|
| Subjects of the electoral process | Weighted Value of women in the candidate lists The number of women candidates in the top five list | Subjects of the electoral process | Women in top five on list The number of women candidates in the top five list n list |
| People's Leaderships Unification | "0" | All-Ukrainian Unification in Freedom | "0" |
| Bloc of Yulia Tymoshenko | 5 | People's Party "It's Time" | "0" |
| Community Party "It's Time" | 5 | The Public Position | "0" |
| Our Ukraine | 8 | The People's Movement of Ukraine | 1 |
| Party of Greens in Ukraine | "0" | Our Ukraine | "0" |
| Party of Regions | 10 | The Party of Regions | "0" |
| Reform and Order | "0" | Ukrainian National Party | "0" |
| SPU | "0" | Ukrainian Republican Party of Councils | "0" |
| | | Conciliar Ukraine | 1 |
| | | "Front of Change" | "0" |

owing to the unstable public situation in conjunction with the impover-
ishment of a large part of the populace. On the micro-level, village and
other rural settlements councils can be judged by the public activization
of women—their rising numbers in leadership roles in village and other
rural settlements. Currently, their leadership roles exceed 40 percent in
only two administrative regions. In eleven districts the figure drops to less
than 20 percent.

Agreement on positions to be filled in women's organizations, and
support of local delegates is totally subjective, and depends upon interpersonal relationships. There is no informed women's civic movement, although two years ago an educational/practical gender school was founded
in Lviv with the aim of coordinating the efforts of public activists and
educators working in the field to raise gender awareness among Lviv's
inhabitants.

## Crime

Crime is yet another sphere where gender differences are extensive. In
times of crisis or in transitional economies, the combination of rising unemployment, lowered living standards, and low level of government safety
nets frequently lead to a bypassing of the legal system, to taking matters
into one's own hands. Among those who committed crimes as a result,
women comprised 13 percent. Generally speaking, the number of such
crimes since 1996 has decreased, but convictions rose to 16 percent in
1996, 14 percent in 2000, and 19 percent in 2005. Constituting nearly
one-fifth of the criminal element, women differ in their criminal tendencies from the general population, most notably in a rotation out of
narcotics use and property crimes to theft, cheating, appropriation or
embezzlement of property, or abusing it in some official capacity. The
majority of crimes committed by men are either drug-related (16 percent)
or property crimes (47 percent).

Factors influencing the formation of women's criminality in the region
can be either innate or acquired. Most illustrative are age and sex. Females
constitute 9 percent of the minors who commit crimes. Throughout the
oblast most convictions fall to women 30–50 years of age (42 percent),
followed by 50–65 year olds (20 percent). In the city of Lviv, almost 30
percent of the women convicted of crimes fall between the ages of 30–50,
and 35 percent are between the ages of 18–30. The age cohort is closely
connected to the level of education. Higher education is important, although not a guarantee of, preventing the growth of a criminal personality. The greatest number of criminal acts falls to women with a completed
secondary education. Men in the same cohort have a completed secondary

or incomplete higher education. An advanced degree tends to moderate the pattern of criminal behavior. Only one in ten convictions is handed down to women with a higher education.

The majority of female criminals in the region are unemployed working-age women with a completed general education who are no longer studying. Evidence suggests that women with a secondary education will not necessarily pursue further study, and tend instead to seek income from extralegal sources. The largest number in this category are located in high unemployment areas, where the only prospects are part-time work. Nearly one-quarter of all women convicted of crimes belong to socially unprotected sectors of society and are supported by the state—mostly pensioners and invalids. Clearly their basic needs, especially medicine and medical care, are not being met, and this breeds criminal activity. Specific to these women, however, is a low rate of recidivism. A geographical analysis revealed that the focus of women's crimes in the western region moves from the center to the periphery, and twice as many crimes are committed in these regions than in points farther east.

Recidivism is directly related to the so-called risk group, characterized by alcohol and narcotics abuse among the homeless. This is understandable, inasmuch as the customary behavior patterns of this group are conducive to crime. Of all women convicted of a crime in 2004, 4 percent were under the influence of alcohol (among men the figure is 8 percent). Individuals such as the homeless, or those who have left the normal lifestyle, fill the ranks of risk groups. Minors, especially boys, occupy a special niche there.

Diverging once more from the Lviv Oblast paradigm, Oselia—in the district of Kyiv—demonstrates a particularly humanitarian attitude toward the homeless. It provides hot meals, clothing, and shelter for the homeless. Another is the Regional Center for Social Adaptation. More than half the time it is women who are the victims of crimes, basically robbery and theft. Most noticeable among these are pensioners, doctors, government workers, foreigners, and managers of private enterprises. In sum, the overall economic decline in the country has led to a significant overall increase in crime.

## State of Women's Health in Lviv Oblast

The decline in the overall health and expected life span of Ukrainian citizens is without precedent since WWII. Research has shown that the three main problems are: low level of individual incomes, inadequate government-financed health care, and inability to pay for private medical treatment. People have become indifferent to their state of health, and disillusioned over the possibility of free health care. Added to this is the inaccessibility of so many medications and effective medical treatment, etc., owing to their prohibitive cost. All such factors influence their state of health, and translate to infrequent visits to medical facilities for timely diagnoses. A significant number of patients also resort to self-medication or they simply ignore the early stages of pathologies and consult health professionals only when a disease has advanced to the chronic, incurable stage. Finally, the inclination to seek medical help differs between the sexes. Of those who seek medical care for the first time, 44 percent are women. Follow-up visits change dramatically. On average one hundred women see a doctor 170 times for subsequent visits. Illness among women is also differentiated by age and gender. For instance, more women become invalids during their working years—two-thirds of the total number. The trend (8 percent) toward succumbing to this debilitating condition, however, is now beginning to surface at an increasingly young age, with signs of its onset beginning as early as the age of 16.

## Conclusion

The primary problems inherent in the challenges of a demographic reconstitution of the women's population in Ukraine were reflected on a smaller scale in the Lviv region. Progressive depopulation, the aging process, low birth rate, mounting family instability, new marriage practices such as common-law unions, increased family planning, and the accelerated migration of women during their childbearing years are all contributing factors.[4]

From the socioeconomic standpoint we also have evidence of the changes that are transforming the post-Soviet Ukrainian society: the mononational composition of women, and the dominance of the Ukrainian church contributing to a relatively homogeneous spiritual and cultural environment; women's high educational and professional qualifications while offering no absolute guarantee of career advancement; the increased incidence of women's age-related illnesses; limited opportunities for decision making at the legislative and executive levels to the women's detriment; the low rate of recidivism among women committing crimes.

This study has used Lviv Oblast as a microcosmic model for reflection on the larger national trends and developments in post-Soviet Ukraine. Among them are the advantages (if not guarantees) in the workplace for women with a higher education; the continued move of qualified women out of traditional women's areas of employment; their increasing engagement in small business; a progressive decrease of crimes committed by women; growing numbers of women engaging in mainstream politics;

and an ongoing decline of older women with deteriorating health in the labor force.

**Halyna Labinska** received her Kandydat degree from Ivan Franko National University in Lviv, where she concentrated her studies on an examination of the lives and migration patterns of women in the region of Lviv. This interest prompted her to contribute a study of their patterns of internal and external migration to the present volume, adding it to some forty articles written on various aspects of the population in western Ukraine, among others. Other areas of research include demographic configurations, Ukrainian topography, and tourism and recreation in Crimea. She currently (2014) serves as docent in the Kyiv Mohyla Academy Department of Geography.

# Notes

1. An international conference on trafficking took place as early as 1895. In 1949 the UN General Assembly approved the International Convention against Trafficking in Humans. By 1996, 151 countries (more than two-thirds of the entire membership) had ratified the document.
2. Ukrainian Greek Catholic Monasteries.
3. "Women in education: Past, present, and future," *Materials from the International Conference on Education* (3–4 December 1999). Kyiv, 288.
4. Divergences from the Lviv model have been duly noted.

# Bibliography

*Central Statistical Office, Lviv Region.* http://www.stat.lviv.ua.
*Demohrafichna Kryza v Ukraini. Problemy Doslidzhennia, Vytoky, Skladovi, Napriamy Protydii.* 2001. Ed. Valentyna Steshenko. Kyiv: Instytut Ekonomiky NAN Ukrainy.
Kolodii, Antonina. 2002. *Na Shliakhu Hromadans'koho Suspil'stva.tychni Zasady I Sotsiokul'turni Peredymovy Demokratychnoyi Transformatsiyi v Ukraini.* Lviv: Chervona Kalyna.
Labinska, Halyna. 2002. "Uchast' zhinok v hromadskii, osvitnii, ta naukovii robotakh na pochatku XXst v Halychyni," in *Materialy Druhoyi Mizhnarodnoyi, Naukovopraktychnoyi Konferentsiyi "Zhinka v Nautsi ta Osviti: Mynule, Suchasne, Maibutnie."* Kyiv: 280–290.
———. 2006. "Mihratsiina aktyvnist' zhinochoho naselennia Lvivskoi Oblasti: demohrafichny, genderny, ta heohrafichny aspekty," in *Materialy Vseukrainskoi Naukovo-Praktychnoyi konferetsiyi "Podolannia Gendernoi ta vikovoyi dyskryminatsiyi na Rynku Pratsi v Ukraini: Realiyi ta perspektyvy."* Lviv: Lviv Polytechnic National University, 61–72.
*Lvivshchyna Konfesiina: Informatsiino-statystychny Dovidnyk.* 2006. Lviv: Manuscript.

*Materialy Sotsiolohichnoho Obstezhennia.* 1998. "Sotsial'ne Stanovyshche Sil'skoyi Zhinky v Ukraini. Kyiv: Akadampres.

*Materialy Sotsiolohichnoho Obstezhennia.* 1998. "Sotsial'ni Problemy Stanovy-shcha Sil'skoyi Rodyny v Umovakh Rozbudovy Nezalezhnoyi Ukrainy." Kyiv: Akadampres.

*Mihratsiini Protsesy v Lvivskii Oblasti u 2000 rotsi.* 2001. Lviv: Lvivske Oblasne Uprav-linnia Statystyky.

*Monasteri Ukrainskoyi Hreko-Katolytskoi Tserkvy.* 2006. Lviv: Svidchado.

Smoliar, Liudmyla. 2001. *Zhinochy Rukh Ukrainy iak Chynnyk Gendernoyi Rivnovahy ta Gendernoyi Demokratiyi v Ukrainskomu Sotsiiu.* Kyiv: Tsentr Innovatsii ta Rozvytku.

Stashenko, Valentyna, ed. 2001. *Demographic Crisis in Ukraine: Problems of Research, Conclusions, Components, and Reactions.* Kyiv: Ukrainian Academy of Sciences.

Vlasenko, Nataliia, Ella Libanova, Oleksandr Osaulenko, ta inshi. *Pershy Vseukrain-sky Perepys. Naselennia Istorychni, Metodolohichni, Sotsial'ni, Ekonomichni, Etnichni, Aspekty.* Editorial Collective: Ivan Kuras, Serhii Pirozhkov. Kyiv: Derzhkomstat Ukrainy.

# CHAPTER 11

# Gender Strategies in Research on Family Marriage Practices

## Assessment of Contemporary Youth

Lyudmyla Males

This chapter builds primarily upon the intersections of three sets of problems: traditional and modern gender strategies in matrimonial conduct, their proliferation throughout Ukrainian society, and changes in their adoption during the socialization process of the post-Soviet generation.

To date, post-Soviet sociologists have produced a relatively modest number of sociocultural analyses of the most gender-oriented of all social institutions: the family. Among them are the bibliographic analyses of Victor Horodianenko (2001) and Sergey Golod (1993); works by Russian scholars under the supervision of Natalia Rimashevskaia (1999); and several manuals on the sociology of family by Anatoly Antonov and Victor Medkov (1996), using a statistical-demographic approach, prefaced by a rigid normal family paradigm. Examples of more in-depth sociocultural examinations of the family exist in Western European anthropological studies such as those of Jean-Pierre Almodovar (1992); Victoria Semenova (1996); Richard Seider (1987); and Sergey Oushakine (2004). Such historically specific studies are often passed over in contemporary Ukrainian research however. For our primary source material we turned to sociological and statistical data, and to papers written by senior college students in partial fulfillment of their practicums (practical application of previously studied theory), centered on an examination of folksongs portraying day-to-day activities. Consistent with sensitivity to possible repercussions and requests for anonymity, only given names of student authors and their course titles will be provided.

Inasmuch as the current sociology of family is devoted primarily to contemporary society, both the temporal framing and the sources consulted have far-reaching academic and social implications. To begin with, we have a limited view of the family—monogamous, nuclear, and with few children, the characteristics of which are dictated by the demands of industrialization and urbanization. This image is disseminated by the media and advertising, from which a healthy, smiling, prosperous married young European-type couple, with one or two children, looks out at us. In this context, deviations from such a norm—incomplete families, childless or families with many children—are represented as being somehow deficient. State ideology, many of the churches, and political movements, all actively supporting the commercial advertising images, are conducting an aggressive campaign of essentialism favoring the so-called complete family. Today's traditional family consists of an extended multigenerational entity that rarely establishes a single household. Its members are scattered among various sites and cities and they tend to congregate only on special occasions such as weddings, wedding anniversaries of senior family members, and funerals.

Popular and academic texts dealing with family relationships call attention to the birth and rearing of children within the bonds of marriage. They are predisposed to judge and terminologically stigmatize all other combinations, without conducting a detailed examination or proper analysis of the existing state of affairs. For example, singles are labeled unmarried and lonely, unmarried and separate; parents are described as mothers without husbands, childless couples are portrayed as incomplete families by choice, and so on. This tendency is reinforced by the resentment of those who favor professional fulfillment. Their choices are regarded as poor excuses for postponing or suspending reproductive intentions, irrespective of the age group within which such decisions are made.

The "complete" family lost its monopoly back in the Soviet era, but as far as Ukrainian reality is concerned families headed by women became typical so long ago that it is unrealistic to label them deviant today, all the more so because single parenthood has become such a widespread and intentionally adopted plan. Over the course of many decades more than 20 percent of all children in Ukraine have been born to women out of wedlock, although some mothers do live in common-law unions (Tymoshenko 2009: 301). This trend toward establishing female-headed households with children born out of wedlock is supported by statistical data. Their numbers have vacillated between 17.3 percent (2000) and 20.9 percent (2008), and within the different oblasts (regions) they have fluctuated between 5.9 percent (Ternopil—urban dwellers) to 38 percent (rural residents in Kirovohrad and adjacent regions). In 2008 there were 93,000 such families, or 55 percent of the total number formed from divorced couples; the five years prior saw 26,000 such households, representing two-thirds of all divorced couples. The reader is reminded that whatever the reasons, Ukraine's culture legally granted divorces do not automatically grant paternal custody; that would be a rare and unnatural (for Ukraine) exception (Hladun 1993; Stelmakh 2004; Tymoshenko 2009).

The main theses of contemporary Ukrainian gender discourses emphasize marriage not only as a legalizing factor, but as an important legitimization of family relationships. Marriage is listed as the center and focal point of reference for family status and its reproductive behavior in demographic discourse, in which the designations *not married, married,* or *awaiting marriage* are likely to be applied. Generally speaking, discussions of gender strategies, marriage, and family—nuclear and extended—are conducted synonymously, although they are separate entities, and distinctions should apply. The entire aggregate of blood relationships designates an extended family; it serves to promote generational continuity as well as transmission of tradition and values from generation to generation.

Our understanding of family will be the form of organized social life consisting of various combinations of members working together to meet their social-psychological and spiritual needs, the birth of children, maintenance of a shared household, etc. Marriage is the institutionalized legalization of an acceptable family standard for a given society, and the origin of its rights and responsibilities within the framework of prevailing laws. Naturally this legalization, with its economic, legal, and moral implications, leads to the principal dissemination of those family structures that resonate with the public's conception of what marriage should be about. That is why we can commonly refer to one or another typical marriage for a given country, although this by no means exhausts all of its possible family formations. Other types are simply forced to the margins, erased from view, or they represent different types of social relationships (for instance next of kin, friendship, professional, and others.

That said, one must also be cognizant of certain modifications in academic analyses and their assessments of marriage-family relationships, such as a significantly more neutral attitude toward unregistered marital unions (Libanova 2008) than is customary outside of academe. Together with the preservation of relatively positive male and female attitudes toward establishing a family, today's institutionalization (civil marriage) also does not suit all Ukrainian women and men. Attesting to this is the growth in popularity of a much earlier institutional form of the church wedding ceremony—the betrothal—even though it no longer carries the same judicial weight as it once did, as well as the development of the alternative prearranged forms of cohabitation. Conversely, prearranged alternative forms of cohabitation remain rather limited. The all-Ukrainian population census of 2001 placed their number at a modest 7 percent, and projects a future increment to just below 10 percent.

According to data compiled by European social research in 2006–2007 nearly one-half of the Ukrainians polled exhibited a negative attitude toward cohabiting couples, one-third said they found a response difficult, 17 percent of the women and 18 percent of the men approved of the arrangement, and 4 percent had no idea how to evaluate it.[1] As is evident from the table below, the Ukrainian level of support is the lowest of all European societies. It falls substantially below Western countries, and its rigorousness outstrips even those socialist countries that participated in the survey.

If the rules of supporting family, reproductive, and marriage strategies are established primarily by social marriage institutions, and debated publicly in the media and social networks, the values and motives applicable to variations in the behavioral aspects of these strategies are not accessible to the wider public. They are lodged within closed circles—in families and neighboring communities, as well as among colleagues, friends, and other agents of socialization. These agents are difficult to establish by sociological research and virtually impossible by statistical accounts. In light of this, one might look to other methods, derived from a variety of alternate sources, as will be shown below.

First we turn to traditional sociological surveys that currently offer the lion's share of information on social questions. Research indicates that Ukrainian matrimonial conduct today is dictated by a hierarchy of mo-

**Table 11.1.** *Level of Support in 2007 of Europeans toward Cohabitation Outside of Marriage*

| Country | Mean score* | | Country | Mean score* | |
| --- | --- | --- | --- | --- | --- |
| | Women | Men | | Women | Men |
| Austria | 3.48 | 3.45 | Portugal | 3.40 | 3.43 |
| Belgium | 3.91 | 3.85 | Russia | 2.79 | 2.70 |
| Bulgaria | 3.03 | 3.02 | Romania | 2.63 | 2.69 |
| Great Britain | 3.15 | 3.11 | Slovakia | 2.87 | 2.82 |
| Denmark | 4.47 | 4.50 | Slovenia | 3.54 | 3.37 |
| Estonia | 2.85 | 2.79 | Hungary | 3.31 | 3.23 |
| Ireland | 3.08 | 3.02 | Ukraine | 2.37 | 2.39 |
| Spain | 3.54 | 3.53 | Finland | 3.95 | 3.90 |
| Cyprus | 2.98 | 3.20 | France | 3.60 | 3.51 |
| Latvia | 3.14 | 3.11 | Switzerland | 3.36 | 3.37 |
| Netherlands | 3.91 | 3.92 | Sweden | 3.88 | 3.68 |
| Norway | 4.25 | 4.16 | Germany | 3.21 | 3.19 |
| Poland | 3.03 | 3.08 | | | |

*Mean level of support according to a scale of from 1 to 5: unequivocally do not support, do not support, difficult to say, support, support unreservedly.

tives that predispose couples to exchange marriage vows.[2] Marriage as a social institution is based on romantic love, desire for children, avoiding loneliness, and a relationship with a person sharing one's views and values. In sum, leading motives for both sexes are recognized as emotional and psychological. For men fatherhood might serve as an incentive to embrace marriage because it is the only way to legitimize paternity. Married women avoid the social censure of an illegitimate birth, although this no longer has the devastating effect that it once did—in the past the only label available to a child born out of wedlock was the stigma of bastard. Marriage also secures for women the legal assurance of rights and expectations stemming from shared parenthood, although in point of fact this might amount to little more than a formality.

The economic security that marriage offers women is an example of the role that financial considerations play in creating the entire patriarchal system. Survey data and the mass consciousness demonstrate this to be an exclusively women's issue, for which they are often unjustly criticized. Allegedly this confirms one popular conviction that women favor a patriarchal system over emancipation, but this is too simplistic. Drawing upon the terminology of Jürgen Habermas, in contemporary Ukrainian society the "lifeworld" (*Lebenswelt*) of the people and the system coexist in an acutely conflicted relationship. Currently, the market dominates in confirming the logic of this bifurcation as a form of macroeconomics. The labor market especially not only fails to anticipate the existence of conditions that support a fully valued life and human development, but in reducing it to the status of a workforce it discredits those women who are pregnant and give birth, who raise children, and care for the sick—in essence these are women who are not in a position to devote all of their time and energy to wage labor.

As for the state favoring tactics over strategy, which is tantamount to a colonizing policy toward its own people, this too regulates itself according to the dictates of market efficiency (minimum outlay for maximum profit). The net effect of this is elimination of the state as a source of support in the people's life activity and development by shifting the burden onto the family and its internal resources. In most cases those resources consume the women's leisure and recreation time, added to which are the contributions of grandparents and older children to domestic work and family survival.

Women who aspire to motherhood confront a dilemma in today's world: should they rely solely on their own resources, turn into "inferior workers" and become female poverty statistics, or strive to share both parental joy and sorrow with the children's father, although few men would choose sorrow. It is important for women to convince men to stop resisting marriage, and to share in the costs of a child's upbringing. Such expedients provide at least a modicum of legal guarantees for mothers even in the event of divorce.

These data[3] confirm the asymmetricality in preparedness to share parental responsibility. Men view expenditures on a child solely from a material perspective, not as necessary personal financial outlays, whereas for women such expenditures are very personal. Their contributions draw upon the women's time, health, and abilities—all of the child's needs are considered women's needs. This explains the apparent financial motive of female respondents—costs of giving birth, childcare, and financial security. It is not, as so frequently charged, motivated by a selfish desire tantamount to wishing to become a millstone around someone's neck.

Once again we encounter asymmetry in the value that a woman places on family (on marriage) in her self-sacrifice for the sake of the children and domestic harmony. Patriarchal propaganda equates this with women's true

**Table 11.2.** *Values of Ukrainian Women and Men, 2007*

| Values | Men | | Women | |
|---|---|---|---|---|
| | % | Position in hierarchy | % | Position in hierarchy |
| Creating a family | 49 | 2 | 80 | 1 |
| Material provision for family | 51 | 1 | 35 | 7 |
| Children's happiness | 40 | 5 | 77 | 2 |
| Personal health | 43 | 4 | 40 | 4 |
| Openness in relationships | 32 | 6 | 39 | 5 |
| Presence of steady employment | 44 | 3 | 19 | 9 |
| Calm and comfort in the family | 21 | 10 | 41 | 3 |
| Professional growth | 31 | 7 | 8 | 13 |
| Ownership of one's dwelling | 23 | 9 | 14 | 11 |
| Sexual satisfaction | 29 | 8 | 10 | 12 |
| Interesting and creative employment | 20 | 11 | 16 | 10 |
| Proper personal appearance | 9 | 16 | 37 | 6 |
| Love | 11 | 15 | 34 | 8 |
| Good food | 21 | 10 | 6 | 15 |
| Interesting and happy leisure | 15 | 13 | 6 | 15 |
| Participation in community life | 13 | 14 | 6 | 15 |
| Cultural and spiritual self-perfection | 8 | 17 | 10 | 12 |
| Continual improvement of knowledge | 9 | 16 | 7 | 14 |
| Other | 1 | 18 | 1 | 17 |

happiness. At the same time these allegedly "women's only" values are not their sole consideration. Such factors as love, sexual satisfaction, a fulfilled and joyful leisure are also important to women, yet the family ignores them throughout the entire gendered socialization of girls. This leads to numerous future conflicts, misunderstandings, and breakdowns in family relationships. For men family values are more differentiated. Among them are a wide variety of considerations for entering into marriage and establishing a family—personal, social, sexual, etc. The men's desire for a marital union is lower on the scale (49 percent) than it is for women (80 percent). As for changes in contemporary gender strategies, modernization and globalizational displacement have been moving Ukrainians in the general European direction of a demographic transition and women's emancipation.

## The Past as a Factor in Ukrainian Identity

Reflecting on Ukraine's complex history of changing marriage traditions is not as simple as it might seem. Folkloric texts—those transmitters of traditional norms and images—are being recreated today, or reborn as pseudo rituals. We will now focus more closely on student analyses of the texts in question and what they have discovered in the process of working on their assignments. Although seemingly unscholarly, the aggregate of some two hundred student works assembled over the past five years does provide vital information on certain basic issues that are worthy of celebratory narratives. They form a solid basis for student evaluations of former Ukrainian customs, and provide insights into their interpretations by today's young people. They also contribute to the tendency of youth to overrate the traditional gender profiles and marriage strategies (choice of partner, limiting the marriage circle) of a hundred-year-old past in the process of fulfilling their senior-year practicum requirements.

In their analyses of traditional folklore and lyrical songs, coupled with Soviet posters featuring women, the students observed behavioral patterns and attitudes toward women as these are revealed in both traditional folklore and Soviet ideology. Using double hermeneutics in assessing these materials, we show how students also expose their personal attitudes toward the issues in question, and their own reflection of contemporary values and realities.

To begin with we will look at those works that tend to demonstrate sensitivity to gender and its indispensable priorities from the nonparticipant perspective of the young people's current portrayal of Soviet reality. Sensitive students regarded the stereotypical masculinization of Soviet women as degrading when they are publicly represented as an exploitable labor force, such as the way they are seen in a poster titled "The Road to

Collectivization," for instance: "It shows three men standing alongside a woman exhorting her to resume her public duties on a collective farm (in the name of equality), while they stand around supervising" (Yuilia K). The figure of the woman is massive, she has a classical Soviet-style intelligent face (Kateryna So) and powerful hands. Her red attire connects her to the communist world (Kateryna Su). Students are impressed by those huge, sunburned hands and the woman's strong countenance (Yulia K). Such changes in the anthropological code were the stuff of public discourse and propagandistic displays of human images during the Soviet epoch. "This ideological portrayal exemplified women as nothing more than units in a work force" (Maryna D). Aside from the female sturdiness depicted, students are moved by the women's exhausted countenances (Yulia K). This altered anthropological code during the Soviet era contrasts sharply with the typically gendered family represented in the commercial and social advertisements of contemporary Ukraine.

## The Past as Refracted through Contemporary Eyes

It is plain to see that value-laden illustrations of the marriage circle have undergone some fundamental changes over the past hundred years. Student assignments for a second practicum did not fail to lay emphasis on this. In this case the course was titled "Sociology of the family," the practicum was named "Gender strategies and marriage circles," and the assignment was an analysis of the Ukrainian marriage circle. A typical comment in response to the assignment was: "It is as though we find ourselves in a different world where every word carries an aggregate of thoughts and sacred acts. Already, from the perspective of our culture and thoughts, its meaning is difficult to ascertain without suitable direction. All the more so when it comes to marriage traditions, disrupted as they were first by urbanization, next by Soviet ideology, then the aggressive incursion of Western values" (Ksenia S).

Some of the brighter students provided extensive analyses of the cultural changes that occurred over time, while their less "sociologically engaged" peers simply judged the former rituals according to contemporary norms of family relationships. Both approaches have merit; each is informative in its own way. All such studies reflected former practices that have lost their original meaning, yet their messages continued to resonate with today's youth—the need for separate living arrangements, and profusion of generational conflicts—references to which can still be found in songs of bygone days.

Conforming to accepted methodology, and communicated by the use of appropriate terminology, practicums frequently concluded that traditional society yielded parallels with today's social world, except for their description in contemporary terms. One student found a new meaning in contemporary military campaigns as they related to the stories of former heroics. Another observed parallels between earlier and contemporary military campaigns, although personally she could not reconcile herself to either. "Love [for a woman] spurred *kozaky* on to victories in past battles, rendering them virtually immortal" (Iryna M). The contemporary equivalent exists in the practice of many a soldier going into battle with a picture of his beloved to sustain him.

## Creating a Marriage Circle

The beginning of a marriage circle can be traced to an initial flirtation between two people during the ritual known as *vechornytsi*—evening meetings of young people that often went beyond flirtation, and led to sex. According to the students' findings the first formal meeting on an appointed day took place in secret outside the home, typically in the evening after a workday, on a public street. In some cases a homonym modernized the acquaintance process, rendering it more spontaneous, more democratic, more demonstrative, especially as the street represented a site of mutual leisure activity rather than just a public space. As they tracked the formation of a future affianced couple students also noted the occasional parental warnings and presence of various obstacles to the match. These might include outright parental (read: mothers') cautions, which frequently signaled attempts to break up the couple and reorient children toward another marital candidate, or simply prohibited the proposed match. "The injunction: 'Be home no later than ten' (folk rituals aside) were heard frequently in the past. Just as they do today (if in somewhat different guise) mothers attempted to protect their daughters from excessive contacts with 'undesirable' young men. Daughters ignored such parental warnings in the past and do so in the present, often to their regret later" (Maryna P).

Time was when unremitting external mediation influenced the norms of morality in the form of numerous parental restrictions on personal freedom, or the gossip and rumors of neighbors and the community at large. This dwindled to virtually nothing in the urbanized twentieth century, in which sex became one of the most flexible of values, although certain agents such as freedom restricted by parents and relatives, as well as gossip, scandal, disapproval voiced by neighbors and others might still have been at work. And when such oversight needed to be reinforced, it was justified by claims that it was designed to protect love and prevent bitter mistakes. Cruel behavior toward the offspring and savage beatings as tokens of parental love and good intentions no longer resonate with contemporary readers; on rare occasions corporal punishment might be applied in an effort to break a cycle of sinful conduct: "Mother was the authority figure in the family, the head of the household and she discharged the role of stern parent, even though raising her daughter to be modest ran counter to her own youthful conduct" (Inna S). It was no accident that the futility of such attempts at caution was so often analyzed (Almodovar 1992: 101). Added to these cautions were external factors capable of separating lovers for long periods, sometimes for life—military campaigns, forced unions, death. Students also reported that girls were overwhelmingly victimized: "It was the girls who suffered when a loved one was forced to go to war, seek employment abroad, or when parents interfered in the interest of some demands of their own" (Kateryna B).

Likely enough, once they had familiarized themselves with some widely known folk songs and rituals, students began to think about the complexity and ambiguity of family relationships, in sharp contrast to their representation as part of the romanticized simplicity of village life in days gone by. They began to recognize the gender imbalance in many of the traditions, the authoritarianism of the older generation, and its dismissal of youthful views. "Often with the best of intentions, mothers doomed their own children to unhappiness and suffering" (Olena Po), and this impelled students to criticize those idealized practices of bygone days. Today, sure of themselves and their future, young women are no longer prepared to identify unequivocally with the tragic fate of girls of more than a hundred years ago. Contemporary young women refuse to accept the former romantic celebration of a chosen mate with her pledge of eternal love, and death if the beloved failed to return. Revenge also became a frequent variation on the theme—"if I can't have him, no one will" (Olena Pe). Although extremely rare, this is not altogether unknown in contemporary society.

Consistent with Ukrainian custom the future married couple became the primary actors in a marriage circle. In noting the relatively great degree of independence in the formation of unions, and the possibilities of spending time together as they became acquainted, including insinuations of premarital relations, one student concluded (surprisingly) that we cannot gainsay certain influential exogenous factors such as magic. "Marital happiness is achievable through fortune telling (only thus can mutual love be guaranteed)" (Olena Pe).

Along with the young principals in the marriage circle, parents, kinfolk, friends, the community, neighbors, and acquaintances (mostly women) might also become agents. They were all empowered to participate in the second phase of the wedding preparations. Many of the student works emphasized the popular saying that "mothers are the time-honored bearers of traditions." One student pointed to the "frequent repetition of the word mother, often accompanied by the exasperated expression oiy" (Marina Kh), leading the contemporary reader to assume that such an emotional outburst was motivated by the student's personal worldview. Today's family council must also take into account the growth in the role of education, the media, comradely exchanges, and the significant weight of personal experience in the choice of a partner, unlike the situation in the past when mothers played such a prominent role.

> Disregarding the relatively unconstrained formation of the marriage circle, the overall strategy and legitimization of the marital choice might still rely on the need for parental consent—usually from the mother of the bride. If wealth consolidation was an issue influence would pass to the mother of the groom. Capital was transferred through patrilineal descent, but the transmission itself was overseen by the most senior woman on the groom's side—the matriarch or "Berehynia."[3] Strategies such as these frequently diverged from the personal desires of young women and men, conditioned by their commitment to the ideals of romantic love. (Sergii L).

With some sense of satisfaction, students found in the romance of former premarital relations certain lighthearted qualities that resonated with them, especially those reflected in the playful songs about multiple relationships, flirting, premarital sex, and excessive concentration on the externalities and youth of the couple. A comparative analysis calls attention to the fact that traditional premarital relations, which found their expression in folk songs, were characterized by a high level of democratic leanings differing little from contemporary models (Kateryina Sok).

Personal attributes that drew a couple together revealed the overwhelming number of unions formed independently, and marriage circles created by consent. Beauty, grace, and affection are the first to come to mind. Once a decision to establish a new family was initiated, however, the emphasis shifted to boldness and industriousness on the part of both sexes. "When a union was announced, the importance of good household management came into play. The candidacy for marriage of a widow who was a good housekeeper trumped that of a homely single girl" (Oxana S). Conversely, a forced marriage elicited criticism in the form of charges of ugliness, stupidity, laziness, alcoholism, and violence. Generally speaking, contemporary students of both sexes, accustomed to a worry-free pop culture, pointed to the frequency with which folk songs highlighted unhappy marriages, with their betrayed love, separations, and other anxiety-ridden tendencies, or as one student explained: "In songs about family life we encountered a panoply of sorrowful and mournful ones" (Liudmila Sh).

Romantic sympathies aside, today's youth is also capable of acknowledging the importance of wealth as a defining motive, whether it is used to augment or preserve the family holdings should this become an issue. In such a case, the chosen mate might be relabeled as inferior. One of the students placed special emphasis on the fact that the mother of the groom appeared to have the paramount interest in material issues. As she put it: "The mother of the groom showed the greatest concern about wealth" (Olena Po). No less important were considerations such as class, most frequently expressed as the dichotomy between free and enserfed. It is also a truism that during the aristocratic era, and even later, there were many instances recorded of a young woman being forced into a loveless match with a wealthy man (Liudmila Sh). Another problem arose when men exaggerated their social status, claiming to be Russian soldiers ("Muscovite"), or *kozaky* (cossacks). These seductive allegations were concealed from the public only to create problems for the bride later in life. Mothers often cautioned against choosing such a partner with: "that *kozak* is always on the move" (Maia T). Absences, whatever the cause, were known to destroy unions, giving rise to incomplete families. In light of this evidence, the student works shattered today's ubiquitous and illusory positive stereotype of the knightly *kozak* as the masculine ideal, the enviable party so characteristic of the androcentric version of Ukrainian history. They also noted the frequency with which the marriage circle's criterion of "a suitably stable life" was reducible to endogamy, and exclusion of foreigners.

Homogamy, as students rightly commented, was a typical tactic, as a result of which a great age difference, or family compositions that included widowhood, or "female soldier," became subjects of songs as variants of the norm, or exceptions to it. Consider such examples as taking as a bride a woman abandoned by a lover because of his military service, or employment abroad. This could have a humane implication, with good people accepting this good girl. Such socially approved behavior on the part of the groom's parents was equated with good people, as did a prospective bride's willingness to wait for the return of her affianced soldier (Maksym Z). Nonetheless, Maksym continued to characterize her situation as a state of marital marginality—"the prospective bride was neither one without a past, nor a widow," emphasizing the undesirability of the match. The status of widowhood was ambivalent—attractive by experience but repulsive by reputation. It was also commonly held that if a couple was unable to follow through on the marriage plans it was because they were being subjected to God's punishment.

Gender inequality was also evident in the wedding arrangements: "During the final selection phase the young man began to take note of the woman's reputation" (Olena Ro), closely observing her conduct. Adverse behavior left him free to reject her on the grounds that she had failed to meet his expectations. Conversely, the prospective groom was not subjected to the same scrutiny. The gender sensitivity of the student writing this reveals itself in the lack of information provided about the role of a father in the marriage proceedings. Another gender-sensitive student commented upon married life by noting, "a picture of a happy wife and mother in the marriage was difficult to come by."

Apart from the characterization of the family's role in a description of the marriage circle, the more dedicated students provided a gender analysis.

> The folk songs, with their external banality, mark the intersection of oppression—gender and age—that created the patriarchal system. Accordingly, a young wife found herself in an untenable situation, where a woman from an older age cohort became the agent of her oppression. And even if her husband succeeded in integrating himself firmly into the public sphere, be it state building or some mundane peasant occupation, a young wife was unable to assume her socially mandated position because a senior woman—the mother-in-law—was in charge and her authority could not be challenged. (Yury Z)

## Conclusion

This brief sketch is the first attempt in the study of a larger subject; it is designed to reveal the dearth of research on the wide array of contemporary marriage-family practices, and to inspire reflections on the past, where similarities or differences also reveal certain aspects of our own culture—a procedure that the American anthropologist Phillip Bock called culture shock. An effort was made either to restructure or refute some of the numerous unjustified generalizations and established conceptions of marriage-family relationships in order to provide a more accurate gender analysis and offer some constructive criticism. This essay touches on a migration pattern that differs from the contemporary labor migration process, but it does portray the outmigration of women from one physical space to another, from home to an alien environment. We are left with the thought that it is overwhelmingly the women who make the transfer from the "known" to the "unknown."

**Lyudmyla Males** is a sociologist and doctor of science (PhD in 2003, Habilitat in 2013), and associate professor at Taras Shevchenko National University in Kyiv. She has published textbooks and numerous articles on gender analysis and family relations in Ukraine, along with a monograph, *Studying the Texts of Culture. Sociocultural Analysis as a Knowledge-Acquisition Strategy for Sociology.*

## Notes

1. Figures compiled from ESS-3 data. http://zacat.gesis.org/webview/.

2. Results based on sociological survey carried out by the Ukrainian Institute of Social Research within the framework of the 2002 project titled "Forming gender parity in the context of contemporary socio-economic conversions."
3. Known as Berehynia (protectress), she assured generational continuity. Owing to the fact that she presided over the hearth where all decisions were taken during the clan stage of human development, she wielded considerable influence and power. Accordingly, she came to represent the empowerment of women, but her role in Ukrainian culture has been, and continues to be the subject of great controversy.

# Bibliography

Almodovar, Jean-Pierre. 1992. "Rasskaz o zhizni i individual'naia traektoriia: sopostavlenie masshtabov analiza," *Problemy sociologiyi* 1(2): 98–103.

Antonov, Anatoliy, and Victor Medkov. 1996. *Sociologiia semeyi*. Moscow: Moscow State University, International University of Business and Administration.

Bertaux, Daniel, et al. 1996. *Sud'by liudei: Rossiia XX vek. Biografiyi semei kak ob'ekt sociologicheskogo issledovaniia*. Moscow: Institute of Sociology, Russian Academy of Sciences.

Bock, Philip, ed. 1970. *Culture Shock: A Reader in Modern Cultural Anthropology*. Washington, DC: Press of America.

Giddens, Anthony. 1993. *New Rules of Sociological Method: A Positive Critique of Interpretative Sociologies*, 2nd edition. Stanford, CA: Stanford University Press.

Golod, Sergey, ed. 1993. *Annotirovannaia bibliografiia po problemam semyi*. Moscow: IS RAN.

Habermas, Jürgen. 1981. *Theorie des kommunikativen Handelns*, Band 2. *Zur Kritik der funktionalistischen Vernunft*. Frankfurt: Suhrkamp Verlag.

Hladun, Olexandr, ed. 1993. *Naselennia Ukrainy, 1992. Demohrafichny shchorichnyk*. Kyiv: Tekhnika.

Horodianenko, Viktor, ed. 2001. *Sociologiya semyi. Chastichno annotirovanny bibliograficheskii ukazatel' literatury za 1980–2000 gody*. Dnipropetrovsk: DNU.

Libanova, Ella, et al. 2008. *Shliub, Sim'ia ta Ditorodni Orientatsiyi v Ukraini*. Kyiv: ADEF-Ukraine.

Oushakine, Sergey A., ed. 2004. *Semeine uzy: modeli dlia sborki*, vols. 1–2. Moscow: New Literary Review.

Rimashevskaia, Natalia, et al. 1999. *Okno v russkuiu chastnuiu zhizn'. Supruzheskie pary v 1996 godu*. Moscow: Akademiia.

Seider, Reinhard. 1987. *Sozialgeschichte der Familie*. Frankfurt am Main: Surkampf Verlag.

Semenova, Viktoria, ed. 1996. *Sud'by liudei: Rossia XX vek. Biografiyi semei kak obiekt sociologicheskogo issledovaniia*. Moscow: Institute of Philosophy, Russian Academy of Sciences.

Stelmakh, Lubov, ed. 2004. *Naselennia Ukrainy za 2003 rik. Demohrafichny shchorichnyk*. Kyiv: Derkomstat of Ukraine.

Tymoshenko, Halyna, ed. 2009. *Naselennia Ukrainy za 2008 rik. Demohrafichny shchorichnyk*, Kyiv: Derkomstat Ukrainy.

# PART IV

# Paradigm Shifts

# CHAPTER 12

# Gender as the "Blind Spot" in Ukrainian Psychology

Marfa M. Skoryk

There is nothing new in the idea of systematizing the direction of the Ukrainian psychology studies that have been examined from a gender-theory perspective in order to determine their full potential. Research consistently benefits from self-reflection, especially the kind of rapid conceptualization and methodical integration of gender issues currently taking place in Ukrainian social sciences and the humanities. At issue here, however, is not merely disciplinary self-revision; presently we are observing increasing manifestations of a somewhat unusual understanding of the application of gender in Ukraine's scientific, circum-scientific, and unscientific spheres (Hrydkovets 2011). This includes proposals for practical applications of gender in national government and regional policies (*Proekt*).

Contrary to measures adopted by international experts for addressing the issues of (in)equality through interdisciplinary measures, in Ukraine gender as a concept, still inadequately understood by many, has been confined to the gender-identity domain. Consistent with its Soviet legacy, the entire body of post-Soviet educational literature leans in this direction, where the term in question is being promoted as a singular substitute for *sex* (sexual dimorphism), with no distinction made between the two sexes, thereby implying an absence of the individual essence. This trend might also be observed in religion-linked movements (*Rivne, UPGKC*). They position gender-related self-realization as the key component of their ideology, and their political watchword. Ukraine's political, cultural, and religious elites tend to view the study of psychology as a logical point of entry for developing an understanding of gender. Meanwhile, gendered structural inequalities, still widely unacknowledged, continue to languish in a "blind spot."

## Recent Research and Publications

From time to time the numerous transformations of gender issues, especially in the context of post-Soviet studies, have captured the attention of psychologists in Ukraine. For instance, at the dawn of the new millennium Ukrainian experts began their assessments of normative courses and educational programs in the humanities (*Genderna Ekspertyza*), enabling them to identify potential entry points for the inclusion of gender in their psychology programs. Professionals, such as Iryna Klëtsina, addressed the theory and methodology of a gender-based approach to psychology and identified problems inherent in this method (1998, 2002, and 2005). Nadia Radina looked into the potential of a gender analysis in psychological research (1999). Tetiana Repina described the thorny path that leads from the theory of sex-role socialization to gender psychology (1987). Liudmyla Males systematized the results of the biological, psychological, and sociocultural elements of gender (2004). Liudmyla Stepanova examined the overall problems of a gender approach in Ukraine's post-Soviet psychology (2006), while Lubov Volkova analyzed empirical research on gender (1990–2009), and Tetiana Yevmenova delineated the studies in Ukrainian political psychology, together with the ongoing research on the impact of women's leadership in mainstream politics (2011). Each of these works is considered a separate theoretical study relating to the way scholarship is, or can be, organized and connected to the introduction of gender in psychology. The systematized ideas of the part that gender-related disciplines play are important scholarly and practical considerations (Smoliar 2004; Skoryk 2006).

During the Soviet era and into the post-Soviet period Ukrainian scholars published many of their basic works on gender in the form of informational and analytical surveys of foreign literature on genderized psychology. This practice continues, and in fact has been expanded by the addition of handbooks and various kinds of reference works. Other genres have also been added to this growing body of literature on the subject. Despite such a quickened flurry of activity, however, Ukrainian scholars have not kept pace with the burst of methodological works on gender issues being produced in the West.

Ukrainians are also paying more attention than ever to the process of translating outstanding foreign works on feminist theory and methodology. This, in turn, is facilitating the adaptation of gender issues to serious scholarly studies in various disciplines, but lends itself most readily to the study of psychology. As a result Ukrainian researchers are now successfully creating a kind of autonomized gender "ghetto" within a discrete Ukrainian research space, a necessary one that allows them to bypass foreign sources as they carve out their own distinct stream of scholarship.

## Description of the Problem Under Study

This chapter aims to scrutinize the ways in which gender issues have been inserting themselves into Ukrainian psychology for the past fifteen years, and to delineate the core conflict lines (terminological, conceptual, structural, and so forth). In other words, the objective is to identify the prioritized course of gender psychology already completed, and to scrutinize it in its new developmental stage. Post-Soviet scholars working in the discipline of psychology apply a theoretical framework to the analysis of publications on gender issues.

Gender studies enjoyed a long prehistory in the Soviet social sciences. Most interesting was the widespread discourse on the relationship between the social and the biological that began in the 1970s. Drawing on this Soviet legacy, academic interest in gender and the appearance of scholarly studies on the topic in Ukraine can be dated to about the mid-1990s. This interest extends to almost all of the social sciences, with the works of linguists, literary scholars, and sociologists considered the most dynamic and methodologically sound.

Let us return for a moment to the "sex/gender" dichotomy to view the range of gender applicability in psychology. In the past thirty years or so the dichotomy developed its own history, concluding with an emphasis on the cultural production of knowledge about the body as the rationale for rejecting an autonomous definition of *sex*. That was one aspect. Another is the problematization of sex as part of a given dichotomy, similar to the fate of our understanding of gender, as explained in the West by Susan Bordo (1993). Under the circumstances a retrospective look at the so-called authentic initial formulations of this discussion would also be productive.

As we know, biological reductionism was the main concept against which the gender approach was aimed, and the motive for its adoption. In her article "Toward a redefinition of sex and gender," considered a classic for our purposes, Rhoda Unger explained that at the time of its publication in 1979 the term *gender* was used to describe the "non-physiological components of the sex culturally ascribed to men or to women." Its application served to reduce the received parallels between biological and psychological sex, or at least to call attention to certain assumptions regarding them. The fundamental message of the gender approach is a refutation of the exploitation of sexual differences as a basis for creating schemes for interpreting sociocultural phenomena, even as the same differences are deemed appropriate for descriptive purposes.

Gender studies as an interdisciplinary sociocultural project deserve a reference here, inasmuch as their relevance varies according to the different disciplines into which they are incorporated. What is most important for us is that as the crucial issue of biological determinism was being discussed, psychology turned out to be the discipline that articulated the division between a gender approach and the ensuing terminological wars.

Whereas sociology, literary criticism, and philosophy are able to ignore or even to jettison their biodeterministic definitions, in psychology such dismissals appear far less likely. Since the mid-nineteenth century, according to Stephanie Shields, psychology (in the West) has had a tradition of studying sex differences based upon the perception that the brains of women and men differ structurally, producing disparity in intellect and character, as well as a hypothetical variation in men's intellect and creativity. This observation was disseminated in educational and social venues, triggering the perception of a "woman's unique nature." It, in turn, invited an entire array of psychological "facts" such as the "maternal instinct," "women's sexual passivity" (1975: 30, and 739–754), and "women's intuition" among her so-called leading attributes, according to the indigenous pop-psychology. Small wonder, then, that Shields arrived at the conclusion that the history of sex differences constitutes a research field that has never lacked for social prejudice. Biological differences, as Sandra Bem observed, have been at the forefront of nearly all American reflections on the differences between the sexes, especially on the part of psychologists (1997).

Justifiably, such discussions prompted a reaction from professionals. For instance, through experimentation Leta Hollingworth attempted to verify precisely which sexual differences are to be found in the various psychological traits. She was the first among such professionals working in psychology to pursue systematic experimental research on these disparities. Holingsworth published her findings in a series of works that became classics in the field (1914, 1916, and 1918). It bears noting that during the entire twentieth century the problem of biological explanations for sexual differences was left to the discipline of psychology to pursue. Within it the framework of feminist psychology took shape. A steady stream of publications offers eloquent testimony to this. Since the end of the past century, as Ukrainian scholars increasingly acquired access to Western studies, similar historical and psychological projects have appeared in post-Soviet Ukrainian scholarship. In her study, published in the late 1990s, Natalia Khodyreva strove to delineate the discourse of the "natural" views of the body as a historical attribute, and the evolution of its perception in the nineteenth-century scholarship of Russian psychologists. A partial explanation of this phenomenon can be found in Rhoda Unger's study, in which she demonstrates that together with the biological accounts gender-oriented interpretational schemes in psychology on the list there were possible explanations.

Contrary to data accumulated through experimentation, and formulated over the course of just under a hundred years in the West, until it compromised itself bio-determinism was not refuted in psychology. It is arguable that the reason lies not only in routine methodological interventions, especially in biology, but is inherent in the very disciplinary field of psychological limitations.

It is obvious that explanatory limitations of the dominant argument for women's unique nature, or more specifically a woman's nature, are revealed in disciplines such as sociology, political science, and philosophy rather than in psychology, with its greater visibility. From the very beginning, however, the concept of a woman's unique nature, that is to say conceptions about the essence of a woman or her natural destiny revealed its interpretive inability to explain the changes in the status of the sexes, which began to emerge in industrialized countries.

The allegedly natural tendencies of either sex were called into serious question as a consequence of the French Revolution followed by Europe's industrialization in the mid-nineteenth century, resulting in the ultimate breakdown of traditional societies. This resulted in radical changes in the status of the sexes, as well as relations between them, within countries and in local societies, in families and individuals alike. Having created a problem, these changes soon required regulating, and in this form finally made their way into the political sphere. In this context the entire conceptual defenselessness of biodeterministic definitions manifested itself with alacrity. If sex based traits are truly conditioned biologically they must remain constant, unchangeable. This deprives us of any possibility, even at a minimum, to explain the apparent and drastic changes in the status of men and women as members of sociosexual groupings. The only generalization possible from this theoretical standpoint is the claim that the nature of woman and man deteriorates, although within these parameters no actual causes can be specified. It is even less possible to articulate a positive program that would specify what must be done to influence human nature in order to avert these consequences. This had the effect of peeling off the mask of biodeterministic explanations, which betray themselves as an ideology and not as scientific explanations. Required is an analysis of the causes and a recognition of further developments in the social enlightenment processes. The biodeterministic approach, beginning with a search for sexual differences in biology and neuropsychology with their ability to explain disparities in the status of social sexual groups, in sociobiology, in evolutionary or differential psychology, in cultural studies, even in philosophy is without a practical application. The biodeterminist approach cannot build a political strategy or program without the conceptual tools needed to influence phenomena linked to sex differences and identified in contemporary social sciences as gender related. This is true in sociology, political science, philosophy, and linguistics (expressed as *gen-derlect*), where the conceptual limitation and methodological impotence of biodeterminism is obvious.

Simultaneously, it is very clear even from what has been written here how little these discussions and their consequences have influenced the disciplinary field of psychology, especially in Ukraine. In and of itself, scholarship in psychology does not deal in social or statistical general-izations, in which the allegedly biological differences between the sexes engender a socially undesirable gender gap in the various spheres of their daily life. The problem simply does not exist from the standpoint of the discipline, with its long-standing and respected tradition of illuminating psychological differences between the sexes and their biological origins. It is noteworthy that once this list of biological differences was reviewed and shortened, stemming from a series of experimental works in American psychology, the fundamental explanations shifted toward psychological arguments (Unger 1979). As an example, "basic female/male traits" were used to explain politics as a basically male profession, or some other so-cially prominent phenomenon.

Compared to psychology in general, the Ukrainian equivalent has even more grounds for producing rationalizations of this kind, and for formu-lating mainly essentialist arguments. For instance, if we consider the sit-uation in greater detail we will observe that the minimal influence on the discipline of psychology revealed in our discussions cannot be explained by its structure, uneven evolutionary progress, and developmental direc-tions, where, to repeat, the psychology of personality so clearly dominates. One offshoot in particular is the fact that the number of psychologists as well as departments and universities that train them, have kept pace with the steep growth in societal demand for psychological guidance, coun-seling, and therapy, all of which are expanding exponentially. Although the psychology of personality is dominant in the practice and discipline of psychology, while potentially gender-rich subsets such as industrial psychology or organizational psychology are still virtually nonexistent in Ukraine, even nominally sociopsychological themes and empirical re-search in the methodological designs and the psychology of personality are able to achieve dominance in the sociopsychological sphere, and em-pirical research.

What this means in practice is that the gender theory becomes hostage to interpretational schemes of the psychology of personality; that delimi-tation of gender/sex (or more precisely the *connection* between gender and sex) will assume the mantle of a key disciplinary discussion; and gender issues will continue to be treated as problems of the individual rather than as social structures. In other words, the psychology of personality mod-ifies the theme, as well as the conceptual grounds, and methodological apparatus of gender studies to fit the needs and possibilities of its subdisciplinary field.

At the same time, this situation has a positive component in its prospects for the implementation of a gender orientation. To begin with, it lies within the autonomy of results obtained by such research, and more precisely within the question of how long these results can be produced and remain conceptually self-replicating in a closed disciplinary circle. Obviously, the issue here is not simply the application of the notion of (biological) "sex" as an interpretational scheme of social origins in empirical psychological research, or in allied disciplines. The issue also consists in the heuristic potential of a gender approach that enables previously socially significant phenomena, unnoticed in earlier scientific procedures, to emerge, thereby facilitating their predictability and producing explanations for them. Rejection of gender as an analytical category, and the gender approach as an interpretational scheme, separate elements of which can be observed in indigenous psychological studies, is more dangerous in this respect. It removes psychology from the mainstream of social analytics and pushes psychology studies away from the mainstream of social analysis, reducing the discipline to the marginal realm of the pseudo-academic.

Another aspect of this situation is the societal accumulation of poorly studied, even unexamined socio-psychological phenomena such as, for instance, domestic (gender) violence, male suicides, or psychological predisposition to prostitution, which are gradually but insistently accumulating and slowly shifting from the category of private issues to day-to-day political agendas. In this axiomatic position the administratively relevant research questions are formulated as problems of administrative relevance that cannot be ignored indefinitely, as Dorothy Smith once explained it (1987).

## Conclusion

The present chapter serves as a "revisiting" of the gender approach in indigenous Ukrainian psychology. Our analysis has shown that psychology serves at once as the frontier of the gender approach and the turf of its terminological wars, inasmuch as discussions central to sex/gender discourses, biological determinism, and other such issues are taking place within that disciplinary field. Our major conclusions lead us to the practical impotence of biodeterministic or essentialist rationalizations, as they first became visible in the social sciences as ideological concepts.

Alternatively, psychological studies in and of themselves do not participate in either social or statistical generalizations, where sexual differences so obviously reach the level of a gender gap between men and women as sociosexual groupings in the many spheres of their daily existence. In our judgment, this is exactly why psychology has greater grounds for resorting to essentialist approaches. We link its peripatetics to the introduction of a gender approach, and its further prospects in the interdisciplinary lines of conflict in the indigenous socio-humanities, all of which have already left their mark on gender studies in Ukraine. Another significant aspect of our analysis is its relevance to psychology's well-established status in gender studies as an interdisciplinary phenomenon, offering numerous non-psychological departure points.

We believe that including gender studies within the parameters of Ukrainian psychology is controversial not only because of the insignificant influence of the discourses on the discipline of psychology. The structure and uneven directional development in Ukrainian psychology—dominated as it is by the psychology of the individual, not to mention the absence of such potentially gender-rich subsets as industrial psychology or organizational psychology—makes its introduction premature. Whether this will mean a further dependence of gender theory on interpretational schemes grounded in the psychology of the individual; whether the gender/sex dichotomy (or, more precisely, identification of gender with sex) will continue as the key disciplinary discourse; whether gender issues will be treated as problems of the individual, as opposed to social structures, are all questions that invite further research.

**Marfa M. Skoryk** is a senior researcher of the Institute of Social and Political Psychology of National Academy of Pedagogical Sciences of Ukraine. She heads the Kyiv Gender Studies Institute. Her expertise lies in performance of the governmental programs (2007, 2008, and 2009), the methodology of gender studies, and Ukrainian women's political participation, and she has written more than twenty papers on the subjects. She is a gender analyst, in which capacity she authored several national documents on gender equality: "Strategy of gender transformations of the Ukrainian society" (2005) and the "State program on the maintenance of equality between women and men in Ukraine" (2005).

# Bibliography

Anastasi, Anne. 1981. "Sex Differences: Historical Perspectives and Methodological Implications," *Developmental Review* 1(3 September): 187–206. http://www.apa.org/education/k12/sexual-inequality.aspx.

Bem, Sandra Lipsitz. 1993. *The Lenses of Gender: Transforming the Debate on Sexual Inequality: From Biological Difference to Institutionalized Androcentrism.* New Haven, CT: Yale University Press.

Bordo, Susan. 1993. *Feminism, Post Modernism and Gender Scepticism: Unbearable Weight Feminism, Western Culture*. Berkeley: University of California Press.

*Genderna Ekspertyza Navchal'nykh Prohram Sotsio-humanitarnoho Tsyklu*. 2001. Kyiv: Kyiv Gender Studies Institute.

Haaken, Janice. 1988. "Field dependence research: A historical analysis of a psychological construct," *Signs: Journal of Women in Culture and Society* 13: 311–330.

Hollingworth, Leta. 1914. "Variability as related to sex differences in achievement: A critique," *American Journal of Sociology* 19(4): 510–530.

———. 1916. "Sex differences in mental traits," *Psychological Bulletin* 13(10): 377–384.

———. 1918. "Comparison of the sexes in mental traits," *Psychological Bulletin* 15(12): 427–432.

Holovashenko, Iryna O. 2004. *Stanovlennia Teorii Genderu. Osnovy Teorii Genderu: Navchal'ny Posibnyk*, eds. Larysa S. Kobelyanska, Vira P. Aheeva, and Marfa M. Skoryk. Kyiv: Kyiv Gender Studies Institute.

Hrydkovets, Liudmyla. 2011. *Gendenorivnistny Extremism iak Faktor Riunatsiyi Rodyny. Naukovi Studii iz Sotsial'noi ta Politychnoi Psykholohiyi: Zbirnyk Stattei*, eds. Mykola M. Sliusarevsky, 27(30). Kyiv: Milennium. ispp.org.ua/bibl_4.htm.

Khodyriova, Natalia. *Arkheologiia Psykhologii. GROSSVITA* no. 5. http://giacgender .narod.ru/n5t3.htm.

Kletsina, Iryna S. 1998. "Genderny podkhod v sistemy Psikhologicheskoho Obrazovaniia," in *Gendernyie Issledovaniia: Feministkaia Metodologiia v Sotsial'nykh Naukakh*. Materialy 2oi Mezhdunarodnei Letnei Shkoly Gendernym Issledovaniam—X. Kharkiv: Kharkiv Center for Gender Studies, 193–215.

———. 2002. "Razvitie gendernykh issledovanii v psikhologiyi," *Obshchestvenniie Nauki i Sovremennost'* 3: 181–191.

Voronina, Olga A. 2005. *Genderna Ekspertyza Uchebnikov dlia Vysshei Shkoly*. Moscow: Soltex Publ.

Males, Liudmyla V. 2004. "Biolohichni, psykholohichni ta sotsiokul'turni chynnyky genderu," in *Osnovy teoriyi Genderu: Navchal'ny Posibnyk*, eds. Larysa S. Kobelyanska, Vira P. Aheeva, and Marfa M. Skoryk. Kyiv: Kyiv Gender Studies Institute, 109–132.

Proekt recommendatsiyi hromads'kykh slukhan' na temu "Ziasuvannia sutnosti gendernoi polityky ta problem I ryzykiv iaki vona nese Ukrainskomu suspil'stvu." Vidpovidno do rishennia Volynskoi Oblasnoi Rady vid 6/21/2012, no. 12/13, 10 lypnia 2012 roku. http://volynrada.gov.ua/news/10-lipnya-sesiinislukhannya-materiali.

Radina, Nadezhda K. 1999. "Ob ispol'zovanii gendernoho analiza v issledovanniakh," *Voprosy v Psykhologiyi* 2 (1999): 22-27.

Repina, Tatiana A. 1987. "Analiz teorii polorolevoi sotsializatsiyi v sovremennoi Zapadnoi psikhologiyi," *Voprosy v Psykhologiyi* 2: 158–165.

*Resolutsiia uchasnykiv kruhloho stolu*. "Suchasni problemy vprovadzhennia statevoho vykhovannia, gendernoi polityky, ta iuvenal'noi iustytutsiyi v osvitniu systemu Ukrainy," Bat'kivs'kyi Komitet Ukrainy 24–25 liutoho, 2012 roku. *News from the Christian World/Pro Church.Info*. http://prochurch.info/index.php/news/more/22932.4449

Shields, Stephanie A. 1975. "Functionalism, Darwinism, and the psychology of women: A study of social myth," *American Psychologist* 30: 739–754.

———. 1982. "The Variability Hypothesis: The History of a Biological Model of Sex Differences in Intelligence," *Signs* 7: 769–797.

Smith, Dorothy E. 1987. "Women's Perspective as a Radical Critique of Sociology," in *Feminism and Methodology: Women's Perspective*. Tver: Center for Women's History and Gender Research, Tver State University. http://tvergenderstudies.ru/main.php?subaction=showfull&id=1294236240&archive=&start_from=&ucat=68&do=.

Stepanova, Liudmyla N. 2006. "Aktual'nyie problemy gendernoi psikhologiyi v usloviakh sovremennykh integratsionnykh protsesov," in *Actual'nyie Problemy Sotsial'no-humanitarnykh Nauk v Usloviakh Sovremennykh Integratysionnykh Protsesov*, eds. Stepan Fedorovych, Sokol, et al. Minsk. www.mycoach.at.tut.by/gender.html.

Thompson, Helen B. 1903. "The mental traits of sex," in *Classics in the History of Psychology*. http://psychclassics.yorku.ca/Thompson/.

Unger, Rhoda K. 1979. "Toward a redefinition of sex and gender," *American Psychologist* 34: 1085–1094.

———. 1998. *Resisting gender: Twenty-five Years in/of Feminist Psychology*. London and Thousand Oaks, CA: Sage Publications.

*UPGKC*. "Public organizations' appeal to Lviv's City Council," in *The Family* under *the Virgin's Cover*. http://www.pokrov.lviv.ua/?cat=3.

Volkova, Lyubov O. 2012. "Gender u psykhologichnykh doslidzhenniakh (na materialakh dysertatsiinykh robit iz psykholohiyi 1990-1009 rokakh," in *Problemy Gendernoi Sosializatsiyi Suchasnoi Molodi*. Kryvy Rih: State Higher Education Institution. National University of Kryvy Rih, 33–40.

Yevmenova, Tetyana M. 2011. "Genderni pytannia v politychnii psykholohiyi: stan rozroblenosti ta perspektyvy (Za materialamy dysertasiinykh robit, 1995–2010)," in *Psykholohichni Perspektyvy: Spetsvypusk Psykholohichni vymiry Ukrainskoho sotsiokul'turnoho prostoru*. Kyiv, 132–139.

# CHAPTER 13

# The Ukrainian Woman Elects Patriarchy
## *Who Benefits?*

### Hanna Chernenko

Although sufficient data are available on women in contemporary Ukrainian society to provide an intelligible picture of preferred family models, any attempt to apply the same methodology to study the preferences of Soviet-era women becomes more problematic. Their recollections are shrouded by more than two decades of Ukrainian independence. Currently, our most reliable information comes from their comments submitted to women's journals over the course of nearly a century, especially letters revealing women's attitudes toward men. These are now accessible to researchers.

For purposes of this research, *Zhinka* (Woman), a Soviet-era publication targeting Ukrainian women and in existence for over twenty years in independent Ukraine, provides a sound foundation for comparing Soviet women's views with those voiced in post-Soviet Ukraine. The journal's history goes back to 1920, when it first appeared under the title *Communard,* and then was renamed *Radianska Zhinka* (Soviet Woman) in 1939. Once Ukrainian independence became a reality, the journal's publisher refused to use the term *Soviet* in the title, so it was renamed *Zhinka*. All references were reclassified in the card catalog of the Vernadsky Scientific Library in Kyiv under the letter *X*, which was typed over the original entry.

This is a unique publication not only owing to its prolonged existence, but because of its close connection to our country's history, not to mention its refusal to metamorphose into one of those sleek, "glitzy" magazines portraying the recent emergence of "glamour" in the women-oriented mass media. Here is how today's editor in chief, Lidia Mazur, formulated the publisher's credo: "Yes, we have preserved the ... fundamental tendencies of our predecessors. Our heroine is not your sexually unbalanced woman, nor is she the one who sees pleasing a man as her basic calling, or perhaps indulging herself by acquiring some gaudy bauble or other. We operate on the premise that every single woman is an individual, with her own range of interests, a job she loves, and one who wishes to bring up happy, healthy children" (Lavrinenko 2001). In addition to these issues, running a household, maintaining personal relationships, and following the latest fashion, social-political, and cultural events are routinely featured. Other sections include references to manufacture in the UkSSR (Ukrainian SSR), and business in independent Ukraine.

In conducting this research, it was important to bear in mind that published letters are invariably marked by editorial policy, that they have undergone a process of selection and correction; notwithstanding, the women's voices have remained irrefutably their own. On the one hand such texts are instruments for disseminating a particular ideology, and on the other they more or less expose a broad spectrum of collective attitudes. They also create a unique mirror reflecting dominant social ideologemes.

For sources unmarked by women's thoughts as they were filtered through a publisher's house policy, the researcher might choose to turn to items from the Internet forums, as well as to an array of humorous writings, one of the functions of which is to reveal women's semi-censorable public pronouncements. Indeed, anecdotes are today's most prevalent humorous subject matter, although their authorship, male or female, is virtually impossible to ascertain. As for forums, here we lack sufficient data to make adequate comparisons with Soviet Ukrainian (hereafter UkSSR) data.

## Methodology

We used the cognitive-discursive and content analysis methods in analyzing the women's letters to the journal to gain insights into their views regarding the various family models. Negative comments about men served as our primary research resources about them. They provided direct evidence of what the women rejected, relieving us of the need to rely on stereotypical examples implying that women do not understand their own needs. Linguists who study speech evaluation affirm that such discourse demonstrates a clear asymmetry between negative and positive poles of an axiological coordinate. Our inclination was to use conformance as the norm, although deviations would have been easier to understand. Indeed, it is often possible to recognize norms by tracking their breaches (Arutiunova 1987).

Presumably, the number of letters in which positive assessments of men dominated never exceeded one-tenth of the overall number received. That is the reason why they were not considered a viable research resource. Evaluations were classified in accordance with a semantically unmarked positive modality. For instance, "We cannot live in our home because of a drunken father"[1] was a negative evaluation against which a sober way of life as the desirable mode of conduct functioned as the unmarked paradigm reflecting women's demands.

Criteria used in the evaluation process, organized into a hierarchical structure, represented the range of values. The higher the position occupied by external features, for example, the more likely we were to judge people by their physical attributes such as "a slim figure" or "ideal facial characteristics." If the evaluation contained evidence of these traits, descriptions such as the following would be appropriate: *barefoot* and *beggar,* or conversely, *prosperous* and *well-to-do.* A summary of the dominant evaluative criteria in the reader's letters enabled us to acquire a sense of the values that were important to them, and facilitated the compilation of a descriptive list, with examples arranged in order of frequency of occurrence.

Relying on the views of patriarchal and egalitarian family models constructed within genderological studies, we concluded that in a patriarchal family certain values are less tolerated than others (listed below, ordered according to the number of references published). They run from reliability within the most intimate relationships ("Keep your word when you give it to your wife and children") to a man's self-respect. The egalitarian model is more attuned to qualities ranging from emotional intelligence to independence from the natal family.

As already suggested, the division is relative and in no way gainsays the fact that the woman who favors the patriarchal model will automatically reject her husband's help with domestic chores, or his emotional support. On the other hand, a woman who prefers the egalitarian family model might still choose a husband who assumes responsibility for the family finances, leaving her free to realize her own potential by following her chosen (even if poorly paid) profession. Because it is not easy for a man to conform to the ideals of both models, the absence of a partial set of values might well be the price that women need to pay for the presence of others. At times, however, a woman will adamantly declare her preference for one model (without any sign of deviation), in which case all values of the other will be refused. A case in point might be the rejection of a man's gallantry by adherents of the egalitarian model who support the feminist movement. Gestures like hand kissing or opening doors for women will be construed as patriarchal, implying inequality. Other women might object to the division of labor roles in an egalitarian family. Let us take as one example a television interview with the wife of Russian writer and Nobel prizewinner Alexander Solzhenitsyn. She responded angrily to an interviewer's question, "Does your husband help with raising the children?" "That's all he needs," she replied sarcastically, "to spend his time changing diapers!" And here is an Internet forum comment from a woman who criticized her husband's propensity for compromise, in other words his social intelligence which she interpreted as "spinelessness": "He prefers to avoid arguments or quarrels, to give in … he is nothing but a wimp, a rag to be used for wiping one's feet then unceremoniously tossed aside; that is my opinion."[2]

The following list represents absent values that are less tolerated by patriarchal families (once again arranged according to frequency of appearance in the journal *Zhinka*):

> Reliability in personal relationships (complaints of betrayal and dissolution of marriage ties): "My former husband simply vanished and that was that.…[3]
>
> I caught my first husband cheating with my girl friend, then he moved in with her."[4]
>
> Financial responsibility for the family: "He contributes practically nothing to the family budget.[5]
>
> He lives with his lover Larysa, gives her and her children most of his salary, and all we get is a pittance, even less than the alimony ordered."[6]
>
> Economic exploitation: "My former husband even insisted on his right to some of my assets.… Everybody covets my possessions—a magnificent Opel and a suburban house"[7]
>
> Physical and moral strength: "I feel so sorry for the men. They have become, if you will excuse my saying so, ineffectual, helpless"[8]
>
> "Perhaps it's because I am such a fighter. Neither my husband nor even my daughter are as well adapted to life."[9]
>
> Gallantry: "Who stands in public transport weighed down by bags? We women, that's who. And who sits reading newspapers? Men!"[10]
>
> Where are all those chivalrous knights now?"[11]
>
> Competence in customary domestic tasks (technical repairs): "If we can agree that sewing and embroidery is the woman's domain, then why is it that so many men cannot repair, let us say, an iron, and feel no shame?"[12]
>
> Self-respect. "Where, is it, that self-respect?"[13]
>
> Husband's over dependence on parents: "I once had a family, but it fell apart; neither I nor my parents suited my mother-in-law."[14]

The following represents the absence of values in men to which the egalitarian family model is most sensitive, also according to frequency of appearance:

> Emotional capacity: lack of sympathy, and disinclination to understand woman's problems, or even to bring home a wage in a timely fashion. "He arrives from work and heads straight for the television, or immediately takes a nap. And who will give me a smile, offer sympathy if I have had a hard day."[15]

How I long for a kindhearted husband with an earnest soul. They just don't exist?"[16]

Equal distribution of domestic obligations: "My workday is just like his, and we all know how much of the domestic work falls to the woman. ... The husband comes to a home where everything is waiting for him and he doesn't even appreciate it."[17]

Vadym did not come to me out of love, it was a desire for his own comfort, and routine services."[18]

Interest in family life: "One fault that most men share is that they live their own separate lives, totally disconnected from that of the family."[19]

"My husband lives in a total state of autonomy, virtually outside the life of his family."[20]

Sensitivity to romance: "My husband helps me with everything. He can cook, he cleans. But his attitude toward me has changed. There is no tenderness."[21]

The following are attributes that did not fit easily into either model—patriarchal or egalitarian. Most fall into the category of universal human values:

Respect for a woman's mind: "My third husband wanted to move us to Poland immediately after the marriage ceremony, even though this decision did not fit in with my plans."[22]

"Not a trace of a concession to my point of view."[23]

Involvement in raising the children: "Although I have a husband I am raising our son alone. I take him to festive celebrations, to concerts."[24]

A sober lifestyle (complaints of drunkenness): "Our home is the site of a perpetual state of fear because of my husband's drunkenness." "Some men are just plain drunks."[25]

Honor: "Promises are nothing more than empty words."[26]

Meeting parental obligations: the husband has no inclination to spend time with his children (and he denies us all material support, etc.): "No alimony, no contact."[27]

"We have never known a father's kindness, no caring word, no help."[28]

Aggression, violence: "My husband ridicules me, calls me stupid."[29]

"His fists are his most convincing argument."[30]

Self-centeredness: "Our father is tall, with hazel eyes, and is incredibly handsome. He is always busy ... with his own affairs."[31]

Men are concerned with only themselves."[32]

No generosity: "All my husband talks about is money."[33]

No longer able to tolerate his mercenary nature, she divorced her husband while she was still young."[34]

Spirituality or intellect: "If only one spiritually rich man would write to me, although I know that such men do not exist in this country."[35]

Conscience: "Where is their awareness, their conscience?"[36]

Responsibility (men shift the responsibility for resolving problems, and for their own shortcomings, onto women; they are irrational in this): "In the beginning my husband maintained that the most important things in life are love and compatibility, not education. ... My daughters grew, went to nursery school ... and the time came for me to go to work. But where? I have no formal training. Then my husband started in on me: "What were you thinking?"[37]

"Why does he smoke? Because he has a bad wife, is his answer. And why does he drink? Because there is no harmony between them. Why are men unfaithful? It's the woman's fault. This is the way he explains his shortcomings."[38]

These lists, compiled from the most frequently repeated complaints, illustrate the kind of men's faults that aggravate Ukrainian women the most. The positive values that emerged during the interviews resonate with the qualities women desire in men, and as such appear to have formed a new set of criteria against which to measure male behavior. Insofar as the evaluations came to light out of the most intimate of male-female relationships, the list represents a unique axiological profile—a system of family values favored by women. Having thus established the separate values that conform to each of the patriarchal and egalitarian models, we were in a position to determine which model Ukrainian women favored during the years 1884–1990, and which was most to their liking in 2004–2010.

## Changed Perceptions of Individual Values

We scoured all issues of *Zhinka* from 1984–1990 and 2004–2010—168 in all, or 84 for each period. The list of women's negative appraisals of men, compiled from their letters for 1984–1990 (27) and 2004–2010 (18), produced the following number of censorious evaluations: for the period 1984–1990 there were 88; for 2004–2010 there were 89; for a total of 177. Nonetheless, as suggested above, the specific division of criteria and relatively small volume of material available yielded limited information about each value individually, so we are able to point only to general tendencies, which can now serve as hypotheses for future research: a reduced number of evaluations associated with legality (complaints of aggression), and unfairness in the distribution of domestic duties; an increase in the number of evaluations relating to altruism (complaints of egoism), and hope for personal relationships without an ulterior motive.

Such changes do not automatically reflect objectivity. Reduced complaints of aggression and unjust division of domestic duties, for instance, do not necessarily indicate that violence no longer has a place in the Ukrainian family, or that men are obliged to share in domestic responsi-

bilities. Also significant in the dynamic of indicators is the changing attitude toward relevant values and men's behavior on the part of the women
themselves, and in the editorial offices where letters for publication are
selected. Let us take domestic violence, for instance. We can assume that
a more active educational program, the formation of negative public attitudes toward abuse, and a variety of media publications on denouncing
violence have changed the stereotypical thinking, "He beats me and that
means he loves me." The new family awareness that violence is unacceptable, that it is a crime might also have led to some women feeling too
ashamed and embarrassed—even fearful—to write about it. Perhaps editorial policy should be oriented more toward portraying reality in a more
positive light, and avoiding emotionally laden subjects such as violence.

We must also approach with caution the reduction of complaints about
injustice in the division of household labor. This tendency ought to be
studied in conjunction with another—rising objections to the male ego. In
each instance the issue comes down to a similar reality: men avoid family
obligations; in daily life they are consumers of women's labor.

In letters from 1984–1990 the man is convinced that his sole obligation toward the family is to contribute his paycheck in a timely way. Who
will help me? Who spends time after work slaving over a hot stove? We
women, that's who. And who sits watching television? They do."[39] Evidence derived from the 2004–2010 period points to the fact that all men
are self-absorbed egoists:[40] "They think only of themselves. My vacation
time consists of plans that conform only to his wishes."[41]

These examples contain the following differences: letters published
during the Soviet era correlated such behavior with the value of "a just division of household labor," explained by the uniqueness of the man's role
within the framework of the dominant family model. This is the reality
in which men still exist, without inquiring whom it benefits, whether or
not it is just. From this we obtain maximum objectification and generalization of the existing situation: "he believes it is his duty"; "as everyone
knows"—note the we/they dichotomy. In letters written during the contemporary period the emphasis shifts from the general state of affairs to
individual men. They are not epitomized as objects, and their actions are
not subordinated to tendencies in the established order. Instead they function as subjects who make conscious choices about an equitable division
of responsibilities, convenient for them but unfair to the woman: "men
are concerned only with themselves."

This shift in focus can be explained in a number of ways. On the one
hand it signifies the emancipation of women who have come to a realization of men's egotistical position in the division of household labor and
are now open to discussing it. On the other hand, it does not judge the
model, but rather individual human beings. The fact that responsibility

for men's behavior toward women has shifted to the men themselves is not a bad thing. What *is* bad is that this kind of patriarchal thinking is allowed to slip away from the enlightened field of consciousness, where it can be viewed as an established social ideology of contemporary Ukraine enjoying strong support, not as a flaw in men.

## Division of Values Relative to Family Models

Computations indicate that compared with 1984–1990, in 2004–2010 there was a fundamental increase—actually a doubling—in the percentage spread of patriarchal values at the expense of general humanitarian and egalitarian ones. Although this tendency has been fixed on the basis of a somewhat insignificant breadth of analysis, its continuity will assure the validity of our findings.

This makes the claim for universality based on an analysis of a single women's publication feasible. We recall that it was this same journal that positioned itself as the one designed for the contemporary working woman who cares about her personal development. What, then, should we look for in the other, mostly glossy journals, which do not strive for an enrichment of ideas? Looking at it from another perspective, it is plausible that among the readers of glamorous publications aimed at the materially secure women, many of whom own their own businesses, there might be less concern about the existence of patriarchal values. Therefore, as we have demonstrated, the Ukrainian women's rejection of or indifference to egalitarian values—such as a man's willingness to share in domestic duties—often stem from unhappiness over the family's material status, as Internet forums have indicated:

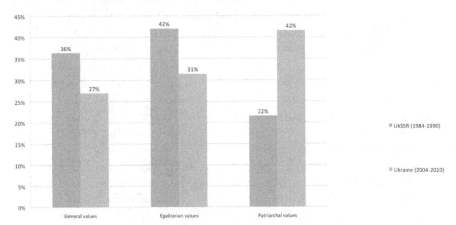

**Figure 13.1.** *Values of* Zhinka's *women readers.*

On another note, let us consider the younger men who are constantly on the look-out for girls who will pay to get them into a discotheque and buy them a beer. Or when on a date she discovers that he has no money? Should she send him away? *Then* there is the one who calls on a girl at her home. Later, he will cook for her, yet never take out the trash. Driving in a nail is a problem for him, but he can make borshch on the fly. After they marry it turns out that he is incapable of earning a living, yet is quite adept at changing pampers. Then who will bring home the bread? Either the parents will step in or it becomes the wife's responsibility. That is one important motive in her search for a good provider."[42]

On the basis of this information we must conclude that a segment of Ukrainian women (further research is required to determine its dimension) believe that they would prefer to live in a family structured according to the patriarchal model. We say *"believe* that they would prefer" here because, in our judgment, many of these women have an imperfect impression of what a true patriarchy, or genuine egalitarianism for that matter, means to family life. We will attempt to explain this below.

## Reasons for Change

The recorded dynamic involving a rise in female supporters of the patriarchal family model might signify:

- changes in the conduct of the men themselves, who have begun to disregard the norms of patriarchal values more frequently;
- changes in the women's attitudes toward men's behavior when the needs of the former coincide with patriarchal values and become more important than egalitarian ones;
- changes in editorial policy in addressing more meaningful purposes.

We believe that each of these elements has a role to play in real life, but since our aim is to ascertain the desires of women we will direct our attention to them. What might have motivated Ukrainian women, especially contributors to the journal *Zhinka,* to change their preference to the patriarchal model in contrast to the global tendency of establishing gender parity? Here are some of our assumptions, illustrated by announcements from women's Internet forums least subjected to the editing process by a publisher.

First, the emancipation of Ukrainian women in the UkSSR resulted in millions of them moving into the public sphere, where they functioned well, yet men were in no rush to improve their domestic skills. This produced the infamous double burden.

It is agreed that women are changing, but not so the men. They have pushed the women to the fore, and compelled them to function financially, on an equal footing, yet it never occurred to them to assume at least some of the responsibility for building the 'cozy nest.' As for their inclination to focus exclusively on their own comforts, what is there to say? The husband sits watching television for two hours and as soon as I cross the threshold, he asks: 'When do we eat?' Then, 'bring me some tea'. After that, it's 'make love to me.' But where do I find the time or the energy?!![43]

Today's Ukrainian women blame feminist movements for this sorry state of affairs, as if to say that in the past, within the patriarchal system, women could stay at home and look after the household while the "knightly" husband provided for his family. Those who shouted: "We have equal rights" must have given scant thought to the inevitable consequences of their demands. What did these matter as long as women could stay at home in comfort and look only after themselves! Doors were opened for them, hand kissing with each encounter was routine, as was bowing deeply before them, treating them like goddesses, and winning their kiss was the men's greatest joy."[44]

This somewhat simplistic picture does not necessarily reflect the entire situation. During the patriarchal era not every woman could afford to stay home to manage a household. Some found it necessary, as so frequently happens today, to work in the public sphere, under much worse conditions, without social guarantees or protected motherhood. In view of the idealized vision of patriarchy, however, desire for a patriarchal relationship is becoming increasingly evident among Ukrainian women. Most never suspect that the family model under which society obliges them to live has little to do with gender justice. Appropriately, researchers in Lithuania, among others, refer to this family model as neotraditional (Tereškinas 2010). As for the egalitarian family, constructed according to principles of equality, it is as though such a concept does not exist, even in the minds of some Ukrainian sociologists. In describing the various types of family models (nuclear, extended, traditional, etc.) they routinely neglect to mention this one (Dvoretska 2002).

Second, the rejection of prerevolutionary "bourgeois" norms of communication led to a palpable lacunae in courtesy (Zolotova 2000), as well as a decline in the overall level in the culture of relationships in the UkSSR. "Changes in the nature of relations revealed the dangers to which the nullification of social and interpersonal distances can lead" (Arutiunova 1989: 120). Hand kissing, giving up a seat to women, making way for them—all these gallant gestures have become a rarity. And, although in Western Europe and the United States such courtesies are now considered signs of gender inequality, in Ukraine the decline in this conduct on the part of men is viewed as a sign of an overall cultural decline. A nongallant man is one who ignores sexual differences, and does not respect women.

Is it so difficult to hold open a door for a woman, or to give up your seat for her on public transportation, extend a helping hand if she should happen to fall, give her your place in a queue, and so forth? And to do this regardless of her age, physical beauty, sense of style, but only because you are a man and she is your 'weaker half.' Dear men, doesn't a woman's smile, her appreciation for such this agreeable gesture at least bolster your self-esteem?[45]

"Where *are* those genuine knights"?[46]

What do we have now? A woman carrying heavy bags passes by, and not one of you scum will even glance in her direction, at her heavy load; suddenly everyone is in such a hurry. When she enters a room somewhat shabbily dressed, not wearing heels, no makeup (she just wasn't in the mood for such things) not only will a man not rush to open a door for her, he will gawk at her for moving so slowly, or impatiently push her aside, and she faces the danger of being run down at a pedestrian crossing. In principle, we don't give a fig for having doors opened or held open for us, or being kissed on the hand when we meet, we have the same rights as you, and men don't go around kissing other men's hands, nor do they open doors for one another, or offer flowers. ... The true worth of a woman has been lost in today's world. To be sure, we are now self-sufficient, strong, but at the same time we have lost our value as full human beings. It is now up to us to express our feelings, take the first step in cultivating relationships.[47]

In the third example (of the message from the forum) disrespect for women is equated with emancipation and a retreat from patriarchal relationships. This sentiment on the part of Ukrainian women found its way, for one, into Lina Kostenko's poem, "Petals of An Ancient Romance."

The old man sang without grease-paint, without mimicry.
The words were fiery but outmoded.
O, sing a romance to a girl!
Women are tired of being unbeautiful.

Third, nostalgia for the patriarchal model might also be connected to dissatisfaction with the Ukrainian men's infantilism, brought on by decades of living under a totalitarian regime, as well as centuries of colonial dependence upon an autocratic state (Layton 1994; Zabuzhko 2001; Aheieva 2004). Although some twenty years of independence was a sufficient interval for women to revise their expectations, apparently it was not enough time for men to learn how to meet the women's demands.

Finally, the media naturally play their part in the formation of women's views. Monitoring of Ukraine's mass media today frequently reinforces the fact that women are used as instruments with which to impose patriarchal stereotypes.[48]

In our estimation the Ukrainian woman who is tired of "not being beautiful" identifies her double burden and lack of respect from men, their infantilism, as something caused by social-political circumstances and emancipation. Inflamed by the mass media, she places her hopes on a change in the family model in the belief that when all is said and done the patriarchal model will be seen as far superior to the egalitarian one.

## Patriarchal Ideal: Source of the Average Citizen's Problems

Few Ukrainian men possess the resources that would allow them to live in accordance with the patriarchal model without the financial contributions to the family budget of their wives. Men's inability to conform to the ideal of the so-called hegemonic masculinity demanded of the average male leads to various complexes and stresses. Fortunately, Ukrainian society is becoming aware of the problem, albeit only gradually; scholars are beginning to address it.[49] Added to this were initiatives such as roundtables organized around the theme of "Men's standing in Ukraine," held on 19 February 2009 (regarding guarantees of equal rights and opportunities for both women and men). Women's anticipation of a patriarchal arrangement, and men's distress over their inability to conform to its dictates, both made their way into the belles lettres.

> This last circumstance, conveying men's seeming powerlessness to change anything, applies to all men in Ukraine who fear that their wives will turn to feminism and send them all to perdition." Tonight we don't even attempt to make love; I have an inferiority complex over my inability to change anything, affect anything, so why bother to embrace my wife; she sees that I am nothing ... I am so intimidated. I know that I need to earn a living, but the competition is so fierce just now; if I can't keep up—I fall off the conveyer belt.... The thing I fear most is contempt, and this fear demeans me too. A man should feel like a winner, so his wife can find him interesting. But basically I can only win over myself." 'You want to eat?' Tatiana's eyes narrow: 'Give me some money ... I will serve you three meals a day...'" This scornful 'curve ball' pierced his heart.[50]

Unable to find at home the qualities they consider to be worthy in men, some women seek personal happiness abroad. There, they believe, men are equipped to assume the burden of responsibility for a family, including financial responsibility. At the same time, however, many women who sought the good life in a foreign land became disillusioned with their marriages. Researchers believe that the main reason for those failed unions lies in the fact that the women were not willing to subordinate themselves to their husbands, to divest themselves of their own voice, for the sake of a successful role as a wife in a patriarchal family (Kononenko 2001).

Therefore, in the same manner as the average woman, albeit to a lesser degree, the contemporary man does not aspire to live in a patriarchal situation too much, although he too considers it an ideal. This destines them both to a life of misery.

## Social Questions Illuminated in *Zhinka*: 1984–1990 and 2004–2010

Here the Latin concept of *cui prodest* (who benefits?) comes into relief. Logic suggests that the imposition of the ideal patriarchal family model benefits only those actively engaged in pursuing it, in a word the ones with adequate resources. This begs the question: what benefits do advocates of patriarchal values derive from them?

In search of an answer, we turned once more to the readers' letters sent to the editor of *Zhinka*. We examined issues on the activities of Ukrainians able to exert authority in areas such as pension allocation, help for single parents, families with many children, protection for mothers and children, labor regulations pertaining to employers and workers, etc. These are questions that relate to the state's implementation of its social obligations. We analyzed the letters for the same periods as before (1984–1990 and 2004–2010). Here are some examples:

> Dear publisher: we request that you plead our cause before the parliament so that we can have no fear of work termination after a few days of an unavoidable absence ... it is as though we work to earn a little spare cash. How can my pay be considered spare cash when I have three children to support and my wages amount to seventy rubles? I do have three children. My husband no longer lives with us. And now I have lost my job. Why? Because I was absent ... but I informed my employers at the outset that I would not be able work the night shift. And I told the foreman about four-year-old Dmytryk's illness in plenty of time. They never gave a thought to how I would feed my children.[51]

> We women ask that the men view us not only as colleagues, but as women ... and show some concern for our financial dilemma .[52]

In the journals published during the Soviet era we found eighteen rubrics containing letters devoted to social issues. The miscellany of rubrics and large number of letters began to appear in 1986 with the commencement of "Perestroika" and its proclaimed freedom of expression. Prior to this, such headings as "A vacuum cleaner is not electrical; it is satirical" and "Every Soviet woman needs ..." were featured.

In the 2004–2010 editions of *Zhinka* we observed a different tendency: the merging of social rubrics. It is difficult to establish whether or not this indicated a loss of freedom of speech and the genesis of a different form of censorship—this time imposed by proprietors rather than the party. What is plain is the fact that the publisher systematically shifted the readers' attention away from their concentration on social issues. Of all the rubrics examined only one is in existence today—"Consulting with a Lawyer," where letters from readers with questions more or less pertaining to social safeguards are published.

Alterations in the quality and volume of the letters have also undergone some changes. Whereas for 1984–1990 we counted 160 letters, during the 2004–2010 period the journal received a mere 101. As for their contents, for purposes of comparison we divided those according to the positive or negative tone of social protection offered by the state, and those that were protection-neutral.[53]

Among those containing negative evaluations: "Is it possible that I, a mother of many children, without a place to live, with a husband in prison, should not be protected by some sort of social safety net?"[54] "Who will give me back my father, a victim of Chernobyl? I have been allocated a pension of forty-two rubles."[55] "Veterans were promised a raise long ago. When is this going to happen?"[56]

Some examples of those containing positive evaluations: "Because of my pregnancy I requested and received a lighter workload. How would this impact my salary I wondered?"[57] "Will the mechanism for implementing the Regulation on temporary government assistance to children of fathers who avoid paying alimony still hold?"[58]

Finally, among the neutral evaluations: "How does a private business person document a permanent work record in the labor book [*trudova knyzhka*]?"[59] "Do I have the right to the title 'heroine mother'?[60] "How much should parents be expected to pay for meals served to their children in pre-and boarding schools?"[61]

A comparison of the number of texts cited for the researched periods indicated a significant (4.5 times) decrease in letters with negative evaluations of governmental social assistance programs. This was offset by an upsurge in the number of letters focusing on positive aspects (a fifteenfold

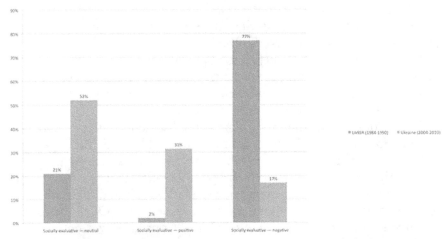

**Figure 13.2.** *Evaluation dynamic of social protection found in readership letters to* Zhinka, *1984–1990 and 2004–2010.*

increase) and neutral evaluations (more than double). Letters submitted during the Soviet period containing positive evaluations were conspicuous by their virtual absence.

These figures might be the result of: objective improvements in social guarantees made by the government; the fact that such social guarantees for Soviet citizens were perceived as the norm and simply went unnoticed, as opposed to the independent era in Ukraine where they remain subjects of ongoing discourse, and the enhanced dynamism in the legislative process in independent Ukraine. This tends to enliven interest in various normative acts, the aim of which is to raise the level of social assistance.

This said, the data do diverge from numerous other findings (Koper 2006; Rudenko 1999) and surveys (Sharma and Serpe 2010), as well as public declarations by leaders of social organizations whose members require social protection—various groups of invalids, veterans, victims of Chernobyl, etc. (Mykytenko 2011; Chervonopyskyi n.d.). They testify to the inadequate governmental assistance, and even its absolute deterioration. At the beginning of 2011 this is what research data, compiled by the Research & Branding Group, revealed to the public: 70 percent of all Ukrainians make public their dissatisfaction with the country's financial standing in *Novyny Ukrainy* (Ukrainian News). In December of 2010, during the national census-taking period initiated by the Democratic Initiatives Fund, public defenders disclosed that in Ukraine, in addition to the cultural and personal rights of citizens, economic rights were violated most frequently (Removska 2010).

By the end of the 1990s, the situation had become so critical that the government was finally obliged to acknowledge it. An addendum to the 18 October 1997 Edict (*Ukaz*) "On the Fundamental Direction of Social Politics," no. 166/97, announced that social protection had declined for the most vulnerable stratum of society—children, pensioners, invalids, singles, the unemployed, and families with many children. The level of social and employment rights and guarantees for citizens had also decreased.

In addition, we have data derived from comparative research by sociologists who asked their respondents to evaluate whether or not their lives had improved since the demise of the USSR. These indicated that 54.3 percent of respondents polled by professionals from Kyiv's International Institute of Sociology answered that up to the time of Perestroika their lives were better than they are today. Those who argued that their lives were worse under the Soviet regime totaled only 15.1 percent (Kyrychenko 2011).

Paraphrasing another longitudinal study completed in 2009 and titled *End of Communism Cheered but Now with More Reservations* we find that ordinary citizens gained far less from the market reforms than did the business elite or the politicians. If in 1991 some 52 percent of the populace supported the move to capitalism, by 2009 this level of affirmation had dwindled to a mere 36 percent. Meanwhile 62 percent of the respondents were of the opinion that the current living standard was much worse than it had been under the communist regime. And although the general level of satisfaction with one's life rose from 8 percent to 26 percent, the data do give rise to some serious misgivings. In 1991, 8 percent of the respondents registered their satisfaction with life—a normal reaction in light of the widespread expectation that life was bound to improve. Conversely, a rise in this number to 26 percent by 2009 was considered low, stemming as it did from a general disenchantment over Ukrainian-style market reforms, and diminished expectations of a better life.

## Conclusion

Through our research, two paradoxes became evident. First, there was a desire on the part of female contributors to live according to the patriarchal model. They rejected the egalitarian model despite the greater rights and respect that it offered. Second, compared with the Soviet period, there has been a marked increase in the number of positive assessments of state social policies published in the journal during the period of independence. This ran counter to the findings of sociological research and surveys indicating an upward trend in dissatisfaction with government-sponsored social protection measures.

In our opinion, these conflicts find their resolutions one at a time. The desire for a patriarchal type of family relationship on the part of the wife, as we have already observed, is also a desire for the husband to assume full responsibility for the social status of his family: go to work, provide economic security, and create conditions enabling the wife to perform the domestic chores and look after small children. In opting for the dominance of the patriarchal ideology, the woman shifts responsibility away from the state and transfers her demands to the man. This adds a new dimension to the guardians of social security. Propagation of a patriarchal family model in Ukrainian society in this fashion functions as a kind of "lightning rod" by channeling public dissatisfaction over social security guarantees away from the post-Soviet state to individual men. In light of the high level of dissatisfaction, we can argue persuasively that diverting responsibility in this manner is advantageous only for those in high positions of authority in Ukraine's governing structure.

As a result of the expansion of a patriarchal ideology, in which readers and letter writers to *Zhinka* were instrumental, men found themselves between "Scylla and Charybdis." On the one hand patriarchy appeared attractive because of its authoritative function in the family, together with

the lure of an obedient domesticated wife. On the other the head of a patriarchal family not only has rights, but obligations, which most Ukrainian
men are unable to discharge. Women can also fall into this snare of contradictions. They do face the attractive option of submerging themselves
in the patriarchal model and feeling protected, but at the same time many
find themselves reluctant to forget their individuality, to reject their professional self-realization, in order to submit to the will of a husband.

These contradictions, along with a host of other factors, conspire to
destabilize the Ukrainian family. As we see it, the only solution lies in a
resolve to build relationships based on the individual attributes and in-
clinations of each member, while bearing in mind that dissemination of
the patriarchal model by the Ukrainian media is advantageous neither for
women nor for men. Rather it serves the interests of a ruling structure
interested in: eliminating women from the labor market, thereby reducing
competition for employment; shifting dissatisfaction with the social situation in the country from state to individuals; and imposing upon men a
feeling of inadequacy, a complex of inferiority, owing to their fear of not
measuring up to the ideal of patriarchal masculinity. This complex is an
active means of suppressing the social and political activity of citizens,
which might otherwise be channeled toward some productive changes.

**Hanna Chernenko** holds the degree of Kandydat in philological science,
and is a researcher at Taras Shevchenko National University of Kyiv. She is
a prolific writer of scholarly articles (numbering some eighty) and numerous media publications on the problems of cognitive linguistics, sociolin-
guistics, and culturology.

# Notes

1. *Radianska Zhinka* (hereafter *R Zh*), 1984, 2:15.
2. http://posydenky.lvivport.com/archive/index.php/t-24602.html.
3. *R Zh*, 1988, 3:27.
4. *Zhinka* (hereafter *Zh*), 2005, 12:26.
5. Ibid., 1986, 4:26.
6. *Zh*, 2006, 2:26.
7. *R Zh*, 1989, 5:12*Zh*, 2007, 12:26.
8. *Zh*, 1990, 11:25.
9   9. *Zh*, 2005, 6:26.
10. *R Zh*, 1990, 3:28.
11. *Zh*, 2005, 5:26.
12. Ibid., 1989, 8:12.
13. Ibid., 1986, 9:15.
14. *R Zh*, 1988, 4:27.

15. Ibid., 1987, 1:24.
16. *Zh*, 2007, 12:26.
17. *R Zh*, 1986. 4:26.
18. *Zh*, 1988, 12:26.
19. *R Zh*, 1989, 4:3.
20. *Zh*, 2008, 9:26.
21. Ibid., 1990, 12:12.
22. Ibid., 2007, 12:26.
23. Ibid., 2010, 5:26.
24. Ibid., 2008, 9:26.
25. Ibid., 2007, 1:26.
26. *R Zh*, 1989,7:30.
27. *Zh*, 2006, 3:26.
28. *R Zh*, 1984, 2:15.
29. Ibid., 1990, 5:22–23.
30. Ibid., 1988, 12:24.
31. Ibid., 2008, 9:26.
32. Ibid., 2006, 8:26.
33. Ibid., 1986, 4:26.
34. *R Zh*, 2006, 112:126.
35. Ibid., 1989, 3:28.
36. Ibid., 1986, 9:15.
37. Ibid., 1987, 1:25.
38. Ibid., 1990, 3:28.
39. Ibid., 1990, 3:28.
40. Ibid., 2006, 8:26.
41. Ibid., 2009, 12:26.
42. http://lady.tochka.net/ua/9026-a-nuzhna-li-zhenshchine-semya-somnevayutsya-muzhchiny/comments/desc/15.
43. Ibid.
44. http://clubbing.in.ua/forum/showthread.php?t=213&page=1.
45. http://misto.ridne.net/viewthread.php?tid=7898.
46. *R Zh*, 2005, 5:26.
47. http://clubbing.in.ua/forum/showthread.php?t=213&page=1.
48. Gender resources of the Ukrainian mass media, 2004.
49. Consult Meshcherkina 2002 and Konovalov 2005.
50. In Vasyl' Slapchuk 2006, 61.
51. *R Zh*, 1990, 4:7.
52. *R Zh*, 1987, 11:26.
53. Evaluations, especially positive ones, in such letters can also be expressed implic-
    itly. More frequently, semantically speaking they take on the form of presuppo-
    sitions—there is a need in such an unavoidable situation for a comprehension of
    precisely this assertive part. Thus, for instance, such a seemingly neutral question
    as: "What sort of mechanism exists for the implementation of the Regulation
    on temporary government assistance to children of fathers who avoid paying
    alimony?" A covert positive evaluation of governmental assistance to children in
    lieu of support from fathers found in *Zhinka*, 2006, 7:27.
54. *R Zh*, 1989, 12:23.

55. Ibid., 1990, 11:14.
56. *Zh,* 2007, 4:27.
57. Ibid., 2006, 2:27.
58. Ibid., 2006, 7:27.
59. Ibid., 2005, 10:27.
60. Ibid., 2006, 12:27.
61. Ibid., 2006, 1:26.

# Bibliography

Aheeva, Vira. 2001. "Materyvbyvstvo ii cholovicha infantyl'nist'," in *Gender i Kul'tura,* eds. Vira Aheeva and Svitlana Oksamytna. Kyiv: Fakt, 131–144.

Arutiunova, Nina D. 1987. "Anomalii i iazyky k probleme iazykovoi kartine mira," in *Voprosy iazykoznania.* Moscow: Institute of Linguistics, USSR Academy of Sciences, 3:3–20.

———. 1999. *Iazyky i Mir Chelovieka.* Moscow: Languages of Russian Culture.

Chervonopys'kyi, Serhii. n. d. "Veterany—hordist'—hidnist' i oplot suspil'stva," *Ukrainska Spilka Veteraniv Afganistanu.* http://usva.org.ua/mambo3/index.php?option=com_content&task=view&id=526&Itemid=48.

Dvoret'ska, Halyna. 2002. *Sotsiolohiia,* 2nd. edition. Kyiv: Kyiv National Economic University. http://193.19.153.65/rada/control/uk/publish/article/news_left?art_id=144616&cat_id=37http://usva.org.ua/mambo3/index.php?option=com_content&task=view&id=526&Itemid=48486.

*End of Communism-Cheered but Now with More Reservations* 2009. *20 Years After the Fall of the Berlin Wall.* http://pewglobal.org/2009/11/02/end-of-communism-cheered-but-now-with-more-reservations/.

Kononenko, Evheniia. 2001. "Rizni bazhannia i rizni dumky. Yiaki z tykh dodatkiv skladet'sia suma?" in *Gender I Kul'tura,* eds. Vera Aheeva and Svitlana Oksamytna. Kyiv: Fakt, 145–150.

Konovalov, Dmytro O. 2005. *Gender i Natsional'nyi Subiekt: Konstruiuvannia Maskulinnostiv v Konteksti Postradians'koi Ukrainy.* Avtoreferat dysertatsiyi na zdobuttia naukovoho stupenia kandydata filosofs'kykh nauk. Kharkiv: V.N. Karazin Kharkiv National University.

Koper, N. Ie. 2006. "Sotsial'na pereorientatsiia promyslovosti regioniv Ukrainy v umovakh rynkovykh peretvoren'; problemy i prioriotety," *Naukovi Zapysky Vinnytskoho Derzhavnoho Pedagogichnoho Universytetu im. M. Kotsiubynsky. Seria Geografiyi,* 112–120.

Kostenko, Lina. 2011. *Zapysky Ukrainskoho samashedshoho.* Kyiv: *A-BA-BA-HA-LA-MA-HA.* http://www.ehttp://www.ereading.org.ua/bookreader.php/1000996/Kostenko Lina Zapiski_ukrainskogo_samashedshogo.html.

Kyrychenko, Iryna. 2011. "Perebudova chy zoria postkomunizmu?" Kyiv: *Dzerkalo Tyzhnia.* http://dt.ua/articles/76807.

*Lady.tochka.net.* http://lady.tochka.net/ua/9026-a-nuzhna-li-zhenshchine-semya-som nevayutsya-muzhchiny/.

Lavrinenko, Oleksandra. 2001. "Chomu Ukraintsi zrobyly svoim symvolom khatu pid strikhoiu," Kyiv: *Den'.* http://www.day.kiev.ua/60296/.

Layton, Susan. 1994. *Russian Literature and Empire: Conquest of the Caucasus from Pushkin to Tolstoy.* Cambridge: Cambridge University Press.

*Kul'tura Cholovikiv u Stavlenni do Zhinok.* 2010. http://misto.ridne.net/viewthread.php?tid=7898.

Meshcherkina, Elena. 2002. "Bytie muzhskoho soznaniia: opyt rekonstruktsiyi maskulinnoi identychnosty srednevo i rabochevo klasa," in *O muzhestvennosti.* Moscow: Novy-Literaturny Obzor, 268–288.

Mykytenko, Oleksii. 2011. "'Danylenko: Podvyh Chornobyl'tsiv iak I vyrishennia yikhnikh problem, vymahaiut' ne bezdumnoi patetyky, a real'noi otsinky ta vidpovidnoho stavlennia do nykh," *Vechirny Kyiv.* http://eveningkiev.com/2011/04/viktor-danylenko-podvyh-chornobyltsividpovidnoho-stavlennia.

*Posydenky.lvivport.com.* http://posydenky.lvivport.com/archive/index.php/t-24602.html

*Radians'ka Zhinka.* 1984–1990. Nos. 1–12.

Removs'ka, Olena. 2010. "Ukraintsi ne zadovoleni dotrymanniam svoyikh konstatutsiinykh prav," *Radio Svoboda.* http://www.urist.in.ua/showpost.php?p=2998 85&postcount=1.

Rothmeir, Renate. 2009. "Novaia russkaia vezhlyvost'—moda delovoho yietiketa ili korennoie pragmaticheskoie izmeneniie," in *Voprosy Iazykoznaniia.* Moscow: Institute of Linguistics, USSR Academy of Sciences, 63–82.

Roundtable. 2009. "Kruhlyi stil na remu: 'Stanovyshche cholovikiv v Ukraini," *The Ukrainian Parliament News.* Kyiv: K.I.C. http://193.19.153.65/rada/control/uk/publish/article/news_left?art_id=144616&cat_id=37486.

Sharma, Rakesh, and Lauren Serpe. 2010. "Change on the Horizon? Public Opinion in Ukraine before the 2010 Presidential Election." Findings from an IFES November 2009 Survey. Washington, DC: International Foundation for Electoral Systems, US Agency for International Development.

Shved, Bohdan. 2011. "Na siohodni Ukraintsiv nezadovoleni, a zadovoleni zhyttiam, iake vony vedut'," *Novyny Ukrainy.* Kyiv: News Market. http://www.newsmarket.com.ua/2011/03/70-ukrayintsiv-nezadovoleni-ekonomichnim-stanovishhem-v-krayini.

Skoryk, Marfa, and Mykola Sydorenko, eds. 2004. *Genderni Resursy Ukrainskykh Mas-media: Tsina i Iakist'.* Kyiv: K.I.C.

Slapchuk, Vasyl. 2006. "Osin' za shchokoiu." Kyiv: *Fakt,* 61.

*Stusunky.* http://clubbing.in.ua/forum/showthread.php?t=213&page=1.

Tereškinas, Artūras. 2010. "Between the Egalitarian and Neotraditional Family: Gender Attitudes and Values in Contemporary Lithuania," *Kultūra ir Visuomenė Socialinių tyrimų žurnalas,* No. 1(1). Kaunas, Lithuania: Vytautas Magnus University Press.

*Zhinka.* 2004–2010.

Zabuzhko, Oksana S. 2001. "Zhinka-avtor u koloniial'nii kul'turi abo znadoby do Ukrains'koi gendernoi mitolohiyi," in *Khronika vid Fortinbrasa.* Kyiv: Fakt, 152–193.

Zolotova, Halyna. 2000. "Funktsiyi I disfunktsiyi sovremennoi Russkoi rechi," in *Russkii Iazyk Segodnia,* ed. Leonid Krysin. Moscow: Azbukovnik, 122–136.

# CHAPTER 14

# Men in Crisis
## *Moral Panicking, Media Discourse, Gender Ideology*

Tetyana Bureychak

Ukrainian academic, political, and public discourses recently turned their attention to the subject of masculinity. They have begun to raise questions about men as both individual and collective social agents, especially with reference to the social norms that regulate their behavior and the peculiarities of their respective lifestyles. Among the numerous sociologists currently addressing these issues we find Tamara Martsenyuk (2008), Tetyana Bureychak (2009), Bradley A. Janey (2009), Anastasia Riabchuk (2008), and Olena Strelnyk (2009). Roundtables are routinely organized for the purpose of discussing these issues,[1] and men's community organizations are springing up in search of practical solutions to the problems (Bureychak 2009, 2011)[2]. The "discovery" of masculinity as a social concern worthy of attention has moved the focus to men's gendered experience—acknowledging the fact that men are what they are not only because of their biological heritage, but as products to a significant degree of historical, political, economic, social, and cultural forces. This view also stems from a conviction that their situation can be problematical—that is to say that they are known to react to the current social transformations in negative or destructive ways. Transformations of traditional perceptions of masculinity and its dominant frameworks contribute to destabilizing a normative discourse of masculinity and are often framed as an indicator of the crisis of masculinity.

The contemporary Ukrainian mass media increasingly contribute to this discussion through appeals to "men's devaluation,"[3] social and physical degradation,[4] and their shortage. Some suggest classifying men as a threatened species.[5] The absence of clear identifying criteria for the crisis of masculinity, and contradictions in ascertaining its reasons and consequences are common across many academic and public discussions on these issues. This triggers numerous questions. Does such discourse appeal to a crisis of masculinity or crisis of representation? Is there a clear basis for concern or is it mostly moral panicking? What are the reasons for such concerns? How can they be considered politically charged? How are they related to men's life experiences? Is the crisis of masculinity a matter of fact or is there a threat of it in the future? The conceptual differentiation between crisis of masculinity as a category problematizing shifts in dominant understandings of masculinity, and the category describing the problematic men's experience (men in crisis) often remains vague. Media play a particularly important role in articulating and popularizing this discussion. This chapter attempts to reveal and discuss the construction of the crisis of masculinity and of men in crisis, as well as the modes of their resolution and legitimization according to reports from the Ukrainian mass media.

## Crisis of Masculinity and Men in Crisis: Theoretical Interpretations

Before moving on to the question of media representations of the problematic men's experience it is important to establish the meaning of the terms *crisis of masculinity* and *men in crisis* (as they are used here), often treated as synonymous or equivalent concepts. In current academic thinking the concept of plural masculinities prevails, along with the impossibility of describing the multidimensional masculine experience by a single interpretation. Therefore, in any discussion of the crisis of masculinity, the typical reference is not to masculinity in general, but rather to a definition that corresponds to its dominant meaning, representations, and practices.

R. W. Connell defines this masculinity as hegemonic and declares that typically it aspires to dominance, is work oriented, demonstrates physical prowess, and lacks an emotional component. Hegemonic masculinity is a response to the legitimization of patriarchy and is constructed in relation to other forms of masculinity and femininity, each of which is subordinate to it (Connell 1987).

The concept of crisis is somewhat problematic when pairing it with masculinity. This has to do with the fact that hegemonic masculinity functions on an array of social levels, and relative to this its crisis state is able to operate in fundamentally different ways. Were we to consider the crisis of masculinity as one of self-identification, it could present itself as a particular problem of identity performance in the social space, producing destructive behavior aimed at oneself and others. This might be exhibited as depression, pessimism, conduct disorder, alcohol abuse, narcotics addiction, aggression, violence, suicide, and any other such destructive behavior. Most frequently, the crisis of identity is associated with social alterations and the difficulty in adapting to them.

Crisis can be viewed as a permanent aspect of identity. It can also be the result of some concrete problematic life experience. I would argue that in the present situation it would be more appropriate to refer to the condition as "men in crisis" or "the crisis experience of men." While a concept of crisis of masculinity is more suitable for describing shifts in dominant social discourses of masculinity, this might put into question its hegemony.

At the same time, theoretical discussions of the categories "men in crisis" and "crisis of masculinity" are not always differentiated, which we perceive as a problem insofar as they represent separate phenomena. It is especially important to emphasize the fact that the crisis of masculinity does not necessarily have to cause a crisis experience in men, and the reverse is also true. These phenomena do exert an influence, but they are not unavoidably responsible for one another. To underscore this we have the Scandinavian example, where the perceptions of femininity and masculinity over the past decades have experienced considerable transformations due to a decrease in binary opposition and heightened criticism of hegemonic masculinity. Unlike the situation in other countries, however, the duration and quality of men's lives did not deteriorate as a result, proving that even under such circumstances it is possible to speak of a crisis of masculinity as a concept, but not as a destructive factor in men's life experience (Bureychak 2011).

An emerging awareness of the theoretical variability of the term "crisis of masculinity" has motivated some researchers to propose a separation of certain trends in its conceptual operationalization. For instance, Tim Edwards addresses both the so-called crisis from without and crisis from within (2006: 7–8). The "crisis of masculinity from without" denotes empirically fixed changes in men's social standing in institutions of family, education, and work. Above all, the point to consider here is the men's weakened authority in the area of established privilege. The crisis from within anticipates greater complexity in the empirically fixed alterations of their experience and exertion of authority. This trends toward a feeling of helplessness, futility, purposelessness, and ambiguity, all stemming from the men's diminished role in society. Central to both is the question of power indicated by the acknowledgment and overall comprehension of masculinity and the state of its crisis.

Based upon an analysis of contemporary sociological works on these issues a classification of the main approaches to an examination of the crisis of masculinity is proposed—historical, essentialist, and critical (Bureychak 2011). We begin with the historical, which emphasizes the fact that the crisis of masculinity is an unprecedented phenomenon caused by social, cultural, economic, and political transformations that began in the mid-nineteenth century and are still with us (Faludi 1999; Clare 2000;

Segal 2006). Then we proceed to the second classification—essentialist—one that offers an opposing viewpoint: this crisis has always existed. It is an inseparable component of masculinity with a tendency to realization and intensification during particular historical eras. The majority of such discussions stem from psychology and psychoanalysis (Thompson and Pleck 1986; Burn 2002). Finally the third—critical—approach argues that moral panicking produces speculations about the crisis of masculinity. It is a discursive product with scant relationship to reality. Whatever the emphasis on the theoretical deconstruction of the crisis of masculinity, the very existence of these discussions attests to a growing visibility of men's experiences, and highlights an issue that has languished so long on the peripheries of academic and popular appeal.

## Institutional Privileges and Costs of Masculinity for Ukrainian Men

The notion of institutional privileges, as Michael Messner refers to them (1997), or patriarchal dividends, in the words of R. W. Connell (1995), focuses on the institutionalized practice of supporting the dominance, prestige, and social significance of a group of men at the cost of women's concerns and those of other men. As a rule, this applies to white, heterosexual men from the middle or upper middle class. In the Ukrainian reality institutional privileges for all men have been enhanced over the course of the past two decades. The post-Soviet regime is characterized by a strengthening of neo-traditionalism—habitually presented vertically and horizontally by gender segregation—all of which fortifies patriarchal domination. Its expression is routinely found in men's privileged access to power, prestige, and prioritized male success in the public sphere, while encouraging women's self-fulfillment primarily in the private domain. This tendency bears a strong institutional imprint, and is reinforced by symbolic mechanisms of displacing women and downgrading their contribution to the public sphere. It is systematically expressed in the sexist discourse of the most highly placed Ukrainian politicians and ubiquitous sexist and misogynist hype. As an example one might offer the fact that since Ukrainian independence in 1991 the country's parliament has averaged more than 90 percent men, big business and corporations have been almost entirely controlled by men, and the median wage of female employees performing the same tasks as men constitutes, at most, 70 percent of the latter's earnings (*Zhinky i Choloviky* 2007: 16). The problem of gender inequality becomes especially acute when expressed through family violence. According to GfK survey fifty-three percent of the battered women who participated in the research informed that up to age

18 they suffered from domestic violence inflicted by their fathers, and 80 percent of those over age 18 claimed violent abuse at the hands of their husbands (GfK 2010). Irrespective of the ubiquity of domestic violence in Ukrainian society public discussions of both the violence and strategies to combat it continue to be marginalized.

Irrespective of the men's institutional privileges, their life experiences are problematic. This is especially true regarding their health and median life span, currently twelve years shorter than that of women. In 2009–2010 the average life expectancy at birth for men was 63.5 years, and 75.5 for women (*Zhinky i Choloviky* 2011: 25). The data also signified a shorter life span for men during their most productive years. Particularly indicative is the fact that men between the ages of 20 and 45 are 3–3.5 times more likely than women to face an early death (*Zhinky i Choloviky* 2011: 17). Social factors govern this disparity to a significant degree. To the latter, men's engagement in risky behavior, dangerous employment practices in manufacturing, criminal activity, etc., account for their greater vulnerability. Indicators of men suffering violent deaths also exceed those of women. Men commit suicide noticeably more often than women (*Zhinky i Choloviky* 2007: 24). In addition, socially induced illnesses account for this basic gender division, especially tuberculosis, which reached epidemic proportions in 1995. According to unofficial figures) it has affected 1.5 million inhabitants of Ukraine, with men 2–2.5 times more likely than women to contract it (*Zhinky i Choloviky* 2011: 38). Men are six times more susceptible than women to alcohol-induced illnesses, and they surpass women by 7.5 times in drug abuse (*Zhinky i Choloviky* 2011: 36). Men's exaggerated opinions of their own robust health, their unwillingness to appear weak, and their craving for risk taking are all reinforced by the prevailing double standards of conduct and tolerance for these same traits. This turns them into hostages of traditional views of masculinity, for which they pay with their health, even their lives. We will explore the interpretations and portrayals of these issues in Ukrainian media discourses below.

## Research Methodology

An analysis of the documents is the basic method in this study of media reports on men's crisis experiences. The procedure consists of identifying and examining the contents and social significance of the issues under analysis (Altheide 1996). Documents were found on the Internet in articles on the men's crisis, but it needs to be underscored that most of the texts are also available in hard copy in the archival holdings of local or national mass media outlets of Ukraine. A total of thirty-five publications from 2006 to 2010 were analyzed. The selection was purposive, targeting titles and texts containing words relating to the crisis of men. Key terms included *men, crisis, crisis of men, men in crisis,* and *crisis experience, etc.*

Two methods of analyzing documents were combined in conducting this research: qualitative content analysis and discourse analysis. Qualitative content analysis presupposes that the categories of analysis are identified during the course of the research process. Similar to what happens in the quantitative analysis procedure, a systematic method is indispensible, although only qualitative analysis remains flexible throughout the research process. It also anticipates taking the context and appearance of the given category into account. Generally speaking, the results are presented either in computer descriptive or symbolic form (Mayring 2000). Discourse analysis is at once a theoretical model and a method of textual analysis, and it supports a variety of traditions and approaches in its application. Its fundamental epistemological principle rests on the premise that the social is constructed and transformed with the assistance of language and discourse—in other words it is a reciprocal relationship between signs and the symbolic system implying a specific explanation and means of legitimizing social reality. One of the foremost receptions of discourse analysis is textual deconstruction, that is to say disclosure of the discrete mechanisms with the help of which the connotation of a text passes for truth. This demonstrates the ideological constructiveness of the text and its meaning in a concrete social context. As a rule, discourse aims at gaining knowledge of (1) the organization of a text (for example, the form of its presentation, its structure, the means of connecting its elements, stylistics, and so forth), (2) analysis of its convictions (for instance, ideological and moral convictions displayed in the texts, references to prior knowledge, expert evaluations of emotional appeals, etc.), and (3) interpretations of the contents of a text (analysis of polysemantic information, omissions, references to "unmarked" concepts, meanings of both active and latent content (Parker 1999; Gee 2005; Djik 2006).

In analyzing the crisis of masculinity, one perceives that publications tend to concentrate on three areas: pointing at problems, providing reasons, and suggesting potential solutions. It must be made clear, however, that not every article offers such a comprehensive analysis of the problems. Most tend to stress the problematical experiences of contemporary men and offer interpretations. We will examine each of the most common interpretations in greater detail.

## Men in Crisis: Indicators of the Problem

Media accounts of the crisis uncovered a wide spectrum of issues related to the life experiences of contemporary Ukrainian men. We propose to separate them into three basic groups: (1) demographic and social/medical issues; (2) men's destructive practices; and (3) men's nonconformance to social norms and expectations.

Men's demographic and medical-social problems are mentioned in twenty-one publications under study here, attesting to the assessment of their significance. The following problems are part of this group:

- Significant gap in the life span of Ukraine's women and men. Accounts on this subject generally include statistical information, emphasizing the fact that on average women live twelve years longer than men (Blokhtur 2010; Denisova 2009; Korespondent 2009; Kovalenko 2009; NEWSru 2009; Polishchuk 2006). According to the experts cited here, compared with other countries the imbalance in the average lifespan of Ukrainian women and men is the greatest in all of Europe (Klymkovska 2009; Polevska 2008; Korespondent 2009; UNDP 2009).

- Numerical predominance of women in Ukraine's population. Although, generally speaking, at issue is the relationship between the men and women of working age, and pensioners, media accounts seldom explain this. As a rule, the issue is presented as an overall shortage of men (Kostyshyn 2010). It is interesting to note that the illumination of this issue suggests a women's problem: "What this means is that for every ten young women, there are no longer nine bachelors, as the proverbial song goes, but eight and one-half. Where have all the bachelors gone?" (TCH 2010). The shortage of men is translated as the women's inability to establish a family, which, as far as the media are concerned, problematizes their life experience.

- Men's early demise. The untimely death of employable men, compared with women in the same category, is significant. In this case, the mass media resort to statistical-demographic data, which place the men's mortality rate at three to four times higher than it is for women. The publications stress that apart from childbearing complications men die from virtually the same causes as the women (Govorukhina 2007; Klymkovska 2009; Korespondent 2009; Mykoliuk 2008, 2009; Yarmoshchuk 2009). They also point out that men succumb during their most labor-productive years—between the ages of 30 and 50 (Polishchuk 2006). In addition men's early passing is linked to the hazardous professions in which they engage—lifeguards, pilots, miners—which tend to shorten their lives (Klymkovska 2009; Kostyshyn 2010; Mykoliuk 2009; Polevska 2008).

Destructive behavior is the next problem to be addressed by the media to illustrate the crisis experience of Ukrainian men. This includes:

- Suicide. According to various publications these are committed overwhelmingly by men, who account for 90 percent of all self-inflicted fatalities. Causes vary from unemployment to depression, and men's general propensity to keep emotions bottled up (Blokhtur 2010; Polevska 2008; Shtohryn 2009; UNDP 2009).

- Men's tendency to defer medical attention. Only a limited number of publications underscore this but without offering any interpretation (Kostyshyn 2010; Ukrainska Gazeta Plus 2008).

- Men's poor habits and unhealthy lifestyles. Alcohol abuse and smoking are cited as the most detrimental (Korespondent 2009; Medychna Gazeta 2009; Polevska 2008; Ukrainska Gazeta Plus 2008), with failure to exercise a close second (Klymkovska 2009; Mykoliuk 2009).

- Domestic violence. Notwithstanding its acute nature and widespread existence in Ukrainian society, not to mention that the major perpetrators are men who resort to physical, economic, and sexual abuse against women in the domestic realm, the issue remains on the peripheries of media coverage. It too is seldom marked as a men's problem (UNDP 2009).

Men's failure to conform to social norms and expectations falls into a separate category of "male crisis." It embraces somewhat different issues:

- External appearance and sexual deviance. Among the reasons for anxiety over male experiences one might list the transformation of their external features, especially the assumption of certain female traits stemming from alcohol abuse; beer is seen as the chief culprit: "The organism of a man who consumes too much beer leads to an accumulation of female hormones. The result is a feminine appearance in men. This increases the milk glands, the belly inflates, thighs broaden, fatty layers distend, and premature baldness sets in" (Godovanets 2008). Most remarkable here is the fact that the media determine a connection between deterioration of men's bodily appearance and the acquisition of feminine features, thus equating the latter with the abnormal and deviant. The media point to the testimony of certain doctors as convincing evidence of this allegation.

- Failure to live up to the masculine ideal. Besides articulating the concrete problems attendant on men's experience, the mass media accentuate the fact that men are becoming more enfeebled and helpless (UNIAN 2009), therefore they suffer from escalating deterioration (Godovanets 2008; Yarmoshchuk 2009).

- The crisis of fatherhood. This works in tandem with the mass media, reinforcing the fact that too few men are willing to assume the responsibilities entailed with bringing up their children (Kostyshyn 2010). On the one hand men are predisposed to detachment, and on the other they seldom gain custody of their children in the event of divorce (Klymkovska 2009; Mykoliuk 2009; UNDP 2009). Publications do stress the positive effect of engaged fatherhood on the men's self-esteem: "A good, caring father, accustomed to spending time with his children, and is happy within his own family circle, tends to live longer than the proverbial 'cat prowling around in its own closed world'" (Kostyshyn 2010). We must also be aware of the fact, however, that the media seldom analyze this phenomenon even as they underscore both the patriarchal and egalitarian norms, to neither of which contemporary Ukrainian men are inclined (or able) to conform.

## Media Interpretations of Men's Crisis Experience

Aside from descriptions of the experiences of contemporary Ukrainian men, most publications analyzed also interpreted reasons for the problems associated with them. These can be separated into two large groups: pressure of traditional gender norms and the endorsement of women. The pressure from traditional gender norms is expressed in the following:

- Norm of emotional endurance. On the one hand this finds its representation in the triumph over any outward show of weakness and failure, as well as control over one's emotions. On the other it anticipates men's exhibition of strength, indifference to risk taking, and suppression of fear (Kostyshyn 2010).

- Norm of physical endurance. Conveyed by the widespread assumption that men are strong enough to play the role of protector, and this ties into their exaggerated pretense of good health (Mykoliuk 2009; Klymkovska 2009; Kostyshyn 2010).

- Norm of dominance in the family. This is problematic for men inasmuch as it relies on their inadequate experience in dealing with contemporary life, and ignores the consequences of women's emancipation (Mykoliuk 2009; Klymkovska 2009).

- Norm of professional and financial success. This finds its representation in the idea of responsibility for fulfilling the role of breadwinner (Mykoliuk 2009). Especially detrimental to men are the effects of job losses, which to a significant degree are occasioned by unfavorable economic circumstances and the financial crisis in the country (Klymkovska 2009; Mykoliuk 2009; UNDP 2009). The pressure for financial success is responsible for at least a segment of the men joining the ranks of labor migrants abroad. This is presented in the media as a potential factor in the men's deteriorating health, even the risk of an untimely death. "When abroad, they are known to die or become crippled while performing the most arduous and dangerous work" (Denisova 2009).

In the publications we also found references to norms responsible for the stereotypical socialization, and pressure exerted by unrealistic media portrayals of men's responsibilities to which most are incapable of measuring up.

Another set of reasons for the men's crisis of experience, based on media-induced unrealistic expectations, are the women's endorsements of these expectations:

- Indulging women. This can lead to such destructive actions by men as domestic violence. The paradox is explained in the media by the women's fear of abandoning a domestic tyrant owing to their inability to find another partner in light of Ukraine's demographic circumstances and shortage of men. "As one woman explained: I cannot say no to my husband when he becomes violent because just beyond the threshold three women are eagerly waiting to take my place" (Denisova 2009).

- Devaluing women. This takes account of female promiscuity, provocative dress, moral degradation, and increase in illnesses, prostitution, alcohol abuse, as well as diminished fertility (Godovanets 2008). According to media reports, these tendencies can all have a negative impact not only on men, but on the moral, physical, psychological, social, and economic state of nation and country.

- Women's leadership capacity. This is undesirable because it encourages men's enfeeblement (Kovalenko 2009), and the destabilization of family relationships. "Strong, capable women, those breadwinners who have replaced the traditional 'submissive' guardians of the domestic hearth, and are not in accord with their other halves, who can drive a man to drink" (Kostyshyn 2010).

It is important to note that the mass media accounts of the reasons for the crisis of Ukrainian men point to their victimization. They are depicted as passive victims of a bad situation in which they are divested of all responsibility for their own experience. In most instances, it is claimed that men suffer from the effects of traditional gender norms.

## Overcoming the Crisis of Men's Experience

According to the mass media, because men are so little accountable for their own suffering, as a rule the road to overcoming their crisis seldom takes under consideration their own behavior. The two basic agents expected to assume responsibility for improving this state of affairs are women and the state. The media exacerbate the problem with their contradictory advice. Either they prescribe an environment that reinforces traditional (hegemonic) masculinity, or suggest revising the dominant gender expectations of men. As a result, women are expected to function as agents for bolstering traditional views of masculinity and helping men to realize their aspirations. Simultaneously, the media portray the state as that agent of change that must promote the destruction of traditional gender norms. In order to accomplish the first objective the publications urge women to protect men by manipulating them: "It costs nothing at all to arrive at a good decision by pretending that it was the man who initiated it. Right? Nothing will happen to the women while men are bound to grow in stature as a result, at least in their own eyes, as long as we are loving wives and fine homemakers" (Kostyshyn 2010). "In a family of well fed men they will be healthier; this can add three years to men's lives. A loving wife is the best protection against stress, and this can add two years more" (Ukrainska Gazeta Plus 2008). The state's agency in overcoming the crisis of men consists of developing an array of programs designed to motivate men to change their lifestyle. Above all, the emphasis becomes one of promoting a healthy existence (Klymkovska 2009; Ukrainska Gazeta Plus 2008; UNDP 2009), encouraging involved fatherhood, and struggling against domestic violence (Mykoliuk 2009).

# Men in Crisis: Discursive Variations

In terms of discourse analysis, the issue of men's crisis of experience can be designated as the central discussion point in the mass media, with rather distinct discourses that channel its particular explanation. This attests to the discursive struggle for a way to establish the significance of the question, various ways to demonstrate the crisis of men, and routes to its resolution. In sum, we specify four of the most compelling media discourses: neutral, patriarchal, mixed patriarchal, and gender egalitarian.

Neutral media discourse anticipates the production of statistical data without interpreting them. Most frequently this refers to the average life span of men, their mortality, and level of illness in any of its static, dynamic, or comparative manifestations. Captions in such publications commonly tend to emphasize and problematize the decrease of males in Ukraine's population: "Ukraine already has a 3.6 million shortfall of men. What comes next?" (Ukraina i Svit 2009); "Ukraine's deficit in men—3.6 million" (TCH 2009); "Ukrainian men are dying out?" (Korespondent 2009). Neutral media discourse is so named provisionally because even the absence of an evaluative articulation of the problem facilitates the visibility and framing of the men's crisis.

Patriarchal and mixed patriarchal media discourses judge as critical the experience of contemporary men in resulting from the loss of their dominant positions. In the first instance, popular reflections on the situation and its negative social impact are implied, and in the second, statistical and demographic data containing appeals for a resumption of traditional gender norms are offered. The media publications aim to attract public attention by titles such as "Deterioration of Ukrainian men persists" (TCH 2010); "Devaluation of men, or who should Ukrainian women marry?" (Godovanets 2008); "The enfeebled strong sex" (Kovalenko 2009); "The crisis has clad men in skirts" (Druzhbliak 2010); "Ukrainian men are dying out. We will have matriarchy. Hurrah?" (Govorukhina 2007). The titles of these pieces all underscore the "deterioration," "devaluation," and "weakening" of Ukrainian men. Implicit in such media discourses is the emphasis on men's mounting inability to remain strong and maintain their leadership positions, so women are forced to assume them. The media portray women as more adaptable to unfavorable conditions. Generally speaking, publications regard the tendency toward a reduction of men's leadership roles and reversal of gender roles as an affirmation of social deviance. In light of this, prevailing over the crisis of men's enfeeblement would allegedly be possible only through a return to traditional gender relations and roles. Typical of this line of thinking is the fact that such comments and conclusions is the province of journalists (Godovanets 2008; Druzhbliak 2010; Kostyshyn 2010), or individuals whose functions are not tied to any professional research of these problem, but rather to celebrities and public figures such as lawyers, trend setters, sports commentators, and the like (Kovalenko 2009; Druzhbliak 2010; Yarmoshchuk 2009).

According to gender-egalitarian discourse, the crisis of men's experience is linked, first and foremost, to pressure from traditional gender expectations of men's conduct. The publications view the current patriarchal gender relations as both inadequate for today's life experiences, and destructive in light of their influence on men. It is, however, possible to overcome these negative consequences thanks to the promotion of an awareness of the problem, and endorsement of changes in traditional gender models. The titles of some of the publications reflect the emphases on egalitarian gender methods of interpreting problems, and legitimization of appropriate routes to their resolution: "Gender imbalance in society hurts Ukrainian men" (UNDP 2009); "What do we want with gender?" (Mykoliuk 2008); "Formula for happiness: The more time that men spend with their children the more likely they are to live longer" (Mykoliuk 2009); etc. In this kind of presentation of the problem, expertise is characteristic—that is to say commentaries from individuals professionally engaged in studies of the state of Ukrainian men (these might include demographers, statisticians, sociologists) (Klymkovska 2009; UNDP 2009), or to its improvement (for instance political activists) (Mykoliuk 2008, 2009; Shtohryn 2009; UNDP 2009), and representatives of NGOs (Mykoliuk 2008; UNDP 2009).

Drawing parallels with academic interpretations of men's destructive practices, especially the three ways of conceptualizing the crisis of masculinity—historical, essentialist, and critical—facilitates the argument that it is uncharacteristic for the mass media to arrive at any kind of wide-ranging generalizations, or to explain the transformation of views on masculinity, either from a global or a local perspective. Only an insignificant number of reports (six of thirty-five) contain mentions of the term *gender* and the label *masculinity* does not figure in any. At the same time it is evident that gender-egalitarian media discourse is consonant with the historical conceptualization of the crisis of masculinity, relative to which is a gender imbalance in contemporary society. This too complicates men's ability to fulfill their traditional roles. Instead, the patriarchal media discourse in question does not fit any academic conceptualization of the crisis of masculinity in light of the pro-feminist orientation of current gender research, and the perception of similar views as gender discriminatory.

A further vital question in the context of this research is the reason for the media problematization of the male experience in recent years. In view of the time frame during which these articles appeared, it is obvious that

**Table 14.1.** *Mass Media Publications on Men's Crisis Experience*

| Year | Number of Publications |
|------|------------------------|
| 2006 | 1 |
| 2007 | 2 |
| 2008 | 4 |
| 2009 | 23 |
| 2010 | 5 |

their numbers have risen sharply since the world financial crisis in 2008, which also had a significant impact on Ukraine's socioeconomic situation. Although presentation of this research is still provisional, in light of the purposive data sampling techniques the time dynamic is suitably instructive.

Most of the articles published in 2009 (twenty-three) refer to the negative social consequences of the economic crisis on the state of men. This underscores, yet again, the importance of men's financial and professional achievements when it comes to evaluating their masculinity (in traditional terms). When men face the impossibility of conforming to social expectations because of certain objective circumstances, the media tend to portray the situation as a crisis of men, underscoring thereby the existing moral alarm. The possibility of constructing media images of this is, to a significant degree, a reflection of the dominant patriarchal gender ideology in today's Ukrainian society. Thus, the discourse on men in crisis becomes a politicized question reinforcing conservative rhetoric.

## Conclusion

The analysis of mass publications testifies to the practice of reinforcing a traditional gender ideology, suggesting patriarchal discourse in identifying the crisis of men's experience, and stimulating its redefinition, appealing to egalitarian gender models of explanation and resolution of the problem. This is explained by the tendency to academize gender research in today's Ukraine and include expert media evaluations of the situation. Another, parallel, tendency is the institutionalization of a state mechanism for regulating gender parity by allowing for the men's circumstances when contemplating implementation of gender policy.

Publicizing men's experience in today's mass media illuminates the plurality and the contentiousness of discursive determinations of the problem. The media are not inclined toward an overall analysis of gender-relationship transformations, especially when it comes to masculinity. It is plain to see that academic discussions of men's experience are avoided. An exceptional example of this is the absence of the term *masculinity* itself. The problem is most frequently reduced to a discussion of men's life experience on an individual level with an emphasis on its problematical nature. Essentializing the meaning of masculinity—which is to say ignoring the fact of its relativity and sociocultural specificity—is a typical occurrence. The relegation of all men to a single homogenous social group and neglecting variation of status, age, experience, and practices of men are also scrupulously traced.

Three fundamental indicators of the men's crisis experience are: demographic and social/medical problems, evidence of destructive behavior, and failure to conform to social norms and expectations. An analysis of the mass media publications attests to the presence of patriarchal and gender-egalitarian discourses on the crisis of men's experience. Despite principal differences in approach toward overcoming the crisis, common to both discourses is an emphasis on men's victimization and their inability to conform to either model. Stressing the importance of women and state agencies in overcoming the problem effectively removes the men's responsibility for their crisis experience. In sum, according to the media men are simply passive casualties of experiences that they are powerless to alter. Others must do this for them.

**Tetyana Bureychak** holds a Kandydat Nauk degree in sociology. In 2012 she was appointed open position fellow at the Department of Gender Studies at Linköping University (Sweden). Prior to that she was an assistant professor in the Department of Sociology, Ivan Franko National University in Lviv. Her research interests lie in critical studies on men and masculinities, nationalism, post-socialism, gender politics, consumerism, and visual culture. She has published more than thirty articles in Ukrainian and international academic journals, and a book, *Sotsiolohia Maskulinnosti* (Sociology of Masculinity).

# Notes

1. A Roundtable "The role of men in family and community," Komsomolsk NGO Center for the Development of Child and Family RODIS, held on 25 February 2010. Roundtable on "Men's gender problems" organized by Kharkiv's Main Administration for Family, Youth and Sport, on 5 November 2010. A Parliamentary Roundtable on "The state of men in Ukraine" held in 2009. A Roundtable on "Attracting men to the struggle against gender violence," supported by the UN Population Fund in Ukraine, and others, was held in Luhansk in 2008.

2. In recent years the following organizations were active in Ukraine: the Ukrainian-Swedish Project OLEH, in Vinnytsia; the Adaptational Men's Center, in Ternopil; the International Union of Courageous Daddies, in Sloviansk, Donetsk Region; "TORO Daddy School, in Kirovohrad; School for Fathers' Competence: "Stanislav's Father," in Ivano-Frankivsk; the Community Centers "Men against Violence," in Kherson and Luhansk; the Association of Courageous Daddies of Vinnytsia, in Vinnytsia; and others.

# Bibliography

Altheide, David L. 1996. *Qualitative Media Analysis*. London: Sage.

Blokhtur, Aliona. 2010. "Ukraintsiv stalo menshe: Kryza Chy Tendentsiia?" *Glavkom*. http://glavcom.ua/articles/685.html.

Bureychak, Tetyana. 2009. "Cossacks in Ukrainian Consumer Culture: New Old Masculinity Model," Eds. Jeff Hearn and Alp Biricik *Proceedings from GEXcel. Theme 2: Deconstructing the Hegemony of Men and Masculinities Conference, 27–29 April*. Linköping: Institute of Thematic Gender Studies, 215–226. http://www.genderexcel.org?q=webfm_send/55.

———. 2011. "Pohani Chasy Dlia Cholovikiv? Sociolohichni Interpretatsiyi Kryzy Masculinnosti," *Sociolohiia: Teoriia, Metody, Marketyng*. Vol. 1, 79–94.

Burn, M. Shawn. 2002. *Gender Psychology*. Saint-Petersburg: Prime-Evroznak.

Clare, Anthony. 2000. *On men: Masculinity in Crisis*. London: Chatto & Windus.

Connell, R.W. 1987. *Gender and Power*. Stanford: Stanford U P.

———. 1995. *Masculinities*. Cambridge: Polity Press.

Denisova, Liudmyla. 2009. "Naibil'she vid kryzy v Ukraini poterpaiut' choloviky," *Ukrinform news*. http://www.ukrinform.ua/ukr/order/?id=823854.

Djik, Teun A. van. 2006. "Discourse, Context, And Cognition," *Discourse Studies*. Vol. 8, 1, 159–177.

Druzhbliak, Natalia. 2010. "Kryza vbrala cholovikiv v spidnytsi," *Vysokyi Zamok* 134(4266). http://www.wz.lviv.ua/print.php?atid=84658.

Edwards, Tim. 2006. *Cultures of Masculinity*. London: Routledge.

Faludi, Susan. 2000. *Stiffed: The Betrayal of the Modern Man*. London: Vintage.

Gee, James Paul. 2005. *An Introduction to Discourse Analysis*. London: Routledge.

GfK Ukraine. 2010. "Rozpovsiudzhenist' Nasyl'stva v Ukrainskyh Simiakh. Zvit," Project of UNDP Ukraine. http://www.undp.org.ua/files/en_5843415_JAN_violence_prez_fin_UKR.pdf.

Godovanets, Olga. 2008. "Devaliuvatsiia cholovikiv, abo za koho vykhodyty zamizh Ukrainskym zhinkam?" *Glavred*. http://glavred.info/archive/2008/07/24/114129-7.html.

Govorukhina, Maryna. 2009. "Ukrainski choloviky vymyraiut'. Bude Matriarchat. Ura?" *Ukrainska Helsinska Spilka*, 11 July 2007. http://helsinki.org.ua/index.php?id=1184161132.

Janey, Bradley A. et al. 2009. "Masculinity In Post-Soviet Ukraine. An Exploratory Factor Analysis," *Culture, Society, & Masculinity*, Vol. 1.2, 137–154.

Klymkovska, Nina. 2009. "Macho v nebezpetsi!" *Demokratychna Ukraina*. http://www.dua.com.ua/2009/008/9.shtml.

Korespondent. 2009. "Ukrainski choloviky vymyraiut'." http://ua.korrespondent.net/tech/726543.

Kostyshyn, Lilia. 2010. "Berezhit' cholovikiv!" *Vilne Zhyttia* 14(15126). http://vilne.org.ua/index.php?option=com_content&view=article&id=3932:bere zhyt-cholovikiv&catid=20:naperehr&Itemid=27.

Kovalenko, Natalia, and Oleksandr Lashchenko. 2009. "Kvola syl'na stat'. Chy spravdi v Ukraini vymyraiut' choloviky?" *Radio Svoboda*. http://www.radiosvoboda.org/content/article/1737383

Martsenyuk, Tamara. 2008. "Formuvannia Masculinnosti u Ditei Shkil'noho Viku." *Ia*, Vol. 2, 16–20.

Mayring, Philipp. 2000. "Qualitative Content Analysis Forum," *Qualitative Social Research*. Vol.1.2. http://www.inteligentsiacolectiva.org/principal_proyectos_met odologia.qca.pdf

Medychna Gazeta. 2009. "Ukrainski choloviky vymyraiut?" 6(981). http://www.vz.kiev.ua/pop/06-09/5.shtml#2.

Messner, Michael. 1997. *Politics of Masculinities*. Lanham, Md: Altamira Press, 1–14.

Mykoliuk, Oksana. 2008. "Navishcho nam gender?" *Den*. http://www.day.kiev.ua/253910/.

———. 2009. "Formula shchastia: Chym bil'she cholovik provodyt' chasu zi svoimy dit'my, tym dovshe vin zhyve," *Den*. http://www.day.kiev.ua/264884.

NEWSru. 2009. "Ukrainski choloviky ledve dozhyvaiut' do 62 rokiv cherez piantstvo ta travmy." http://www.newsru.ua/ukraine/30jan2009/choloviki.html.

Parker, Ian. 1999. *Critical Textwork. An Introduction to Varieties of Discourse and Analysis*. Buckingham: Open University Press.

Polevska, Liudmyla. 2008. "Chomu vymyraiut' Ukrainski choloviky?" *Vysokyi Zamok* 210 (4834). http:/archive.wz.lviv.ua/articles/66898.

Polishchuk, Mykola. 2006. "Strashnishe vid holodu, chumy i viiny," *Dzerkalo Tyzhnia*. http://www.dt.ua/3000/3450/52944/.

Riabchuk, Anastasia. 2008. "Destruktyvni Masculinnosti u Postradianskomu Konteksti na Prykladi Zhyttievykh Istorii Kyivskykh Bomzhiv," *Conference Materials: Men's Problems in the Context of Equal Rights and Opportunities*. Vinnytsia: Vidkryte suspil'stvo, 12–13.

Segal, Lynn. 2006. "Men at Bay: the Contemporary "Crisis" of Masculinity," *Men and Masculinities. Critical Concepts in Sociology*. Vol. 1, Part1, London: Routledge, 272–281.

Strelnyk, Olena. 2009. "Genderna Rivnist' ta Aktual'ni Problemy Cholovikiv iak Klientiv Sotsialnoi Roboty," *Metodoloiia, Teoriia i Praktyka Sociolohichnoho Analizu Suchasnoho Suspil'stva*. Vol. 15, 547–50.

Shtohryn, Iryna. 2009. "Kryza naibil'she bie po cholovikam," *Radio Svoboda*. http://www.radiosvoboda.org/articleprintview/14.

Thompson, Edward H. and Joseph H. Pleck. 1986. "The Structure of Male Role Norms," *American Behavioural Scientist*. Vol. 29, 531–543.

TCH. 2009. "V Ukraini sposterihaiet'sia rizkyi defitsyt cholovikiv," *News of TV channel "1+1"*. http://tsn.ua/ua/ukrayina/v-ukrayini-sposterigayetsya-rizkii-defitsit-cholovikiv.html.

———. 2010. "Ukrainski choloviky vymyraiut' cherez sposib zhyttia." *News of TV channel "1+1"*. http://tsn.ua/ukrayina/ukrayinski-choloviki-vimirayut-cherez-sposib-zhittya.html.

UNDP. 2009. "Genderna rozbalansovanist' shkodyt' Ukrainskym cholovikam." UN-DP's discussion of the situation of women and men as a result of the economic crisis. http://www.undp.org.ua/ua/media/41-democratic-governance/821-undp-initiates-discussion-on-the-state-of-women-and-men-in-times-of-economic-crisis.

Ukraina i Svit. 2009. "V Ukraini vzhe 3,6 milliona defitsyt cholovikiv. Shcho dali?" http://ua-inter.net/archives/1958.

Ukrainska Gazeta Plus. 2008. "Choloviky Vymyraiut'." 45(185): 8–31. http://ukr gazeta.plus.org.ua/article.php?ida=1685.

UNIAN. 2009. "Defitsyt cholovikiv v Ukraini–3.6 miliona." http://www.unian.net/ukr/news/news-321652.html.

Yarmoshchuk, Tetiana. 2009. "Vyrodzhennia cholovikiv tryvaie," *Radio Svoboda*. http://www.radiosvoboda.org/content/article/175.

*Zhinky i Choloviky v Ukraini. Statystychnyi zbirnyk.* 2007, 2011. Kyiv: State Committee of Statistics of Ukraine.

# Index